The encouragement of critical reading and thoughtful discussion is Professor Park's primary objective in this Third Edition of his widely used book on the philosophy of education. Suitable for use as a text or a source book, the volume includes the writings of many of the principal contributors to the field.

Carefully selecting materials that reveal significant points of view, the editor, a leading scholar in the field, quotes each author at considerable length to make his theories fully comprehensible. Biographical sketches follow the first selection from each author. The editor also provides an introduction to each part offering a general commentary on the topic and specific comments about each selection.

Part I is devoted to the role of philosophy in the study of education. The remaining six parts consider the pragmatic philosophy of education; idealism; realism; religious thought and education; existentialism; and analytical philosophy of education. The editor points out that his general headings are convenient rubrics but that a "schools approach" to the philosophy of education in which the student learns what each school is supposed to advocate is boring and likely to be sterile. Rather, he encourages the student to deliberate on the problems raised in each selection, reexamine his current views on education and compare and contrast them with those of the writers presented, and attempt to formulate for himself a philosophy of education that he can defend intelligently.

Two modern movements, existentialism and philosophical analysis, are given extended treatment in this volume. The

Third Edition also features recommended reading lists at the end of each part, organized under two separate headings: *philosophy* and *philosophy of education.* It is hoped that students will explore the ideas in these writings further, and be stimulated to read in their entirety the books from which selections have been taken.

A unique feature of the Third Edition is an annotated bibliography of some of the most important works in philosophy and education. Representative rather than exhaustive, it enables the student to make his own departure into deeper philosophical problems.

ABOUT THE EDITOR:

JOE PARK is the author of two other books on education, *Bertrand Russell on Education* (1963) and *The Rise of American Education: An Annotated Bibliography* (1965), in addition to more than sixty articles. He was awarded a Ford Foundation Grant in 1953-54, served as President of the Philosophy of Education Society, Midwest Region, 1960-62 and is currently Secretary-Treasurer of The National Philosophy of Education Society. Associated with Northwestern University since 1944, and Professor of Education there since 1953, he has also taught in the Evansville, Illinois public school system, the University of Michigan, Evansville College, and, during summer sessions, at Johns Hopkins and the University of Colorado. He is a member of Phi Delta Kappa, Pi Gamma Mu, and Phi Kappa Phi.

Selected Readings in
the PHILOSOPHY
of EDUCATION

Selected Readings in

the PHILOSOPHY

of EDUCATION

THIRD EDITION

EDITED BY Joe Park

NORTHWESTERN UNIVERSITY

The Macmillan Company, New York
Collier-Macmillan Limited, London

Library of Congress catalog card number: 68–10034

THE MACMILLAN COMPANY, NEW YORK
COLLIER-MACMILLAN CANADA, LTD., TORONTO, ONTARIO

PRINTED IN THE UNITED STATES OF AMERICA

Preface

The purpose of this collection of readings is to make available in one volume some of the best-known works in the philosophy of education. The collection has been designed to serve as a textbook or source book for students of the philosophy of education. The first and second editions served in one or both of those capacities in many colleges and universities.

In compiling the collection, I tried to select from the writings of some of the foremost men in the field those quotations that most nearly reveal some of the most significant points of view. My policy, in general, has been to quote each author at considerable length in order to make his particular philosophical theories as understandable and coherent as possible. Biographical sketches have been prepared for each author quoted, and each sketch follows the first selection from that author. Introductory background statements, which include comments on the major topic and each selection, appear at the beginnings of the seven parts.

Part One is devoted to the role of philosophy in the study of education. The remaining six parts are grouped under the following topics: the pragmatic philosophy of education, idealism, realism, religious thought and education, existentialism, and analytic philosophy of education. These rubrics should be thought of as general headings, and not as hard-and-fast schools of philosophy. They represent merely *one* convenient system for categorizing philosophical writings. They are useless otherwise, because the labeling of philosophers solves no problems and sometimes leads to over-simplification.

Students will discover that the selections in this book require critical reading and careful discussion. The serious student should take time to think through the selections deliberately and thoroughly. Insofar as possible, each student should re-examine his current views on education, and compare and contrast them with those of men who are distinguished in

v

the field. This procedure is recommended with the hope that the student will develop those critical philosophical skills that will enable him to formulate for himself a tentative philosophy of education which he will be able to defend intelligently. He should try to find time to read in its entirety each of the books from which these selections have been taken— first, to get a more comprehensive view of each author's position, and second, to get from many of the sources a number of very important ideas that could not be included in this collection because of the limited space available.

I should like to acknowledge the cooperation of the various authors and publishers whose permissions to quote made this collection possible. I am grateful for the aid and suggestions offered toward the improvement of the volume by those who advised The Macmillan Company as the manuscript was being prepared.

I am especially indebted to Herbert Johnston, University of Notre Dame; J. Donald Butler, Macalester College; Ernest E. Bayles, The University of Kansas; George L. Newsome, Jr., The University of Georgia; Allan Hart Jahsmann, The Lutheran Church–Missouri Synod; Bruce Baker, Purdue University; Francis Villemain, Southern Illinois University, Edwardsville; Hugh Petrie and Robert Browning, Northwestern University; Eli Krumbein, University of Illinois, Chicago Circle Campus; Sister Anne Marie, College of New Rochelle, New York; and to my assistant, Mrs. Ronald Gottsegen, and my secretary, Mrs. James Beloungy.

I should not complete this preface without thanking my former students who helped to clarify some of my thoughts concerning the philosophy of education. They taught me more than they may realize. Most of all, I wish to express my appreciation to my wife and daughter for their help, encouragement, and tolerance while working on this revision.

J. P.

Evanston, Illinois

Contents

PART THREE
Idealism

PART FOUR
Realism

PART FIVE
Religious Thought and the Philosophy of Education

PART SIX
Existentialism

PART SEVEN

Philosophical Analysis

The Place of Philosophy in the Study of Education

Introduction to Part One

THIS INTRODUCTION will attempt to define philosophy of education, provide a few suggestions to students who use this book, and make some comments about the readings in this section.

Historically, philosophy (*philos,* fond of, and *Sophos,* wise) has varied considerably both in meaning and in scope. Plato used the term in the most general way in his *Republic,* applying it to ". . . those who see the absolute and eternal and immutable . . . those who love the truth in each thing." Thus, all knowledge was fused by him into a semireligious synthesis. It remained for Aristotle, with his methodic intellect, to separate the vast field of philosophy into the disciplines we recognize today as logic, psychology, ethics, aesthetics, metaphysics, etc.

Philosophy, however, has not remained the grand subject it was in ancient times, for it has been rocked to its very foundations by the advance of knowledge and by natural science in particular. Much of what was once epistemology has become the chief concern of the physiologist and the psychologist. Cosmology has yielded to research in astronomy and physics, while logic has been greatly modified by the work of the mathematical logicians. Meanwhile, metaphysics and ethics have not gone unscathed. Today there are those philosophers who would completely reject all metaphysical statements as nonsense, for they believe them to be unverifiable, at least as the term commonly is used. These same philosophers are likely to think of ethical statements as imperative sentences that express the attitudes of the persons uttering them.

Even though not all philosophers are as skeptical as some of the comments above would indicate, it is true, nevertheless, that philosophy is no longer the pretentious and all-inclusive subject it was in the days of Plato, for much of its subject matter, as well as the absolute, eternal, and the immutable, has been eroded away, even for many of those who are not skeptics.

The philosophy of education likewise has undergone, and is now undergoing, some very profound changes. Whereas a score of years ago an author could discuss the philosophy of education without going beyond the realists, idealists, and pragmatists, now he must extend his

3

consideration to encompass the thinking of the existentialists and the critical analysts. But in spite of the necessity for extending the boundaries of philosophy of education, the traditional problems of philosophy are still apparent. Thus, it is defensible to define the philosophy of education ✓ as an attempt to find answers to questions some would call ultimate. The philosopher in education desires to learn what can be known and what this has to do with education. He is interested in the nature of reality, sources of value, and what these may mean for education—aims, curriculum, and method. He may or may not believe that he can know the nature of ultimate reality. He may or may not believe that values are discovered by intuition or revelation. He may or may not reduce all knowledge to observation and experimentation. But whatever his views on metaphysics, epistemology, and axiology, he is concerned with their implications for education.

This very general definition perhaps will become more meaningful if some illustrations are given to show the differences of opinion among philosophers, all of whom recognize the same problems, but each of whom would take a different view toward them. From among the writers in contemporary philosophy of education, the works of J. Donald Butler, Sidney Hook, and D. J. O'Connor will be selected to illustrate the point.

J. Donald Butler divides knowledge into two kinds: (1) specific discoveries which are tentative descriptions produced by the sciences and (2) truth, a kind of knowledge which seems to go beyond discoveries. Perhaps his ultimate values fall into this category of truth. Butler believes that the cosmos partakes of the nature of selfhood, and that God speaks to man through "a cosmic movement which is the equivalent of the coming of God to man." God is existence, and man has a personality that is more than what is seen by the psychologist or the sociologist. His personality includes a spiritual element. God intends goodness for man, but man can only achieve this goodness when he brings himself close to God.

Butler thinks that his metaphysics, and most particularly his value theory, have a direct bearing upon the kind of education he recommends. He feels that the school should be conceived as a value-realizing institution next in importance to the church. At the same time, he doubts that the common school in America can give us the kind of education he seeks. Instead of all education going on in public schools, a "composite of institutions" will be needed to achieve the ends he seeks. J. Donald Butler, then, is an excellent example of a philosopher who still holds steadfastly to the ultimate and immutable. He is in the grand tradition that has descended to us from Plato.

Sidney Hook, on the other hand, represents the pragmatic school of thought that has held sway in America for most of this century. Professor Hook rejects the religious and metaphysical approach of men like Butler, for he believes that such an approach seeks to deduce what men *should* be from what men are *thought* to be. In other words, to Hook, this approach is sheer tautology. Hook would discover the nature of men in the developing careers of men in time and in relation to the world. The nature of man is nothing more and nothing less than a set of conditions that limits the possible educational aims, allowing us to select from among the many aims those that are most desirable. Hook couples this cultural relativity with the method of intelligence. This method of intelligence becomes the center of his "liberal philosophy," because it undercuts the absolutes that stand in the way of the development of new knowledge and insights. "Method should be central in educational activity because it not only evaluates the funded tradition of the past, but enhances the capacity to enrich it." Hook appears to reject most, if not all, metaphysical considerations, reduces values to hypotheses, and conceives of knowledge as that which is produced as a result of human experience. Education is a human endeavor, with human purposes, procedures, and subject matter, and the process of education is subject to human error and correction of this error by the exercise of the method of intelligence.

More recently the analytic philosophers, such as D. J. O'Connor, have emerged on the scene and have concerned themselves with problems in education. Although analytic philosophy may be called a "school of thought," it does not advocate a system of philosophy. Instead, it repudiates systems of philosophy. Analytic philosophers strongly contend that truths about human experience and the universe cannot be discovered by philosophical intuition or speculation. They question the idea of a logical unity of truth, goodness, and beauty. Within the analytic school of thought there are numerous differences of opinion. Some stress informal logic and common language, while others are chiefly concerned with symbolic logic and philosophy of science. Analytic philosophers do seem to agree on one thing, and that is that the function of philosophy is to clarify. This can be done by and through philosophical analysis (logical and linguistic) of what men say and write (statements, sentences, or propositions). These statements can be clarified, made meaningful, or exposed as nonsense. Since analytic philosophy is devoted to the clarification of language, one philosophizes about almost anything. This being the case, the analytic philosopher has, on occasion, turned his attention to education. He hopes to develop some defensible statements about education. He plans to do this by analyzing the language used by most educators, i.e. "needs," "real experience," "lifelike situations," etc. Finally, he hopes to provide some models, to state criteria for establishing meaning and verification, and in general to "unsnarl the logical and linguistic tangles in pedagogical knowledge."

These three illustrations should serve to warn those who try to understand philosophy of education that it would be wise to proceed with caution. Except in the most general way, what philosophy of education is to one philosopher is not philosophy of education to another. The safest thing to do when studying philosophy of education is to seek to understand what each writer means when he philosophizes on matters educational.

In order to do this, one needs to keep several suggestions in mind. Look for the presuppositions, explicit or implicit, that underlie the philosophy of each writer. It is well to remember that usually these will fall into three groups: Metaphysical presuppositions are statements about first principles, descriptions of ultimate reality, opinions about the origin and nature of the universe, and beliefs about the nature of man; such presuppositions are especially noticeable in the work of some philosophers, less so in others. Epistemological presuppositions are closely allied with those of metaphysics, and deal with the origin, nature, method, and limits of knowledge. Axiological presuppositions are statements about value, and are especially significant so far as education is concerned. All our educational objectives, for example, appear to be value judgments. In some instances the student may not find presuppositions explicitly stated. In these cases, they may lie under the surface of an argument, remaining implicit, and may have to be discovered by pausing to read between the lines.

Be alert to the justifications for presuppositions. Is there a basis in fact for what the writer has to say? Or are his arguments unsubstantiated and nakedly dogmatic? Examine the writer's arguments to see whether they follow from his presuppositions. Discover the implications and recommendations for education. Finally ask, "What is there in this man's work that should cause me to rethink my own position?" One does not have to accept everything an author recommends; neither does he have to reject all of it. He may seek to maintain a foot in one philosophical camp, but reserve the right to borrow from whomever he studies. He may wish to be an eclectic, selecting from one position a point and from some other position still another point, but never committing himself to any particular philosophy. Some may wish to identify themselves with one philosophy and reject all others. A student is entitled to do this, but he should recognize that most philosophers are agreed that THE TRUE PHILOSOPHY has not been constructed and is not likely to be developed in the fore-seeable future.

The readings in this part deal with the function of the philosophy of education, the growth of interest in philosophy of education, and the dangers in discipleship.

In Chapter One, Professor Ducasse suggests that there are three fun-damental questions on which the philosophy of education can throw light. What is the cosmic destiny of man? Why do human beings need formal education as well as informal education? What is the nature of man? Professor Ducasse then considers the chief dimensions of education, resting his considerations upon certain presuppositions concerning the nature of man.

In Chapter Two, Professor Levison explains the nature of philosophy and indicates the major ways in which it can and cannot be of help to educators.

In Chapter Three, Professor Kircher warns against the dangers of discipleship and the cry for *one* philosophy.

1

What Can Philosophy Contribute to Educational Theory?*

C. J. DUCASSE

THE QUESTION selected as topic of the present symposium has ultimately in view, I take it, a state of affairs which is not exactly new, but which for a number of reasons has in recent times exploded into public notice. What I refer to is the chaos of irresponsibility, fads, vested interests, and inefficiency which exists in various degrees and at various levels in American education today. Hardly a week now passes without some book or article appearing that asks why Johnny can't read, why Mary can't count, or more generally why our educational institutions turn out so large a proportion of uneducated and undisciplined young people. Our problem is then specifically what practical contribution philosophy can make to the urgent task of bringing intelligent order, responsibility, and efficiency into that chaotic educational situation.

1. *The Equipment Required for Responsible Educational Reform.* Discernment of the answer to this question will be easier if we first list the rather obvious items of equipment required for performance of a task of educational reform.

The *first* of them consists of adequate knowledge of the existing state of affairs in our educational institutions; and a *second*, of likewise ade-

* C. J. Ducasse, "What Can Philosophy Contribute to Educational Theory?" *Harvard Educational Review*, Vol. XXVIII, No. 4, Fall, 1958, pp. 285–297. Used by permission of the author and *Harvard Educational Review*.

quate knowledge of the social, political, and economic conditions under which one or others of these institutions actually have to operate. In the *third* place, powers of action are needed, sufficient under those conditions to put into effect the reforms that come to be judged desirable.

And a *fourth* item consists of a responsible conception of what education is, and of the functions it ought to perform at each of its various stages, in each of its possible dimensions, and for what classes of persons. For only in the light of such a conception is responsible judgment possible concerning the defects and merits of the existing state of our educational institutions, and concerning the specific changes that would make them function more satisfactorily than they now do.

2. *Nature of the Practical Utility Peculiar to Philosophy.* Evidently, the last of these four items of equipment is the only one philosophy can contribute to the reform of education; and, that only philosophy can contribute it becomes evident too when one bears in mind that whereas the practical utility of the natural sciences, in so far as they have any, consists only in the power they give man to predict or to control the course of events; the practical utility of philosophy, on the other hand, when it has any, consists in the power it then confers on man to use wisely and responsibly, instead of foolishly and arbitrarily, such powers of prediction or of control of events as he happens to have on given occasions. That is, in so far as philosophy has practical value, this consists in making clear what, *in given circumstances* and *on the whole, is the best use to make* of such powers as one happens to have, or what is *the best means to employ,* out of several at one's command, in order to achieve a chosen end.

3. *Some Fundamental Problems of the Philosophy of Education.* What then, more specifically, are the fundamental questions on which the philosophy of education can throw light, and thereby provide the broad perspective necessary for wise instead of doctrinaire or emotional evaluation of given educational practices or of proposals for the reform of our educational institutions?

One such question, and one that indeed overarches all the others, is that of the cosmic destiny of the individual and of the significance in the light of it of his life on earth. Does its brief duration comprise all there is to the life of a man? Or are those few years, as the majority of mankind has always believed, only a small part of his total life but a part that determines the nature of all the rest? Obviously, the orientation appropriate for education in the latter case might be very different from that which might recommend itself in the former.

Today, unfortunately, man's *post mortem* destiny, if any, is for us not a matter of knowledge but only of faith. That is, a variety of opinions about it exist, but none of them is definitely verifiable or confutable by us now. We may believe or disbelieve one or another of them, but we just do not really know. For on the one hand the facts alleged to show that man's consciousness survives the death of his body are few and appear possibly open to a different interpretation; while, on the other hand, the allegation sometimes met with that science has proved life after death to be impossible turns out on examination to be based either on a definition *ad hoc* of "life" exclusively in physiological as distinguished from psychological terms, or else on the materialistically pious but hazardous speculation that since *some* psychological states have physioloigcal causes, *no* psychological state at all is possible without some physiological cause.

Thus, because the question as to man's ultimate destiny is not conclusively decidable by us now, I shall in what follows confine myself to questions that relate to man's life between birth and death and that, with the powers of observation and of reason man now possesses, he can investigate.

The first of those that are relevant to our present purpose is what, in the most general sense it is, "to educate"; and how educating is related to instructing, to indoctrinating, and to training.

A second question is why human beings need artificial education, in addition to the automatic education they gain from their experiences.

And a third question concerns the nature of this being, called Man, who is to be educated. That is, just as in the case of a physical object we speak of length, breadth, and depth as its three dimensions, so here we must ask what are the several dimensions of the nature of man, along any one of which his education may proceed, and along all of which it must proceed if it is to be education of the whole man. Also, what is the relative importance of each, for what classes of persons, and under what circumstances.

Let us consider those three chief questions in turn.

4. *Education, Instruction, Training, Indoctrination*. The first asks what exactly it is, "to educate." Etymologically, to educate, is to lead out or bring out; and that which is to be brought out and developed can only be capacities that man has but that remain more or less dormant or embryonic until something acts upon him that awakens, nourishes, and exercises them.

Among the capacities or potentialities latent in man, however, some are good and others bad, absolutely or relatively to the particular social and other circumstances under which he has to live. Hence we occasionally speak of education in crime, or in vice, and so on. But in most cases we mean by "education" development of capacities that are valuable, not pernicious; and it is with education in this narrower but more frequent sense that we shall here alone be concerned.

The processes through which education takes place would seem to be mainly three: *instruction, training and indoctrination;* and, in the last two of these, a substantial part is played by observation and imitation of what is observed, as well as by linguistic communication between teacher and learner.

Etymologically again, to *instruct* is to build something in. Specifically, it is to build knowledge into the mind—knowledge of facts, relations, rules, laws, or principles of one kind or another. Instruction is thus the process that incorporates *information* into the mind. *Training,* on the other hand, is the process of imparting to someone the *skill* to perform some operation or set of operations whether mental or physical, and whether acquisition of the skill is or is not accompanied by understanding of the principles on which the operations depend.

But, besides information and skills, there is need to insert into the individual also various sets of dogmas. These are beliefs and allegiances as distinguished from knowledge, and they operate to shape the conduct, dispositions, and feelings of the person concerned in such manner that these will fit in with those of the persons with whom or among whom the individual will have to live.

The process of thus implanting dogmas constitutes *indoctrination* rather than instruction. Hence we distinguish religious indoctrination, civic or political indoctrination, or the indoctrination of military personnel, from the imparting of information about religion, civics or politics, or military matters. Indoctrination takes place mainly through the psychological process called *suggestion,* which essentially consists in getting beliefs into a person's mind in one or another manner that by-passes such powers of critical judgment as he may have and thus insures automatic acceptance by him of the belief concerned; whereas in *instruction* the process employed is that which may comprehensively be called *submission of evidence*—including thereunder the calling of attention on the one hand to facts, and on the other to the inferences which the facts warrant.

Indoctrination, then, rather than instruction, is what psychologically *adapts* the child to—as distinguished from only *informing him about*— the social context in which he lives. This social context consists of the beliefs, customs, and allegiances—whether these be in fact foolish or wise —that actually are those of the community of which he is a member.

5. *Man's Need of Education.*   We come next to the question of man's

peculiar need for education. It arises from the fact that, among all the animals, he is perhaps the one most ill-equipped with instinctive mechanisms for dealing with his environment. Many living things are ready to fend for themselves from birth; and in many others that have a period of helpless infancy the mechanisms they need for adult life are soon gained as a matter of growth, rather than by learning. Man, on the other hand, not only has a long period of dependent infancy, but in him the ability which he later gains to take care of himself is, much more than in any other animal, a matter of education rather than of maturation of instincts. He is the most plastic and teachable of all the animals, but he is also the one most in need of teaching.

The teaching he gets, however, is in some directions and in some degree automatic rather than deliberately instituted. In the natural course of his life, each of us meets experiences he had not set out to seek; learns lessons he had not set out to learn and which no one else had planned to have him learn; and develops abilities which the immediate needs of his situation call for, but which neither he nor anyone else had designed that he should acquire.

But as compared with the development that can be brought about in a man designedly, the development that would come unaided simply out of the pressure of events would ordinarily be very limited; and man is never content with only this. Perception by him of the need of his fellows, and in particular of his children, for education, motivates him to undertake it. In primitive tribes as well as in our society, each generation has a conception, based partly on experience and partly on tradition blindly accepted, of things the next generation should learn, of powers and skills it should acquire, of experiences it should undergo, and of beliefs it should harbor. Each generation accordingly takes steps specifically intended to make the children acquire the equipment and develop the abilities it regards as desirable. Such education may therefore be described in the words of C. H. Judd as "an attempt on the part of the adult members of a human society to shape the development of the coming generation in accordance with its own ideals of life."

In primitive tribes, where individualism is not encouraged and indeed hardly allowed, the whole of education would be covered by this definition. But more advanced societies recognize the desirability of providing opportunities for the cultivation of individual gifts, and for the development of man as a free human being rather than as only a cog in the social machine. Enlightened societies assume that—again in Judd's words—"the best forms of communal life will be fostered by an education which regards *social activities as a necessary medium for the development of the higher stages of individual life* rather than as something to which the claims of individual development must be subordinated." (Italics supplied.)

But, besides the educating of others, whether children or adults, there is also such a possibility as self-education. An individual can take into his own hands his education in certain directions or beyond certain points, and can thus unfold in himself as an individual, capacities which society makes little or no attempt to develop in its members either because it lacks the means to do so or because it attaches no great value to their development. Among all the animals, man seems to be the only one capable of observing himself and curious of doing so. He is the animal that looks at himself in mirrors—whether physical mirrors, or the mental mirror called reflection. And what he finds when he does this seldom pleases him altogether. Man is thus the animal capable of self-criticism, and hence of self-improvement. As Nietzsche and before him Epictetus pointed out, man is the animal who is forever ashamed of himself. He is incurably an idealist—dissatisfied not only with external things as they are but also with himself as he is, and ever striving to improve both.

To the question, "Why educate?," the answer which man returns when he observes himself and his fellows is thus that each and every man is more undiscerning, ignorant, blundering, clumsy, uncouth, insensitive, undiscriminating, callous, weak, unhealthy, foolish, undisciplined, unjust, unskilled, selfish, miserable, and so on, than he need be; and that these shortcomings all stand squarely in the way of the happiness of himself and his fellows. Man recognizes this at first dimly, but more and more clearly as his development progresses; and with realization of it grows the importance he attaches to education. The sufficient justification for education is thus ultimately the same as for every other justifiable human enterprise—namely, to decrease the wretchedness and the suffering that affect sentient beings, to promote their welfare, and to raise them to levels of greater and more secure happiness and beneficence.

6. *The Dimensions of the Nature of Man.*   I come now to the third of the main questions listed at the outset—that of the nature of this being, Man, in whose education we are interested.

Many have been the attempts to say what man essentially is. Some trait or capacity possessed by no other animal often has been picked out as constituting the very core of man's being. The capacity for self-observation and self-criticism, which we have just noticed, was what Nietzsche had in mind when he said that man is the animal with red cheeks—that is, the animal alone capable of the blush of shame. Again, man has been described as the animal endowed with reason; and on this account he has been called *homo sapiens*. And, if rationality is his essence, it has sometimes been held to follow that his feelings and emotions are then accidents, or even diseases of his reason. But it has also been contended that man's very core consists rather of his will—of his impulses, desires, cravings, purposes; and that his cognitive powers are—to use Schopenhauer's metaphor—but a light, which his will has kindled to illuminate its way. Again, man has sometimes been conceived as being not essentially an individual, but rather a member of a society; that is, really but an organ— a cell, as it were—in a greater, inclusive organism; his importance or significance being then only or mainly derivative from something external to himself.

But the conception of the nature of man which I would advocate is more inclusive than any of these. It proposes to regard the cognitive powers of man, his emotional capacities, his impulses and volitional capacities, his physical powers, his need of and capacity for membership in a society, and so on, as so many aspects or dimensions of his nature. This is to say that man's essence is not simple, but consists in the complex of these various ingredients. They are present in different proportions in different men, and in some men a particular one of these ingredients—for example, his cognitive powers—may come to occupy a ruling position, to which the other parts of his nature are then subordinated. But they remain parts of him nonetheless—parts which have a role to play in the total economy of his life. Education therefore is not to ignore them or suppress them. Its task, rather, is to foster their development in the appropriate measures, and to integrate them; that is, to weave them together into an organic unity. This conception of the nature of man, although not identical with that of Plato, is nevertheless of the same general type.

What I now propose to do is to consider in turn the chief dimensions of education. They will correspond, of course, to those of man's nature.

7. *Intellectual Education.*   I begin with what ordinarily first comes to mind when education is mentioned, namely, intellectual education. It is the sort of education to which schools, colleges and universities have mainly been instruments, and for which they are the main instruments. It is education of man in the dimension of his nature which consists in knowing and thinking.

One occasionally hears it said nowadays in connection with education of this kind that it does not matter much whether a man acquires any particular stock of information; and that the important thing is that he should learn to think, and develop intellectual initiative and the capacity for independent intellectual exploration. However, I believe this is but an extreme view, excusable at all only as a reaction against the opposing extreme which conceives intellectual education as chiefly the learning of a lot of facts.

To me, the truth seems to be that, for each age and place, there is a minimum amount of information each individual ought to have, and it would be a very good thing if he should have much in addition to this minimum. For, lacking this, he is in life much like a man in a wilderness without a map or compass. His sense of direction, of the resources available to him, of the tasks he should undertake, of the nature of his environment, and so on, is then limited strictly to the relatively small area about him that he can personally explore. I therefore believe that the education of man ought to include acquisition of as large and diverse a stock as possible of what I like to call *map knowledge* or *surface knowledge*. It is knowledge in breadth, not in depth. To seek it is, as the phrase goes, to seek to know something about everything.

The complement of this, of course, is in the corresponding phrase, the attempt to know everything about something; or, more literally, to gain knowledge detailed, precise, and thorough about some things. A certain amount of such knowledge in depth is as necessary as is knowledge in breadth; for after all each mind—however much in need of a map wherewith to orient itself—has a home ground of its own; and, for the work it has to do there, knowledge merely superficial would be of little use.

But although acquisition of a stock of knowledge of both the kinds mentioned is an indispensable part of intellectual education, it is neither the whole of it nor its most intimate and abiding part. The latter consists rather in development of the intellectual powers; for example, the power of objective and careful observation and of precise and logically ordered formulation of what has been observed, and of any ideas one may have about it. Again, the power of rigorous inference; practical grasp of the nature of experimental procedure; the habit of verification; the ability to read understandingly and critically; and development of the intellectual independence and initiative which consists so largely in the capacity to think of questions not before raised about matters already familiar.

These are mental powers as distinguished from the mental furniture or material which information constitutes. These powers are developed only through exercise, and the process which exercises them is that of actually searching for knowledge. It is to the development of them that the maxim, "learn by doing," properly applies. This maxim, however, is often unthinkingly taken to mean that learning, in the sense not only of learning how but also of learning facts, is best done by discovering the facts for oneself. But this is of course not true. On the contrary, when important facts which it took hours or days or years to discover can be learned in a few minutes from the records handed down by their discoverers, it would be only stupid not to learn them in this easy way as far as possible. The ability to learn from others is one of the most valuable a man can have; for, as Franklin remarked, "experience [that is, personal experience] keeps a dear school; yet fools will learn in no other."

These remarks on the specific range within which the educational catchword, "learn by doing," is valid, but outside of which it becomes silly, constitute an example of the kind of practical service which philosophical reflection—insisting as it does on always asking where? when? why? and what for?—can render to education. Other stereotypes similarly calling for philosophically critical scrutiny would be "Democracy in education," "Education for adjustment," "The educational process should be made enjoyable," and so on. In what follows, we shall have occasion to comment on some of them.

8. *Physical Education.* From intellectual education, we may now turn to the education of other aspects of man's nature.

Irrespective of what we may conceive the relation to be between a man's mind and his body, the fact remains that he does have a body, and that his body, like his mind, is capable of education. What physical education, viewed in terms of its contribution to a distinctively human life, should aim at is perhaps best suggested by saying that man's body is the most useful of his domestic animals. It is the physical vehicle and basic implement of all the experiences and undertakings of his life on earth. Physical education should then aim to do in general for the body what the intelligent owner of a valuable horse would do for the horse. On the positive side, this would mean the establishment of physical habits conducive to health and to fitness of the body to do its work, and development of the versatility that renders the body quickly adaptable to the specialized physical tasks or situations which life may thrust upon it. On the negative side, physical education does not mean asceticism, but only restraint of bodily cravings or impulses within the limits compatible with health and bodily efficiency. It means also that such muscular development and agility as those of the fabulous Tarzan might be sensible ideals for apes, but hardly for civilized men. The justification of athletic sports from the point of view of physical education is either, as in the play of children, development of bodily powers needed later; or, as in the play of adults, recreation and maintenance of valuable bodily powers that otherwise would atrophy.

9. *Vocational Education.* Next to physical education a word should be said about vocational education; but only to point out that it is not

education of any specific aspect of human nature, but is essentially development to a high degree of efficiency of such of a man's capacities as relate to the particular vocation he proposes to follow. These capacities would be physical ones in the case of a vocation, such as an acrobat's, dependent chiefly on bodily agility, strength, or dexterity; but, for diverse vocations, the capacities to be developed would be of corresponding diversity.

10. *Education in Social Dexterity.* There is a certain human capacity, the educating of which is of considerable importance to man simply as a social being; that is, in his relation with his fellow men. It is difficult to find a suitable name for the dimension of education I am referring to, but it may perhaps be called education in manners, or more comprehensively, education in social dexterity. It is education of an ability usually well developed in politicians, but valuable equally outside of politics; namely, the ability to deal effectively with other human beings *as they are,* in the variety of relations one may have with them—the ability to make contact with them—the ability to make contact with them easily, to enlist their good will and cooperation, and to avoid antagonizing them. It is true that there are occasions when competing with others, or opposing them rather than getting along with them, is the task that faces a man; but even then the ability to engage the aid of third parties on his side stands him in good stead.

11. *Education of the Will.* Another dimension of education, about which in general little is said, was called education of the will by a French writer, Jules Payot, in a book which appeared a good many years ago. What he meant by that phrase was development of the capacity to make oneself do the things which one has the ability to do and desires to do. It is education in the overcoming of inertia, sloth, and procrastination; in perseverance, in firmness of purpose, in courage under difficulties, and in readiness to take pains and to take care. In short, it is education in the translating of dreams into deeds. How important this is, any teacher realizes who has seen highly gifted young men or women, for whom he anticipated a great future, sometimes get nowhere for lack of the capacity to make themselves come through with what they are capable of.

12. *Aesthetic Education.* Next to be considered, and at somewhat greater length, is what in a broad sense may be called aesthetic education. It includes, for one thing, education of man's capacity for fine discrimination in his sensory impressions. Concerning colors, shapes, tones, textures, odors, and flavors, it is possible to cultivate the ability to discern differences and other relations of which one was before unconscious. Sensitivity to such relations is the very basis of what is called taste or

aesthetic appreciation as concerns the various kinds of perceptible objects.

But there is also such a thing as sensitivity and appreciative discernment in matters of human relations. There we give to taste rather the name of tact. What it depends on, however, is not sensory discrimination but comprehensiveness of one's horizon of acquaintance with the immense variety and the subtle nuances of human emotions, sentiments, moods, feelings, and attitudes. For the education of man in this dimension of his being, the most adequate formal instrument consists of literary works—such as novels, poems, dramas, biographies—that depict diverse human characters in situations of various kinds. Into these, the reader can project himself in imagination and, losing for the time being his own identity, he can gain vicariously many experiences which he could neither obtain nor afford in his objective life. Moreover, although the situations depicted in those literary works are lived through by the reader only in imagination, nevertheless the feelings, sentiments, moods, or attitudes thereby generated in him are not imaginary but quite real for the time being, and may constitute emotional insights genuinely novel to him. But these insights, it must be emphasized, result not from reading *about* such literary works, or from dissecting their structure and history, but only from reading the works themselves, and reading them in the manner which consists of intensely living through in imagination the situations they depict.

A similar remark applies to the education of the sensations. For it, the works of painters, of sculptors, of musicians, and of other creative workers in the arts and crafts, are the analogues of what scientific treatises are for education in the sciences. But development of sensitivity to subtle modulations of sensory qualities and of forms results, not from listening to discourses about the technique of art or from reading about the history of art, but from abundant, prolonged, intense, and diversified contemplation of works of art at first hand. This is said not to disparage in any way interest in the history of the arts, in the technical analysis of works of art, or in the lives of their creators, but only to emphasize that interest in *these* matters is essentially intellectual, not aesthetic. It is intellectual interest in aesthetic objects; and this is very different from aesthetic interest in them—as different as, on the other side, aesthetic interest in scientific apparatus would be different from scientific interest in such apparatus. Aesthetic contemplation is something radically different from intellectual curiosity. This greatly needs to be remembered by those who teach courses in the appreciation of the works of the various arts; for aesthetic contemplation is what is directly relevant to aesthetic appreciation; whereas historical and technical knowledge about works of art is at best an aid to aesthetic appreciation, and at worst diverts one's interest altogether from contemplation.

If the term "aesthetic education" is to be taken in the broad sense I have proposed, it must then also cover the active side. It must include cultivation of the capacity to give objective expression to one's insights into the realm of sensations and sentiments; and this means development of the individual's latent artistic abilities. Great natural gifts in this direction are of course as rare as in any other; but the capacity to express oneself in some art medium is no rarer and no more difficult to bring out than is the capacity to express one's ideas in writing exemplified in, for instance, a freshman theme or a letter to a friend. If the capacity for artistic self-expression seems more wonderful, it is only because fewer persons as yet cultivate it. The truth, however, probably is that most of the paintings, music, poems, and other works of art created each day in the land are about on the same level of difficulty, or originality, or of merit as are most of the essays written by students in college.

Much could be said concerning the human importance of aesthetic education. If art and aesthetic experience are thought by many persons to be at best of secondary moment in the life of man, it is I think chiefly because these persons tacitly but mistakenly assume art to be the sort of thing found only in art galleries, studios, museums, concert halls, or the like. The fact, however, is much rather that art and aesthetic experience are among men everywhere and at every moment, and have been so throughout the history of the race. In producing objects of even the most practical utility, men have generally utilized more thought and work than is demanded simply for their practical function. In almost every case, much time, thought, and effort have been given also to the attempt to make the object pleasing to the senses. And the consumer willingly pays for this.

13. *Moral and Religious Education.*   But there are two other dimensions of education—namely moral education and religious education—on which, because of their importance, it might have been expected that I should have touched before now.

Many persons believe that religion is the indispensable basis of morality, but although this can, I think, easily be disproved, there is no doubt that a certain close relation often exists between them. For its specific nature to become evident, it is necessary first of all to have a definite idea of what each essentially is; and I shall approach this question through a reference to the contention of Plotinus that, in respect of spiritual worth, men can be divided into three classes. Some, he said, may be described as beasts among men; others, as men among beasts; and others yet as gods among men. But instead of three classes, I shall distinguish four, and describe each in less picturesque but more literal terms.

The lowest class is that of malicious men. Malice is disinterested evil-doing. A man is malicious in so far as he does evil not as a means to advantage of some kind to himself, but for the mere pleasure he finds in doing it, even perhaps sometimes at some cost to himself. The terms "sadism" and "vandalism" describe some of the manifestations of this trait.

Next above the malicious man is the selfish man. He is the man who considers only what benefits him, and strives for it irrespective of what the cost of it to others may be. He does not seek to injure others nor to benefit them, but is quite ready to do either if only it works to his own profit. He does not care what happens to others.

Next higher in the spiritual scale is the moral or righteous man. He is the man whose rule in dealing with others is merely that of justice—or fair exchange or compensation. He is equally scrupulous to give others their due and to demand of them his due. He complies strictly with his obligations and expects others to do likewise; but he feels no impulse to do for others more than his obligations require, or to forgive them any part of what their obligations to him call for. His philosophy is simply that of the square deal.

Duty, justice, or righteousness, in the sense just defined is what I shall here assume to be the province of morality as distinguished from generosity. Morality, as so conceived, is about as much as the laws of the land have generally attempted to codify. It has been the most that a man's fellows felt they had the right to require of him, but it has been also the least they expected of him, since the unrighteous, unjust, undutiful man is in so far a burden or a plague to them. Generosity of spirit is no part of righteousness, which, therefore, does not call forth love; but it rightly calls forth esteem and respect, for it is of great social value. Development of morality is therefore one of the proper objectives of a total education of the individual.

On the other hand, religious education, in so far as it concerns itself with man's disposition towards his fellows, seeks to make him not merely just, but good; that is, freely benevolent. The good man is the man who, going beyond what merely justice or duty requires of him, is kind, merciful, compassionate, helpful. He is the altruistic man, the man who finds his own greatest happiness in bringing happiness to others or in promoting their welfare. He is the polar opposite of the malicious man. The latter does evil disinterestedly, for the sheer love of it. The altruist, on the other hand, does good disinterestedly, for the sheer love of it.

Cultivation in individuals, in social classes, and in nations, of the capacity to interest themselves benevolently and actively in the welfare of others is in our day perhaps the most urgent educational task. The education that undertakes it might be called education of the heart. It is this, I think, which great religious teachers such as the Christ and the Buddha were basically concerned to promote. The particular dogmas of the religions they founded are, from this point of view, significant essentially as premises for arguments in favor of brotherhood among men. Hence, by religious education, I mean in the present context not necessarily instruction in the scriptures or the beliefs of one or another of the historical religions of mankind; but, essentially, education of the heart—cultivation of altruistic feelings, impulses, and conduct, irrespective of whether this be done by means of indoctrination in the theology of a religion, or in some other way.

In this connection, it is essential to remember that, as a person acts, so does he tend to feel. Hence, in the education of the heart, the first step is to get the person concerned to act beneficently—that is to do good to others—even if he feels no direct impulse to do so. Only in the act of doing good to others can one discover the happiness which resides in the very doing of it. Virtue, we are told, is its own reward; but, to discover the reward inherent in altruistic action, it is necessary first to *act* altruistically, that is, in ways that benefit others, even if, to begin with, one so acts out of perhaps remotely egoistic motives, such as hope for a future life in a heaven.

14. *Liberal Education.*   We have now considered the principal aspects of human personality and the corresponding chief possible dimensions of the education of man. When we come to drawing concrete educational counsels from these considerations, however, a number of empirical factors enter the picture. One of them is the fact that, even if all human personalities have all of the kinds of potentialities mentioned, a given man is always more highly gifted with certain ones of them than with certain others. This would, in any given case, influence decision as to which ones of those aspects we ought to select as the ones upon which to concentrate the major part of the limited time and educational resources available in the particular case. The fact that the time and resources to be devoted to a given person's education are always short of what we might wish is thus a second empirical factor. What would in itself be desirable for the fullest development of an individual's potentialities is one thing; but what society, which ultimately pays in one kind of coin or another for his education and for his lack of it, can afford, is

another thing. And what is to be done in each concrete case is necessarily a compromise between the two.

Granting this, however, the counsels which would flow from the foregoing analysis of the generic nature of man, would be such, for example, as that the so-called "practical" aims, in education, should not be the only ones taken into account; that the success or failure of an education—or indeed of a life—should not be measured wholly or even mainly in terms of fruits of the conspicuous kinds, such as wealth, honors, position, power, popularity, or renown. Again, that the truly important thing about democracy is not that it performs the objective tasks of government better than could any other system—for this probably is not true—but that it is the one form of government which can in the long run automatically educate the citizen in social and individual responsibility, and which thus tacitly recognizes the fact that the most important thing for him is not that he should be well governed, but that he should have the opportunity to make his own mistakes and to gain wisdom from them. Again, that not only self-expression should be encouraged in the educational process, as has been the fashion in recent years; but also development of the capacity most men are even more likely to need throughout most of their life— namely, the capacity to do and to do well tasks which they perhaps do not like, but which are imposed on them by their own commitments or by the pressure of external necessity.

The essential import of the point of view I have been presenting may perhaps now in the end be summarily put by saying that an education is *humanly* right in proportion as it is as *liberal* as the circumstances of the individual concerned permit.

Essentially, liberal education is *liberating* education. It is not the education of men who are free, but the education that makes men free. More specifically, it is the kind of education designed to free man from his own ignorance, prejudices, and narrowness, by making him aware of them; it aims to give him a comprehensive view of the ranges of human knowledge, human achievements, and human capacities; and to develop in him an appreciative insight into the typical values for which men live. That is, liberal education is education essentially for perspective; and the value of perspective is that it brings freedom of choice of aims, and of judgment. Such freedom consists in awareness of the alternatives there are to choose between. The man who knows but one course, or sees but one aspect of things, or appreciates but a limited range of values, has no choice or but little choice as to the direction he takes. Unaware of his own blind spots and prejudices, he is held by them in an invisible jail. *The task of liberal education is to tear down its walls.*

C. J. Ducasse (July 7, 1881—) was born in Angouléme, France, but he earned his A.M. degree at the University of Washington in 1909 and his Ph.D. three years later at Harvard University. Upon completing his graduate training at Harvard, he returned to the University of Washington as an instructor. He became assistant professor of Philosophy in 1916, and was advanced to associate professor in 1924. In 1926 he accepted a position at Brown University as associate professor of Philosophy. He became professor of Philosophy in 1929 and head of the Department of Philosophy in 1930. He served as acting dean of the graduate school from 1947 to 1949, and became professor emeritus in 1958.

Professor Ducasse has lectured during the summer sessions at such well-known universities as California, Michigan, Chicago, Cornell, and Columbia. He has been elected president of a number of learned societies, including the Association for Symbolic Logic (1936–38), the American Philosophical Association, Eastern Division (1939), American Society for Aesthetics (1945), and the Philosophy of Science Association (1958–61). His published works include Causation and the Types of Necessity; The Philosophy of Art; The Relation of Philosophy to General Education; Philosophy as a Science; Art, the Critic, and You; Nature, Mind, and Death; A Philosophical Scrutiny of Religion; *and* A Critical Examination of the Belief in a Life After Death. *Professor Ducasse has contributed articles to such well-known professional journals as* The Philosophical Review, Mind, Synthése, Philosophy of Science, The American Scholar, Revue Internationale de Philosophie, The Review of Religion, *and the* Centennial Review.

"What Can Philosophy Contribute to Educational Theory?" was delivered at a symposium on philosophy and education held at Northwestern University during the summer of 1958.

2

The Uses of Philosophy and the Problems of Educators[*]

ARNOLD B. LEVISON

WHEN THIS TOPIC was first suggested to me, "In what ways can philosophy be of use to educators?", my inclination was to reply "None," or at least "None that would be relevant to the educator in his professional capacity."[†] But when I set myself to work out the implicit considerations which had led me to make this judgment I found that the conditions were more complex than I had envisioned. I found that although there was one sense at least in which it would be wrong to claim that philosophy could be of special help to educators, there were other senses in which it would not be so. For originally I had thought of the educator as a professional person whose primary interest was in education as a "practical" science, that is to say a science which seeks knowledge of what to do in the teaching situation. But upon reflection I found that the notion of "teaching situation" was ambiguous and that there were at least three senses in which the teaching situation could present itself according as the educator was (1) an educational theorist, (2) a planner of curricula, and (3) a classroom teacher. And the way in which philosophy could or could not be of assistance to educators, I found, was simi-

[*] Arnold B. Levison, "The Uses of Philosophy and the Problems of Educators," *Educational Theory*, Vol. XI, No. 4, April, 1961, pp. 123–128. Used by permission of the author and *Educational Theory*.

[†] A paper read at the 12th Annual Meeting of the Philosophy of Education Society (Southeastern Section), February 5–6, 1960.

larly no univocal matter but depended on whether philosophy was conceived as (1) an autonomous activity, (2) a certain type of institution, or (3) an expression of a broad human concern. This last category is vague but not necessarily insignificant. In view of this complexity, I have revised my original opinion so that it now seems to me that there are definite ways in which one *can* speak of philosophy being of help to educators, provided that the sense in which philosophy *cannot* be of such assistance is first clearly comprehended. For it must be kept in mind that philosophy is a field of study in its own right, and is not especially oriented to education any more than it is oriented to the problems of other special fields outside its own province. The same, of course, is true of education; and in the sense in which both philosophy and education are independent, autonomous areas of study with their own standards, goals, ends, and requirements, it is downright impertinent to speak of one being of any special help to the other. But recognizing the integrity and independence of each as a branch of human knowledge and concern, it is permissible to speak of ways in which they can be of help to one another. In this paper, I shall speak from the side of philosophy only, and of how I conceive that it can and cannot be of assistance to educators.

To begin, I must devote some space to telling you what, in my opinion, philosophy is. I should observe, first of all, that to me philosophy is something that one "does," as opposed to something that one merely "talks *about*" or "reports," i.e. philosophy is first of all an activity of a certain kind and only secondarily a subject-matter consisting of a definite body of literature. But it is an activity which is accomplished through talking and writing, and for this reason is regarded by many people, who view all talking as "just talking" and never see that talking can be a kind of doing, as a rather silly or idle preoccupation. They take this attitude because they see philosophy only from the outside. From the inside, a different picture emerges. Here philosophy reveals itself as the analysis or systematic interpretation of general problems such as meaning, truth, perception, proof, knowledge, and so on. It seeks to say what can be said, logically and evidentially, about such general problems *as* general. It is thus, professionally regarded, a highly circumscribed activity, but one with an intense intrinsic value and interest for those who practice it.

Now philosophy in this sense, as an activity in its own right, is of no earthly use to educators or anyone else except those whose whole interests happen to be for that time philosophically engaged. Thus it would be absurd for a public school teacher to undertake to establish the reality of the external world prior to deciding how to discipline a recalcitrant pupil. In the same way, it would be ridiculous for an educator planning a curriculum for a system of public schools to concern himself with the question whether, if Hume is right, tomorrow will be like today or indeed whether there will be any schools at all in which to apply his program. These things are absurd and silly, but they would not be absurd and silly if the activity of philosophizing *were* directly relevant to the activities of an educator. It would be logically just as absurd to judge on the basis that philosophizing is of no value to educators that it has no value or use *whatever*. The usefulness and value of philosophy as such is to be judged wholly by those whose interests are philosophical, and not by those whose interests are in something else. Philosophy is essentially to be conceived, then, as an activity in its own right, cognitive, yet distinct from science and art, and in this sense the activity of philosophizing is wholly irrelevant to the activities of the educator.

But this way of viewing philosophy, as a certain distinctive type of human activity, is not the only one. Thus philosophy conceived as a certain type of institution *can* be of assistance to educators. I shall argue that philosophy in this respect is of assistance not so much to classroom teachers as to educational theorists and program planners. I will now proceed to elaborate this point.

Philosophy, I have said, is essentially to be conceived as an activity in its own right, cognitive, yet distinct from science and art. But the use of the word "philosophy" is not limited to this sense. There is another sense of the word "philosophy" in which what is referred to is an institution belonging to a complex social nexus of institutions. Philosophy conceived as an institution among institutions is an ill-defined community of diverse activities, some of which are not distinctively philosophical in the sense in which I have defined the philosophical activity. The philosophical community, as it exists today, contains many activities which I should call essentially "scientific", but I do not wish to say that they are for that reason out of place in that community. One of the peculiar characteristics of the philosophical activity is that it can be practiced on subjects not themselves distinctively philosophical. There is always room for the activity of probing into our deeper perplexities, in the very general way that is characteristic of philosophers, even when such perplexities are "philosophical" only because they are not sufficiently well-defined to be amenable to scientific treatment. Many of the problems of educators are of this nature, that is to say they are "scientific" in character and yet not sufficiently well-defined to be amenable to scientific treatment. Consequently, these problems come to rest for the present in the roost of the philosophers.

So far as we have any knowledge, it seems that there will always be such perplexities, however far back the frontiers of positive scientific knowledge are pushed. The general activity of probing into ultimate perplexities, some of which may be amenable to eventual scientific investigation and some of which may not, forms a large part of the activities and concerns of people operating within the institution of philosophy. Taking first those problems which may never be amenable to scientific treatment, it is still possible to attempt to come to some kind of systematic conclusion with regard to them, the best that one can, logically and evidentially. These are the problems that philosophers concern themselves with under the titles of epistemology, metaphysics, cosmology, etc. But, and this is the point, *other* problems presently occupying the attention of people within the philosophical community may eventually prove so productive as to develop into new sciences or at least contribute substantially to the improvement of an existing science. In this way the philosophical community may function as the mother of new sciences, as an influential force in the development of existing sciences, or as the permanent home of problems which will never be anything but philosophical.

Thus, people working within the philosophical community, whether we call them scientists or philosophers, can be of help to educators, especially educational theorists and program planners, in the following ways. 1. They can undertake to conduct, at least in the preliminary stages, the necessary empirical investigations which will establish the basic concepts of an educational theory. 2. They can assist in the development of tests for judging the truth and adequacy of any hypothesis which is advanced in educational science. 3. They can develop and supply the techniques for analyzing the words or concepts of educational discourse, in order to remove verbal conflicts and resolve inconsistencies in the language of education.

Since the philosophical community functions as the natural harbor and refuge for problems, whatever their real character, which are homeless and wandering, and since many of the problems of educators at the present time are of this nature, it is natural for educators to look to philosophy and philosophers for aid, especially in the matter of offering sound hypotheses and general programs for educators to try out in the teaching situation, in the manner of John Dewey. But it must be pointed out that when philosophers function in this way, they are functioning not as people whose interests are wholly absorbed in philosophical activities as such, but as scientists, offering hypotheses and formulating objective tests for validity. I have not tried to develop for you the concrete ways in which philosophy conceived as an institution can be of help to educators. I have concentrated rather on specifying the ways in which philosophy *logically* could and could not be of help to educators.

There is yet a third way, it seems to me, in which philosophy could be of help to educators, this time not to the educational theorist or program planner, but to the classroom teacher. And this involves the conception of philosophy not as an autonomous professional activity, nor as an institution among other institutions, but as an expression of a broad type of human concern. In this broader or vague sense philosophy is of peculiar importance to the classroom teacher because it typifies a kind of concern which is common to all mankind. The classroom teacher, whose profession is practiced on human beings as subjects, is peculiarly in need of a strong dose of philosophy in this sense. In order to bring out my meaning, however, I must take some space to develop an aspect of philosophizing which has not so far been made explicit.

I have said that philosophy is essentially to be conceived as an activity, cognitive, yet distinct from science and art. Its distinction from art may be assumed, but I have not yet made clear for you how it is to be distinguished from science. You will understand that I am here using the word "science" in a somewhat limited sense, that is, merely to denote such sciences as mathematics, physics, biology, anthropology, and so forth. They are sometimes called the "special sciences". In what way, then, is philosophy distinct from these special sciences? The answer to this question lies, I believe, in the fact that the philosophical activity incorporates as a part of its methodology the peculiar limitations of the human condition, that is to say, the fact that our results in an investigation must be affected by the presence of an observer or desirer such as man. The notion of complete non-intervention in the facts, or of maintaining an attitude of stolid passivity in the examination of pure data, which has been rendered sacrosanct by the special sciences, has really no place in philosophy.

You will tell me, of course: "Yes, but scientific results are testable by observation, and are therefore perfectly objective and imply no subjective intervention which might distort their character." But this seems to me to involve a false conception of "observation". What you say may well be true in the sense that it describes, for all practical purposes, the way in which a biologist or chemist goes to work, but it is not true as a theoretical statement about "observation". Observation is *not* an utterly passive activity. It is not merely the confrontation of a set of pre-labeled facts by a passive perceiver. The analogy of the man watching the behavior of the goldfish in the goldfish bowl is only one kind of observation, and a rather trivial one at that. The results of scientific investigation have their peculiar status and value not merely because they can be tested by observation but because large groups of human beings, namely, those whom we call scientists, know what to take them for. There are, of course, important reasons why a significantly large group of human beings *can* know, in that precise sense of "knowledge", how to take the results of a scientific investigation. It is because the whole sense of a "scientific" investigation is that it creates perfectly general standard conditions under which any scientist can follow out the specified procedure and arrive at the same results. But though there are analogues between this scientific procedure and the philosophical one, the essential difference remains that a purely philosophical investigation cannot proceed in ignoration of the fact that it is undertaken by man. The fact that the person conducting the philosophical investigation may affect the results is not considered as an unhappy chance to be avoided so far as possible, but *as itself something that requires investigation and explanation.*

It is for this reason that a philosophy, from the time of Socrates, has always been in part the views of a certain individual, and since the time of Socrates, society has never been quite unambivalent in its feeling for such an individual. Socrates felt that it was the peculiar office of the philosopher to be a goad or "gadfly" in relation to his fellow citizens. You all know the story in the *Apology*. My contention is that philosophers continue to fulfill this social function as defined by Socrates, especially in their own classrooms. They still administer the paralytic shock to those of their pupils who imagine that their "knowledge" rests on perfectly secure foundations.

It is part of the distinctive function of philosophy, as opposed to science, to get out into the open this aspect of cognition, on which our beliefs are so largely founded, namely, what we claim to know through personal experience and through the personalities of important individuals in our lives, such as classroom teachers. We all know that classroom teachers have an enormous influence over the choices made by their pupils as the latter mature in life. Yet this type of knowledge, namely, that which we claim to have through personal experience, though precious, is probably the most precarious and the least secure of all our forms of knowledge. This fact does not preclude its being the most often used. In most of the practical and important decisions we make in life, we cannot call upon the disclosures of science to back us up. What we normally rely upon are the personalities of influential people in our lives, such as our teachers. We come to regard certain people as arbiters of taste and right conduct, and attempt to guide our lives according to their approvals and disapprovals. Teachers are certainly high on the list of those who influence us in this way.

Teachers, therefore, even more than most people, have the responsibility of freeing themselves from prejudice and from irrationally formed opinions. The relation of a teacher to a classroom filled with pupils is symbolic of the tremendous danger in the human situation. There is no way of eliminating the type of danger inherent in this situation and preserving the distinctive character of human society, as opposed, for instance, to insect society or a society of perfect automatons. Now of course if people could be persuaded to form their opinions on the basis of expert testimony exclusively, except where they could through investigation formulate their opinions directly on the basis of evidence, this particular danger would be greatly averted. And that in a sense is the goal towards which we here are striving. But in the meantime the facts are otherwise. One of the facts about our human nature appears to be that we would rather have our beliefs vindicated, whatever the consequences, than to examine them to see whether or not they are worthy.

The responsibility of the teacher is at least in part not to pass on to his pupils the prejudices and unanalyzed, subconscious desires of his own generation, so far as he can help himself. And philosophy, it seems to me, is peculiarly apt to be of help to the teacher in gaining the requisite self-knowledge to discharge this responsibility. For how can a teacher fulfill this responsibility if he himself is not aware of the danger? Now in contrast to all other forms of cognitive activity, philosophy begins not by filling a person's mind full of propositions which he must take for granted, but by emptying his mind (ideally) of *all* uninvestigated and unanalyzed beliefs. The rule in philosophy is that no belief, however indispensable to practical life, is to be regarded as *true* without supporting evidence. It is this fact that makes some philosophical questions appear so peculiar, such as questions about the reality of an external world. But in no better way, it seems to me, than through the study of philosophy, can a teacher come to realize the lack of secure foundation for most of our beliefs. And the insight thus gained into the lack of justification we have for many of our beliefs naturally results in a disposition to be cautious with respect to stating those beliefs which, though held, cannot be securely supported. Furthermore, by coming to appreciate the way in which personality *can* affect results, the teacher is less likely to be dogmatic about anything, even science.

To come to the point at last, philosophy can be of help to the classroom teacher by the fact that it is training in the activity of evaluating our beliefs, and thus, in effect, training in the art of self-knowledge.

Philosophy instructs us in that knowledge of one's own ignorance generally which is indispensable to the improvement of the human mind, and since the professional task of classroom teachers is this improvement, a philosophically cultivated habit of thought can greatly assist a teacher, it seems to me, in the discharge of his responsibilities.

I will end with a note of reassurance. Human beings, and that includes philosophers and educators, are entitled to a degree of prejudice. Prejudice is a luxury, and one of which it would be unwise, I think, to seek to deprive ourselves altogether. Some prejudices are silly because they are plainly refuted by the evidence. Others are harmful, at least when practiced on a social scale. But many of our prejudices are quite harmless and it would be inhuman to expect anyone to be completely free of them. I think that the teacher, like the rest of us, is entitled to his measure of prejudices, but it is one thing to be the victim of a prejudice in ignorance of its true nature, and another thing to give expression to a prejudice in awareness of the fact that it is, or may be, nothing else.

To sum up, I have tried in this paper to make clear for you the major ways in which philosophy logically could and could not be of help to educators. Philosophy as an institution can be of practical and concrete assistance to educational theorists and program planners; and as an expression of a broad human interest in the foundations of our beliefs, it is of help to the classroom teacher in the discharge of his most fundamental responsibility. But as an autonomous activity, demanding complete absorption in the philosophical problem for its own sake, philosophy is of no special use or assistance to educators or anyone else outside its province.

Arnold B. Levison (December 2, 1929—) was born in Philadelphia and educated at the New School for Social Research and at the University of Virginia. He received the Ph.D. degree from the latter institution in 1959, writing his dissertation on the "Concept of Proof." Professor Levison has devoted almost all his energies to pure philosophy with an occasional excursion into the philosophy of education. He has contributed articles to Mind, Inquiry, Philosophy and Phenomenological Research, Monist, *and* Educational Theory. *In 1966 he edited and prepared a critical introduction to a collection of papers in the philosophy of history by Karl Löwith, entitled* Nature, History and Existentialism. *He has taught at the University of Georgia, Northwestern University, University of Virginia, and at present is an assistant professor of philosophy at the University of Illinois at Chicago Circle.*

3

Philosophy of Education– Directive Doctrine or Liberal Discipline?*

EVERETT JOHN KIRCHER

LIKE MOST CULTURES, American democracy has evolved to its present state without benefit of any single formal system of philosophy. This is not to deny that the philosophic mind has been present nor that the general character of our culture has benefited at one time or another from a rich diversity of both formal and informal philosophies. It is rather to deny that our culture has been self-consciously constructed along the lines of any one comprehensive system of thought which was first theoretically formulated and subsequently actualized into a whole way of life. In other words we have not built our American democracy deliberately according to any pre-selected system of philosophy. Conversely, modern Russia is an example of a culture in which it was belatedly decided to do just this.

Marx was a philosopher with a disposition toward philosophy which has become more and more popular throughout the world. He was a philosopher who inclined to the notion his disciples wholly embraced that the discipline of philosophy could recover itself only if it largely abandoned its role as one of the liberal disciplines and became literally directive of human affairs. Since the teaching of philosophy, like other

* Everett J. Kircher, "Philosophy of Education—Directive Doctrine or Liberal Discipline?" *Educational Theory*, Vol. V, No. 4, October, 1955, pp. 220–229. Used by permission of the author and *Educational Theory*.

of the liberal studies, has often been unimaginative and sterile and has failed to function as an intellectual leaven in our common culture, it was easy for him to conclude along with many another in other systems of thought that philosophy fell into either one of two categories. Either it was ivory tower and irrelevant to the moving concerns of men or it was an ultimate commitment, doctrinally conceived, and effectively directive of the practical affairs of the market place. Faced with these two alternatives, he concluded that philosophy should be changed from its esoteric status and be made to bake bread. Such a proposal was not only congenial to the Marxist reformers who followed him, it has been congenial to the academic reformer in America. The idea has intrigued us. Preplanned systems in the large, theoretically formulated world views, inspire the imagination with a high hope. And reformers respond to the notion that a system of philosophy can be used as a reliable referent in the conduct of the confusing, inconsistent and conflicting forces of the human enterprise.

One in this mood looks at the social scene and asks what it adds up to other than over-all, meaningless and incoherent confusion. One sees only a welter of disparate and conflicting social forces in the fields of religion, economics, and politics. One senses that the gods looking down from the Olympus see us running helterskelter like ants at cross purposes with one another in a state of endless frustration and conflict. What any culture and finally the world desperately needs, we are then told, is an over-all system of thought, an integrating world-view, which would establish a common purpose for mankind and mutually consistent subordinate goals. Some all-comprehending philosophy within whose generous circumference men could find themselves at peace; a common way of life in which social forces were harmonized and the culture convincingly integrated is what is required. Then men would enjoy a community of mind and spirit, social harmony would be approximated and the brotherhood of man would become a reality on this earth. Such is the philosopher's dream, and all it would take to realize this cultural millennium would be the long-sought discovery of the philosopher's stone.

This is a noble dream which the over-agitated and the over-eager recurrently discover that they are destined to fulfill in reality. In other words, men who seek the philosopher's stone too expectantly soon find it. There is a compulsion in their quest which guarantees its premature discovery. And upon such an occasion they look down upon struggling man and know what he must do. This is where Hegel finally stood. It is where Marx stood. And it is where every philosopher-reformer is destined to stand who lays claim to the exclusive adequacy of his philosophy for any culture or for the world. This evil role in which knowledgeable man succumbs to the temptation to play God because he is surrounded by men without sufficient knowledge to controvert his system of thought does not pertain only to philosophies we have come to look upon as evil. It pertains alike to those philosophies we have come to look upon as good. The evil and the suffering ultimately entailed derives from misrepresentation on the grand scale. Philosophic man presumes to an adequacy of systematic knowledge that he does not have, and other men follow in an unwarranted faith eternally destined to disaster.

Yet men in the large hold themselves perennially prepared to believe again that the philosopher's stone has been found. Consequently there is a social climate conducive to the notion that a philosophy of freedom has been found, a philosophy that is inherently not susceptible of subversion to evil ends. What is so alien to our thought is that the very claim to have found such a philosophy makes that philosophy inimical to human freedom. To claim that one has found the true or the ultimately adequate philosophy is to claim that one has found the philosophy of philosophies, that the philosophic quest in the large has been completed. The philosophy of Marx speculatively projected and creatively entertained would not have jeopardized the philosophic enterprise nor human freedom on this earth. The Communist institutionalization of this system of philosophy as a wholly adequate world doctrine is the point at which the philosophic enterprise and all human freedom was cast into jeopardy. The evil is not inherently in the speculative system but in the disposition of those who would universalize it. It is therefore unfortunate that so many of us have been so preoccupied with the notion that the Russian error was in the selection of a wrong philosophy that we have neglected to note their more fundamental error; namely, that they embraced the inhumanity of attempting to integrate their social order, and finally the world, in accordance with some one pre-planned and elaborately conceived philosophy. Their fatal error in judgment revealed itself in their uncompromising conviction that a distinguished system of thought could be made so logically adequate that it could be put into practice without fundamental modification. Their error did not seem greater to them than ours does to us when we also incline to the notion that a comprehensive and carefully conceived theory could be made reliably adequate to the conduct of human affairs. We too indulge, from time to time, in the unwarranted faith that the academic mind at its best is equal to the task of providing a system of philosophy that will prove itself adequate to the complex exigencies of fact. And the systematic academic mind is understandably susceptible of this persuasion whenever reforming zeal runs high. Conversely, the creative and dedicated scholar is uniquely impervious to this profane presumption himself and always suspicious of it in the many varied forms it takes in others.

Education and the One Philosophy

There have been many theorists and some formal philosophers in the history of American culture who have periodically proposed to involve us in the same error. It is the common aspiration of theorists, and their recurring presumption, to have worked out a system of ideas that would adequately harmonize and integrate the American social order. It is to the credit of our own culture that it has largely resisted persuasion in this matter up to the present time. Not only in the culture at large have we resisted the temptation to be wholly logical according to some one system of logic, we have largely resisted this temptation in the public school systems of the state. Consequently, our educational program shows neither the theoretical benefit nor the actual deterioration which would result from the adoption of the central doctrine of a one-philosophy state. In other words, public education in the United States is not, and never has been, conducted according to any one system of philosophy. *It is significant to note, however, that it has become the prevailing mode of our time to lament this fact.* The past generation of educational theorists have been at great pains to show that this has been unfortunate in the past and promises to be disastrous in the future. We are told that the welter of prevailing philosophies and theories in conflict can logically result only in general confusion, cultural disintegration and the ultimate frustration of both the American teacher and the rising generation. To many academic minds intent upon effecting logical coherence and cultural integration, this is self-evident.

Since it is the primary function of the intellectual to knit the desparate and disarrayed tag ends of things into clear and consistent meaningful wholes in every area of learning, nothing could be more natural than for each to envision the whole as finally organized, integrated and explained in terms of the generalized insights of his own distinctive philosophy, religion or academic discipline. Not only is this natural, to a certain degree it is inevitable, and there is a sense in which it is proper. It is proper as forever unfinished aspiration.

The social and educational theorist is faced in a more dramatic way with the same paradox which faces every man and every culture. For his own sanity, he must hold to the somehow rightness of his own personal-intellectual point of view. He cannot be forever qualifying, denying and doubting himself. And yet, in any free society, and in the world at large, every man's carefully intellectualized outlook on life is in fact qualified, denied or doubted by men and cultures of equal intellectual equipment and equal intellectual integrity. To believe in one's self and yet to honor the person and the thinking of those who find it necessary to deny one's own beliefs, presents finite and inevitably biased man with a dilemma he does not have the cosmic mind finally to resolve. All extant theories for the resolution of this problem end in one more theory which attempts to persuade man that he actually is intellectually competent to resolve this dilemma after all. And the native presumption of men is always prepared to rise once more and to believe again that a new device has been created that will allow him to transcend those limits of his finitude that it is not reasonable to believe he can surmount with any distinctive point of view or any unique system of logic. Indeed, to be distinctive and to be unique is to be *other than* other forms of distinction and uniqueness that forever rise to confound the intellectual resolution of uniqueness.

One must grant that there is no more adequate evidence of learning and personal culture than the progressive enlarging of one's own understanding of the world from his own unique perspective. One's coherent distinctiveness is doubtless the greatest contribution one has to make to the world. But the all too human tendency to universalize this uniqueness and presume to assimilate all relevant diversity into one inclusive perspective, the fatal end toward which all systematic rationality inclines, fails to recognize the strategic limits of intellection and robs a diversity of men of the only real freedom in the world, the freedom to engage life with integrity each on his own terms.

Growth of Any One Philosophy

There is no open-minded philosophy in the sense that each often boasts that it is. No philosophy is open to other than its own assumptions, its own methods, its own distinctive pattern of meanings and, above all, its own ultimate propagation. No philosophy frees a man in all directions for any or all assumptions or values. Every philosophy releases man into the full and generous arena of the only universe there is—the materialistic, the idea-istic, the realistic or the empirical—but the only universe there really is; and it is designed to explain all the others away. If there is anything characteristic of any system of philosophy, it is that it is sufficient unto itself. Of all the things it logically does not need in the world, it is the conflicting and denying assumptions and propositions of other philosophical systems. Or if it does need these, it needs them as the materials for its own assimilation and development. It needs them as the negative to its own positive, the error to demonstrate its own truth. It needs them as food upon which to feed, a process which results in the disintegration of the food and its assimilation into a growing body of thought which is designed to prevail through the disintegration of its opposition.

In a sense, a system of philosophy is like a cat in the forest. It grows by what it feeds upon and by transforming what it feeds upon into itself. It has no way of doing justice to other forms of life except from its own point of view. And from this point of view, other forms of life look like a means of growth and development for itself. Its promise of the good life to what it regards lesser forms is a promise to assimilate them into a nobler structure that is more glorious in the sight of gods or men. Sometimes they are promised that this will be a painless transformation. Sometimes they are promised a special place of residence that will not do violence to their own distinctive form. And yet it seems to be the fact with both the organic system of the cat and the organic system of a philosophy that undigested foreign matter must ultimately be assimilated or be passed off, and this on pain of death. Regardless of high promises on the part of any system of thought to protect the distinctiveness of other organic forms within its own system, we would do well to recall that no matter how many birds a compassionate cat may eat, it never becomes more birdlike. Rather, it becomes a bigger cat. A philosophy lives upon the assimilation into its own organic system of the facts of life, the problems of men and the relevant aspects of all other philosophies. It is modified in this process but not in a way congenial to the forms assimilated.

There is a fundamental sense in which all philosophies are, therefore, philosophies of growth. Each struggles to grow into a state of universal explanation of the only real world it acknowledges. Anything not yet assimilated into the organic structure of any philosophy leaves it still hungry and growing. Philosophies which would distinguish themselves as philosophies of growth have a doubtful distinction for they are as ungenerous in the large as any other philosophy. They are always characterized by growth toward their own fulfillment through a disintegration of other logical forms and by a digestive process distinctively designed to this end. It is consequently the dilemma of all systematic intellection that it is carried on in such a way as to perpetuate its own distinctive form and proceed from its own perspective whereas it aspires to enfold a variety of forms and it wishes to appear inclusive of a wide diversity of perspectives. The implicit denial of this which occurs when any philosophy aspires to universalization and to becoming directive of a whole way of life sounds the knell of philosophic thought, makes a mockery of the liberal university and introduces into any culture the rational conditions for the denial of freedom to all who choose to define it differently from the prevailing rationale.

In simple point of fact, a philosophy can no more afford to assimilate the total complex of life into its own system than a cat can afford to assimilate the total complex of forest life into its own system. For a philosophy to explain the world, and finally all other philosophies, a not uncommon presumption of comprehensive world-views, is literally to embrace self-extinction. The ongoing life of both philosophies and cats depends upon the continuing existence of other organic forms. In the case of the cat, these other forms must be both an abundance of birds and other cats. No matter how many of the former are consumed and the latter bred or killed in combat, cats die from this earth when they assimilate into themselves all that they prey upon, fertilize or engage in mortal combat.

Remarkably similar observations can be made of integral and organic systems of philosophy. In order to keep healthy, vital and growing, they need what they commonly hasten to deny; they need an abundance of as yet unexplained problems, aspects of the natural world and of the human enterprise that they have as yet been unable to assimilate into their own organic structure. Moreover, they need cross-fertilization with other systems of philosophy which they commonly attack with the intention of annihilation. The perennial claim of exclusive adequacy for any philosophy is the expression of an unwitting presumption calling for the abandonment of the philosophic enterprise. Contests of explanation among the philosophies and creative engagements over the problems that beset us result both in health and procreation of a rich diversity of philosophies. But the determination, once and for all to win the field results in a declaration of war. The philosophic temper and intention is abandoned; and if the war is successful, the winner will have devasted the field in which he was wont to forage. Yet there are educational philosophers reminiscent of such cats, for they leave the survival of the philosophic enterprise not to intention but to chance. Like the forest tom, many a philosophy would have annihilated the condition of its being except that it was not able to assimilate the whole field.

We must conclude, therefore, that no system of philosophy, not even the presumed right one should be allowed to gain the uncontested status of being the exclusively adequate philosophy of free men. Freedom resides not in a system of philosophy but in the acceptance of a state of consciously maintained diversity which thereupon becomes a state of ethical diversity. In saying this, we have dealt only with the ought; no philosophy ought to aspire to universal and exclusive adequacy. We may go on to say that any philosophy uniquely designed to guarantee freedom among men not only ought not be universally adopted, it probably cannot be universally adopted. The complex enormity of the world appears to protect the philosophic enterprise from self-annihilation. There is just too much in the world for any one organic structure to assimilate. Even in Soviet Russia the original Marxist philosophy has not only been grossly modified in process of Communist application but there is reason to believe that large and silent sectors of the people have never accommodated themselves to its fundamental assumptions. In the attempt to translate any one system of philosophy into a whole way of life, we are therefore confronted with an aspiration that not only ought not but cannot finally be realized. A very real evil and much suffering results from the attempt and the partial success that is attained.

It is probably safe, then, to say that no philosophy has ever fully realized itself in any culture without fundamental compromise. Moreover, it is probably true that no formal system of philosophy has ever taken up unqualified residence in the life of any single man. A man, like a culture, is forever more than any theory about him. Each encompasses not only a logic but a mystery beyond the logic. Consequently, while it is apparently possible for both a man and a culture to identify themselves with some comprehensive rational theory, it is not possible for them to conduct their lives strictly in accordance with any such theory. The whole man is never encompassed by any rational theory but suffers unaccountable modification and growth out of the mysterious heart of him. Whether the intellectual system is Christian, Marxist or pragmatist, it appears impossible to fulfill the theorist's dream and strategically or forcefully to actualize any formal theory either in the free society or in the totalitarian state.

There is, of course, some basis for believing that the integration of a social order in terms of some one philosophy of life can be more fully attained in the totalitarian state. Certainly this is widely assumed. Yet there is reason to doubt that the overt conformity to the state philosophy is expressive of the vital and living principles of that philosophy. It is doubtful if the philosophy lives as philosophy in the hearts and minds of those it appears to motivate and direct. Perhaps in such seemingly mono-lithic states philosophy is largely dead and only the philosophic skeleton remains to give the appearance of philosophic structure to the social body. In such cases, conventions, ritual, habit and formal directives take the place of action enlightened by philosophic principles. However this may be, no one philosophy can endure indefinitely in any culture without stimulating alternative and conflicting systems of thought. The formal regulation of life according to some rational system cannot finally bring about the stultification of the human spirit. It would therefore behoove us in all of modern culture, but in the schools of the state particularly, to ask ourselves whether or not we are incorporating into our teacher train-ing the assumption that one of the formal systems of philosophy in our time holds the promise of freedom for the human spirit. In other words, we must ask whether we are openly or subtly imparting the notion that there is one wholly adequate philosophy of democracy.

Development of Discipleship

There is reason to believe that creative philosophers themselves tend to divide on this issue even though the great majority of them have long made the assumption that the freedom and vitality of the philosophic enterprise depended, among other things, upon a rich diversity in philo-sophic speculation. Yet it appears that some philosophers are more con-tent than others simply to bring into being a new perspective on life for the general enlightenment of men. Others incline to the notion that they have conceived a theoretical formulation of such adequacy that it merits universal acquiescence. Santayana was typical of the former and there-fore finds it natural to say in the preface to his *Skepticism and Animal Faith*,

Here is one more system of philosophy. If the reader is inclined to smile, I can assure him that I smile with him. . . . I think that common sense, in a rough dogged way, is technically sounder than the special schools of philoso-phy, each of which squints and overlooks half the facts and half the difficulties in its eagerness to find in some detail the key to the whole.[1]

Conversely, Friedrich Hegel is widely known to have grown congenial to the notion that his dialectical system of thought finally led to the possi-

[1] George Santayana, *Skepticism and Animal Faith*. New York: Charles Scribner's Sons, 1923, p. V.

bility of an ultimate synthesis on its own terms in the German state of his time.

Between these two extremes there rests the great majority of philosophic minds about whose location on the scale we may only speculate. This much may be said however; the character of some systems of philosophy appear to solicit followership in ways almost too subtle to define. Others seem to effect the conditions which make discipleship next to impossible. Of the former, the disciples are characteristically unphilosophic and essentially doctrinal in their thinking. And one of the hidden sources of their power and of their cruelty is that they are oblivious to this fact. The doctrinal mind of the disciple who is following the authority of a pre-fabricated system of thought finds what he calls freedom in this enterprise, and he would like to enroll as many others as possible into this kind of freedom. In speaking of his commitment he often refers to it as the philosophy of freedom. But the genuinely philosophic mind is of an entirely different order. It finds its freedom in creating distinctive modes of thought out of the philosophic heritage and the occasion of its time. Former systems of thought are reconstructed rather than simply followed, implemented and applied. Any philosopher worthy of the name is therefore the beneficiary of the philosophies of the past but never the victim of any one of them.

The transition from the creative thinking which results in a system of philosophy to a doctrinal acceptance of the system is very subtle. One lives through the creative process with the original mind, knows the delight of an unfolding organization of thought and discovers life more richly meaningful than he had known it before. In this state of intellectual excitement it is a very great temptation to identify one's self with the master and with his system of thought, envision one's self as a co-partner in the evolution and the extension of his ideas and become a champion of his views. If one's distinguished mentor is living, it is common to be desirous of his public approval and deeply enthralled by his expression of endorsement and affection. The long struggle to be worthy of discipleship then follows. The rewards for acceptance are very great, for the disciple himself becomes an authority through his identification with an undeniable authority. Competition for favor among the disciples always sets in and much bitterness attends every followership. Among such disciples every face is turned toward the central philosophy; their teaching and discussion centers upon philosophy; they are primarily concerned with philosophy—and yet natively philosophic minds look upon them in wonderment, for the philosophic enterprise has mysteriously been abandoned. A cult has developed, and the cult struggles in vain to fill the philosophic vacuity left by a great and seminal mind.

Much good work is done by disciples and much necessary work but much evil ensues from the very deception that they are philosophers who have inherited the authority that originally attached to an intellectual enterprise of great scope and integrity. They do not know how to wear the authority, for their power stems from their commitment and their commitment denies them the privilege of fundamentally reconstructing the philosophic source of their authority. Yet it was this privilege that kept the original philosophers free and philosophic. He was free to abandon or rebuild anything he constructed; he was free to indulge in doubt about his most fundamental premises; he was free to wonder about the adequacy of his system. Consequently, he was free to listen to other competing and conflicting philosophies and, across the bridge of his wonderment and his doubt, meet other philosophic minds also stepping out to the precarious edge of their thought. He was free to join in the transcendent community known to all philosophic minds of integrity, the key to which is the qualified commitment to what one has rationally proved to be true and necessary. The qualified commitment to one's own rational system and an unqualified faith in an undiscovered future or an unknown God that transcends systematic rationality—these are the conditions of the philosophers' community of mind in the midst of their inevitably diverse rational systems. Yet these freedoms and this transcendence are characteristically what the disciple abandons. He is, therefore, not only not a philosopher, he is not free. He is the victim of his appropriated system and he is the uncompromising enemy of those systems of thought which are in conflict with his own. With him literal rationality takes precedence over the philosophic temper and the philosophic quest. He cannot say with Whitehead that at its best all philosophy becomes poetry. Refusing to admit poetic transcendence over literal rationality at the higher levels of insight, he wages unremitting war over literal and exact differences in doctrine. This is the common fate of the man who goes through life on the ultimate authority of another. And it is thus that he makes the transition from freedom to slavery through a philosophy of freedom.

Dewey's Philosophy of Freedom

One is constrained to believe that this is essentially the transition that has taken place between John Dewey, the philosopher, and many of his disciples. Their native presumption in the face of other social, religious and academic philosophies must derive from an essentially unqualified commitment to their naturalistic empiricism. The arbitrary denials of other philosophies of life can hardly mean other than that they really believe Dewey found the philosopher's stone and passed it on to them. This allows them the presumption that their philosophy is different in the sense that it is the only truly democratic, the only truly adequate philosophy of freedom. Over the last generation unnumbered students have been given to believe that this philosophy is so exclusively adequate, in this sense so universally true, that a democratic society has no need to sponsor and teach other conflicting systems of philosophy. Consequently, in a largely Christian-Hebraic culture, this nontheistic philosophy is commonly spoken of as THE democratic philosophy. It implies, we have been told, a whole *Weltanschauung* waiting for explicit realization which may properly be thought of as the only adequate conception of the democratic way of life. Yet what this turns out to be is the implementation of the formal philosophy of Dewey-pragmatism as a whole American way of life. Bode's *Democracy as a Way of Life*[2] turns out to be naturalistic empiricism as a way of life. Such indirection on the part of one of the many formal systems of philosophy in American culture may be strategic and persuasive among American teachers who are not philosophically oriented, but to many professional philosophers in the last generation it has appeared unwarranted and unwise. Indeed, it has appeared inimical to freedom in the name of freedom because the literal identification of freedom with one system of thought violates the most fundamental faith of free men; namely, that no one system of philosophy finally defines freedom in a culture which is dedicated to being inclusive of a diversity of philosophies speculatively entertained.

Progressive education is the educational counterpart of the naturalistic philosophy of John Dewey, and probably William Heard Kilpatrick has been its most celebrated exponent. Gentle, patient and persuasive, Professor Kilpatrick oriented himself steadfastly to this one philosophy of life and in a lovable, temperate, and compromising approach to all his teaching inclined untold thousands of teachers in our time toward a philosophy of life whose fundamental principles he has not compromised. The comprehensive statement of his position in his later years[3] reveals his steadfastness, his dedication and his uncompromising philosophic

2 Boyd H. Bode, *Democracy as a Way of Life*. New York: The Macmillan Company, 1939.
3 William Heard Kilpatrick, *Philosophy of Education*. New York: The Macmillan Company, 1951.

commitment. The American teacher to whom the book is largely addressed is gently dissuaded from believing in other less adequate philosophical views with an artfulness and sincerity that can hardly offend them even when they wonderingly differ. But the philosophically astute who hold self-consciously to a Christian, idealist, or other system of philosophy may be offended by what they properly take to be caricatures of their philosophical positions. To them, this gentle man is an unfair partisan, and many of them are as gentle and liberal in the entertainment of their views as he. Most of them are also unconditionally committed. And here we are confronted with the human dilemma again. How is a committed man to make good his boast of impartiality in the presentation of views contrary to the truth as he sees it?

Some hold to the proposition, herein denied, that it is the distinguishing character of a certain system of philosophy that is uniquely impartial toward all philosophies. Some hold that their philosophy is inevitably biased toward all others but that they have the capacity to stand outside of their philosophy and present all the rest as sympathetically as their own representatives would. Still others incline to the notion that teachers in training can only get a fair presentation by the representatives of each position. There may be one more alternative. From time to time, there are teachers of history, and literature and of philosophy in the tradition of the liberal university who have no ultimate commitment relative to systems of thought. Such men present a variety of philosophies with the kind of sympathy which comes from genuine indebtedness to each and genuine reservations with respect to each. Such a teacher's faith may be of another order. It is the faith of the pilgrim rather than the disciple. It is the commitment to the unending quest in which one's way is enlightened by all systems of thought but not finally directed by any one of them. It is the commitment of the doctrinally uncommitted scholar. It is the faith of liberal learning in which the teacher knows more but learns with his students in a distinctive sense. For about one thing he does not finally know. He does not finally know what really is the best rationalized ultimate commitment for mankind even though he does know more than his students do about what man's ultimate commitments have been and more of the arguments for and against them. In other words, he has much more knowledge than his students do, but his knowledge has led him not to an ultimate dogma but to wisdom. And in a state of wisdom he discovers that, in all his knowledge, he does not finally know. It is the students' sense of this fact, when it is a fact that sets them at one with their teacher in ultimate wonderment. It is this fact that sets them free. And it is dedicated inquiry in this state of disciplined freedom through knowledge in which the liberal university at its best puts its final faith. Qualified commitment at all levels of knowledge may very well be the condition of ethical community in the free society. If so, such teaching would tend to extend it by example and by contagion.

In contrast to the basic motivation of such men, there are those who incline to the conviction that a social order must be integrated along the lines of a comprehensively coherent system of thought. They ask that a philosophy be actualized into a whole way of life, that it become practical and directive of the human enterprise rather than merely enlightening of it. They ask that philosophy abandon its sterile role as one of the liberal disciplines, that it take up residence in the market place and that it become self-consciously the ideological center of reference for the culture. They are asking, in deference to practicality and their highest partisan hope, that philosophy abandon its liberal status for a doctrinal status. This has been the fundamental error of the pragmatist-progressive school of thought; namely, that they would rescue human freedom by substituting one philosophy of freedom for another, in this case the philosophy in which Dewey found his freedom. But they have forgotten to note that he found his freedom both negatively and positively—negatively, by not committing himself to any extant philosophy in his heritage, positively, by constructing his own system of thought out of this heritage and the occasion of his time. His is the kind of freedom we honor and he took the only sure pathway to it. Thus must each philosophic mind and each generation hew its own freedom from the raw rock of life.

Everett John Kircher (January 29, 1906—) received his A.B. degree from the University of Wisconsin in 1931. He taught English for four years at the Appleton, Wisconsin, high school, during which time he received his M.A. degree from Ohio State University. With graduate work transferred from the University of Wisconsin and Teachers College, Columbia University, Kircher was awarded the Ph.D. degree at Ohio State University, 1938, where he had been assisting Boyd H. Bode. He was then appointed assistant professor of Language Arts, University School, Ohio State University. In 1941 he went to Tulane University as associate professor of Education, returning to Ohio State as associate professor of Philosophy of Education upon the retirement of Boyd H. Bode in 1944. In 1945 he went to Cairo, Egypt, as visiting professor of Education in the Graduate Institute of Education, and in 1947 he served as visiting lecturer at the University of Louisville. In 1949–50 Kircher served one session as a consultant on General MacArthur's civilian staff in Tokyo, Japan. Since

1955 he has held the rank of professor of Education at Ohio State University.

Dr. Kircher has traveled and lectured throughout the United States and in several foreign countries. He has contributed to Essays in Educology, *edited by Lowry W. Harding, and has a chapter in* Teacher Education and Religion, *edited by A. L. Sebaly, 1959. He is a contributor to* Progressive Education *and* Educational Theory.

Recommended Readings for Part One

Students are urged to consult the annotated bibliography at the end of this volume for information on the books cited here.

The following books in philosophy and philosophy of education should be especially helpful.

A. Philosophy:

A. J. Ayer, *The Revolution in Philosophy*
W. T. Jones, *History of Philosophy*
John Passmore, *A Hundred Years of Philosophy*
Hans Reichenbach, *The Rise of Scientific Philosophy*
Bertrand Russell, *A History of Western Philosophy*
Herbert W. Schneider, *A History of American Philosophy*
G. J. Warnock, *English Philosophy Since 1900*
Morton White, *The Age of Analysis*

B. Philosophy of Education:

Marc Belth, *Education as a Discipline*
George Z. Bereday and Joseph A. Lauwerys, *Education and Philosophy*
William K. Frankena, *Philosophy of Education*
Nelson B. Henry (ed.), *Modern Philosophies and Education*
D. J. O'Connor, *An Introduction to the Philosophy of Education*
Louis Arnaud Reid, *Philosophy and Education*

Pragmatism and Education

Introduction to Part Two

PRAGMATISM is an American philosophy originated by Charles S. Peirce and extended and enriched principally by the efforts of William James and John Dewey, but there were in Protagoras (481–411 B.C.) some of the same elements to be found in contemporary pragmatism.

Charles S. Peirce (1839–1914) has been called the most versatile, profound, and original philosopher that America has ever produced.* The son of a Harvard mathematician, he was early initiated into the fascinating problems of mathematics, physics, and astronomy. He earned his bachelor's and master's degrees at Harvard, and was employed for a time as a physicist and an astronomer by the United States Coast and Geodetic Survey. For a while he was an instructor in Logic at Johns Hopkins University, but his classes drew few students and he was dropped from the faculty. He died in extreme poverty, and it is reported that there was no money for a decent burial. His widow sold his manuscripts to Harvard University for $500.

Peirce had been interested in so many complex and difficult subjects that he never took time to publish a book; he characterized his life as a "mere table of contents, . . . a very snarl of twine."

William James suggests that Peirce first formulated pragmatism as a doctrine in the article "How to Make Our Ideas Clear," which Peirce published in *Popular Science Monthly*, January, 1878. In this article Peirce relates the words "doubt" and "belief" to the starting of any question "no matter how small or great." He speaks of the indecision that arises in the mind as one debates whether to drop a nickel or five pennies into the container in a horsecar. Doubt arises from such indecision, and it is this doubt that stirs the mind to action. By reflection, some rule of action or *habit* is arrived at. "As it appeases the irritation of doubt, which is the motive for thinking, thought relaxes, and comes to rest for a moment when belief is reached . . . The *final* upshot of thinking is the exercise of volition, . . . belief is only a stadium of mental action . . ."

* Philip P. Wiener (ed.), *Values in a Universe of Change: Selected Writings of Charles S. Peirce, 1839–1914.* New York: Doubleday Anchor Books, 1958, pp. 113–136.

Peirce's argument was that the only road to knowledge was the scientific method and that philosophy should imitate the sciences. All knowledge had to be based upon experience, and verifiable knowledge was obtainable through observation and experimental testing. The conceptions of a particular object exist only in connection with that object, and the whole meaning of an intellectual conception resides in the practical consequences that follow from acting upon conception. The totality of the practical effects constitute the meaning of the conception. Thus, truth arises from experimental testing, and theories must be tested in practice in order to discover their consequences. If an idea does not work out as it is supposed to, then it is false. Peirce went on to show that in the last analysis the test of ideas is a social test, that is, that the true idea is the one that is eventually agreed upon by an infinite community of observers.

William James (1852–1910), the second of the founders of pragmatism, popularized pragmatism and demonstrated wherein it was a revolt against the traditional philosophies. He applied pragmatism to many realms of life, especially to those practical affairs of ethics, religious experience, art, science, law, government, and, of course, education. In all these realms he taught that our inherited ideas should be reexamined or tested to determine what consequences they were producing in action. It should be noted that James' pragmatism was more individualistic than that of Peirce, even though he agreed with the former that ideas must be defined in terms of the difference they make. James' influence was quite great on a number of Americans—Edward L. Thorndike and John Dewey, in particular.

In the essay included in these readings it is well to notice that James maintains that the scope of pragmatism is, first, a method, and second, a generic theory of what is meant by truth. With regard to the first, he suggests that it is an attempt to interpret each notion by tracing its practical consequences. Pragmatism is shown to turn away from categories, first things, principles, and supposed necessities and to look instead toward consequences, facts, fruits, and last things. It is empirical. As a generic theory of truth, it holds that ideas become true "just insofar as they help us get into satisfactory relations with other parts of our experience." Note further the place of theological ideas in James' discussion and his reference to instrumentalism when he speaks of the work of Dewey at the University of Chicago.

John Dewey (1859–1952) began his philosophical career as an idealist, but he soon broke away from the "mentalistic and spiritual" aspect of idealism, although he kept some elements of Hegel's thought. He was greatly influenced by the work of Darwin, and conceived of man as an organism that lives in a constant state of transaction with the environment "of" which he lives. He early accepted the empirical and scientific assumptions of Peirce and James, and he extended their pragmatic theory of knowledge. He was likewise influenced by his colleague at the University of Chicago, George Herbert Mead, who taught him to value the social concept of mind and self.

It is, of course, impossible to summarize the main items in Dewey's writings on education here, but the "laboratory habit of mind," a term Dewey borrowed from Peirce, was the very center of his philosophy of education.

Education, to Dewey, is the process of learning to inquire systematically by using the method of science, and its aim is to continue the educative process, because the existential situations constantly change and final answers are unavailable to man. Dewey referred to Colonel Francis Parker as the "Father of Progressive Education," but it has been customary to pin this same label on Dewey himself. Yet, although Dewey was active in the progressive-education movement, it is incorrect to say that he was in complete agreement with those who called themselves his disciples. One has only to read *Experience and Education* to see the concern Dewey felt about some of the things that were going on in the name of progressive education.

As Brubacher has explained, the progressive-education movement was divided into three camps.† One of these was the Dewey camp, sometimes called "the sober wing" of the progressive movement. (This group is represented here by the selections from Dewey.) Kilpatrick falls into the second camp, in spite of the fact that he considered himself in complete agreement with Dewey. A closer examination of Kilpatrick's writing, however, indicates that he was in reality an exponent of the child-centered, activity-oriented camp, which placed considerably less emphasis upon reflection and subject matter than did Dewey.‡

The third camp may be called reconstructionism. This group of progressive educators began to form at the time of the Depression, and found in *Dare the School Build a New Social Order?* an expression of their concern for social issues. Brameld is the most prominent contemporary reconstructionist. The progressive movement collapsed soon after the

† John Brubacher, "The Challenge to Philosophize about Education," *Modern Philosophies and Education,* Chapter I, *Fifty-fourth Yearbook of the National Society for the Study of Education.* Chicago: Distributed by the University of Chicago Press, 1955, Part I, pp. 8–16.
‡ George Swimmer, "A Comparison of the Intellectual Development of John Dewey and William H. Kilpatrick with Implications for Differences in their Educational Theories." Northwestern University, unpublished doctoral dissertation, 1957.

Second World War, and one reason for the collapse was the schism that we have been discussing. The selection from McMurray provides some insights into what may be the future of pragmatism in American education.

4

What Pragmatism Means[*]

WILLIAM JAMES

SOME YEARS AGO, being with a camping party in the mountains, I returned from a solitary ramble to find every one engaged in a
ferocious metaphysical dispute. The *corpus* of the dispute was a squirrel
—a live squirrel supposed to be clinging to one side of a tree-trunk; while
over against the tree's opposite side a human being was imagined to
stand. This human witness tries to get sight of the squirrel by moving
rapidly round the tree, but no matter how fast he goes, the squirrel
moves as fast in the opposite direction, and always keeps the tree between himself and the man, so that never a glimpse of him is caught. The
resultant metaphysical problem now is this: *Does the man go round the
squirrel or not?* He goes round the tree, sure enough, and the squirrel is
on the tree; but does he go round the squirrel? In the unlimited leisure
of the wilderness, discussion had been worn threadbare. Everyone had
taken sides, and was obstinate; and the numbers on both sides were even.
Each side, when I appeared therefore appealed to me to make it a
majority. Mindful of the scholastic adage that whenever you meet a contradiction you must make a distinction, I immediately sought and found
one, as follows: "Which party is right," I said, "depends on what you
practically mean by 'going round' the squirrel. If you mean passing from
the north of him to the east, then to the south, then to the west, and then
to the north of him again, obviously the man does go round him, for he

* William James, *Pragmatism: A New Name for Some Old Ways of Thinking.*
New York: Longmans, Green and Co., 1907, pp. 43–81. Copyright 1907 by William
James. Permission to reprint granted by Paul R. Reynolds & Son, 599 Fifth Avenue,
New York, N.Y.

occupies these successive positions. But if on the contrary you mean being first in front of him, then on the right of him, then behind him, then on his left, and finally in front again, it is quite as obvious that the man fails to go round him, for by the compensating movements the squirrel makes, he keeps his belly turned towards the man all the time, and his back turned away. Make the distinction, and there is no occasion for any farther dispute. You are both right and both wrong according as you conceive the verb 'to go round' in one practical fashion or the other."

Although one or two of the hotter disputants called my speech a shuffling evasion, saying they wanted no quibbling or scholastic hair-splitting, but meant just plain honest English 'round,' the majority seemed to think that the distinction had assuaged the dispute.

I tell this trivial anecdote because it is a peculiarly simple example of what I wish now to speak of as *the pragmatic method.* The pragmatic method is primarily a method of settling metaphysical disputes that otherwise might be interminable. Is the world one or many?—fated or free?—material or spiritual?—here are notions either of which may or may not hold good of the world; and disputes over such notions are unending. The pragmatic method in such cases is to try to interpret each notion by tracing its respective practical consequences. What difference would it practically make to any one if this notion rather than that notion were true? If no practical difference whatever can be traced, then the alternatives mean practically the same thing, and all dispute is idle. Whenever a dispute is serious, we ought to be able to show some practical difference that must follow from one side or the other's being right.

A glance at the history of the idea will show you still better what pragmatism means. The term is derived from the same Greek word πράγμα, meaning action, from which our words 'practice' and 'practical' come. It was first introduced into philosophy by Mr. Charles Peirce in 1878. In an article entitled 'How to Make Our Ideas Clear,' in the 'Popular Science Monthly' for January of that year[1] Mr. Peirce, after pointing out that our beliefs are really rules for action, said that, to develop a thought's meaning, we need only determine what conduct it is fitted to produce: that conduct is for us its sole significance. And the tangible fact at the root of all our thought-distinctions, however subtle, is that there is no one of them so fine as to consist in anything but a possible difference of practice. To attain perfect clearness in our thoughts of an object, then, we need only consider what conceivable effects of a practical kind the object may involve—what sensations we are to expect from it, and what

[1] Translated in the *Revue Philosophique* for January, 1879 (vol. vii).

reactions we must prepare. Our conception of these effects, whether immediate or remote, is then for us the whole of our conception of the object, so far as that conception has positive significance at all.

This is the principle of Peirce, the principle of pragmatism. It lay entirely unnoticed by anyone for twenty years, until I, in an address before Professor Howison's philosophical union at the university of California, brought it forward again and made a special application of it to religion. By that date (1898) the times seemed ripe for its reception. The word 'pragmatism' spread, and at present it fairly spots the pages of the philosophic journals. On all hands we find the 'pragmatic movement' spoken of, sometimes with respect, sometimes with contumely, seldom with clear understanding. It is evident that the term applies itself conveniently to a number of tendencies that hitherto have lacked a collective name, and that it has 'come to stay.'

To take in the importance of Peirce's principle, one must get accustomed to applying it to concrete cases. I found a few years ago that Ostwald, the illustrious Leipzig chemist, had been making perfectly distinct use of the principle of pragmatism in his lectures on the philosophy of science, though he had not called it by that name.

"All realities influence our practice," he wrote me, "and that influence is their meaning for us. I am accustomed to put questions to my classes in this way: In what respects would the world be different if this alternative or that were true? If I can find nothing that would become different, then the alternative has no sense."

That is, the rival views mean practically the same thing, and meaning, other than practical, there is for us none. Ostwald in a published lecture gives this example of what he means. Chemists have long wrangled over the inner constitution of certain bodies called 'tautomerous.' Their properties seemed equally consistent with the notion that an instable hydrogen atom oscillates inside of them, or that they are instable mixtures of two bodies. Controversy raged, but never was decided. "It would never have begun," says Ostwald, "if the combatants had asked themselves what particular experimental fact could have been made different by one or the other view being correct. For it would then have appeared that no difference of fact could possibly ensue; and the quarrel was as unreal as if, theorizing in primitive times about the raising of dough by yeast, one party should have invoked a 'brownie,' while another insisted on an 'elf' as the true cause of the phenomenon."[2]

2 'Theorie und Praxis,' *Zeitsch. des Oesterreichischen Ingenieur u. Architecten-Vereines,* 1905, Nr. 4 u. 6. I find a still more radical pragmatism than Ostwald's in an address by Professor W. S. Franklin: "I think that the sickliest notion of physics,

It is astonishing to see how many philosophical disputes collapse into insignificance the moment you subject them to this simple test of tracing a concrete consequence. There can *be* no difference anywhere that doesn't *make* a difference elsewhere—no difference in abstract truth that doesn't express itself in a difference in concrete fact and in conduct consequent upon that fact, imposed on somebody, somehow, somewhere, and somewhen. The whole function of philosophy ought to be to find out what definite difference it will make to you and me, at definite instants of our life, if this world-formula or that world-formula be the true one.

There is absolutely nothing new in the pragmatic method. Socrates was an adept at it. Aristotle used it methodically. Locke, Berkeley, and Hume made momentous contributions to truth by its means. Shadworth Hodgson keeps insisting that realities are only what they are 'known as.' But these forerunners of pragmatism used it in fragments: they were preluders only. Not until in our time has it generalized itself, become conscious of a universal mission, pretended to a conquering destiny. I believe in that destiny, and I hope I may end by inspiring you with my belief.

Pragmatism represents a perfectly familiar attitude in philosophy, the empiricist attitude, but it represents it, as it seems to me, both in a more radical and in a less objectionable form than it has ever yet assumed. A pragmatist turns his back resolutely and once for all upon a lot of inveterate habits dear to professional philosophers. He turns away from abstraction and insufficiency, from verbal solutions, from bad *a priori* reasons, from fixed principles, closed systems, and pretended absolutes and origins. He turns towards concreteness and adequacy, towards facts, towards action, and towards power. That means the empiricist temper regnant and the rationalist temper sincerely given up. It means the open air and possibilities of nature, as against dogma, artificiality, and the pretense of finality in truth.

At the same time it does not stand for any special results. It is a method only. But the general triumph of that method would mean an enormous change in what I called in my last lecture the 'temperament' of philosophy. Teachers of the ultra-rationalistic type would be frozen out, much as the courtier type is frozen out in republics, as the ultra-montane type of priest is frozen out in protestant lands. Science and

---

even if a student gets it, is that it is 'the science of masses, molecules, and the ether.' And I think that the healthiest notion, even if a student does not wholly get it, is that physics is the science of the ways of taking hold of bodies and pushing them!" (*Science*, January 2, 1903.)

metaphysics would come much nearer together, would in fact work absolutely hand in hand.

Metaphysics has usually followed a very primitive kind of quest. You know how men have always hankered after unlawful magic, and you know what a great part in magic *words* have always played. If you have his name, or the formula of incantation that binds him, you can control the spirit, genie, afrite, or whatever the power may be. Solomon knew the names of all the spirits, and having their names, he held them subject to his will. So the universe has always appeared to the natural mind as a kind of enigma, of which the key must be sought in the shape of some illuminating or power-bringing word or name. That word names the universe's *principle,* and to possess it is after a fashion to possess the universe itself. 'God,' 'Matter,' 'Reason,' 'the Absolute,' 'Energy,' are so many solving names. You can rest when you have them. You are at the end of your metaphysical quest.

But if you follow the pragmatic method, you cannot look on any such word as closing your quest. You must bring out of each word its practical cash-value, set it at work within the stream of your experience. It appears less as a solution, then, than as a program for more work, and more particularly as an indication of the ways in which existing realities may be *changed.*

Theories thus become instruments, not answers to enigmas, in which we can rest. We don't lie back upon them, we move forward, and, on occasion, make nature over again by their aid. Pragmatism unstiffens all our theories, limbers them up and sets each one at work. Being nothing essentially new, it harmonizes with many ancient philosophic tendencies. It agrees with nominalism for instance, in always appealing to particulars; with utilitarianism in emphasizing practical aspects; with positivism in its disdain for verbal solutions, useless questions and metaphysical abstractions.

All these, you see, are *anti-intellectualist* tendencies. Against rationalism as a pretension and a method pragmatism is fully armed and militant. But, at the outset, at least, it stands for no particular results. It has no dogmas and no doctrines save its method. As the young Italian pragmatist Papini has well said, it lies in the midst of our theories, like a corridor in a hotel. Innumerable chambers open out of it. In one you may find a man writing an atheistic volume; in the next someone on his knees praying for faith and strength; in a third a chemist investigating a body's properties. In a fourth a system of idealistic metaphysics is being excogitated; in a fifth the impossibility of metaphysics is being shown.

But they all own the corridor, and all must pass through it if they want a practicable way of getting into or out of their respective rooms.

No particular results then, so far, but only an attitude of orientation, is what the pragmatic method means. *The attitude of looking away from first things, principles, 'categories,' supposed necessities; and of looking towards last things, fruits, consequences, facts.*

So much for the pragmatic method! You may say that I have been praising it rather than explaining it to you, but I shall presently explain it abundantly enough by showing how it works on some familiar problems. Meanwhile the word pragmatism has come to be used in a still wider sense, as meaning also a certain *theory of truth*. I mean to give a whole lecture to the statement of that theory, after first paving the way, so I can be very brief now. But brevity is hard to follow, so I ask for your redoubled attention for a quarter of an hour. If much remains obscure, I hope to make it clearer in the later lectures.

One of the most successfully cultivated branches of philosophy in our time is what is called inductive logic, the study of the conditions under which our sciences have evolved. Writers on this subject have begun to show a singular unanimity as to what the laws of nature and elements of fact mean, when formulated by mathematicians, physicists and chemists. When the first mathematical, logical, and natural uniformities, the first *laws*, were discovered, men were so carried away by the clearness, beauty and simplification that resulted, that they believed themselves to have deciphered authentically the eternal thoughts of the Almighty. His mind also thundered and reverberated in syllogisms. He also thought in conic sections, squares and roots and ratios, and geometrized like Euclid. He made Kepler's laws for the planets to follow; he made velocity increase proportionally to the time in falling bodies; he made the law of the sines for light to obey when refracted; he established the classes, orders, families and genera of plants and animals, and fixed the distances between them. He thought the archetypes of all things, and devised their variations; and when we rediscover any one of these his wondrous institutions, we seize his mind in its very literal intention.

But as the sciences have developed farther, the notion has gained ground that most, perhaps all, of our laws are only approximations. The laws themselves, moreover, have grown so numerous that there is no counting them; and so many rival formulations are proposed in all the branches of science that investigators have become accustomed to the notion that no theory is absolutely a transcript of reality, but that any one of them may from some point of view be useful. Their great use is to summarize old facts and to lead to new ones. They are only a man-made language, a conceptual shorthand, as someone calls them, in which we write our reports of nature; and languages, as is well known, tolerate much choice of expression and many dialects.

Thus human arbitrariness has driven divine necessity from scientific logic. If I mention the names of Sigwart, Mach, Ostwald, Pearson, Milhoud, Poincaré, Duhem, Ruyssen, those of you who are students will easily identify the tendency I speak of, and will think of additional names.

Riding now on the front of this wave of scientific logic Messrs. Schiller and Dewey appear with their pragmatistic account of what truth everywhere signifies. Everywhere, these teachers say, 'truth' in our ideas and beliefs means the same thing that it means in science. It means, they say, nothing but this, *that ideas (which themselves are but parts of our experience) become true just in so far as they help us to get into satisfactory relation with other parts of our experience,* to summarize them and get about among them by conceptual shortcuts instead of following the interminable succession of particular phenomena. Any idea upon which we can ride, so to speak; any idea that will carry us prosperously from any one part of our experience to any other part, linking things satisfactorily, working securely, simplifying, saving labor; is true for just so much, true in so far forth, true *instrumentally.* This is the 'instrumental' view of truth taught so successfully at Chicago, the view that truth in our ideas means their power to 'work,' promulgated so brilliantly at Oxford.

Messrs. Dewey, Schiller, and their allies, in reaching this general conception of all truth, have only followed the example of geologists, biologists and philologists. In the establishment of these other sciences, the successful stroke was always to take some simple process actually observable in operation—as denudation by weather, say, or variation from parental type, or change of dialect by incorporation of new words and pronunciations—and then to generalize it, making it apply to all times, and produce great results by summating its effects through the ages.

The observable process which Schiller and Dewey particularly singled out for generalization is the familiar one by which any individual settles into *new opinions.* The process here is always the same. The individual has a stock of old opinions already, but he meets a new experience that puts them to a strain. Somebody contradicts them; or in a reflective moment he discovers that they contradict each other; or he hears of facts with which they are incompatible; or desires arise in him which they cease to satisfy. The result is an inward trouble to which his mind till then had been a stranger, and from which he seeks to escape by modifying his previous mass of opinions. He saves as much of it as he can, for in this matter of belief we are all extreme conservatives. So he tries to change first this opinion, and then that (for they resist change very variously), until at last some new idea comes up which he can graft upon the ancient stock with a minimum of disturbance of the latter, some idea that mediates between the stock and the new experience and runs them into one another most felicitously and expediently.

This new idea is then adopted as the true one. It preserves the older stock of truths with a minimum of modification, stretching them just enough to make them admit the novelty, but conceiving that in ways as familiar as the case leaves possible. An *outrée* explanation, violating all our preconceptions, would never pass for a true account of a novelty. We should scratch round industriously till we found something less eccentric. The most violent revolutions in an individual's beliefs leave most of his old order standing. Time and space, cause and effect, nature and history, and one's own biography remain untouched. New truth is always a go-between, a smoother-over of transitions. It marries old opinion to new fact so as ever to show a minimum of jolt, a maximum of continuity. We hold a theory true just in proportion to its success in solving this 'problem of maxima and minima.' But success in solving this problem is eminently a matter of approximation. We say this theory solves it on the whole more satisfactorily than that theory; but that means more satisfactorily to ourselves, and individuals will emphasize their points of satisfaction differently. To a certain degree, therefore, everything here is plastic.

The point I now urge you to observe particularly is the part played by the older truths. Failure to take account of it is the source of much of the unjust criticism levelled against pragmatism. Their influence is absolutely controlling. Loyalty to them is the first principle—in most cases it is the only principle; for by far the most usual way of handling phenomena so novel that they would make for a serious rearrangement of our preconception is to ignore them altogether, or to abuse those who bear witness for them.

You doubtless wish examples of this process of truth's growth, and the only trouble is their superabundance. The simplest case of new truth is of course the mere numerical addition of new kinds of facts, or of new single facts of old kinds, to our experience—an addition that involves no alteration in the old beliefs. Day follows day, and its contents are simply added. The new contents themselves are not true, they simply *come* and *are*. Truth is *what we say about* them, and when we say that they have come, truth is satisfied by the plain additive formula.

But often the day's contents oblige a rearrangement. If I should now utter piercing shrieks and act like a maniac on this platform, it would make many of you revise your ideas as to the probable worth of my philosophy. 'Radium' came the other day as part of the day's content, and seemed for a moment to contradict our ideas of the whole order of nature, that order having come to be identified with what is called the conservation of energy. The mere sight of radium paying heat away indefinitely out of its own pocket seemed to violate that conservation. What to think? If the radiations from it were nothing but an escape of unsuspected 'potential' energy, pre-existent inside of the atoms, the principle of conservation would be saved. The discovery of 'helium' as the radiation's outcome, opened a way to this belief. So Ramsay's view is generally held to be true, because, although it extends our old ideas of energy, it causes a minimum of alteration in their nature.

I need not multiply instances. A new opinion counts as 'true' just in proportion as it gratifies the individual's desire to assimilate the novel in his experience to his beliefs in stock. It must both lean on old truth and grasp new fact; and its success (as I said a moment ago) in doing this, is a matter for the individual's appreciation. When old truth grows, then, by new truth's addition, it is for subjective reasons. We are in the process and obey the reasons. That new idea is truest which performs most felicitously its function of satisfying our double urgency. It makes itself true, gets itself classed as true, by the way it works; grafting itself then upon the ancient body of truth, which thus grows much as a tree grows by the activity of a new layer of cambium.

Now Dewey and Schiller proceed to generalize this observation and to apply it to the most ancient parts of truth. They also once were plastic. They also were called true for human reasons. They also mediated between still earlier truths and what in those days were novel observations. Purely objective truth, truth in whose establishment the function of giving human satisfaction in marrying previous parts of experience with newer parts played no rôle whatever, is nowhere to be found. The reasons why we call things true is the reason why they *are* true, for 'to be true' *means* only to perform this marriage-function.

The trial of the human serpent is thus over everything. Truth independent; truth that we *find* merely; truth no longer malleable to human need; truth incorrigible, in a word; such truth exists indeed superabundantly—or is supposed to exist by rationalistically minded thinkers; but then it means only the dead heart of the living tree, and its being there means only that truth also has its paleontology, and its 'prescription,' and may grow stiff with years of veteran service and petrified in men's regard by sheer antiquity. But how plastic even the oldest truths nevertheless really are has been vividly shown in our day by the transformation of logical and mathematical ideas, a transformation which seems even to be invading physics. The ancient formulas are reinterpreted as special expressions of much wider principles, principles that our ancestors never got a glimpse of in their present shape and formulation.

Mr. Schiller still gives to all this view of truth the name of 'Humanism,' but, for this doctrine too, the name of pragmatism seems fairly to be in the ascendant, so I will treat it under the name of pragmatism in these lectures.

Such then would be the scope of pragmatism—first, a method; and second, a genetic theory of what is meant by truth. And these two things must be our future topics.

What I have said of the theory of truth will, I am sure, have appeared obscure and unsatisfactory to most of you by reason of its brevity. I shall make amends for that hereafter. In a lecture on 'common sense' I shall try to show what I mean by truths grown petrified by antiquity. In another lecture I shall expatiate on the idea that our thoughts become true in proportion as they successfully exert their go-between function. In a third I shall show how hard it is to discriminate subjective from objective factors in Truth's development. You may not follow me wholly in these lectures; and if you do, you may not wholly agree with me. But you will, I know, regard me at least as serious, and treat my effort with respectful consideration.

You will probably be surprised to learn, then, that Messrs. Schiller's and Dewey's theories have suffered a hailstorm of contempt and ridicule. All rationalism has risen against them. In influential quarters Mr. Schiller, in particular, has been treated like an impudent schoolboy who deserves a spanking. I should not mention this, but for the fact that it throws so much sidelight upon that rationalistic temper to which I have opposed the temper of pragmatism. Pragmatism is uncomfortable away from facts. Rationalism is comfortable only in the presence of abstractions. This pragmatist talk about truths in the plural, about their utility and satisfactoriness, about the success with which they 'work,' etc., suggests to the typical intellectualist mind a sort of coarse, lame, second-rate, makeshift, article of truth. Such truths are not real truth. Such tests are merely subjective. As against this, objective truth must be something nonutilitarian, haughty, refined, remote, august, exalted. It must be an absolute correspondence of our thoughts with an equally absolute reality. It must be what we *ought* to think unconditionally. The conditioned ways in which we *do* think are so much irrelevance and matter for psychology. Down with psychology, up with logic, in all this question!

See the exquisite contrast of the types of mind! The pragmatist clings to facts and concreteness, observes truth at its work in particular cases, and generalizes. Truth, for him, becomes a class-name for all sorts of definite working-values in experience. For the rationalist it remains a pure abstraction, to the bare name of which we must defer. When the pragmatist undertakes to show in detail just *why* we must defer, the rationalist is unable to recognize the concretes from which his own abstraction is taken. He accuses us of *denying* truth; whereas we have only sought to trace exactly why people follow it and always ought to follow it. Your typical ultra-abstractionist fairly shudders at concreteness: other things equal, he positively prefers the pale and spectral. If the two universes were offered, he would always choose the skinny outline rather than the rich thicket of reality. It is so much purer, clearer, nobler.

I hope that as these lectures go on, the concreteness and closeness to facts of the pragmatism which they advocate may be what approves itself to you as its most satisfactory peculiarity. It only follows here the example of the sister-sciences, interpreting the unobserved by the observed. It brings old and new harmoniously together. It converts the absolutely empty notion of a static relation of 'correspondence' (what they may mean we must ask later) between our minds and reality, into that of a rich and active commerce (that anyone may follow in detail and understand) between particular thoughts of ours, and the great universe of other experiences in which they play their parts and have their uses.

But enough of this at present? The justification of what I say must be postponed. I wish now to add a word in further explanation of the claim I made at our last meeting, that pragmatism may be a happy harmonizer of empiricist ways of thinking with the more religious demands of human beings.

Men who are strongly of the fact-loving temperament, you may remember me to have said, are liable to be kept at a distance by the small sympathy with facts which that philosophy from the present-day fashion of idealism offers them. It is far too intellectualistic. Old-fashioned theism was bad enough, with its notion of God as an exalted monarch, made up of a lot of unintelligible or preposterous 'attributes'; but, so long as it held strongly by the argument from design, it kept some touch with concrete realities. Since, however, Darwinism has once for all displaced design from the minds of the 'scientific,' theism has lost that foothold; and some kind of an imminent or pantheistic deity working *in* things rather than above them is, if any, the kind recommended to our contemporary imagination. Aspirants to a philosophic religion turn, as a rule, more hopefully nowadays towards idealistic pantheism than towards the older dualistic theism, in spite of the fact that the latter still counts able defenders.

But, as I said in my first lecture, the brand of pantheism offered is hard for them to assimilate if they are lovers of facts, or empirically minded. It is the absolutistic brand, spurning the dust and reared upon pure logic. It keeps no connexion whatever with concreteness. Affirming the Absolute Mind, which is its substitute for God, to be the rational pre-supposition of all particulars of fact, whatever they may be, it remains supremely indifferent to what the particular facts in our world actually are. Be they what they may, the Absolute will father them. Like the sick lion in Esop's fable, all footprints lead into his den, but *nulla vestigia retrorsum*. You cannot redescend into the world of particulars by the Absolute's aid, or deduce any necessary consequences of detail important for your life from your idea of his nature. He gives you indeed the assur-ance that all is well with *Him,* and for his eternal way of thinking; but thereupon he leaves you to be finitely saved by your own temporal devices.

Far be it from me to deny the majesty of this conception, or its ca-pacity to yield religious comfort to a most respectable class of minds. But from the human point of view, no one can pretend that it doesn't suffer from the faults of remoteness and abstractness. It is eminently a product of what I have ventured to call the rationalistic temper. It disdains em-piricism's needs. It substitutes a pallid outline for the real world's rich-ness. It is dapper, it is noble in the bad sense, in the sense in which to be noble is to be inapt for humble service. In this real world of sweat and dirt, it seems to me that when a view of things is 'noble,' that ought to count as a presumption against its truth, and as a philosophic disqualifica-tion. The prince of darkness may be a gentleman, as we are told he is, but whatever the God of earth and heaven is, he can surely be no gentle-man. His menial services are needed in the dust of our human trials, even more than his dignity is needed in the empyrean.

Now pragmatism, devoted though she be to facts, has no such materi-alistic bias as ordinary empiricism labors under. Moreover, she has no objection whatever to the realizing of abstractions, so long as you get about among particulars with their aid and they actually carry you some-where. Interested in no conclusions but those which our minds and our experiences work out together, she has no *a priori* prejudices against theology. *If theological ideas prove to have a value for concrete life, they will be true, for pragmatism, in the sense of being good for so much. For how much more they are true, will depend entirely on their relations to the other truths that also have to be acknowledged.*

What I said just now about the Absolute, of transcendental idealism, is a case in point. First, I called it majestic and said it yielded religious comfort to a class of minds, and then I accused it of remoteness and sterility. But so far as it affords such comfort, it surely is not sterile; it has that amount of value; it performs a concrete function. As a good pragmatist, I myself ought to call the Absolute 'true in so far forth,' then; and I unhesitatingly now do so.

But what does *true in so far forth* mean in this case? To answer, we need only apply the pragmatic method. What do believers in the Absolute mean by saying that their belief affords them comfort? They mean that since, in the Absolute finite evil is 'overruled' already, we may, therefore, whenever we wish, treat the temporal as if it were potentially the eternal, be sure that we can trust its outcome, and, without sin, dismiss our fear and drop the worry of our finite responsibility. In short, they mean that we have a right ever and anon to take a moral holiday, to let the world wag in its own way, feeling that its issues are in better hands than ours and are none of our business.

The universe is a system of which the individual members may relax their anxieties occasionally, in which the don't-care mood is also right for men, and moral holidays in order,—that, if I mistake not, is part, at least, of what the Absolute is 'known-as,' that is the great difference in our particular experiences which his being true makes, for us, that is his cash-value when he is pragmatically interpreted. Farther than that the ordinary lay-reader in philosophy who thinks favorably of absolute idealism does not venture to sharpen his conceptions. He can use the Absolute for so much, and so much is very precious. He is pained at hearing you speak incredulously of the Absolute, therefore, and disregards your criticisms because they deal with aspects of the conception that he fails to follow.

If the Absolute means this, and means no more than this, who can possibly deny the truth of it? To deny it would be to insist that men should never relax, and that holidays are never in order.

I am well aware how odd it must seem to some of you to hear me say that an idea is 'true' so long as to believe it is profitable to our lives. That it is *good*, for as much as it profits, you will gladly admit. If what we do by its aid is good, you will allow the idea itself to be good in so far forth, for we are the better for possessing it. But is it not a strange misuse of the word 'truth,' you will say, to call ideas also 'true' for this reason?

To answer this difficulty fully is impossible at this stage of my account. You touch here upon the very central point of Messrs. Schiller's, Dewey's and my own doctrine of truth, which I cannot discuss with detail until my sixth lecture. Let me now say only this, that truth is *one species of good*, and not, as is usually supposed, a category distinct from good, and co-ordinate with it. *The true is the name of whatever proves itself to be good in the way of belief, and good, too, for definite, assignable reasons.* Surely you must admit this, that if there were *no* good for life in true ideas, or if the knowledge of them were positively disadvantageous and false ideas the only useful ones, then the current notion that truth is divine and precious, and its pursuit a duty, could never have grown up or become a dogma. In a world like that, our duty would be to *shun* truth, rather. But in this world, just as certain foods are not only agreeable to our taste, but good for our teeth, our stomach, and our tissues, so certain ideas are not only agreeable to think about, or agreeable as supporting other ideas that we are fond of, but they are also helpful in life's practical struggles. If there be any life that it is really better we should lead, and if there be any idea which, if believed in, would help us to lead that life, then it would be really *better for us* to believe in that idea, *unless, indeed, belief in it incidentally clashed with other greater vital benefits.*

'What would be better for us to believe'! This sounds very like a definition of truth. It comes very near to saying 'what we *ought* to believe'; and in *that* definition none of you would find any oddity. Ought we ever not to believe what it is *better for us* to believe? And can we then keep the notion of what is better for us, and what is true for us, permanently apart?

Pragmatism says no, and I fully agree with her. Probably you also agree, so far as the abstract statement goes, but with a suspicion that if we practically did believe everything that made for good in our own personal lives, we should be found indulging all kinds of fancies about this world's affairs, and all kinds of sentimental superstitions about a world hereafter. Your suspicion here is undoubtedly well founded, and it is evident that something happens when you pass from the abstract to the concrete that complicates the situation.

I said just now that what is better for us to believe is true *unless the belief incidentally clashes with some other vital benefit.* Now in real life what vital benefits is any particular belief of ours most liable to clash with? What indeed except the vital benefits yielded by *other beliefs* when these prove incompatible with the first ones? In other words, the greatest enemy of any one of our truths may be the rest of our truths. Truths have once for all this desperate instinct of self-preservation and of desire to extinguish whatever contradicts them. My belief in the Absolute, based on the good it does me, must run the gauntlet of all my other beliefs. Grant that it may be true in giving me a moral holiday. Nevertheless, as I conceive it,—and let me speak now confidentially, as it were, and merely in my own private person,—it clashes with other truths of mine whose benefits I hate to give up on its account. It happens to be associated with a kind of logic of which I am the enemy, I find that it entangles me in metaphysical paradoxes that are inacceptable, etc., etc. But as I have enough trouble in life already without adding the trouble of carrying these intellectual inconsistencies, I personally just give up the Absolute. I just *take* my moral holidays; or else as a professional philosopher, I try to justify them by some other principle.

If I could restrict my notion of the Absolute to its bare holiday-giving value, it wouldn't clash with my other truths. But we cannot easily thus restrict our hypotheses. They carry supernumerary features, and these it is that clash so. My disbelief in the Absolute means then disbelief in those other supernumerary features, for I fully believe in the legitimacy of taking moral holidays.

You see by this what I meant when I called pragmatism a mediator and reconciler and said, borrowing the word from Papini, that she 'unstiffens' our theories. She has in fact no prejudices whatever, no obstructive dogmas, no rigid canons of what shall count as proof. She is completely genial. She will entertain any hypothesis, she will consider any evidence. It follows that in the religious field she is at a great advantage both over positivistic empiricism, with its antitheological bias, and over religious rationalism, with its exclusive interest in the remote, the noble, the simple, and the abstract in the way of conception.

In short, she widens the field of search for God. Rationalism sticks to logic and the empyrean. Empiricism sticks to the external senses. Pragmatism is willing to take anything, to follow either logic or the senses and to count the humblest and most personal experiences. She will count mystical experiences if they have practical consequences. She will take a God who lives in the very dirt of private fact—if that should seem a likely place to find him.

Her only test of probable truth is what works best in the way of leading us, what fits every part of life best and combines with the collectivity of experience's demands, nothing being omitted. If theological ideas should do this, if the notion of God, in particular, should prove to do it, how could pragmatism possibly deny God's existence? She could see no meaning in treating as 'not true' a notion that was pragmatically so successful. What other kind of truth could there be, for her, than all this agreement with concrete reality?

In my last lecture I shall return again to the relations of pragmatism with religion. But you see already how democratic she is. Her manners are as various and flexible, her resources as rich and endless, and her conclusions as friendly as those of mother nature.

William James (January 11, 1842–August 26, 1910) received his liberal education through wide travel, tutors, and attendance at several American and European schools. At eighteen he sought to establish himself as a painter, but, sensing his limitations, he turned his attention to medicine. He entered the Lawrence Scientific School, Harvard University, in 1861, remained until 1863, and entered Harvard Medical School the following year. He withdrew a few months later to accompany a scientific expedition to South America, but resumed his medical studies in the spring of 1866. A year later he went to Germany to study the language and experimental physiology. He returned to Harvard in November of 1868 and received his medical degree the following June. Too ill to begin practice, he devoted himself to extensive reading. During this period he was deeply impressed by the writing of the French philosopher Renouvier, which led him to reject both theological and scientific determinism and to embrace free will.

After he regained his health in 1872, he was appointed instructor in Physiology at Harvard College. Finding himself more interested in the workings of the mind, he shifted his teaching emphasis and became a professor of Psychology in 1875. This seems to have provided him with new physical vigor. He began to write what was eventually published as a two-volume work in 1890, Principles of Psychology, *which is often credited with representing the state of psychology in America at that time. Two years later he condensed this into a single volume,* Psychology: American Science Series, Briefer Course, *which became the country's most popular textbook in psychology. In addition, he published* Talks to Teachers on Psychology *in 1899, which is recognized as a classic in education. However, James lost interest in psychology and turned to philosophy as an outlet for his abilities, becoming professor of Philosophy at Harvard in 1897.*

His study of philosophy inspired him to explore the nature and existence of God, the immortality of the soul, free will, the values of life, and the theory of method. His study of the theory of method caused him to prepare a series of lectures, delivered in Boston, which he later published as Pragmatism. *Here he showed that an idea must ultimately be judged by the fruits it bears, by its consequences.*

5

Democracy and Education*

JOHN DEWEY

The School as a Special Environment. . . . Hence a special mode of social intercourse is instituted, the school, to care for such matters.

This mode of association has three functions sufficiently specific, as compared with ordinary associations of life, to be noted. First, a complex civilization is too complex to be assimilated *in toto*. It has to be broken up into portions, as it were, and assimilated piecemeal, in a gradual and graded way. The relationships of our present social life are so numerous and so interwoven that a child placed in the most favorable position could not readily share in many of the most important of them. Not sharing in them, their meaning would not be communicated to him, would not become a part of his own mental disposition. There would be no seeing the trees because of the forest. Business, politics, art, science, religion, would make all at once a clamor for attention; confusion would be the outcome. The first office of the social organ we call the school is to provide a *simplified* environment. It selects the features which are fairly fundamental and capable of being responded to by the young. Then it establishes a progressive order, using the factors first acquired as means of gaining insight into what is more complicated.

In the second place, it is the business of the school environment to

* John Dewey, *Democracy and Education*. New York: The Macmillan Company, 1916, pp. 23–25, 32, 33–34, 49–53, 54–56, 59–61, 89–92, 100–102, 117, 148–150, 151–152, 163–164, 176–177, 180, 183–184, 193–194, 197–200, 210, 212, 214–217, 397, 398, 414–415. Copyright 1916 by The Macmillan Company. Used by permission.

eliminate, so far as possible, the unworthy features of the existing environment from influence upon mental habitudes. It establishes a purified medium of action. Selection aims not only at simplifying but at weeding out what is undesirable. Every society gets encumbered with what is trivial, with dead wood from the past, and with what is positively perverse. The school has the duty of omitting such things from the environment which it supplies, and thereby doing what it can to counteract their influence in the ordinary social environment. By selecting the best for its exclusive use, it strives to reënforce the power of this best. As a society becomes more enlightened, it realizes that it is responsible *not* to transmit and conserve the whole of its existing achievements, but only such as make for a better future society. The school is its chief agency for the accomplishment of this end.

In the third place, it is the office of the school environment to balance the various elements in the social environment, and to see to it that each individual gets an opportunity to escape from the limitations of the social group in which he was born, and to come into living contact with a broader environment. Such words as 'society' and 'community' are likely to be misleading, for they have a tendency to make us think there is a single thing corresponding to the single word. As a matter of fact, a modern society is many societies more or less loosely connected. Each household with its immediate extension of friends makes a society; the village or street group of playmates is a community; each business group, each club, is another. Passing beyond these more intimate groups, there is in a country like our own a variety of races, religious affiliations, economic divisions. Inside the modern city, in spite of its nominal political unity, there are probably more communities, more differing customs, traditions, aspirations, and forms of government or control, than existed in an entire continent at an earlier epoch.

Each such group exercises a formative influence on the active dispositions of its members. A clique, a club, a gang, a Fagin's household of thieves, the prisoners in a jail, provide educative environments for those who enter into their collective or conjoint activities, as truly as a church, a labor union, a business partnership, or a political party. Each of them is a mode of associated or community life, quite as much as is a family, a town, or a state. There are also communities whose members have little or no direct contact with one another, like the guild of artists, the republic of letters, the members of the professional learned class scattered over the face of the earth. For they have aims in common, and the activity of each member is directly modified by knowledge of what others are doing.

Modes of Social Direction. 1. When others are not doing what we would like them to or are threatening disobedience, we are most conscious of the need of controlling them and of the influences by which they are controlled. In such cases, our control becomes most direct, and at this point we are most likely to make the mistakes just spoken of. We are even likely to take the influence of superior force for control, forgetting that while we may lead a horse to water we cannot make him drink; and that while we can shut a man up in a penitentiary we cannot make him penitent. In all such cases of immediate action upon others, we need to discriminate between physical results and moral results. A person may be in such a condition that forcible feeding or enforced confinement is necessary for his own good. A child may have to be snatched with roughness away from a fire so that he shall not be burnt. But no improvement of disposition, no educative effect, need follow. A harsh and commanding tone may be effectual in keeping a child away from the fire, and the same desirable physical effect will follow as if he had been snatched away. But there may be no more obedience of a moral sort in one case than in the other. A man can be prevented from breaking into other persons' houses by shutting him up, but shutting him up may not alter his disposition to commit burglary. When we confuse a physical with an educative result, we always lose the chance of enlisting the person's own participating disposition in getting the result desired, and thereby of developing within him an intrinsic and persisting direction in the right way.

2. These methods of control are so obvious (because so intentionally employed) that it would hardly be worth while to mention them if it were not that notice may now be taken, by way of contrast, of the other more important and permanent mode of control. This other method resides in the ways in which persons, with whom the immature being is associated, *use things;* the instrumentalities with which they accomplish their own ends. The very existence of the social medium in which an individual lives, moves, and has his being is the standing effective agency of directing his activity.

This fact makes it necessary for us to examine in greater detail what is meant by the social environment. We are given to separating from each other the physical and social environments in which we live. The separation is responsible on one hand for an exaggeration of the moral importance of the more direct or personal modes of control of which we have been speaking; and on the other hand for an exaggeration, in current psychology and philosophy, of the *intellectual* possibilities of contact with a purely physical environment. There is not, in fact, any such thing as the direct influence of one human being on another apart from use of the physical environment as an intermediary. A smile, a frown, a rebuke, a word of warning or encouragement, all involve some physical change.

Otherwise, the attitude of one would not get over to alter the attitude of another. Comparatively speaking, such modes of influence may be regarded as personal. The physical medium is reduced to a mere means of personal contact. In contrast with such direct modes of mutual influence stand associations in common pursuits involving the use of things as means and as measures of results. Even if the mother never told her daughter to help her, or never rebuked her for not helping, the child would be subjected to direction in her activities by the mere fact that she was engaged, along with the parent, in the household life. Imitation, emulation, the need of working together, enforce control.

The Conditions of Growth. In directing the activities of the young, society determines its own future in determining that of the young. Since the young at a given time will at some later date compose the society of that period, the latter's nature will largely turn upon the direction children's activities were given at an earlier period. This cumulative movement of action toward a later result is what is meant by growth.

The primary condition of growth is immaturity. This may seem to be a mere truism—saying that a being can develop only in some point in which he is undeveloped. But the prefix 'im' of the word immaturity means something positive, not a mere void or lack. It is noteworthy that the terms 'capacity' and 'potentiality' have a double meaning, one sense being negative, the other positive. Capacity may denote mere receptivity, like the capacity of a quart measure. We may mean by potentiality a merely dormant or quiescent state—a capacity to become something different under external influences. But we also mean by capacity an ability, a power; and by potentiality potency, force. Now when we say that immaturity means the possibility of growth, we are not referring to absence of powers which may exist at a later time; we express a force positively present—the *ability* to develop.

Our tendency to take immaturity as mere lack, and growth as something which fills up the gap between the immature and the mature is due to regarding childhood *comparatively,* instead of intrinsically. We treat it simply as a privation because we are measuring it by adulthood as a fixed standard. This fixes attention upon what the child has not, and will not have till he becomes a man. This comparative standpoint is legitimate enough for some purposes, but if we make it final, the question arises whether we are not guilty of an overweening presumption. Children, if they could express themselves articulately and sincerely, would tell a different tale; and there is excellent adult authority for the conviction that for certain moral and intellectual purposes adults must become as little children.

The seriousness of the assumption of the negative quality of the possibilities of immaturity is apparent when we reflect that it sets up as an ideal and standard a static end. The fulfillment of growing is taken to mean an *accomplished* growth: that is to say, an Ungrowth, something which is no longer growing. The futility of the assumption is seen in the fact that every adult resents the imputation of having no further possibilities of growth; and so far as he finds that they are closed to him mourns the fact as evidence of loss, instead of falling back on the achieved as adequate manifestation of power. Why an unequal measure for child and man?

Taken absolutely, instead of comparatively, immaturity designates a positive force or ability,—the *power* to grow. We do not have to draw out or educe positive activities from a child, as some educational doctrines would have it. Where there is life, there are already eager and impassioned activities. Growth is not something done to them; it is something they do. The positive and constructive aspect of possibility gives the key to understanding the two chief traits of immaturity, dependence and plasticity. (1) It sounds absurd to hear dependence spoken of as something positive, still more absurd as a power. Yet if helplessness were all there were in dependence, no development could ever take place. A merely impotent being has to be carried, forever, by others. The fact that dependence is accompanied by growth in ability, not by an ever increasing lapse into parasitism, suggests that it is already something constructive. Being merely sheltered by others would not promote growth. For (2) it would only build a wall around impotence. With reference to the physical world, the child is helpless. He lacks at birth and for a long time thereafter power to make his way physically, to make his own living. If he had to do that by himself, he would hardly survive an hour. On this side his helplessness is almost complete. The young of the brutes are immeasurably his superiors. He is physically weak and not able to turn the strength which he possesses to coping with the physical environment.

1. The thoroughgoing character of this helplessness suggests, however, some compensating power. The relative ability of the young of brute animals to adapt themselves fairly well to physical conditions from an early period suggests the fact that their life is not intimately bound up with the life of those about them. They are compelled, so to speak, to have physical gifts because they are lacking in social gifts. Human infants, on the other hand, can get along with physical incapacity just because of their social capacity. We sometimes talk and think as if they simply happened to be *physically* in a social environment; as if social forces exclusively existed in the adults who take care of them, they being passive recipients. If it were said that children are themselves marvelously endowed with *power* to enlist the coöperative attention of others, this would

be thought to be a backhanded way of saying that others are marvelously attentive to the needs of children. But observation shows that children are gifted with an equipment of the first order for social intercourse. Few grown-up persons retain all of the flexible and sensitive ability of children to vibrate sympathetically with the attitudes and doings of those about them. Inattention to physical things (going with incapacity to control them) is accompanied by a corresponding intensification of interest and attention as to the doings of people. The native mechanism of the child and his impulses all tend to facile social responsiveness. The statement that children, before adolescence, are egotistically self-centered, even if it were true, would not contradict the truth of this statement. It would simply indicate that their social responsiveness is employed on their own behalf, not that it does not exist. But the statement is not true as matter of fact. The facts which are cited in support of the alleged pure egoism of children really show the intensity and directness with which they go to their mark. If the ends which form the mark seem narrow and selfish to adults, it is only because adults (by means of a similar engrossment in their day) have mastered these ends, which have consequently ceased to interest them. Most of the remainder of children's alleged native egoism is simply an egoism which runs counter to an adult's egoism. To a grown-up person who is too absorbed in his own affairs to take an interest in children's affairs, children doubtless seem unreasonably engrossed in *their* own affairs.

From a social standpoint, dependence denotes a power rather than a weakness; it involves interdependence. There is always a danger that increased personal independence will decrease the social capacity of an individual. In making him more self-reliant, it may make him more self-sufficient; it may lead to aloofness and indifference. It often makes an individual so insensitive in his relations to others as to develop an illusion of being really able to stand and act alone—an unnamed form of insanity which is responsible for a large part of the remediable suffering of the world.

2. The specific adaptability of an immature creature for growth constitutes his *plasticity*. This is something quite different from the plasticity of putty or wax. It is not a capacity to take on change of form in accord with external pressure. It lies near the pliable elasticity by which some persons take on the color of their surroundings while retaining their own bent. But it is something deeper than this. It is essentially the ability to learn from experience; the power to retain from one experience something which is of avail in coping with the difficulties of a later situation. This means power to modify actions on the basis of the results of prior experi-

ences, the power to *develop dispositions*. Without it, the acquisition of habits is impossible.

Habits as Expressions of Growth. We have already noted that plasticity is the capacity to retain a. d carry over from prior experience factors which modify subsequent activities. This signifies the capacity to acquire habits, or develop definite dispositions. We have now to consider the salient features of habits. In the first place, a habit is a form of executive skill, of efficiency in doing. A habit means an ability to use natural conditions as means to ends. It is an active control of the environment through control of the organs of action. We are perhaps apt to emphasize the control of the body at the expense of control of the environment. We think of walking, talking, playing the piano, the specialized skills characteristic of the etcher, the surgeon, the bridge-builder, as if they were simply ease, deftness, and accuracy on the part of the organism. They are that, of course; but the measure of the value of these qualities lies in the economical and effective control of the environment which they secure. To be able to walk is to have certain properties of nature at our disposal—and so with all other habits.

Education is not infrequently defined as consisting in the acquisition of those habits that effect an adjustment of an individual and his environment. The definition expresses an essential phase of growth. But it is essential that adjustment be understood in its active sense of *control* of means for achieving ends. If we think of a habit simply as a change wrought in the organism, ignoring the fact that this change consists in ability to effect subsequent changes in the environment, we shall be led to think of 'adjustment' as a conformity to environment as wax conforms to the seal which impresses it. The environment is thought of as something fixed, providing in its fixity the end and standard of changes taking place in the organism; adjustment is just fitting ourselves to this fixity of external conditions.[1] Habit as *habituation* is indeed something *relatively* passive; we get used to our surroundings—to our clothing, our shoes, and gloves; to the atmosphere as long as it is fairly equable; to our daily associates, etc. Conformity to the environment, a change wrought in the organism without reference to ability to modify surroundings, is a marked trait of such habituations. Aside from the fact that we are not entitled to carry over the traits of such adjustments (which might well be called *accommodations*, to mark them off from active adjustments) into habits

---

[1] This conception is, of course, a logical correlate of the conceptions of the external relation of stimulus and response, considered in the last chapter [*Democracy and Education*], and of the negative conceptions of immaturity and plasticity noted in this chapter.

of active use of our surroundings, two features of habituations are worth notice. In the first place, we get used to things by *first* using them.

Consider getting used to a strange city. At first, there is excessive stimulation and excessive and ill-adapted response. Gradually certain stimuli are selected because of their relevancy, and others are degraded. We can say either that we do not respond to them any longer, or more truly that we have effected a persistent response to them—an equilibrium of adjustment. This means, in the second place, that this enduring adjustment supplies the background upon which are made specific adjustments, as occasion arises. We are never interested in changing the *whole* environment; there is much that we take for granted and accept just as it already is. Upon this background our activities focus at certain points in an endeavor to introduce needed changes. Habituation is thus our adjustment to an environment which at the time we are not concerned with modifying, and which supplies a leverage to our active habits.

The Educational Bearings of the Conception of Development. We have had so far but little to say in this chapter about education. We have been occupied with the conditions and implications of growth. If our conclusions are justified, they carry with them, however, definite educational consequences. When it is said that education is development, everything depends upon *how* development is conceived. Our net conclusion is that life is development, and that developing, growing, is life. Translated into its educational equivalents, this means (i) that the educational process has no end beyond itself; it is its own end; and that (ii) the educational process is one of continual reorganizing, reconstructing, transforming.

1. Development when it is interpreted in *comparative* terms, that is, with respect to the special traits of child and adult life, means the direction of power into special channels: the formation of habits involving executive skill, definiteness of interest, and specific objects of observation and thought. But the comparative view is not final. The child has specific powers; to ignore that fact is to stunt or distort the organs upon which his growth depends. The adult uses his powers to transform his environment, thereby occasioning new stimuli which redirect his powers and keep them developing. Ignoring this fact means arrested development, a passive accommodation. Normal child and normal adult alike, in other words, are engaged in growing. The difference between them is not the difference between growth and no growth, but between the modes of growth appropriate to different conditions. With respect to the development of powers devoted to coping with specific scientific and economic problems, we may say the child should be growing in manhood. With respect to sympathetic curiosity, unbiased responsiveness, and openness of mind,

we may say that the adult should be growing in childlikeness. One statement is as true as the other.

Three ideas which have been criticized, namely, the merely privative nature of immaturity, static adjustment to a fixed environment, and rigidity of habit, are all connected with a false idea of growth or development,—that it is a movement toward a fixed goal. Growth is regarded as *having* an end, instead of *being* an end. The educational counterparts of the three fallacious ideas are first, failure to take account of the instinctive or native powers of the young; secondly, failure to develop initiative in coping with novel situations; thirdly, an undue emphasis upon drill and other devices which secure automatic skill at the expense of personal perception. In all cases, the adult environment is accepted as a standard for the child. He is to be brought up *to* it.

Natural instincts are either disregarded or treated as nuisances—as obnoxious traits to be suppressed, or at all events to be brought into conformity with external standards. Since conformity is the aim, what is distinctively individual in a young person is brushed aside, or regarded as a source of mischief or anarchy. Conformity is made equivalent to uniformity. Consequently, there are induced lack of interest in the novel, aversion to progress, and dread of the uncertain and the unknown. Since the end of growth is outside of and beyond the process of growing, external agents have to be resorted to to induce movement toward it. Whenever a method of education is stigmatized as mechanical, we may be sure that external pressure is brought to bear to reach an external end.

2. Since in reality there is nothing to which growth is relative save more growth, there is nothing to which education is subordinate save more education. It is a commonplace to say that education should not cease when one leaves school. The point of this commonplace is that the purpose of school education is to insure the continuance of education by organizing the powers that insure growth. The inclination to learn from life itself and to make the conditions of life such that all will learn in the process of living is the finest product of schooling.

When we abandon the attempt to define immaturity by means of fixed comparison with adult accomplishments, we are compelled to give up thinking of it as denoting lack of desired traits. Abandoning this notion, we are also forced to surrender our habit of thinking of instruction as a method of supplying this lack by pouring knowledge into a mental and moral hole which awaits filling. Since life means growth, a living creature lives as truly and positively at one stage as at another, with the same intrinsic fullness and the same absolute claims. Hence education means the enterprise of supplying the conditions which insure growth, or adequacy of life, irrespective of age. We first look with impatience upon immaturity, regarding it as something to be got over as rapidly as possible. Then the adult formed by such educative methods looks back with impatient regret upon childhood and youth as a scene of lost opportunities and wasted powers. This ironical situation will endure till it is recognized that living has its own intrinsic quality and that the business of education is with that quality.

Realization that life is growth protects us from that so-called idealizing of childhood which in effect is nothing but lazy indulgence. Life is not to be identified with every superficial act and interest. Even though it is not always easy to tell whether what appears to be mere surface fooling is a sign of some nascent as yet untrained power, we must remember that manifestations are not to be accepted as ends in themselves. They are signs of possible growth. They are to be turned into means of development, of carrying power forward, not indulged or cultivated for their own sake. Excessive attention to surface phenomena (even in the way of rebuke as well as of encouragement) may lead to their fixation and thus to arrested development. What impulses are moving toward, not what they have been, is the important thing for parent and teacher.

Education as Reconstruction. In its contrast with the ideas both of unfolding of latent powers from within, and of formation from without, whether by physical nature or by the cultural products of the past, the ideal of growth results in the conception that education is a constant reorganizing or reconstructing of experience. It has all the time an immediate end, and so far as activity is educative, it reaches that end—the direct transformation of the quality of experience. Infancy, youth, adult life,—all stand on the same educative level in the sense that what is really *learned* at any and every stage of experience constitutes the value of that experience, and in the sense that it is the chief business of life at every point to make living thus contribute to an enrichment of its own perceptible meaning.

We thus reach a technical definition of education: It is that reconstruction or reorganization of experience which adds to the meaning of experience, and which increases ability to direct the course of subsequent experience. (1) The increment of meaning corresponds to the increased perception of the connections and continuities of the activities in which we are engaged. The activity begins in an impulsive form; that is, it is blind. It does not know what it is about; that is to say, what are its interactions with other activities. An activity which brings education or instruction with it makes one aware of some of the connections which had been imperceptible. To recur to our example, a child who reaches for a bright light gets burned. Henceforth he *knows* that a certain act of touching in connection with a certain act of vision (and *vice versa*) means heat and pain; or, a certain light means a source of heat. The acts by which a scientific man in his laboratory learns more about flame differ no whit in principle. By doing certain things, he makes perceptible certain connections of heat with other things, which had been previously ignored. Thus his acts in relation to these things get more meaning; he knows better what he is doing or 'is about' when he has to do with them; he can *intend* consequences instead of just letting them happen—all synonymous ways of saying the same thing. At the same stroke, the flame has gained in meaning; all that is known about combustion, oxidation, about light and temperature, may become an intrinsic part of its intellectual content.

(2) The other side of an educative experience is an added power of subsequent direction or control. To say that one knows what he is about, or can intend certain consequences, is to say, of course, that he can better anticipate what is going to happen; that he can, therefore, get ready or prepare in advance so as to secure beneficial consequences and avert undesirable ones. A genuinely educative experience, then, one in which instruction is conveyed and ability increased, is contradistinguished from a routine activity on one hand, and a capricious activity on the other. (*a*) In the latter one 'does not care what happens'; one just lets himself go and avoids connecting the consequences of one's act (the evidences of its connections with other things) with the act. It is customary to frown upon such aimless random activity, treating it as willful mischief or carelessness or lawlessness. But there is a tendency to seek the cause of such aimless activities in the youth's own disposition, isolated from everything else. But in fact such activity is explosive, and due to maladjustment with surroundings. Individuals act capriciously whenever they act under external dictation, or from being told, without having a purpose of their own or perceiving the bearing of the deed upon other acts. One may learn by doing something which he does not understand; even in the most intelligent action, we do much which we do not mean, because the largest portion of the connections of the act we consciously intend are not perceived or anticipated. But we learn only because after the act is performed we note results which we had not noted before. But much work in school consists in setting up rules by which pupils are to act of such a sort that even after pupils have acted, they are not led to see the connection between the result—say the answer—and the method pursued. So far as they are concerned, the whole thing is a trick and a kind of miracle. Such action is essentially capricious, and leads to capricious habits. (*b*) Routine action, action which is automatic, may increase skill to do a *particular* thing. In so far, it might be said to have an educative effect. But it does not lead to new perceptions of bearings and connections; it limits rather than widens the meaning-horizon. And since the environment changes and our way of acting has to be modified in order successfully to keep a balanced connection with things, an isolated uniform way of acting becomes disastrous at some critical moment. The vaunted 'skill' turns out gross ineptitude.

The essential contrast of the idea of education as continuous reconstruction with the other one-sided conceptions which have been criticized in this and the previous chapter is that it identifies the end (the result) and the process. This is verbally self-contradictory, but only verbally. It means that experience as an active process occupies time and that its later period completes its earlier portion; it brings to light connections involved but hitherto unperceived. The later outcome thus reveals the meaning of the earlier, while the experience as a whole establishes a bent or disposition toward the things possessing this meaning. Every such continuous experience or activity is educative, and all education resides in having such experiences.

It remains only to point out (what will receive more ample attention later) that the reconstruction of experience may be social as well as personal. For purposes of simplification we have spoken in the earlier chapters somewhat as if the education of the immature which fills them with the spirit of the social group to which they belong, were a sort of catching up of the child with the aptitudes and resources of the adult group. In static societies, societies which make the maintenance of established custom their measure of value, this conception applies in the main. But not in progressive communities. They endeavor to shape the experiences of the young so that instead of reproducing current habits, better habits shall be formed, and thus the future adult society be an improvement on their own. Men have long had some intimation of the extent to which education may be consciously used to eliminate obvious social evils through starting the young on paths which shall not produce these ills, and some idea of the extent in which education may be made an instrument of realizing the better hopes of men. But we are doubtless far from realizing the potential efficacy of education as a constructive agency of improving society, from realizing that it represents not only a development of children and youth but also of the future society of which they will be the constituents.

The Democratic Ideal. The two elements in our criterion both point to democracy. The first signifies not only more numerous and more varied points of shared common interest, but greater reliance upon the recognition of mutual interests as a factor in social control. The second means not only freer interaction between social groups (once isolated so far as intention could keep up a separation) but change in social habit—its continuous readjustment through meeting the new situations produced by varied intercourse. And these two traits are precisely what characterize the democratically constituted society.

Upon the educational side, we note first that the realization of a form of social life in which interests are mutually interpenetrating, and where progress, or readjustment, is an important consideration, makes a democratic community more interested than other communities have cause to be in deliberate and systematic education. The devotion of democracy to education is a familiar fact. The superficial explanation is that a government resting upon popular suffrage cannot be successful unless those who elect and who obey their governors are educated. Since a democratic society repudiates the principle of external authority, it must find a substitute in voluntary disposition and interest; these can be created only by education. But there is a deeper explanation. A democracy is more than a form of government; it is primarily a mode of associated living, of conjoint communicated experience. The extension in space of the number of individuals who participate in an interest so that each has to refer his own action to that of others, and to consider the action of others to give point and direction to his own, is equivalent to the breaking down of those barriers of class, race, and national territory which kept men from perceiving the full import of their activity. These more numerous and more varied points of contact denote a greater diversity of stimuli to which an individual has to respond; they consequently put a premium on variation in his action. They secure a liberation of powers which remain suppressed as long as the incitations to action are partial, as they must be in a group which in its exclusiveness shuts out many interests.

The widening of the area of shared concerns, and the liberation of a greater diversity of personal capacities which characterize a democracy, are not of course the product of deliberation and conscious effort. On the contrary, they were caused by the development of modes of manufacture and commerce, travel, migration, and intercommunication which flowed from the command of science over natural energy. But after greater individualization on one hand, and a broader community of interest on the other have come into existence, it is a matter of deliberate effort to sustain and extend them. Obviously a society to which stratification into separate classes would be fatal, must see to it that intellectual opportunities are accessible to all on equable and easy terms. A society marked off into classes need be specially attentive only to the education of its ruling elements. A society which is mobile, which is full of channels for the distribution of a change occurring anywhere, must see to it that its members are educated to personal initiative and adaptability. Otherwise, they will be overwhelmed by the changes in which they are caught and whose significance or connections they do not perceive. The result will be a confusion in which a few will appropriate to themselves the results of the blind and externally directed activities of others.

The Nature of an Aim. The account of education given in our earlier chapters virtually anticipated the results reached in a discussion of the purport of education in a democratic community. For it assumed that the aim of education is to enable individuals to continue their education—or that the object and reward of learning is continued capacity for growth. Now this idea cannot be applied to *all* the members of a society except where intercourse of man with man is mutual, and except where there is adequate provision for the reconstruction of social habits and institutions by means of wide stimulation arising from equitably distributed interests. And this means a democratic society. In our search for aims in education, we are not concerned, therefore, with finding an end outside of the educative process to which education is subordinate. Our whole conception forbids. We are rather concerned with the contrast which exists when aims belong within the process in which they operate and when they are set up from without. And the latter state of affairs must obtain when social relationships are not equitably balanced. For in that case, some portions of the whole social group will find their aims determined by an external dictation; their aims will not arise from the free growth of their own experience, and their nominal aims will be means to more ulterior ends of others rather than truly their own.

Interest. . . . Interest, concern, mean that self and world are engaged with each other in a developing situation.

The word interest, in its ordinary usage, expresses (*i*) the whole state of active development, (*ii*) the objective results that are foreseen and wanted, and (*iii*) the personal emotional inclination. (*i*) An occupation, employment, pursuit, business is often referred to as an interest. Thus we say that a man's interest is politics, or journalism, or philanthropy, or archæology, or collecting Japanese prints, or banking. (*ii*) By an interest we also mean the point at which an object touches or engages a man; the point where it influences him. In some legal transactions a man has to prove "interest" in order to have a standing at court. He has to show that some proposed step concerns his affairs. A silent partner has an interest in a business, although he takes no active part in its conduct, because its prosperity or decline affects his profits and liabilities. (*iii*) When we speak of a man as interested in this or that the emphasis falls directly upon his personal attitude. To be interested is to be absorbed in, wrapped up in, carried away by, some object. To take an interest is to be on the alert, to care about, to be attentive. We say of an interested person both that he has lost himself in some affair and that he has found himself in it. Both terms express the engrossment of the self in an object.

When the place of interest in education is spoken of in a depreciatory way, it will be found that the second of the meanings mentioned is first exaggerated and then isolated. Interest is taken to mean merely the effect of an object upon personal advantage or disadvantage, success or failure. Separated from any objective development of affairs, these are reduced to mere personal states of pleasure or pain. Educationally, it then follows that to attach importance to interest means to attach some feature of seductiveness to material otherwise indifferent; to secure attention and effort by offering a bribe of pleasure. This procedure is properly stigmatized as "soft" pedagogy; as a "soup-kitchen" theory of education.

But the objection is based upon the fact—or assumption—that the forms of skill to be acquired and the subject matter to be appropriated have no interest on their own account: in other words, they are supposed to be irrelevant to the normal activities of the pupils. The remedy is not in finding fault with the doctrine of interest, any more than it is to search for some pleasant bait that may be hitched to the alien material. It is to discover objects and modes of action, which are connected with present powers. The function of this material in engaging activity and carrying it on consistently and continuously *is* its interest. If the material operates in this way, there is no call either to hunt for devices which will make it interesting or to appeal to arbitrary, semi-coerced effort.

The word interest suggests, etymologically, what is *between*—that which connects two things otherwise distant. In education, the distance covered may be looked at as temporary. The fact that a process takes time to mature is so obvious a fact that we rarely make it explicit. We overlook the fact that in growth there is ground to be covered between an initial stage of process and the completing period; that there is something intervening. In learning, the present powers of the pupil are the initial stage; the aim of the teacher represents the remote limit. Between the two lie *means*—that is, middle conditions:—acts to be performed; difficulties to be overcome; appliances to be used. Only *through* them, in the literal time sense, will the initial activities reach a satisfactory consummation.

These intermediate conditions are of interest precisely because the development of existing activities into the foreseen and desired end depends upon them. To be means for the achieving of present tendencies to be "between" the agent and his end, to be of interest, are different names for the same thing. When material has to be made interesting, it signifies that as presented, it lacks connection with purposes and present power: or that if the connection be there, it is not perceived. To make it interesting by leading one to realize the connection that exists is simply good sense; to make it interesting by extraneous and artificial inducements deserves all the bad names which have been applied to the doctrine of interest in education.

So much for the meaning of the term interest. Now for that of discipline. Where an activity takes time, where many means and obstacles lie between its initiation and completion, deliberation and persistence are required. It is obvious that a very large part of the everyday meaning of will is precisely the deliberate or conscious disposition to persist and endure in a planned course of action in spite of difficulties and contrary solicitations. A man of strong will, in the popular usage of the words, is a man who is neither fickle nor halfhearted in achieving chosen ends. His ability is executive; that is, he persistently and energetically strives to execute or carry out his aims. A weak will is unstable as water.

Discipline. A person who is trained to consider his actions, to undertake them deliberately, is in so far forth disciplined. Add to this ability a power to endure in an intelligently chosen course in face of distraction, confusion, and difficulty, and you have the essence of discipline. Discipline means power at command; mastery of the resources available for carrying through the action undertaken. To know what one is to do and to move to do it promptly and by use of the requisite means is to be disciplined, whether we are thinking of an army or a mind. Discipline is positive. To cow the spirit, to subdue inclination, to compel obedience, to mortify the flesh, to make a subordinate perform an uncongenial task— these things are or are not disciplinary according as they do or do not tend to the development of power to recognize what one is about and to persistence in accomplishment.

It is hardly necessary to press the point that interest and discipline are connected, not opposed. (*i*) Even the more purely intellectual phase of trained power—apprehension of what one is doing as exhibited in consequences—is not possible without interest. Deliberation will be perfunctory and superficial where there is no interest. Parents and teachers often complain—and correctly—that children "do not want to hear, or want to understand." Their minds are not upon the subject precisely because it does not touch them; it does not enter into their concerns. This is a state of things that needs to be remedied, but the remedy is not in the use of methods which increase indifference and aversion. Even punishing a child for inattention is one way of trying to make him realize that the matter is *not* a thing of complete unconcern; it is one way of arousing "interest," or bringing about a sense of connection. In the long run, its value is measured by whether it supplies a mere physical excitation to act in the way desired by the adult or whether it leads the child "to think"—that is, to reflect upon his acts and impregnate them with aims. (*ii*) That interest is requisite for executive persistence is even more obvious. Employers do not advertise for workmen who are not interested in what they are doing. If one were engaging a lawyer or a doctor, it would never occur to one to reason that the person engaged would stick to his work more conscientiously if it was so uncongenial to him that he did it merely from a sense of obligation. Interest measures—or rather *is*—the depth of the grip which the foreseen end has upon one in moving one to act for its realization.

The Nature of Experience. The nature of experience can be understood only by noting that it includes an active and a passive element peculiarly combined. On the active hand, experience is *trying*—a meaning which is made explicit in the connected term experiment. On the passive, it is *undergoing*. When we experience something we act upon it, we do something with it; then we suffer or undergo the consequences. We do something to the thing and then it does something to us in return: such is the peculiar combination. The connection of these two phases of experience measures the fruitfulness or value of the experience. Mere activity does not constitute experience. It is dispersive, centrifugal, dissipating. Experience as trying involves change, but change is meaningless transition unless it is consciously connected with the return wave of consequences which flow from it. When an activity is continued *into* the undergoing of consequences, when the change made by action is reflected back into a change made in us, the mere flux is loaded with significance. We learn something. It is not experience when a child merely sticks his finger into a flame; it is experience when the movement is connected with the pain which he undergoes in consequence. Henceforth the sticking of the finger into flame *means* a burn. Being burned is a mere physical change, like the burning of a stick of wood, if it is not perceived as a consequence of some other action.

Blind and capricious impulses hurry us on heedlessly from one thing to another. So far as this happens, everything is writ in water. There is none of that cumulative growth which makes an experience in any vital sense of that term. On the other hand, many things happen to us in the way of pleasure and pain which we do not connect with any prior activity of our own. They are mere accidents so far as we are concerned. There is no before or after to such experience; no retrospect nor outlook, and consequently no meaning. We get nothing which may be carried over to foresee what is likely to happen next, and no gain in ability to adjust ourselves to what is coming—no added control. Only by courtesy can such an experience be called experience. To "learn from experience" is to make a backward and forward connection between what we do to things and what we enjoy or suffer from things in consequence. Under such conditions, doing becomes a trying; an experiment with the world to find out what it is like; the undergoing becomes instruction—discovery of the connection of things.

Experience and Thinking. So much for the general features of a reflective experience. They are (*i*) perplexity, confusion, doubt, due to the fact that one is implicated in an incomplete situation whose full character is not yet determined; (*ii*) a conjectural anticipation—a tentative interpretation of the given elements, attributing to them a tendency to effect certain consequences; (*iii*) a careful survey (examination, inspection, exploration, analysis) of all attainable consideration which will define and clarify the problem in hand; (*iv*) a consequent elaboration of the tentative hypothesis to make it more precise and more consistent, because squaring with a wider range of facts; (*v*) taking one stand upon the projected hypothesis as a plan of action which is applied to the existing state of affairs: doing something overtly to bring about the anticipated result, and thereby testing the hypothesis. It is the extent and accuracy of steps three and four which mark off a distinctive reflective experience from one on the trial and error plane. They make *thinking* itself into an experience. Nevertheless, we never get wholly beyond the trial and error situation. Our most elaborate and rationally consistent thought has to be tried in the world and thereby tried out. And since it can never take into account all the connections, it can never cover with perfect accuracy all the consequences. Yet a thoughtful survey of conditions is so careful, and the guessing at results so controlled, that we have a right to mark off the reflective experience from the grosser trial and error forms of action.

Thinking in Education. The initial stage of that developing experience which is called thinking is *experience*. This remark may sound like a silly truism. It ought to be one; but unfortunately it is not. On the contrary, thinking is often regarded both in philosophic theory and in educational practice as something cut off from experience, and capable of being cultivated in isolation. In fact, the inherent limitations of experience are often urged as the sufficient ground for attention to thinking. Experience is then thought to be confined to the senses and appetites; to a mere material world, while thinking proceeds from a higher faculty (of reason), and is occupied with spiritual or at least literary things. So oftentimes, a sharp distinction is made between pure mathematics as a peculiarly fit subject matter of thought (since it has nothing to do with physical existences) and applied mathematics, which has utilitarian but not mental value.

Speaking generally, the fundamental fallacy in methods of instruction lies in supposing that experience on the part of pupils may be assumed. What is here insisted upon is the necessity of an actual empirical situation as the initiating phase of thought. Experience is here taken as previously defined: trying to do something and having the thing perceptibly do something to one in return. The fallacy consists in supposing that we can begin with ready-made subject matter of arithmetic, or geography, or whatever, irrespective of some direct personal experience of a situation.

No one has ever explained why children are so full of questions outside of the school (so that they pester grown-up persons if they get any encouragement), and the conspicuous absence of display of curiosity about the subject matter of school lessons. Reflection on this striking contrast will throw light upon the question of how far customary school conditions supply a context of experience in which problems naturally suggest themselves. No amount of improvement in the personal technique of the instructor will wholly remedy this state of things. There must be more actual material, more *stuff*, more appliances, and more opportunities for doing things, before the gap can be overcome. And where children are engaged in doing things and in discussing what arises in the course of their doing, it is found, even with comparatively indifferent modes of instruction, that children's inquiries are spontaneous and numerous, and the proposals of solution advanced, varied, and ingenious.

As a consequence of the absence of the materials and occupations which generate real problems, the pupil's problems are not his; or, rather, they are his *only as* a pupil, not as a human being. Hence the lamentable waste in carrying over such expertness as is achieved in dealing with them to the affairs of life beyond the schoolroom. A pupil has a problem, but it is the problem of meeting the peculiar requirements set by the teacher. His problem becomes that of finding out what the teacher wants, what will satisfy the teacher in recitation and examination and outward deportment. Relationship to subject matter is no longer direct. The occasions and material of thought are not found in the arithmetic or the history or geography itself, but in skillfully adapting that material to the teacher's requirements. The pupil studies, but unconsciously to himself the objects of his study are the conventions and standards of the school system and school authority, not the nominal "studies." The thinking thus evoked is artificially one-sided at the best. At its worst, the problem of the pupil is not how to meet the requirements of school life, but how to *seem* to meet them—or, how to come near enough to meeting them to slide along without an undue amount of friction. The type of judgment formed by these devices is not a desirable addition to character. If these statements give too highly colored a picture of usual school methods, the exaggeration may at least serve to illustrate the point: the need of active pursuits, involving the use of material to accomplish purposes, if there are to be situations which normally generate problems occasioning thoughtful inquiry.

The Unity of Subject Matter and Method. The trinity of school topics is subject matter, methods, and administration or government. We have been concerned with the two former in recent chapters. It remains to disentangle them from the context in which they have been referred to, and discuss explicitly their nature. We shall begin with the topic of method, since that lies closest to the considerations of the last chapter. Before taking it up, it may be well, however, to call express attention to one implication of our theory; the connection of subject matter and method with each other. The idea that mind and world of things and persons are two separate and independent realms—a theory which philosophically is known as dualism—carries with it the conclusion that method and subject matter of instruction are separate affairs. Subject matter then becomes a ready-made systematized classification of the facts and principles of the world of nature and man. Method then has for its province a consideration of the ways in which this antecedent subject matter may be best presented to and impressed upon the mind; or, a consideration of the ways in which the mind may be externally brought to bear upon the matter so as to facilitate its acquisition and possession. In theory, at least, one might deduce from a science of mind as something existing by itself a complete theory of methods of learning, with no knowledge of the subjects to which the methods are to be applied. Since many who are actually most proficient in various branches of subject matter are wholly innocent of these methods, this state of affairs gives opportunity for the retort that pedagogy, as an alleged science of methods of the mind in learning, is futile;—a mere screen for concealing the necessity a teacher is under of profound and accurate acquaintance with the subject in hand.

But since thinking is a directed movement of subject matter to a completing issue, and since mind is the deliberate and intentional phase of the process, the notion of any such split is radically false. The fact that the material of a science is organized is evidence that it has already been subjected to intelligence; it has been methodized, so to say. Zoölogy as a systematic branch of knowledge represents crude, scattered facts of our ordinary acquaintance with animals after they have been subjected to careful examination, to deliberate supplementation, and to arrangement to bring out connections which assist observation, memory, and further inquiry. Instead of furnishing a starting point for learning, they mark out a consummation. Method means that arrangement *of* subject matter which makes it most effective in use. Never is method something outside of the material.

How about method from the standpoint of an individual who is dealing with subject matter? Again, it is not something external. It is simply an effective treatment *of* material—efficiency meaning such treatment as utilizes the material (puts it to a purpose) with a minimum of waste of time and energy. We can distinguish a *way* of acting, and discuss it by itself; but the way *exists* only as a way-of-dealing-with-material. Method is not antithetical to subject matter; it is the effective direction of subject matter to desired results. It is antithetical to random and ill-considered action,—ill-considered signifying ill-adapted.

The Nature of Method. A consideration of some evils in education that flow from the isolation of method from subject matter will make the point more definite. (*i*) In the first place, there is the neglect (of which we have spoken) of concrete situations of experience. There can be no discovery of a method without cases to be studied. The method is derived from observation of what actually happens, with a view to seeing that it happen better next time. But in instruction and discipline, there is rarely sufficient opportunity for children and youth to have the direct normal experiences from which educators might derive an idea of method or order of best development. Experiences are had under conditions of such constraint that they throw little or no light upon the normal course of an experience to its fruition. "Methods" have then to be authoritatively recommended to teachers, instead of being an expression of their own intelligent observations. Under such circumstances, they have a mechanical uniformity, assumed to be alike for all minds. Where flexible personal experiences are promoted by providing an environment which calls out directed occupations in work and play, the methods ascertained will vary with individuals—for it is certain that each individual has something characteristic in his way of going at things.

(*ii*) In the second place, the notion of methods isolated from subject matter is responsible for the false conceptions of discipline and interest already noted. When the effective way of managing material is treated as something ready-made apart from material, there are just three possible ways in which to establish a relationship lacking by assumption. One is to utilize excitement, shock of pleasure, tickling the palate. Another is to make the consequences of not attending painful; we may use the menace of harm to motivate concern with the alien subject matter. Or a direct appeal may be made to the person to put forth effort without any reason. We may rely upon immediate strain of "will." In practice, however, the latter method is effectual only when instigated by fear of unpleasant results.

(*iii*) In the third place, the act of learning is made a direct and conscious end in itself. Under normal conditions, learning is a product and reward of occupation with subject matter. Children do not set out, consciously, to learn walking or talking. One sets out to give his impulses for communication and for fuller intercourse with others a show. He learns in consequence of his direct activities. The better methods of teaching a child, say, to read, follow the same road. They do not fix his attention upon the fact that he has to learn something and so make his attitude self-conscious and constrained. They engage his activities, and in the process of engagement he learns: the same is true of the more successful methods in dealing with number or whatever. But when the subject matter is not used in carrying forward impulses and habits to significant results, it is just something to be learned. The pupil's attitude to it is just that of having to learn it. Conditions more unfavorable to an alert and concentrated response would be hard to devise. Frontal attacks are even more wasteful in learning than in war. This does not mean, however, that students are to be seduced unaware into preoccupation with lessons. It means that they shall be occupied with them for real reasons or ends, and not just as something to be learned. This is accomplished whenever the pupil perceives the place occupied by the subject matter in the fulfilling of some experience.

(*iv*) In the fourth place, under the influence of the conception of the separation of mind and material, method tends to be reduced to a cut and dried routine, to following mechanically prescribed steps. No one can tell in how many schoolrooms children reciting in arithmetic or grammar are compelled to go through, under the alleged sanction of method, certain preordained verbal formulæ. Instead of being encouraged to attack their topics directly, experimenting with methods that seem promising and learning to discriminate by the consequences that accrue, it is assumed that there is one fixed method to be followed. It is also naïvely assumed that if the pupils make their statements and explanations in a certain form of "analysis," their mental habits will in time conform. Nothing has brought pedagogical theory into greater disrepute than the belief that it is identified with handing out to teachers recipes and models to be followed in teaching. Flexibility and initiative in dealing with problems are characteristic of any conception to which method is a way of managing material to develop a conclusion. Mechanical rigid woodenness is an inevitable corollary of any theory which separates mind from activity motivated by a purpose.

It would be much better to have fewer facts and truths in instruction —that is, fewer things supposedly accepted,—if a smaller number of situations could be intellectually worked out to the point where conviction meant something real—some identification of the self with the type of conduct demanded by facts and foresight of results. The most permanent bad results of undue complication of school subjects and congestion of school studies and lessons are not the worry, nervous strain, and superficial acquaintance that follow (serious as these are), but the failure to make clear what is involved in really knowing and believing a thing. Intellectual responsibility means severe standards in this regard. These standards can be built up only through practice in following up and acting upon the meaning of what is acquired.

Intellectual *thoroughness* is thus another name for the attitude we are considering. There is a kind of thoroughness which is almost purely physical: the kind that signifies mechanical and exhausting drill upon all the details of a subject. Intellectual thoroughness is *seeing a thing through*. It depends upon a unity of purpose to which details are subordinated, not upon presenting a multitude of disconnected details. It is manifested in the firmness with which the full meaning of the purpose is developed, not in attention, however "conscientious" it may be, to the steps of action externally imposed and directed.

Subject Matter of Educator and of Learner.   So far as the nature of subject matter in principle is concerned, there is nothing to add to what has been said (see *ante*, p. 158 [*Democracy and Education*]). It consists of the facts observed, recalled, read, and talked about, and the ideas suggested, in course of a development of a situation having a purpose. This statement needs to be rendered more specific by connecting it with the materials of school instruction, the studies which make up the curriculum. What is the significance of our definition in application to reading, writing, mathematics, history, nature study, drawing, singing, physics, chemistry, modern and foreign languages and so on?

Let us recur to two of the points made earlier in our discussion. The educator's part in the enterprise of education is to furnish the environment which stimulates responses and directs the learner's course. In last analysis, *all* that the educator can do is modify stimuli so that response will as surely as is possible result in the formation of desirable intellectual and emotional dispositions. Obviously studies or the subject matter of the curriculum have intimately to do with this business of supplying an environment. The other point is the necessity of a social environment to give meaning to habits formed. In what we have termed informal education, subject matter is carried directly in the matrix of social intercourse.

The Nature of Subject Matter.   The points need to be considered from the standpoint of instructor and of student. To the former, the significance of a knowledge of subject matter, going far beyond the present knowledge of pupils, is to supply definite standards and to reveal to him the possibilities of the crude activities of the immature. (*i*) The material of school studies translates into concrete and detailed terms the meanings of current social life which it is desirable to transmit. It puts clearly before the instructor the essential ingredients of the culture to be perpetuated, in such an organized form as to protect him from the haphazard efforts he would be likely to indulge in if the meanings had not been standardized. (*ii*) A knowledge of the ideas which have been achieved in the past as the outcome of activity places the educator in a position to perceive the meaning of the seeming impulsive and aimless reactions of the young, and to provide the stimuli needed to direct them so that they will amount to something. The more the educator knows of music the more he can perceive the possibilities of the inchoate musical impulses of a child. Organized subject matter represents the ripe fruitage of experiences like theirs, experiences involving the same world, and powers and needs similar to theirs. It does not represent perfection or infallible wisdom; but it is the best at command to further new experiences which may, in some respects at least, surpass the achievements embodied in existing knowledge and works of art.

From the standpoint of the educator, in other words, the various studies represent working resources, available capital. Their remoteness from the experience of the young is not, however, seeming; it is real. The subject matter of the learner is not, therefore, it cannot be, identical with the formulated, the crystallized, and systematized subject matter of the adult; the material as found in books and in works of art, etc. The latter represents the *possibilities* of the former; not its existing state. It enters directly into the activities of the expert and the educator, not into that of the beginner, the learner. Failure to bear in mind the difference in subject matter from the respective standpoints of teacher and student is responsible for most of the mistakes made in the use of texts and other expressions of preëxistent knowledge.

The need for a knowledge of the constitution and functions, in the concrete, of human nature is great just because the teacher's attitude to subject matter is so different from that of the pupil. The teacher presents in actuality what the pupil represents only in *posse*. That is, the teacher already knows the things which the student is only learning. Hence the problem of the two is radically unlike. When engaged in the direct act of teaching, the instructor needs to have subject matter at his fingers' ends; his attention should be upon the attitude and response of the pupil. To understand the latter in its interplay with subject matter is his task, while the pupil's mind, naturally, should be not on itself but on the topic in hand. Or to state the same point in a somewhat different manner: the teacher should be occupied not with subject matter in itself but in its interaction with the pupil's present needs and capacities. Hence simple scholarship is not enough. In fact, there are certain features of scholarship or mastered subject matter—taken by itself—which get in the way of effective teaching *unless* the instructor's habitual attitude is one of concern with its interplay in the pupil's own experience. In the first place, his knowledge extends indefinitely beyond the range of the pupil's acquaintance. It involves principles which are beyond the immature pupil's understanding and interest. In and of itself, it may no more represent the living world of the pupil's experience than the astronomer's knowledge of Mars represents a baby's acquaintance with the room in which he stays. In the second place, the method of organization of the material of achieved scholarship differs from that of the beginner. It is not true that the experience of the young is unorganized—that it consists of isolated scraps. But it is organized in connection with direct practical centers of interest. The child's home is, for example, the organizing center of his geographical knowledge. His own movements about the locality, his journeys abroad, the tales of his friends, give the ties which hold his items of information together. But the geography of the geographer, of the one who has already developed the implications of these smaller experiences, is organized on the basis of the relationship which the various facts bear to one another—not the relations which they bear to his house, bodily movements, and friends. To the one who is learned, subject matter is extensive, accurately defined, and logically interrelated. To the one who is learning, it is fluid, partial, and connected through his personal occupations.[2] The problem of teaching is to keep the experience of the student moving in the direction of what the expert already knows. Hence the need that the teacher know both subject matter and the characteristic needs and capacities of the student.

The Development of Subject Matter in the Learner. It is possible, without doing violence to the facts, to mark off three fairly typical stages in the growth of subject matter in the experience of the learner. In its first estate, knowledge exists as the content of intelligent ability—power to do. This kind of subject matter, or known material, is expressed in familiarity or acquaintance with things. Then this material gradually is surcharged and deepened through communicated knowledge or information. Finally, it is enlarged and worked over into rationally or logically organized material—that of the one who, relatively speaking, is expert in the subject.

Theories of Knowledge. While the content of knowledge is what *has* happened, what is taken as finished and hence settled and sure, the *reference* of knowledge is future or prospective. For knowledge furnishes the means of understanding or giving meaning to what is still going on and what is to be done. The knowledge of a physician is what he has

---

[2] Since the learned man should also still be a learner, it will be understood that these contrasts are relative, not absolute. But in the earlier stages of learning at least they are practically all-important.

found out by personal acquaintance and by study of what others have ascertained and recorded. But it is knowledge to him because it supplies the resources by which he interprets the unknown things which confront him, fills out the partial obvious facts with connected suggested phenomena, foresees their probable future, and makes plans accordingly. When knowledge is cut off from use in giving meaning to what is blind and baffling, it drops out of consciousness entirely or else becomes an object of æsthetic contemplation.

Yet many of the philosophic schools of method which have been mentioned transform the ignoring into a virtual denial. They regard knowledge as something complete in itself irrespective of its availability in dealing with what is yet to be. And it is this omission which vitiates them and which makes them stand as sponsors for educational methods which an adequate conception of knowledge condemns. For one has only to call to him what is sometimes treated in schools as acquisition of knowledge to realize how lacking it is in any fruitful connection with the ongoing experience of the students—how largely it seems to be believed that the mere appropriation of subject matter which happens to be stored in books constitutes knowledge. No matter how true what is learned to those who found it out and in whose experience it functioned, there is nothing which makes it knowledge to the pupils. It might as well be something about Mars or about some fanciful country unless it fructifies in the individual's own life.

The Social and the Moral. All of the separations which we have been criticizing—and which the idea of education set forth in the previous chapters is designed to avoid—spring from taking morals too narrowly,— giving them, on one side, a sentimental goody-goody turn without reference to effective ability to do what is socially needed, and, on the other side, overemphasizing convention and tradition so as to limit morals to a list of definitely stated acts. As a matter of fact, morals are as broad as acts which concern our relationships with others. And potentially this includes all our acts, even though their social bearing may not be thought of at the time of performance. For every act, by the principle of habit, modifies disposition—it sets up a certain kind of inclination and desire. And it is impossible to tell when the habit thus strengthened may have a direct and perceptible influence on our association with others. Certain traits of character have such an obvious connection with our social relationships that we call them "moral" in an emphatic sense—truthfulness, honesty, chastity, amiability, etc. But this only means that they are, as compared with some other attitudes, central:—that they carry other attitudes with them. They are moral in an emphatic sense not because they are isolated and exclusive, but because they are so intimately connected with thousands of other attitudes which we do not explicitly recognize—which perhaps we have not even names for. To call them virtues in their isolation is like taking the skeleton for the living body. The bones are certainly important, but their importance lies in the fact that they support other organs of the body in such a way as to make them capable of integrated effective activity. And the same is true of the qualities of character which we specifically designate virtues. Morals concern nothing less than the whole character, and the whole character is identical with the man in all his concrete make-up and manifestations. To possess virtue does not signify to have cultivated a few nameable and exclusive traits; it means to be fully and adequately what one is capable of becoming through association with others in all the offices of life.

John Dewey (October 20, 1859–June 1, 1952) was educated at the University of Vermont and the Johns Hopkins University. After a brief teaching career in public schools, he began his long life of college work, which took him to the University of Michigan (1884–1888, 1889–1894), the University of Minnesota (1888–1889), the University of Chicago (1894–1904), and finally to the Department of Philosophy at Columbia University in 1904. It was as Director of the School of Education at the University of Chicago that he first began to experiment with his beliefs concerning philosophy and psychology of education. Here he established the now famous Dewey School and began to win the fame that was to be his from that time forward. However, it was not until 1916, when he was well established at Columbia, that he published his best-known volume on education, Democracy and Education.

As a pragmatist, Dewey rejected the authoritarian and classical approach to education, which he thought stressed the ability to talk about things rather than the ability to do things. He built his philosophy on a biological base, pointing out that man is an organism living in an environment, an environment which helps to shape man, but which, in turn, can be modified by man. Dewey thought things were to be understood through their origin and function. To him, the only reality for man was experience; the business of education was to improve the quality of experience that human beings had. This he hoped to accomplish by carefully defining the nature of experience and establishing criteria for judging its value.

Dewey has been called the greatest educational philosopher since Plato. Whether or not this is true, he has produced numerous articles and books that have had profound influence on education, not only in America but throughout the world.

6

Experience and Education[*]

JOHN DEWEY

Traditional vs. Progressive Education

. . . THE TRADITIONAL SCHEME is, in essence, one of imposition from above and from outside. It imposes adult standards, subject-matter, and methods upon those who are only growing slowly toward maturity. The gap is so great that the required subject-matter, the methods of learning and of behaving are foreign to the existing capacities of the young. They are beyond the reach of the experience the young learners already possess. Consequently, they must be imposed; even though good teachers will use devices of art to cover up the imposition so as to relieve it of obviously brutal features.

If one attempts to formulate the philosophy of education implicit in the practices of the newer education, we may, I think, discover certain common principles amid the variety of progressive schools now existing. To imposition from above is opposed expression and cultivation of individuality; to external discipline is opposed free activity; to learning from texts and teachers, learning through experience; to acquisition of isolated skills and techniques by drill, is opposed acquisition of them as means of attaining ends which make direct vital appeal; to preparation for a more or less remote future is opposed making the most of the opportunities of present life; to static aims and materials is opposed acquaintance with a changing world.

[*] John Dewey, *Experience and Education.* Tiffin, Ohio (238 East Perry Street): Kappa Delta Pi, pp. 4, 5–6, 9–10, 13–14, 16, 29–32, 34–35, 38–42, 60–63, 65–66, 69–71, 72, 88–89, 95, 96–97, 114–115. Copyright 1938 by Kappa Delta Pi. Used by permission.

What is indicated in the foregoing remarks is that the general principles of the new education do not of themselves solve any of the problems of the actual or practical conduct and management of progressive schools. Rather, they set new problems which have to be worked out on the basis of a new philosophy of experience. The problems are not even recognized, to say nothing of being solved, when it is assumed that it suffices to reject the ideas and practices of the old education and then go to the opposite extreme. Yet I am sure that you will appreciate what is meant when I say that many of the newer schools tend to make little or nothing of organized subject-matter of study; to proceed as if any form of direction and guidance by adults were an invasion of individual freedom, and as if the idea that education should be concerned with the present and future meant that acquaintance with the past has little or no role to play in education. Without pressing these defects to the point of exaggeration, they at least illustrate what is meant by a theory and practice of education which proceeds negatively or by reaction against what has been current in education rather than by a positive and constructive development of purposes, methods, and subject-matter on the foundation of a theory of experience and its educational potentialities.

It is not too much to say that an educational philosophy which professes to be based on the idea of freedom may become as dogmatic as ever was the traditional education which is reacted against. For any theory and set of practices is dogmatic which is not based upon critical examination of its own underlying principles.

The Need for a Theory of Experience

. . . Any experience is mis-educative that has the effect of arresting or distorting the growth of further experience. An experience may be such as to engender callousness; it may produce lack of sensitivity and of responsiveness. Then the possibilities of having richer experience in the future are restricted. Again, a given experience may increase a person's automatic skill in a particular direction and yet tend to land him in a groove or rut; the effect again is to narrow the field of further experience. An experience may be immediately enjoyable and yet promote the formation of a slack and careless attitude; this attitude then operates to modify the quality of subsequent experiences so as to prevent a person from getting out of them what they have to give. Again, experiences may be so disconnected from one another that, while each is agreeable or even exciting in itself, they are not linked cumulatively to one another. Energy is then dissipated and a person becomes scatterbrained. Each experience may be lively, vivid, and "interesting," and yet their disconnectedness may artificially generate dispersive, disintegrated, centrifugal habits.

Everything depends upon the *quality* of the experience which is had. The quality of any experience has two aspects. There is an immediate aspect of agreeableness or disagreeableness, and there is its influence upon later experiences. The first is obvious and easy to judge. The *effect* of an experience is not borne on its face. It sets a problem to the educator. It is his business to arrange for the kind of experiences which, while they do not repel the student, but rather engage his activities are, nevertheless, more than immediately enjoyable since they promote having desirable future experiences.

CRITERIA OF EXPERIENCE

I return now to the question of continuity as a criterion by which to discriminate between experiences which are educative and those which are mis-educative. As we have seen, there is some kind of continuity in any case since every experience affects for better or worse the attitudes which help decide the quality of further experiences, by setting up certain preference and aversion, and making it easier or harder to act for this or that end. Moreover, every experience influences in some degree the objective conditions under which further experiences are had. For example, a child who learns to speak has a new facility and new desire. But he has also widened the external conditions of subsequent learning. When he learns to read, he similarly opens up a new environment. If a person decides to become a teacher, lawyer, physician, or stockbroker, when he executes his intention he thereby necessarily determines to some extent the environment in which he will act in the future. He has rendered himself more sensitive and responsive to certain conditions, and relatively immune to those things about him that would have been stimuli if he had made another choice.

But, while the principle of continuity applies in some way in every case, the quality of the present experience influences the *way* in which the principle applies. We speak of spoiling a child and of the spoilt child. The effect of overindulging a child is a continuing one. It sets up an attitude which operates as an automatic demand that persons and objects cater to his desires and caprices in the future. It makes him seek the kind of situation that will enable him to do what he feels like doing at the time. It renders him averse to and comparatively incompetent in situations which require effort and perseverance in overcoming obstacles. There is no paradox in the fact that the principle of the continuity of experience may operate so as to leave a person arrested on a low plane of development, in a way which limits later capacity for growth.

On the other hand, if an experience arouses curiosity, strengthens initiative, and sets up desires and purposes that are sufficiently intense to carry a person over dead places in the future, continuity works in a very different way. Every experience is a moving force. Its value can be judged only on the ground of what it moves toward and into. The greater maturity of experience which should belong to the adult as educator puts him in a position to evaluate each experience of the young in a way in which the one having the less mature experience cannot do. It is then the business of the educator to see in what direction an experience is heading. There is no point in his being more mature if, instead of using his greater insight to help organize the conditions of the experience of the immature, he throws away his insight. Failure to take the moving force of an experience into account so as to judge and direct it on the ground of what it is moving into means disloyalty to the principle of experience itself.

In a word, we live from birth to death in a world of persons and things which in large measure is what it is because of what has been done and transmitted from previous human activities. When this fact is ignored, experience is treated as if it were something which goes on exclusively inside an individual's body and mind. It ought not to be necessary to say that experience does not occur in a vacuum. There are sources outside an individual which give rise to experience. It is constantly fed from these springs. No one would question that a child in a slum tenement has a different experience from that of a child in a cultured home; that the country lad has a different kind of experience from the city boy, or a boy on the seashore one different from the lad who is brought up on inland prairies. Ordinarily we take such facts for granted as too commonplace to record. But when their educational import is recognized, they indicate the second way in which the educator can direct the experience of the young without engaging in imposition. A primary responsibility of educators is that they not only be aware of the general principle of the shaping of actual experience by environing conditions, but that they also recognize in the concrete what surroundings are conducive to having experiences that lead to growth.

The word "interaction," which has just been used, expresses the second chief principle for interpreting an experience in its educational function and force. It assigns equal rights to both factors in experience—objective and internal conditions. Any normal experience is an interplay of these two sets of conditions. Taken together, or in their interaction, they form what we call a *situation*. The trouble with traditional education was not that it emphasized the external conditions that enter into the control of the experiences but that it paid so little attention to the internal factors which also decide what kind of experience is had. It violated the principle of interaction from one side. But this violation is no reason why the new education should violate the principle from the other side—except upon the basis of the extreme *Either-Or* educational philosophy which has been mentioned.

The illustration drawn from the need for regulation of the objective conditions of a baby's development indicates, first, that the parent has responsibility for arranging the conditions under which an infant's experience of food, sleep, etc., occurs, and, secondly, that the responsibility is fulfilled by utilizing the funded experience of the past, as this is represented, say, by the advice of competent physicians and others who have made a special study of normal physical growth. Does it limit the freedom of the mother when she uses the body of knowledge thus provided to regulate the objective conditions of nourishment and sleep? Or does the enlargement of her intelligence in fulfilling her parental function widen her freedom? Doubtless if a fetish were made of the advice and directions so that they came to be inflexible dictates to be followed under every possible condition, then restriction of freedom of both parent and child would occur. But this restriction would also be a limitation of the intelligence that is exercised in personal judgment.

In what respect does regulation of objective conditions limit the freedom of the baby? Some limitation is certainly placed upon its immediate movements and inclinations when it is put in its crib, at a time when it wants to continue playing, or does not get food at the moment it would like it, or when it isn't picked up and dandled when it cries for attention. Restriction also occurs when mother or nurse snatches a child away from an open fire into which it is about to fall. I shall have more to say later about freedom. Here it is enough to ask whether freedom is to be thought of and adjudged on the basis of relatively momentary incidents or whether its meaning is found in the continuity of developing experience.

The statement that individuals live in a world means, in the concrete, that they live in a series of situations. And when it is said that they live *in* these situations, the meaning of the word "in" is different from its meaning when it is said that pennies are "in" a pocket or paint is "in" a can. It means, once more, that interaction is going on between an individual and objects and other persons. The conceptions of *situation* and of *interaction* are inseparable from each other. An experience is always what it is because of a transaction taking place between an individual and what, at the time, constitutes his environment, whether the latter consists of persons with whom he is talking about some topic or event, the subject talked about being also a part of the situation; or the toys with which he is playing; the book he is reading (in which his environing conditions at the time may be England or ancient Greece or an imaginary region); or the materials of an experiment he is performing, The environment, in other words, is whatever conditions interact with personal needs, desires, purposes, and capacities to create the experience which is had. Even when a person builds a castle in the air he is interacting with the objects which he constructs in fancy.

Social Control

. . . The school was not a group or community held together by participation in common activities. Consequently, the normal, proper conditions of control were lacking. Their absence was made up for, and to a considerable extent had to be made up for, by the direct intervention of the teacher, who, as the saying went, "*kept* order." He kept it because order was in the teacher's keeping, instead of residing in the shared work being done.

The conclusion is that in what are called the new schools, the primary source of social control resides in the very nature of the work done as a social enterprise in which all individuals have an opportunity to contribute and to which all feel a responsibility. Most children are naturally "sociable." Isolation is even more irksome to them than to adults. A genuine community life has its ground in this natural sociability. But community life does not organize itself in an enduring way purely spontaneously. It requires thought and planning ahead. The educator is responsible for a knowledge of individuals and for a knowledge of subject-matter that will enable activities to be selected which lend themselves to social organization, an organization in which all individuals have an opportunity to contribute something, and in which the activities in which all participate are the chief carrier of control.

I am not romantic enough about the young to suppose that every pupil will respond or that any child of normally strong impulses will respond on every occasion. There are likely to be some who, when they come to school, are already victims of injurious conditions outside of the school and who have become so passive and unduly docile that they fail to contribute. There will be others who, because of previous experience, are bumptious and unruly and perhaps downright rebellious. But it is certain that the general principle of social control cannot be predicated upon such cases. It is also true that no general rule can be laid down for dealing with such cases. The teacher has to deal with them individually. They fall into general classes, but no two are exactly alike. The educator has to discover as best he or she can the causes for the recalcitrant attitudes. He or she cannot, if the educational process is to go on, make it a question of pitting one will against another in order to see which is strongest, nor yet allow the unruly and non-participating pupils to stand permanently in the way of the educative activities of others. Exclusion perhaps is the only available measure at a given juncture, but it is no solution. For it may strengthen the very causes which have brought about the undesirable anti-social attitude, such as desire for attention or to show off.

It is absurd to exclude the teacher from membership in the group. As the most mature member of the group he has a peculiar responsibility for the conduct of the interactions and intercommunications which are the very life of the group as a community. That children are individuals whose freedom should be respected while the more mature person should have no freedom as an individual is an idea to absurd to require refutation. The tendency to exclude the teacher from a positive and leading share in the direction of the activities of the community of which he is a member is another instance of reaction from one extreme to another. When pupils were a class rather than a social group, the teacher necessarily acted largely from the outside, not as a director of processes of exchange in which all had a share. When education is based upon experience and educative experience is seen to be a social process, the situation changes radically. The teacher loses the position of external boss or dictator but takes on that of leader of group activities.

The Nature of Freedom

At the risk of repeating what has been often said by me I want to say something about the other side of the problem of social control, namely, the nature of freedom. The only freedom that is of enduring importance is freedom of intelligence, that is to say, freedom of observation and of judgment exercised in behalf of purposes that are intrinsically worth while. The commonest mistake made about freedom is, I think, to identify it with freedom of movement, or with the external or physical side of activity. Now, this external and physical side of activity cannot be separated from the internal side of activity; from freedom of thought, desire, and purpose. The limitation that was put upon outward action by the fixed arrangements of the typical traditional schoolroom, with its fixed rows of desks and its military regimen of pupils who were permitted to move only at certain fixed signals, put a great restriction upon intellectual and moral freedom. Strait-jacket and chain-gang procedures had to be done away with if there was to be a chance for growth of individuals in the intellectual springs of freedom without which there is no assurance of genuine and continued normal growth.

But the fact still remains that an increased measure of freedom of outer movement is a *means,* not an end. The educational problem is not solved when this aspect of freedom is obtained. Everything then depends, so far as education is concerned, upon what is done with this added liberty. What end does it serve? What consequences flow from it? Let me speak first of the advantages which reside potentially in increase of outward freedom. In the first place, without its existence it is practically impossible for a teacher to gain knowledge of the individuals with whom he is concerned. Enforced quiet and acquiescence prevent pupils from disclosing their real natures. They enforce artificial uniformity.

The other important advantage of increased outward freedom is found in the very nature of the learning process. That the older methods set a premium upon passivity and receptivity has been pointed out. Physical quiescence puts a tremendous premium upon these traits. The only escape from them in the standardized school is an activity which is irregular and perhaps disobedient. There cannot be complete quietude in a laboratory or workshop. The non-social character of the traditional school is seen in the fact that it erected silence into one of its prime virtues.

Progressive Organization of Subject-matter

. . . It is a cardinal precept of the newer school of education that the beginning of instruction shall be made with the experience learners already have; that this experience and the capacities that have been developed during its course provide the starting point for all further learning. I am not so sure that the other condition, that of orderly development toward expansion and organization of subject-matter through growth of experience, receives as much attention. Yet the principle of continuity of educative experience requires that equal thought and attention be given to solution of this aspect of the educational problem. Undoubtedly this phase of the problem is more difficult than the other. Those who deal with the pre-school child, with the kindergarten child, and with the boy and girl of the early primary years do not have much difficulty in determining the range of past experience or in finding activities that connect in vital ways with it. With older children both factors of the problem offer increased difficulties to the educator. It is harder to find out the background of the experience of individuals and harder to find out just how the subject-matters already contained in that experience shall be directed so as to lead out to larger and better organized fields.

That up to the present time the weakest point in progressive schools is in the matter of selection and organization of intellectual subject-matter is, I think, inevitable under the circumstances. It is as inevitable as it is right and proper that they should break loose from the cut and dried material which formed the staple of the old education. In addition, the field of experience is very wide and it varies in its contents from place to place and from time to time.

Once more, it is part of the educator's responsibility to see equally to two things: First, that the problem grows out of the conditions of the experience being had in the present, and that it is within the range of the capacity of students; and, secondly, that it is such that it arouses in the learner an active quest for information and for production of new ideas.

EXPERIENCE—THE MEANS AND GOAL OF EDUCATION

For I am so confident of the potentialities of education when it is treated as intelligently directed development of the possibilities inherent in ordinary experience that I do not feel it necessary to criticize here the other route nor to advance arguments in favor of taking the route of experience. The only ground for anticipating failure in taking this path resides to my mind in the danger that experience and the experimental method will not be adequately conceived. There is no discipline in the world so severe as the discipline of experience subjected to the tests of intelligent development and direction. Hence the only ground I can see for even a temporary reaction against the standards, aims, and methods of the newer education is the failure of educators who professedly adopt them to be faithful to them in practice. As I have emphasized more than once, the road of the new education is not an easier one to follow than the old road but a more strenuous and difficult one. It will remain so until it has attained its majority and that attainment will require many years of serious co-operative work on the part of its adherents. The greatest danger that attends its future is, I believe, the idea that it is an easy way to follow, so easy that its course may be improvised, if not in an impromptu fashion, at least almost from day to day or from week to week. It is for this reason that instead of extolling its principles, I have confined myself to showing certain conditions which must be fulfilled if it is to have the successful career which by right belongs to it.

7

A Modern Theory of Learning

WILLIAM HEARD KILPATRICK*

Suggestions from Biology

How WILL A THEORY of learning to fit the personality demands
stated above [Chapter IX, *Philosophy of Education*] differ from the ordinary theory of learning long dominant in Western education? It may be
that further consideration of biology—*building on what was discussed in
Chapter II* [*Philosophy of Education*]—will help to make this contrast
clearer and at the same time furnish reasons for preferring the new to
the old.

The common or conventional theory, hereinafter called "learning
theory A" (or type A for short), has the following characteristics: (i) it
is primarily a theory for learning from books; (ii) it thus consists typically
of learning the words or statements of others; (iii) it expects the learning
to come in a situation abstracted from life and so (typically) to center
around a content of little or no present meaning to the learner; (iv) it
expects the learning to be got mainly, if not solely, by repetition; and
(v) it counts that the learning will be applied generally, if not always,
in an experience different from that in which the learning takes place,
usually appreciably later.

By contrast the theory here proposed, called herein "learning theory

* William H. Kilpatrick, *Philosophy of Education*. New York: The Macmillan
Company, 1951, pp. 237–247. Copyright 1951 by The Macmillan Company. Used
by permission.

B" (type B), shows the following characteristics: it holds (i) that behaving is typically an essential part of the learning process; (ii) that the learning goes forward best, if not solely, in a situation of concrete personal living; (iii) that the learning comes from behaving, not from mere repetition of words, as with type A; (iv) that the first application of the learning comes, normally, within the experience in which the learning takes place, in fact that the learning comes typically in order to carry on this experience. As a corollary it is here maintained that the best learning under type A really came chiefly when it operated *not* as A—learning in an abstracted situation, to be applied later in life—but when it operated as B (iv), that is, when the content was in fact used to carry on some experience. Study of the biological evolution of man may help us to contrast and evaluate these two learning theories.

It is a recognized principle of evolution that "acquired characters," learned instances of behavior, are not transmitted by birth from parent to child. Evolution does not proceed that way. The theory of evolution does, however, hold that the more useful any organic functioning is for survival, the more surely will a variation in the direction of its better functioning win out in the struggle for existence and so more surely will it be transmitted. For example, ability to learn is highly important to survival; thus increased ability to learn means greater chance of survival and so greater chance of being transmitted.

Two illustrations may thus help at this point. Note how they both illustrate the B type of learning.

Consider first an instance of animal activity prolonged enough and complex enough for an early stage of the activity or experience to enter through the process of learning as a significant factor in a later stage of that same activity or experience. Let us say that a tiger threatens a deer, but at a distance sufficiently great for the deer's superior running ability to get her safely away. Will the deer actually get away? Yes, if she starts in time and runs thereafter for a sufficient length of time. But she will run long enough only if the original impulse (or that reinforced by the tiger's further threats) remains in action sufficiently long after the tiger has been left behind to get the deer fully out of danger. Now the fact that the original impulse to run remains with the deer after the tiger is out of sight gives us, fairly considered, a case of learning; for it is a responding after the original stimulus has ceased to act as an external fact.

A second illustration from human experience will perhaps make the fact of learning more obvious. I wish to talk with a man over the phone. I give the switchboard girl the man's number, and she calls him. Here an interval—short, to be sure—follows between the time the girl hears the number and her use of the number. (Whether the girl first called the number and then wrote it on her report slip or whether she first wrote it and then called the man matters not; in either case, a short but real interval intervened.) That she acted after she heard shows that she learned (remembered) what she heard and then acted on memory (learning). (And the better type of operator keeps in mind the whole incident of the call sufficiently to make sure the call does go through.)

Four questions now confront us: (i) Just exactly what do we mean by learning? (ii) Is Type B really an instance of learning? (iii) Is type B so important biologically that evolution would seize upon it, as asserted above, to fix it, as truly as type A, in the species? (iv) Is not type B really the main source of learning used in mature life? Let us take these in order.

1. Just what do we mean by learning? The definition here chosen is this: Learning is the tendency of any part or phase of what one has lived so to remain with the learner as to come back pertinently into further experience. When such a tendency has been set up, learning has to that extent been effected. To accept anything less of a definition of learning than to expect it to tend so to remain and come back relevantly into experience seems indefensible. If "learning" does not do this, why should it be called learning?

But this definition, the result of many years of study by the author of the problem of learning, is, like every other statement, justified only if it fits the observed facts. How well it does so fit the facts will, it is hoped, become clearer as the discussion continues. In addition, it should be noted, this definition will, as is obvious, fit equally both theory A and theory B.

Various other questions about this definition call for consideration. Just when anything has been *lived* is one such question. But all such points we now postpone to later discussions.

2. Is type B—learning in order to carry on the present experience— really an instance of learning as just defined? The answer is yes. The deer lived the threat of the tiger so vividly that it stayed with her after the tiger had dropped out of sight; she accordingly kept on running until a safe distance had intervened. The girl lived the telephone number when she heard it, she took it in both as a bare number and in its life setting, that is, in the setting of her work; and having thus lived its coming, it stayed with her until she used it. The question of degree of learning enters here. The girl next day probably could not recall the number without looking it up. But even so, it had not entirely gone, for when I called again, she *recognized* it as the same number I had previously used.

We can go on to say that in any complex experience, the earlier stages will ordinarily so stay on with one as to enter pertinently into the later stages, thus giving a connecting unity between earlier and later stages and thereby making the successive happenings into one continuous experience. The point for us here is that the earlier stages actually pervade the later stages and that this fact is essential to the character of the later stages. Without this pervasive effect of learning, the successive happenings would be only physically determined and so would be essentially different from what the pervasive learning makes them. Here is sixteen-year-old Sally talking over the phone with her best friend Mary. Sally learned at the opening of the conversation that it was Mary at the other end; and this consciousness enters into the whole content of the conversation to give it a Sally-Mary character essentially different from a Sally-John conversation and even more markedly different from a Sally-Father conversation.

We conclude, then, that type B certainly is true learning, and that its presence in experience is essential to the very existence of human experience as such.

3. Is type B learning so important biologically that evolution would seize upon it to fix it as an abiding feature in the life of the species? The answer is yes. The importance seen just above would suffice to bring about this effect. Even in subhuman organisms the unity of a life episode is fixed by and in the type B of learning, working, of course, at the same time alongside other kinds of learning from previous experiences. It seems probable that at least some of the deer's fear of the tiger is the result of such previous learning. What happens *now* in *this* activity to give unity to *this* episode or *this* experience is, however, largely the fact of its own B type learnings.

4. Is not type B the principal source of the learning used by the typical adult in life? It is clear that in each life experience this adult learns some things directly in and through this very experience as he works at it to make it go. This learning is of course type B. But the adult in this experience also uses many kinds of learning that have come to him in the past. It is this past learning that we wish to study further. How were these past items learned? Were they learned by the type A process as outlined in the original definition of type A? Or were most of them learned by the type B process? To answer this question consider four possible sources of the past learnings used in this experience: (i) those learned before the adult left school or college, but learned entirely outside of school or college; (ii) those learned in school or college; (iii) those learned since leaving school or college, but learned in and through life; (iv) those learned since leaving school or college, but learned by type A school learning procedures. It is clear that the learning under (i) and

(iii) is type B learning and that the learning under (ii) and (iv) is type A learning. Which pair gives the greater aggregate? Is it not highly probable that the ordinary nonscholarly adult's learning of (iv) kind are very, very few in number, and also that a large proportion of the original (ii) kind have been forgotten? And is it not probable that for any typical adult, (i) and (iii) are largest in number? Is not the answer that type B is the principal source of learning used by the typical adult?

To return now to the bearing of biology on the question of learning, it is generally believed that man has not developed biologically in any significant manner or degree since he became *Homo sapiens;* culturally, yes —greatly so; biologically as regards mind, no, not so far as we can tell. If this be accepted, then man's present capacity to learn was developed during the long period which ended with the coming of *Homo sapiens.* As we contrast theory A with theory B, it becomes clear that B stands closer to man as a behaving organism, and that A came into existence only after *Homo sapiens* had invented writing. As between the two, then, theory B is the only one that certainly appears in the biological evolution of man. Man thus naturally behaves according to B; A belongs solely to cultural development.

This ends our consideration of suggestions from biological evolution of behavior. Its principal suggestion has been to show what the B type of learning is, how it evolved, and somewhat of how it works—works within the experience in which it originates and thereafter as may be needed. Put with this now the discussion of Chapter II [*Philosophy of Education*], where we see what we here call type B learning at work in more detail in any instance of actual experience. The two together constitute the framework for the consideration of education throughout this book.

In the discussion of question (ii) above it was brought out that the earlier stages of any experience *pervade* the subsequent parts of that experience. That is the result seen here. This conception of B type learning, learning to carry on and improve living, will pervade practically all the remaining discussions of this book [*Philosophy of Education*]. It will prove the key element to unlock many of the problems to be considered later.

Additional Conceptions Strategic in Learning

Though the conception of B type learning just discussed furnishes the basic frame of reference for the rest of the book, certain additional and supplementary conceptions should be considered.

1. *The Transitive Verb "to Live" and the Place of Acceptance Therein.* In the definition of learning given above, the verb *to live* played an essential part, implying, if not asserting, that for one to *learn* anything, he must first *live* that thing. This transitive use of the verb to live is so unfamiliar that a word of explanation may be helpful. To *live* anything, as *to live* a feeling or a thought or a bodily movement, belongs grammatically in the same class with singing a song, dancing a waltz, or fighting a battle. In each such case the object of the verb does nothing more than repeat, perhaps more explicitly, the actual content of the verb.

Specifically, what does it mean to say that if I wish my pupil to learn anything, such as a thought or a feeling or a movement, the pupil has to *live* that thought or that feeling or that movement? Suppose as principal of a high school in a fair-sized village, I set as one of my aims or goals that my pupils shall, if I can effect it, learn (acquire, build, develop, each in himself) a spirit of public service to the village. There are really two questions here: (i) What does it mean in such a case to *learn* a thought or a feeling or a movement? (ii) What does it mean to *live* that thought or feeling or movement?

Taking the first question, we can at once name some things which the verb *learn* does *not* mean in this case. It does not mean that any pupil who can get an A on a written examination on the subject has therein learned (achieved) the desired spirit of service. A written examination might disclose *knowledge* (so far as words prove knowledge) *about* such a spirit, but a pupil might have full knowledge *about* the spirit and not have (or feel) the spirit itself. Learning a spirit certainly means more than learning knowledge *about* it. Nor could ability and willingness to say a pledge of allegiance to such a spirit tell us that the pupil had got (learned) the spirit. No, a pupil has not *learned* this desired spirit until he has so got the spirit in him that he will of himself, as opportunity may open, really work for the public good of the community. Learning means, in this case, to build (acquire, develop) the habit, the attitude and the interest of so working; it means so to build this habit and attitude that others can rely on him, when occasion demands, to work this way both outwardly and inwardly. This is what learning means in such a case.

The second question is now more easily answered: What does it mean to *live* such a spirit so as to learn it? The answer is more easily given in words than realized in fact. If my pupils are to live this spirit, they must have the opportunity to respond, and must in fact so respond, with that spirit to some life situations. This means, in practice, the opportunity to embark on some challenging efforts in behalf of, say, some village needs; but, as already implied, opportunity alone does not suffice.

And here comes in *acceptance*, the second essential. As the pupils of a class thus work in behalf of a specific village need, some will enter more wholeheartedly than others into the physical effort and into the wish to help; others will be lukewarm; and a few will perhaps inwardly rebel. These represent different degrees of acceptance, some full acceptance, some but slight, a few negative. And each actual experience of each individual student carries its degree of acceptance; it is an inevitable part of actual life. Acceptance in some degree, positive or negative, is always present in the living then going on; each person, whatever the enterprise, feels his degree of acceptance of that thing at that time under those conditions. *Degree of acceptance of any part of an experience means degree of living that part of the experience.*

We are now ready to state the B type law of learning: *We learn what we live, we learn each item we live as we accept it, and we learn it in the degree we accept it.*

Those pupils who were inwardly rejecting what the class was working at were learning negatively, learning *not to do* that thing. Those who in their hearts accepted it positively were learning *to do* that thing, they were building the positive spirit, and they built it in the degree they accepted it.

It may be well for certain future purposes to restate this law of learning also as follows:

We learn our responses, only our responses, and all our responses; we learn each as we accept it to live by, and we learn it in the degree we accept it.

How this statement of the principle follows from the other statement is easy to see. Life, we may say, consists of (i) happenings, occurrences that affect us, and (ii) our responses thereto in terms of doing, thinking, feeling, or the like. But consider these happenings further. Do I respond to the happening as it actually and objectively took place—"as God sees it," so to say? Or do I respond to it as I understand it, as I take it to be? The more we think about it, the clearer it becomes that I respond to the happening as I see and feel it; I respond to the character which I ascribe to the happening. We may then distinguish three things: (i) the happening, objectively considered; (ii) the happening as I accept it; and (iii) my response to the happening as I understand and accept it. That I may mistake the happening is quite possible; but if so, the clearer does it become that I respond not to the objective happening, but to my mistaken sizing up of it.

What I live, then, is not (i) but (ii), my (possibly) mistaken sizing up, and (iii) my response thereto. But (ii) is my response (mistaken though it may be) to (i), the actual objective happening. As my response, it gives my version of (i). The only part of (i), the true happening, that gets into my life is (ii) which is my understanding of (i). So always do I live exactly (ii) and (iii), each of which is a response of mine. So I live my responses. But we learn what we live, so we learn our responses, each as we accept it.

2. *Degrees of Learning.*   That we learn some things better than others everybody knows. Some things drop out almost as soon as they are over; others we can neither forget nor ignore even if we try. We can then say that one thing has been *better* or *more strongly* learned than another, if it *stays longer* with one to come back into further experience and/or if it has a *stronger tendency* thus to come back into experience.

What is it that makes one thing better learned than another? A full discussion would be long and complex. For our purposes it suffices to name three principal factors. That we learn what we live gives us a starting point; the following gives an illustration: We read in the paper many items of news. Do we remember all and take each equally into account in life from then on? No. Some we size up as unimportant to us and so think no more about them; some we learn strongly, could never forget— as that a dear friend has died or that an opportunity we have long wished for is now open; some we learn weakly, perhaps never to recall them ourselves but still to recognize them if someone refers to them; some we never afterward recall.

(1) We learn any particular item in the degree that we live it, in the degree we count it important to us, in the degree we accept it in our hearts for use in life.

To see the basis of the next principle, try to memorize the following three sets of five syllables each, and see which you have learned best: (i) niz, taf, hig, div, vag; (ii) dog, sin, her, all, big; (iii) the big dog bit her. The three sets are equally long, but differ greatly as to meaning. Hence the second factor in learning:

(2) Other things being equal, we learn any particular item in the degree that it has meaning to us, has meaning in terms of what we already know.

Again, we all know from personal experience that names, faces, numbers, and other items of experience once learned tend to drop out of recall unless they are kept alive, so to say, by use. We may then add a third principle:

(3) Other things being equal, items of experience are recallable in the degree of the frequency and recency of their use.

3. *Cumulative Learning.*   Some things we learn in full strength all at once. When I got a telegram telling me that my long-time friend had passed away, I did not need repeated messages on successive days to

strengthen the learning; the first one sufficed. But my regard for my friend had not come to me thus all at once. It was growing all the years I had known him. Each experience we lived through together contributed its added increment of insight into his character and to my regard for his worth. My feeling for him stands forth as a clear instance of cumulative learning. So likewise is it with our standards, our ideas, our principles of action, as we have previously seen. Each is an instance of cumulative learning.

4. *Simultaneous or Concomitant Learning.*   In any significant experience the human organism acts as an organized whole; thought and feeling, internal glandular secretion, heart and nerve—all act together. Each experience is thus a complex of many interacting parts and aspects. Any similar experience will repeat in some measure certain of the same thoughts or feelings or movements. Suppose now a series of related experiences, such as my successive experiences with my friend just discussed; the related *thoughts* of the successive experiences I had with him, and so of him, were accumulated and organized into my insight into his character. Similarly the *related* feelings of the successive experiences were accumulated and organized into my *attitude* of regard for him.

In this way every school child, in addition to the arithmetic or history or geography which the old type of school sets him to learn, is thinking and feeling and concluding about the teacher, about school, about himself, about the subject. And these successive thoughts about the teacher are being collected to build the cumulative learning we call the child's conception of the teacher, what the child would expect of the teacher, under this, that, or the other condition. Similarly is the child building his attitude toward school as a place to like, or to dislike and leave as soon as possible; toward school work as interesting or the reverse; toward each subject studied and each kind of work taken up; toward each child in the room. In particular is each child building his conception and attitude with reference to himself in relation to the other persons and things about him, a feeling of security in school life or of insecurity, of confidence in himself or, on the contrary, an inferiority complex. A certain child whose eyesight was defective but didn't know it lost confidence in himself and in the people about him when he couldn't see what they said they saw.

Such cumulative learnings are always in process, many going on simultaneously all the active living time of each normal person. As curious as it may seem to us now, the teacher of the past was in effect ignorant of this cumulative simultaneous or concomitant learning. The modern-minded teacher is well aware that out of these cumulative learnings—conceptions, attitudes, ideals, standards, habits, skills, and the like—is the child's character all the time being formed. Even William James seems not to have considered these concomitant learnings, but if we include in the quotation given below the words added in brackets, we have an excellent statement of the accumulated result of all one's learnings:

> We are spinning our own fates, good or evil, and never to be undone. Every smallest stroke of virtue or vice [every accompanying thought or feeling] leaves its never-so-little scar. The drunken Rip Van Winkle, in Jefferson's play, excuses himself for every fresh dereliction by saying, "I won't count this time!" Well, he may not count it, and a kind Heaven may not count it; but it is being counted none the less. Down among his nerve-cells and fibers the molecules are counting it, registering and storing it up to be used against him when the next temptation comes. Nothing we ever do is, in strict scientific literalness, wiped out (88:77f.).[1]

A close and significant relationship exists between the social and moral demands mentioned at the beginning of this chapter and the conceptions of learning just discussed—that we learn what we live, what we accept, the fact of simultaneous or concomitant learnings, and the cumulative nature of learning. This relationship will appear increasingly important in the remainder of this book.

William Heard Kilpatrick (November 20, 1871–February 13, 1965) received his A.B. degree from Mercer University in 1891. He taught mathematics in the public schools of Georgia, and was acting president at Mercer before going in 1909 to Teachers College, Columbia University, as lecturer in Education. He continued teaching at Teachers College, where he received his Ph.D. degree in 1912 and advanced to the rank of full professor in 1918.

*Kilpatrick was a leading exponent and interpreter of Dewey's philosophy of education, and is reported to have said that he could find little in Dewey's philosophy with which to disagree. In spite of this claim, his educational theory was closer to Rousseau than to Dewey. It is for this reason that Kilpatrick is sometimes referred to as a romantic progressive. His writing has been prolific. His books, chapters for the yearbooks of learned societies, published lectures, newspaper and magazine articles, book reviews, and pamphlets won him considerable esteem among ad-*ministrators and public school teachers. Education for a Changing World, How We Learn, Our Educational Task, Education and Social Crisis, The

---

[1] *Talks to Teachers.* Copyright 1899 by Henry Holt and Company, Inc., New York, and used by their permission.

Education Frontier, Remaking the Curriculum, The Teacher and Society, and Group Education for a Democracy *are included in his list of publications.*

Two of Kilpatrick's best-known volumes are The Foundations of Method, *dealing with what he calls the broader meaning of method, and* Philosophy of Education, *in which he describes the conditions necessary to the "good life" and the "good society." The second half of* Philosophy of Education, *a portion of which is included here, indicates the kind of education that he believed was required for the achievement of the "good life" and the "good society."*

8

The Present Status of Pragmatism in Education*

FOSTER McMURRAY

As in the earlier part of this century, pragmatism continues to provide intellectual foundations for educational theory. No other philosophic system has been able to challenge and overthrow it as a nexus of ideas for educational reform. Nevertheless, those ideas and points of emphasis which might be regarded as new within the past decade or two are not pragmatic in origin. They are, in fact, antipragmatic and have been grafted upon the original and still undisturbed pragmatic foundation without awareness of a resulting incongruity.

The incongruity results from efforts to serve a variety of interests that pragmatism cannot honor. These unsatisfied interests include: a concern to clarify relations between human reason or intellect and the more practical cares of daily existence; a desire to avoid scientism and to recognize needs and forces in man's emotional career which scientific method cannot incorporate; and, finally, a desire for a crusade, and a doctrine to support it, in behalf of social unity.

One of the most common complaints against pragmatism is that, by an overemphasis upon the practical worth of ideas, pragmatists tend to denigrate pure reason and pure theory, these being found valuable only in application and not in their own right. Humanists and scholars devoted to the past and to learning for the sake of learning alone are the largest group responsible not only for this criticism, but also for persistent attacks upon the distinctively modern in education. From within their own perspective they are partly right. It is true that pragmatists value ideas only

* Foster McMurray, "The Present Status of Pragmatism in Education," *School and Society*, Vol. 87, No. 2145, January 17, 1959, pp. 14–17.

for what can be accomplished in putting them to work. That is what the word "practical" means as a specially defined term in the vocabulary of pragmatism. But it is a technical meaning, wrongly understood if interpreted as the more usual word of common parlance. A mistake common among humanists is to suppose that pragmatists, like self-made men, would oppose theory to practice and pure science to applied science, finding less value in one than in the other. This mistake is further aggravated by supposing that pragmatism supports anti-intellectualism. Oddly, the truth about pragmatism on such matters is better understood by specialists in education than by academic scholars. Educationalists are inclined to find in pragmatically inspired educational doctrine too much of pure intellectualism and not enough of practicality.

Those who place a highest educational value upon immediately useful knowledge have good reason to feel that pragmatism does not support their practical utilitarianism. According to John Dewey's theory, a good school program is one which leads pupils from an early interest in solving problems of an immediately localized and concrete sort to a more mature interest in solving problems which arise through intellectual curiosity and a desire for abstract knowledge. Clearly, the intent of Dewey's theory was to stimulate more and better learning of arts, sciences, and technologies. There was in this program no concern for immediately practical or directly utilitarian bits of information and technique, nor any process of choosing and organizing information around characteristic activities of daily life. On the contrary, in Dewey's version of pragmatism characteristic activities of daily life were psychologically useful starting points for moving the learner to consideration of meanings increasingly remote, abstract, and related to one another in impersonal systems rather than to practical daily use.

Taking Dewey's theory as representative of pragmatism, then, the emphasis of recent years upon "real life" problems typical of life-adjustment education is not, as might be supposed, a further extension of that emphasis upon learning by problem-solving which pragmatists had originated. It is, in fact, a departure from the methodology of problem-solving and a return to older methods of teaching which pragmatists had decried. In a life-adjustment curriculum, problems common to various stages in human development are preselected and organized into successive units rather than discovered by pupils in the course of their classroom activities. They are problems in which the direction of the learner's growth is toward practical application rather than toward an increased sophistication in the abstractions of a scientific culture. Hence, recent trends toward "common learnings" are a reaction against what some educators find to be an impractical intellectualism.

From a pragmatic viewpoint the simple practicality of life-adjustment education must seem dangerously naive. The intent of the practical-minded educator is to teach pupils precisely what they will need to know in situations characteristic of life outside of school. What is questionable in this worthy aim is the availability of knowledge in simple forms suitably adapted to practical application.

What are called "real life" problems are those which have their most important consequences in the domains of society and human personality. In trying to solve them, anyone who uses intelligence must make many judgments of fact about subject matters which are now being studied within the various social sciences and psychology. But the state of these sciences is such that we know very little with proven assurance. This does not mean that the social sciences are useless. Given a serious problem, it would be foolish to ignore their potential resources. But such resources as we have are largely unproven theories and hypotheses. The question is, How useful are the theories of present-day social science in helping to solve practical problems in personal and social life? Even if we overlook the fact that many of these theories are in conflict with one another, we cannot avoid at least one conclusion: at this stage in history, efforts to solve "real life" problems by actions undertaken deliberately, on the basis of predictions that can be justified as better than blind guesses, must be undertaken with caution, with sensitivity to dangers stemming from ignorance and with a constant readiness to change, adapt, and modify in the face of uncertain or novel outcomes. This is a fact for which pragmatic education is especially suited. It is an education which emphasizes attitudes of experimentalism and which teaches pupils to maintain a quality of corrigibility in ideas constructed for guidance of behavior.

An attitude of tentativeness and corrigibility toward ideas, formerly a center of educational values for pragmatists, has diminished almost to a vanishing point not only for life-adjustment educators, but also for a group who regard themselves as legitimate heirs of pragmatic doctrine. This is the group who call themselves "social reconstructionists." They find pragmatism itself in need of reconstruction, especially because of this emphasis upon scientific caution. It is not so much the Deweyan concept of experimental intelligence which troubles the social reconstructionists—a concept they continue to accept; it is more a matter of finding incompatibility between scientific experimentalism and the urgency of need for social reform. Believing that social tensions have reached a peak of crisis, and believing that catastrophe can be averted only by quick unification, social reconstructionists feel that the pragmatic reliance upon nothing except experimental intelligence is not only much too slow and cautious, but also deficient on at least two counts. Pragmatism is deficient, they say, in supposing that knowledge and the intellect alone can release concerted human action. And it is also inadequate in supposing that judgments of value are a form of knowledge, subject to intellectual hypothesizing and to testing in experience. Finding such deficiencies in pragmatic theory, social reconstructionists have turned to other sources for ideas better suited to their purposes.

No end of alternatives to pragmatism is available. A long line of social theorists, from Marx to Mannheim and Toynbee, provides diagnoses of social crisis and prescriptions for reconstruction. They support the social reconstructionists' feeling that time is running short, demanding from us not only a sense of urgency, but also a nonrational commitment to a more glorious future. To support this commitment, reconstructionists have adopted several typical instruments: beliefs in a class struggle, in deliberately constructed and disseminated myths, in social realism, and above all, in a civic religion. In these respects social reconstructionists share with conservatives and reactionaries one of the most common of all complaints against pragmatism—the complaint, namely, that pragmatism fails to provide for man's spiritual needs or for his emotional longing for a sense of allegiance to a force "bigger than himself." In another respect, however, social reconstructionists may be different from other kinds of religionists. Their concern with spiritual fervor seems to have been stimulated less by a concern for the spiritual as such and more by a conviction that religious-type feelings are a necessary instrumentality to a purely secular goal—in this case, zealous social action and unity of belief and value. To further assure this aim, they propose to use group dynamics as a technique for the deliberate "engineering" of social consensus.

Given a sense of crisis and of need for emotional commitment to rebuilding society, it is not surprising that social reconstructionists find pragmatism wanting. It is true that pragmatism cannot satisfy such needs, and, judging by the popularity of life adjustment and social reconstructionism, it might seem that a hunger for nonrational and noncognitive supports is a widespread feature of our present educational world. At the very least, there seems to be strongly evident a desire among educators for a new stability in manners, mores, and morality, and for a larger core of shared expectations and shared satisfactions with the various roles each person plays. In the kind of pragmatism best known to educators, there would seem to be little or no sympathy for those who seek stability and emotional satisfaction.

What is surprising in these developments is that the experimentalist theory of intelligence is not re-examined. Having accepted it, and having found intelligence of that kind not appropriate to their purposes, social reconstructionists then conclude that, for prompt social action, we must rely upon something other than intelligence. Some of them have gone so far as to sanction a pragmatic theory of knowing and at the same time to reject a pragmatic theory of value in favor of its principal opposite. By thus subscribing to an emotivist theory of value, social reconstructionists are free to separate goals of social action, and their supporting emotional forces, from that which is supported by reason and evidence. This makes it easier to vindicate education by indoctrination, myth-making, and "civic" religion. To a self-consistent pragmatist this splitting of allegiance is logically absurd. The pragmatic theories of knowing and of valuing imply one another and are inseparable.

The struggles of contemporary educators to adapt their pragmatic inheritance to alien values and incompatible ideas may be explained in at least two ways. On the one hand, it may be said that life adjusters and social reconstructionists are not temperamentally suited to the hardheaded quality of pragmatism. They are the tender hearted, seeking warmth and the stability which accompany brotherhood in a cause or in like-mindedness. On the other hand, it may be said that pragmatism is partly at fault. The possibility here is that the charge of scientism, often directed at pragmatists, is partly true—true not in the sense intended by nonpragmatists, perhaps, but in a different respect.

What causes people like the social reconstructionists to supplement their pragmatic base is a feeling that, if intelligence requires experimentalism rather than conviction, scientific detachment instead of loyalty, or open-mindedness instead of like-mindedness, then the antithesis of intelligence must be preserved in some way other than by the use of reason and the appeal to experienced evidence. This reflects a despair that intellectual responsibility can serve values with greater reliability than instruments of a more primitive kind. But the fact is that deliberate thoughtfulness, the use of evidence, and the search for tests in experience are the only methods for guiding social action that is compatible with democracy. When a group holds its ideals for social action apart from critical examination, relying instead upon indoctrinated emotional loyalties, then democracy is endangered. There are social reconstructionists who might admit this. Their difficulty lies in being unable to bring together a variety of values under one embracing theory. As they see it, intelligence is to be valued, but so also are other ends which the Deweyan kind of intelligence would depress. Perhaps a better way out of this impasse is to redefine intelligence so that it does not seem antithetical to feelings of conviction and loyalty.

There is a kind of pragmatism different from the Dewey experimentalist sort, which does not equate the method of intelligence with the methods of experimental science, nor with tentativeness and emotional detachment. This is the kind of pragmatism originally conceived by C. S. Peirce, founder of the school. One of its characteristics is to analyze intelligence as that which guides action, not primarily the action of experimental scientists, but any action which may be perceived as the deliberate behavior of a human being. Within this alternative kind of pragmatic approach, a goal of philosophic analysis is to discover under what circumstances the quality of belief or conviction is justified (as contrasted with verified) and to find criteria for decision-making even when sound knowledge is not available. This places no premium on a preferred attitude but asks instead about the contribution of intelligence to all legitimate strivings, including as potentially intelligent any kind of behavior marked by deliberate intent. Inquiry in these directions gives no support to a social reconstructionist's feeling that, for action in a social crisis, we must go beyond the limited uses of intelligence. Unfortunately, this alternative form of pragmatism has not influenced educational theorists.

A hope that heirs of Dewey's educational theory may continue to refine or to correct their position is not entirely forlorn. In his recent book, "American Pragmatism and Education," John Childs takes issue with a characteristic tenet. In agreement with Dewey, experimentalists have maintained that the method of scientific research, by which new materials are added to knowledge in the public domain, is also the best method for communication of that knowledge to schoolroom learners. It is claimed, in short, that the logic of discovery is the same as the logic of communication. Dr. Childs, on the contrary, doubts that ". . . the problem of the communication and the acquisition of meaning can be equated with the problem of the discovery of meaning in the sense in which the achievement of knowledge through research is ordinarily interpreted." Although he does not push his doubts into the proposal of an alternative, Dr. Childs is sensitive to one of the more serious theoretical inadequacies in the kind of pragmatism that has dominated educational theory.

The problem of communication as related to discovery is one which may be resolved in a different way even within the limits of pragmatism. Between those who support the experimentalist position and those others within pragmatism who would not, there is an underlying issue, more fundamental for pure theory. It concerns the mind and its ideas. Dewey and the experimentalists have maintained that ideas are intermediate between the occurrence of a troublesome situation and its resolution. This suggests that the mind is called into play by an environmental stimulus and then, having served its instrumental role, it ceases to qualify behavior until the next problem has appeared somehow within the existential environment. The alternative to this, which is at least as pragmatic as instrumentalism, is to maintain that mind and its ideas qualify behavior in greater or less degree constantly rather than intermittently. From this it follows that ideas have a part to play in constructing the environment and in discerning what is problematic within it. From this follows a further idea about the logic of communication.

In their creative role, scientists use concepts and constructs as instruments of research. When communicating their findings, however, they use these same concepts in a different way. They use them to narrate and describe some aspect of the world as found. As instruments of narration and description, concepts function for learners in a way different than for researchers. Through the ideas they evoke, concepts function either by pointing to what had been overlooked in the perceived environment, or else, by literary means, they lead a learner to reconstruct in different detail or in greater scope his projection of a surrounding reality. The effect of having comprehended a communication is to modify the intellectual instruments by which reality is interpreted and, hence, to modify sensitivity to environmental stimuli. This is a process which Dewey's instrumentalism had neglected and which may become an area of inquiry for younger pragmatists in the future.

Foster McMurray (August 10, 1914—) grew up in Pennsylvania, and earned his bachelor's degree from Millersville State College in 1938. He was awarded both the M.A. (1940) and the Ph.D. (1952) at Teachers College, Columbia University.

Dr. McMurray's first full-time teaching assignment was at the University of Texas, where he was an instructor for two years (1947–1949). In 1949 he went to the University of Illinois, where he now holds the rank of associate professor. During recent summers he has been a visiting professor at the University of California at Berkeley and the University of Southern California.

At present Professor McMurray is at work on a statement of a pragmatic educational philosophy appropriate to our times. "Intimations of such a modified pragmatic theory" are to be found among his writings in Lee J. Cronbach (ed.) Test Materials in Modern Education (the Fifty-seventh Yearbook of the National Society for the Study of Education, Part I, Basic Concepts in Music Education), and in his article, "The Present Status of Progmatism in Education."

9

Toward a Reconstructed
Philosophy of Education*

THEODORE BRAMELD

Some Characteristics of Reconstructionism

THE FIRST GENERAL CHARACTERISTIC has been treated in the preceding lectures, but I must note it once more. I do not hesitate to call reconstructionism a "crisis philosophy." It is a crisis philosophy in terms not only of education but of culture. For, if we remember that education is part and parcel of culture—indeed, a creation of culture—it follows that a crisis philosophy of education must presuppose a crisis philosophy of culture. Let us recall some of the things said earlier about the nature of the crisis of our time. For example, we are living in an age that is capable, on the one hand, of destroying mankind overnight, and on the other hand, of producing a higher level of civilization on a world scale than man has ever known. We are truly at a crossroad. But many of us are not at all sure which of the two forks we are going to follow—the one toward destruction or the one toward reconstruction.

The reconstructionist is, of course, very clear as to which road mankind *should* take, but he is not at all clear as to which road it *will* take. He has no assurance whatsoever that we are wise enough to choose the road toward reconstruction rather than that toward destruction. But he is convinced that the choice is clear, and that the least education can do is to devote its utmost energy, its utmost responsibility, to making certain that the peoples of the world choose the road of reconstruction.

* Theodore Brameld, *Education as Power.* New York: Holt, Rinehart and Winston, Inc., 1965, pp. 32–40. Quoted by permission of the author and publisher.

Another general feature of this philosophy follows closely and may deepen the previous contention made about the nature of crisis itself. Let us reemphasize the important part that values play in the analysis and interpretation of crisis. For the truth is, of course, that every crisis centers in a dislocation of the value patterns by which all cultures are guided. In such a time many members of the culture simply do not know what to believe as to what is good, as to what is desirable, as to what is purposeful. So many conflicting choices confront them that often they are not sure which choice to make. The reconstructionist contends, therefore, that much of mankind suffers today not only from institutional disequilibrium but from moral confusion and uncertainty. But he maintains also that there are fresh and powerful values to be discovered and to become committed to. The search for and delineation of these values is one of the highest priorities of education.

Reconstructionism is above all, then, a philosophy of values, a philosophy of ends, a philosophy of purposes. It believes that you and I, as teachers and citizens, have the obligation to analyze critically what is wrong with the values that we have been holding and then to decide about the values that we should be holding. The remainder of these lectures will discuss at considerable length the question of the values, the purposes, the moral commitments for which men everywhere should be searching if we are to resolve the dangerous confusions and conflicts which plague us and threaten us with destruction.

One further general characteristic is that reconstructionism, no less than any philosophy worthy of the name, is by no means wholly new. If we define philosophy as the attempt of any culture to give meaning to itself, and so to its ethos, then reconstructionism must in many ways be built upon the rich thinking and experience of other philosophies of life and education. Reconstructionism borrows much from other philosophies, and makes no pretense to the contrary.

From essentialism, for example, it borrows the principle that all education is inevitably transmissive. One of the fundamental tasks of teaching-learning is certainly that of maintaining the continuity of cultural experience.

From progressivism, the reconstructionist borrows particularly the key principle that processes of cultural change are possible through intelligent action. I know of no man in the history of philosophy who has done as much to help us understand the meaning of intelligent action as the greatest philosopher of education in the history of America, John Dewey. In his view, intelligent action should be integral with the processes of education, and both of these in turn should become inseparable from the processes of cultural change.

From the perennialist, I would choose as an important example of influence his insistence that life must be purposeful, that life must have clear goals. To be sure, the perennialist's goals are usually dissimilar to those of the reconstructionist. But the common recognition that the good life must be goal centered and purposeful is one which brings both philosophies together and causes both of them to pay tribute to the influence of such geniuses as Plato and Aristotle.

Some Requirements of Reconstructionism

So much for some general characteristics of reconstructionism. Let us now try to be more specific. First of all, since the reconstructionist, being a crisis philosopher, places heavy stress upon clear, unequivocal goals and purposes, the primary task of education is that of formulating, implementing, and validating such purposes. This contention is tied up with what was said above about the importance of values, for all purposes are saturated with values.

The reconstructionist, accordingly, is searching for what we earlier called, in common with some American social scientists, a value orientation. Is it possible to develop a value orientation that is sufficiently defensible and unified to give us the purposes we now need—one that can galvanize and channel our activities?

Where are such purposes to be found? They will not, I think, be found merely through philosophic analysis. They will be found, if at all, through understanding the abnormal nature of our time, and through recognition of what is required by such a time.

Now there is one requirement today which overshadows all others—a requirement which I noted in my opening chapter and to which I shall return in my closing one. This is a world civilization so powerful, so unified, and so committed to the values we shall presently describe that it can successfully combat and destroy the forces which could lead to the destruction of mankind. World civilization is the great magnetic purpose which education requires today. What does this purpose mean?

Vast problems at once arise when one seriously considers such an encompassing purpose. Certainly it becomes a primary task of education to attack the gigantic difficulties in the way of achieving world civilization. For, as these difficulties are analyzed, the meaning of world civilization itself becomes more and more clear.

Despite the hazards of generalizing about reconstructionism, one thing can be said now that will indicate how it is different, in substantial degree at least, from other philosophies on our continuum: the purpose of a world civilization is a *radical* purpose. It is radical in that it is a thoroughgoing and future-directed goal for mankind. Thus far in its history, mankind has never achieved a world civilization—not even remotely. The world has been split into warring camps that expend much of their energy and resources in hating each other and trying to destroy each other. Hate and destruction are disvalues that often seem to have been more conspicuous in the life of man than the values of love and cooperation and construction. Hence, to propose such a goal as world civilization in which peoples of all races, all nations, all colors, and all creeds join together in the common purpose of a peaceful world, united under the banner of international order, is truly a radical purpose. I suggest to my fellow teachers that should they devote themselves to this great purpose, and in turn help young people to assume responsibility for its achievement, they will become radical teachers. And this, says the reconstructionist, is precisely what they should become.

One more point about the meaning of this supreme purpose may be made in a preliminary way. It is obvious that many people in the world are already prepared to agree on the purpose of world civilization. Where they disagree is on the nature of the world civilization that they favor. To the communist, for instance, the idea of world civilization is perfectly congenial, provided that the civilization is built on communist principles. The remarkable Pope John XXIII also wanted a world civilization. But of course he wanted it in terms of the perennialist conception of man and the universe.

So it is necessary to go further. We need to inquire into the precise meanings of different conceptions of the central purpose. Education should carefully consider, for example, what the communist is advocating. Any school system which prevents children from studying communism fairly, objectively, and thoroughly is not a responsible school system. The same is true in the study of, let us say, the proposals of the Roman Catholic Church; we need to understand critically and comparatively what it advocates also. Similarly we should understand as fully as we can the purpose of world civilization which reconstructionists, or people close to them in viewpoint, most strongly favor.

The essence of this purpose centers in the conception of democracy. We should carefully examine what democracy means. It is, of course, the hope of reconstructionists that if enough people understand what democracy really means, rather than resorting to superficial labels that sound pleasant but mean little, they will come to agree that the kind of world civilization they want most is a democratic world civilization. Here again, we are brought back to the question of value orientations, because democracy itself points toward a definite value orientation.

Reconstructionism and Democracy

What, then, is the nature of a democratic value orientation? At least this: it is one in which man believes in himself, in his capacity to direct himself and to govern himself in relation to his fellows. Politically, this means that a world civilization of the kind reconstructionists advocate is one in which fundamental policies are determined by the majority of people of the world, and in which, at the same time, minorities have the right to criticize and to dissent from policies established by the majority. This does not mean dissent in the sense of disregarding or disobeying such policies, but in the sense of having the privilege of criticizing them and attempting freely to persuade the majority that they are wrong.

Democracy as a political philosophy, therefore, is also bipolar. It cannot possibly function unless both of these principles are constantly at work: majority policy making and minority criticism. Each is necessary to the other. The value orientation behind this bipolarity is a deep conviction that human beings, ordinary human beings in the long run, have more common sense and good judgment with regard to what is ultimately good for them than any one else does—any leader or group of leaders, no matter how allegedly benevolent or wise they may claim to be. Unless we earnestly believe this, and unless we as teachers have profound confidence in the capacity of the majority of people to make the best basic decisions regarding policy, we do not accept democracy.

By this kind of test, I am afraid that we could discover quite a few teachers and students in America who really do not accept democracy, even though they are quick to pay lip service to it. Test yourself: if you want to see the principle of political bipolarity extended to world civilization, you believe that you, in concert with your fellows all over the world, are the final, ultimate judges of what is best for you. You are the ones to establish policy—no minority, no superauthority, no special-interest group —only you. Thus you must have faith not only in yourself but in your fellow citizens. If you possess this faith, you believe in democracy; if you do not possess it, you do not believe in democracy regardless of the words you use.

Means and Resources in Reconstructionism

We have focused thus far upon ends and purposes. But reconstructionism is not just a philosophy of ends—indeed, all philosophies of education worthy of the name are also concerned with means. For education, as an agency through which cultures transmit and modify themselves, is inevitably a process, too. Consequently, we must ask: What is the reconstructionist view of education as means?

For one thing, education as means is only strong when education as an end is strong. We need to know what we want, where we want to go, what our objectives are. Then we can begin to work out ways by which to achieve them. Here is one of the points at which the reconstructionist modifies the progressivist philosophy. The latter emphasizes that ends emerge out of the means we use: if we develop effective means, the ends will eventually come into view. The reconstructionist philosophy emphasizes more strongly that means are also shaped by the ends we decide upon and commit ourselves to. That is, if we are clear about where we are going, we will be more likely to develop the necessary processes by which to get there. To be sure, ends and means are necessary to each other. Nevertheless, education should now concern itself much more deeply and directly than hitherto with the great ends of civilization.

Another definite characteristic of the reconstructionist approach to means, one which could make some claim to distinctiveness, is its stronger-than-average insistence upon the limitations in man's rationality. In many ways, man possesses tremendously powerful unrational drives, both within himself and in his relations with other men. If we are to channel the forces of education effectively toward achievement of such a great purpose as democratic world civilization, it is necessary for us to recognize and utilize these powerful unrational forces—the forces of emotion, the forces of hostility and conflict, as well as the forces of love and harmony. Reconstructionism searches for fresh insights into the nature of man, individually and collectively, in order to understand how he may capitalize upon his energies to the utmost in behalf of imperative new goals.

Where may we search for these resources? Two in particular stand out as intellectual mountain peaks of the last hundred years. The first is the young science of psychiatry. Here, of course, one immediately thinks of that giant in the study of man's emotional complexities, Sigmund Freud (although others as diverse as Carl Jung and Harry Stack Sullivan may also occur to you). More firmly than the other major philosophies of education, reconstructionism contends that sophisticated awareness of these complexities is now so necessary that no teacher can be competently prepared for his work unless he is acquainted with the main principles and practices of this rapidly growing science.

The second major resource for understanding the unrational dimension of man's nature is to be found in those social sciences which examine the phenomena of group behavior, especially class behavior. Here the greatest of all pioneers is, I think, Karl Marx, a profound student of society who exposed the unrational behavior of people, not as individuals, but in their organized social and economic relations. The modern teacher needs to become familiar with the chief contributions of Marx and of later scholars who have modified his interpretation.

Thus the reconstructionist philosophy of education insists upon analysis of the unrational factors in life, both from the point of view of the individual and from the point of view of the group. This is not to say that education as means wishes merely to encourage the release of these unrational factors. This is to say that education as an agency of cultural rebuilding cannot effectively operate rationally unless it takes into full consideration the strength of the unrational. There is a paradox here. It is sometimes contended that the Marxist has no respect for rationality because he stresses the conflicting and sometimes violent nature of the struggle between classes. But this contention overlooks a deeper assumption in Marxian theory: men can never become rational as long as they conceal from themselves their own unrational social behavior. Freudians maintain the same paradox with regard to the individual.

Socrates said twenty-five hundred years ago, "Know thyself." Marx might have said, "If thou art to know thyself, become conscious of thy class relationships." Freud might have said, "To know thyself, examine thy inner emotional forces." The reconstructionist wishes to transform education into a powerful means for social change toward world civilization. But to accomplish this we must learn how to estimate and direct our energies on all levels of personal and cultural nature. The means are ultimately rational, to be sure, but only if and when they succeed in recognizing the power of the unrational.

Let me try to put together what I have been saying. Both the progressivist and the reconstructionist strongly believe in education as cultural modification. They urge you and me as teachers, and as potential if not actual leaders in education, to regard our institution as an agency of change as well as an agency of stabilization.

I am convinced that it makes a world of difference to us whether we approach our work believing primarily that education is a power for the renewal of civilization, or whether we enter with the dominant attitude that our main task is to transmit and to preserve the social heritage. A persuasive case can be made for either approach, and, of course, no teacher can or should hold either one to the complete exclusion of the other. But the reconstructionist view is that, in a crisis age such as our own, the former of the two approaches is much to be preferred to the latter.

Supposing that you agree, many questions remain. How, for example, can the reconstructionist theory be made to work in practice? What is the significance of its very large and difficult idea for us as everyday teachers, confronted as we are with a host of daily tasks, routine assignments, chronic frustrations, limited resources? These are urgent questions, and I hope we may partially deal with them as we proceed.

But let me say now that the reconstructionist point of view means fundamental alteration in the curriculum of the schools all the way from kindergarten up through the high schools, the colleges, and adult education. The processes of learning and teaching will also be radically altered. Finally, the control of education, including its administration and policy-making, will have to be changed. Thus, the curriculum, the teaching-learning process, and the control of education will all undergo transformation. This, again, is what is implied by a democratically radical philosophy. A philosophy which endorses minor, patchwork changes cannot achieve the required goals. Only a far-reaching, reconstructive approach to education as both ends and means will serve an age such as ours.

Theodore Brameld (January 20, 1904—) received his A.B. degree in 1926 from Ripon College, Wisconsin. After receiving his Ph.D. from the University of Chicago in 1931, he accepted an appointment as instructor in Philosophy at Long Island University. He went to Adelphi College as assistant professor in 1935, and was made associate professor in 1938. The following year he joined the staff of the University of Minnesota as associate professor of Educational Philosophy and was promoted to professor in 1945. In a similar capacity, he was a member of the faculty of New York University from 1947 to 1958, at which time he became professor of Educational Philosophy at Boston University, where he now teaches. He has been a visiting member of the faculties of Dartmouth College; The University of Puerto Rico; the University of Wisconsin; Teachers College, Columbia University; The New School for Social Research; and the William Alanson White Institute of Psychiatry. He holds an honorary Doctor of Education degree from Rhode Island College.

Among his best-known works are Ends and Means in Education—A Midcentury Appraisal, Patterns of Educational Philosophy, Philosophies of Education in Cultural Prospective, Toward a Reconstructed Philosophy of Education, Design for America, Minority Problems in the Public Schools, Cultural Foundations of Education, The Remaking of a Culture, *and* Education for the Emerging Age. *In addition, he has contributed regularly to professional journals in education.*

In his book, Toward a Reconstructed Philosophy of Education, *pub-*

lished in 1956, Professor Brameld offered the premise that the progressive-education movement may have served its day of usefulness, and that some logical outgrowth of this movement is needed if education is to go forward. The hope lies, he believes, in reconstruction.

Recommended Readings for Part Two

Students are urged to consult the annotated bibliography at the end of this volume for information on the books cited here.

The following books in philosophy and philosophy of education should be especially helpful.

A. Philosophy:

John Dewey, *Experience and Nature*
———, *How We Think*
———, *Logic the Theory of Inquiry*
William James, *Pragmatism: Four Essays from the Meaning of Truth*
C. I. Lewis, *An Analysis of Knowledge and Valuation*
———, *Our Social Inheritance*
Stephen C. Pepper, *The Sources of Value*
Joseph Ratner, *Intelligence in the Modern World*
Paul Arthur Schilpp, *The Philosophy of John Dewey*

B. Philosophy of Education:

Reginald Archambault, *John Dewey on Education: Selected Writings*
Ernest E. Bayles, *Democratic Educational Theory*
———, *Pragmatism in Education*
Theodore Brameld, *Education as Power*
———, *Education for the Emerging Age*
John Dewey, *The Child and the Curriculum*
———, *The School and Society*
———, *Democracy and Education*
———, *Experience and Education*
Sidney Hook, *Education for Modern Man*
H. Gordon Hullfish and Philip G. Smith, *Reflective Thinking: The Method of Education*
Arthur G. Wirth, *John Dewey as Educator: His Design for Work in Education*

Idealism

Introduction to Part Three

IDEALISM is the philosophy from which pragmatism emerged and against which it revolted. As a philosophy it is opposed to ordinary common-sense dualism, which regards knowledge as the result of the more or less accidental relationship between two separate entities: mind, on the one hand, and the thing with its attributes on the other. The dualism of independent things and thinking persons is eliminated by uniting them under the relation of "determining and determined." Mind and things are viewed as but passing manifestations of a single energy that constitutes the essence of all things. In the words of Horne, whom we shall have occasion to study in these readings: "There is but one vast meaning running through all the facts of existence, like the mind through the body. Mental facts are both facts and meanings, while physical facts also have their mental meaning . . . existence is one unity 'whose body Nature is, and God the soul.'" This, says Horne, is the unverified "guess" of the idealist.

Idealism may be said to have begun with Plato (428–348 B.C.). The clearest statement of what has come to be known as Platonic idealism is to be found in his classical work, the *Republic*. Plato tells us that most men remain on the level of instable facts, not well-understood concrete physical objects. Their knowledge is marked by opinion and guesswork. Some men do proceed to higher levels of intelligence, however, and these levels are scientific truths and a wholeness of vision that is above science. The very highest level consists in seeing the interconnectedness of all things. Here, reality takes the form of permanence and is found in universals, laws, and first principles. As the mind reaches these universals, laws, and principles, it escapes from the world of the senses into the world of ideas.

Plato outlines a system of education for the city-state in his *Republic*, and extends his ideas somewhat later in his discussion of education in the *Laws*. Although he lived in Athens for much of his life, he drew upon Sparta as his model. This has been explained by the decay that was evident in Athenian democracy, and the greater order and permanence that Plato thought he saw in Spartan society.

137

So far as education in the United States is concerned, the roots of the idealistic philosophy of education are to be found in nineteenth-century German idealism and in the work of Hegel in particular. Hegel (1770–1831), however, did not write a treatise on education, although Millicent Mackenzie has pieced together what she believes to be Hegel's system of educational thought.*

Underlying Hegel's educational principles was the belief that ultimate reality was mind, and that progress was the result of the reconciliation of opposites: thesis, antithesis, and synthesis. One of his convictions that found great favor in certain educational circles in this country was that each individual tends to reproduce in miniature the stages of development of the race. G. Stanley Hall of Johns Hopkins University, John Dewey's major professor, was one who embraced it.

But it was William T. Harris who, more than anyone else, brought Hegelianism to the attention of American educators—through his articles in the *Journal of Speculative Philosophy,* a series of books he edited for Appleton, his influence as Superintendent of Schools in St. Louis, Missouri, and as United States Commissioner of Education. In fact, the first book in the Appleton series was a translation of a book written by Rosenkranz, a middle-of-the-road Hegelian. This volume, for a number of years, was the only available textbook in the philosophy of education in the United States.†

Johann Karl Friederich Rosenkranz (1805–1879) believed that the goal of education was to develop the theoretical and practical reason in each person. The general form of education was determined by the nature of the human mind. In the small child below the age of six the mind was essentially undeveloped, and this period was chiefly one of physical development. Soon the mind became absorbed in the observation of surrounding objects and discovered laws and principles in nature. Finally these laws and universal principles were identified with reason. Goodness and truth had absolute power in the universe, according to Rosenkranz. They were never without power in the world, and they were never without means for overcoming anything that stood in the way of their realization. Unconditional obedience to duty was advocated, and religion was viewed as recognizing God's absolute existence above the earthly realm of change and decay. With regard to political education, Rosenkranz recommended a general education for all, arithmetic, writing, and reading—

* Millicent Mackenzie, *Hegel's Educational Theory and Practice.* London: Swan Sonnenschein & Co., 1909.

† J. K. F. Rosenkranz, *The Philosophy of Education* (trans. by Anna C. Brackett). New York: Appleton, 1886.

providing a picture of the world so that citizens could direct the course of their affairs on this planet, and a history of the state so that each citizen might see the circumstances in which he lived as a result of the work of his forebears. Moreover, it was desirable to understand the history of one's country in relation to that of the rest of the world, so that one might estimate the interests of his country. In this respect Rosenkranz appears to have been more liberal than Hegel, who is supposed to have said, ". . . boys should have no present-day political opinion . . . the schools no less than the pupils must consider themselves subordinate to the . . . state."

Herman H. Horne became the first American idealist to prepare a textbook in the philosophy of education; however, he began his teaching career by using the Brackett translation of Rosenkranz. One chapter from the 1927 revision of his own book is included in these readings. This selection is of value mainly from the standpoint of the history of the philosophy of education; nevertheless, the chapter is worthy of careful study, since it was the forerunner of the position of modern idealists.

Among the better-known idealists writing on education today are Theodore Meyer Greene and J. Donald Butler. The selection from Greene deals with liberal education and represents what he had to say in his Inglis Lecture at Harvard in 1952. It is especially interesting to note that Greene begins with three presuppositions taken directly from Dewey, to which he adds a fourth, which represents his idealistic predisposition: ". . . man and nature do not comprise the whole of reality but . . . are . . . grounded in an ultimate reality that transcends space and time and all finite existence." He uses these four presuppositions as a frame of reference when he searches out the basic concepts with which to re-examine the education of free men in a free society.

We have examined Butler's ideas in the introduction to Part One, and thus need not deal further with them here. Suffice it to say that Butler is probably the most prolific and best known among the idealists.

The idealists, in spite of their many contributions to American education, now appear to have relatively little influence. Butler recently wrote that the reason for the wane of idealists is that "there is not sufficient penetration and depth among us . . . we are continuing a kind of holding action against the pragmatists,"‡ and he could have added the realists, analysts, and existentialists as well. He then stated in another place in the same article, "We are no more constructive than the present generation of Dewey-exponents who are mouthing an orthodoxy which has had its

‡ J. Donald Butler, "Idealism in Education Today," *School and Society*, Vol. 87, No. 2145, January 17, 1959, pp. 8–10.

day." Butler is not entirely pessimistic, for he believes that idealism offers the present generation a conviction that "where there is knowledge it is someone's knowledge" and that knowledge is essentially individual and personal and not mechanical. If this is true, then "there is some kind of revelation, or at least discerned insight, in knowledge and learning which is human and personal in essence and value." This would imply that the "humanizing and personalizing" in human life is a more fundamental value than man's achievement in science, for the great danger in science is that it will either destroy us or subvert us to something less than "true humanity."

10

The Philosophical Aspects of Education

HERMAN HARRELL HORNE

Idealism in Education*

. . . THERE IS but one vast meaning running through all the facts of existence, like the mind through the body. Mental facts are both facts and meanings, while physical facts also have their mental meanings. As all Nature fills one space and all events one time, so all existence is one unity "whose body Nature is, and God the Soul." This is the guess of the idealists. In no fact is meaning absent, nor is it unknown entirely to us who know our significant selves, nor is it absent from half existence, nor is it confused in itself, nor is it the counterpart of a no-meaning. It appears fragmentary to us because we see in part, but the whole nevertheless is there giving significance to the parts. The trouble with this guess is that it is not demonstrable. It reads all the facts and in a very simple way, but you cannot prove that the guess is correct. This is of course because the philosopher is not himself the whole meaning. From the nature of the case the guess of the part concerning the whole is not verifiable. Because it seems to have most reason in it, we adopt this last guess of idealism.

Idealism in Educating. Not every man, not every teacher, can idealize his work ethically, or at all. It is our great desideratum. It is by the use of idealism we are to make men and women who can idealize.

* Herman H. Horne, *Idealism in Education*. New York: The Macmillan Company, 1910, pp. 149, 176–177. Copyright 1910 by The Macmillan Company. Used by permission of William H. Horne, executor of the Herman H. Horne Estate.

With the perfecting of the spiritual sense along with the other noble physical, intellectual, emotional, moral, and social capacities of man, we may anticipate the day when the measure of a man will include the physique of the athlete, the reason of the scientist and philosopher, the feeling of the poet, the imagination of the prophet and inventor, and the will of the reformer. Such men will be practical idealists, with vision to see and with energy to execute. Some such fruition as this has already been glimpsed in the greatest characters of human history; those great ones are the earnest of the coming men and women God is making through present men and women. To aid in this work is the true calling of all noble souls. And to aim at this fruition, the perfecting of humanity in the image of divinity, is *idealism in educating.*

The Last Principle of Man-Making. These words contemplate particularly our teachers. Theirs to inform young people aright as to bettering the race by selected heredity, by improved environments, and by good wills; theirs to provide the right environment in the schools; theirs to cultivate their own souls as the most important influence upon their pupils; theirs to aid in building moral character; theirs to receive the wages of going on; theirs to recognize, appreciate, and apply, with all parents and citizens, the last of the first principles in the making of men and women, viz., *eugenics, eutopias, and eunoias are the chosen means of the Divine Purpose in perfecting mankind.*

The Philosophy of Education†

The Method of Philosophy. The characteristic method of philosophy is to take what facts it can find in a given field of human experience and seek to determine their meaning. Each such field is itself a fragment of the whole human experience, and our whole human experience appears itself but a fragment, implying for its interpretation the existence of a still larger and inclusive experience within which all meanings get their fulfillment. Any such chosen section of human experience indicates something as to its own final value and lasting significance. The part implies the whole, and the meaning of the part it is that suggests the nature of the whole. The method of philosophy is to construct the whole from the meaning of some of its parts, just as the complete statue or animal is restored by artist or scientist from its bust or bone. Philosophy has no new

† Herman H. Horne, *The Philosophy of Education.* New York: The Macmillan Company, 1927, pp. 257–285. Copyright 1927 by The Macmillan Company. Used by permission.

facts of its own to consider, it has only to consider the old facts in its own new way. Given such fragments of experience as men possess, to restore the whole, that is the problem of philosophy. What must the final truth be in order to do justice to this fragmentary bit of experience as now known? This is the question of philosophy. The instrument of philosophy is thought, as it attempts to follow out in some final and self-consistent fashion the intimations of partial experiences. The invisible things are really made known in part through the things that do appear, just as Agassiz or Gray could describe the life-history of an animal or plant from tooth or leaf. One thing implies another, things go together, nothing is isolated and unrelated, all things are interdependent in the unity of the whole,—such well-known truths as these philosophy takes seriously, and from such details as it can find it attempts the work of restoration. It is a perfectly legitimate method of mental procedure, as used and vindicated by both science and art; only the whole which philosophy seeks is larger, even reality itself. In brief, the method of philosophy is reflection.

The Question of the Philosophy of Education. From this definition of its method it is apparent that the question of the philosophy of education is this, what are the implications of education? What does the empirical nature of education as already defined through the related sciences of fact suggest as to its ultimate nature? Philosophy has no new educational facts to present; it asks only concerning the significance of the facts already in. It takes our educational experience, already narrated, as given, and concerning so notable a matter of human life, it reflectively inquires as to its meaning. Just as there is a philosophy of art, religion, the state, human conduct, etc., so is there a philosophy of education. Like these other departments of human life, education has its own facts suggesting meanings in their own way. Its facts, of course, are like other facts in that they are closely woven into our unitary human life; and the meanings they suggest in their own characteristic way ought also to fit in harmoniously with the meanings already wrought out in the philosophies of other subjects. All facts ultimately mean the same, but they mean the same in their own unique ways; just as signboards on different roads leading to the same city point by different ways to the same goal. Reality is the heavenly city of philosophy and education is one of its signboards.

Two Preliminary Generalizations. What then is the reality as indicated by education? Attempting first to put the facts of education all together so as to view them as one, two things are seen, viz., education is a world-wide process, and it is a temporal process. Education is a world-process; it is the world at work developing a man into the fulness of his stature. Philosophy with its inclusive view makes us return at once to the broad conception of education as defined in the first chapter; all the experiences of life, as well as those of the school, go into the development of man. Just as it takes all the creative powers in the acme of their exercise to make a man, so it takes all the influences of life to develop a man. Unimaginable ages of creative effort preceded the birth of a human child; unimaginable ages of educational effort must succeed his birth to round out man's power. The heart of humanity in which eternity is set, the mind of man with its eye opened to the infinite, have in our brief span of historic time not yet begun to disclose all their latent secrets to the genial and generous influences of their increasingly educational environment. Education is the process whereby human kind is working out into fruition its own inner nature; it is man's means of realizing his destination, of reaching his goal of largest power, joy, and service. It is a narrow though valuable sense of the term which limits the meaning of education to the influence of the school consciously brought to bear through the agency of the teacher upon the pupil; in the broadest, truest sense of the term, it is the sum total of the influences of life that educate a man. All things develop the human being, whether home or business, church or state, self or others, joy or sorrow, victory or defeat, life or death. The world is busy while men grow. As Browning sings,

> I count life just a stuff
> To try the soul's strength on, educe the man.

A Temporal Process. Education is also a temporal process. Philosophers are not agreed whether time is a characteristic of the ultimate reality or not; that is, some say all reality falls within the stream of time; others say that the stream of time itself flows within the territory of reality. The weight of opinion seems to favor the view that reality is independent of the temporal process, that time is but one of the many ways in which reality exists, but that the temporal process, so far as its nature allows, manifests in finite fashion the nontemporal infinite reality. Education belongs decidedly to the temporal process. In that reality where there is no time, any educational process is unimaginable. Indeed, all things in human experience, except the objects of thought, dwell within the stream of time. We think in time but of things, like truth, which are eternal,—before, behind, and beyond, the growth and decay of time. Time is the presupposition of education, without which as the logical condition of succession, of change from less to more, no development could take place. In time the latent becomes the kinetic, the potential the real, and the actual approaches the ideal. From the fertile womb of time man is born into the world, after which all the events of time combine to nourish him.

It is the growing insight of our own age that the development of organic forms through all the vast periods of uncounted past time is a significant natural process, voicing in long-drawn cadence the word of the Absolute. The one-way, irreversible process of organic evolution is one of the efforts of time to tell the story of the eternal. Just as the nature of justice appeared more plainly to Plato when writ large in the structure of the state, so the nature of reality appears more plainly when writ large through the past centuries of productive change. If the world of matter in its unrepeatable processes of evolution is a parable of the truth, how much more may we expect that the world of mind in its self-conscious development through natural and educational agencies is a revelation of reality? Mental as well as material development must be declaratory of the hidden things. Education is the process of evolution become conscious of itself. The story begun by the fire-mist, the spiral nebulæ, the hot stars, the cooling planets, the inhabitable earth, and the growth of life, ought to be continued in the conscious effort of man to realize his nature and fulfil his destiny. Otherwise the universe cannot complete the story it was able to begin. As a significant conscious process of development in time, whereby immaturity reaches maturity, and the child becomes a man, education ought to be a chapter in the serial which the universe is writing through time in the heavens and upon the earth. The constitution of things is so well framed to educate man that one is easily led through the gate of education back into that reality whence man came and whither he goes. As the rare Paulsen writes, "Thus we are forced to repeat the demand. Out of all the infinite possi- bilities construct a world that would have been better fitted than ours to educate man and would have accomplished more."[1]

If the temporal is just man's present inadequate experience of the eternal, is that measure of the eternal which the mind of man can span, is, in fact, in the eternal without which it would be an abstraction, then a significant, notable, and valuable temporal process like education ought to imply in a certain degree the very nature of the eternal. What are these ultimate implications of education? This is the question of the philosophy of education.

In thus seeing that education from the philosophical point of view is a world-process and a significant temporal process, we are led into the very heart of our whole inquiry concerning the nature and meaning of

[1] Paulsen, "Introduction to Philosophy" (tr. Thilly), p. 326.

education. Any ultimate meanings we can find in the empirical educational process will reflect brighter light upon the nature of that process itself. It is the lower that suggests the higher and the higher that interprets the lower.

The Implications of Education. The implications of education can be grouped about three main concepts, viz., the origin of man, the nature of man, and the destiny of man. The discussion must be limited to the self-consciousness of man, so as to exclude the body, the problems of which belong to the natural sciences.

The Origin of Man. First, as to the origin of man. According to the reflective method of philosophy we must first array our facts and then see their implication. There are three well-known facts of the educational process, selected from the foregoing discussions, which, by suggestion, will partly illumine this subject.

Mind Is Real. (a) Education, as a human process with a meaning to spell concerning the truth, seizes upon *mind* as the final useful appendage to the organism in its upward evolution. That which nature by spontaneous variation, the struggle for existence, and the survival of the fit, bestows as its last best gift to the organism, education seizes upon to improve, thus raising evolution from the unconscious natural to the conscious mental plane. The highest type of selective agency of man,—education, lays hold upon the highest selected product of nature,—mind, for further improvement, thereby indicating mind as the highest type of temporal reality. Education by its emphases practises the saying of Sir William Hamilton, viz., "In the world there is nothing great but man; in man there is nothing great but mind." The school and also the other more general educative agencies of civilization lay all their stress upon mind as the most valuable, the most useful, the most real, element in life. Chosen last as the result of an incalculably long, prehistoric process of natural selection, mind is become first. Education may be pardoned its ontological boldness if it questions reflectively whether the reality it selects as ultimate is not the ultimate reality. Is not reality mental?

The Absolute Mind Is Realized. (b) To take the second familiar fact (since philosophy presents us with no new facts) which may provide us with a thread of meaning, to lead us through the labyrinth of the phenomenal into the open place of the noumenal, viz., education shows us a development, the unrealized powers of mind through exercise becoming actualized. But what in the nature of things is the possibility of development? that education inquires which has begun to scrutinize its ultimate bases. Can something develop from nothing? in disobedience of the dicta alike of mediæval scholasticism and modern biology? Can mind come from something not itself mental? the unlike giving birth to the like. Can maturity of mind develop out of simple immaturity? time thus making additions to the sum total of reality as against what might be called the law of the unity and conservation of the Absolute. Can that develop in the temporal process which is not eternally realized? as against the doctrine of the Stagirite that there is no δύναμις without ἐνέργεια. Education finds itself unable to understand how the development of unrealized mind which it secures can occur without implying that, underneath its whole process and giving power at every point, is the one realized mind. Not a first cause in a temporal series of events does education reflectively and vainly seek, but an adequate cause of its great central fact of development. This it satisfactorily finds only in the existence of a mind which needs no development itself, and so can guarantee the fruitfulness of all educational efforts for development. Thus education upon reflection is forced to hold that the reality it declares mental it must also declare actual.

The Absolute Mind Is Self-active. (c) Man is the only educable being. The horse, the dog,—the lower animals, are trained, not educated. Apparently the lower creature frames to himself no goal to be reached, no moral or intellectual end to be attained, no development to be secured. There is direction, but not self-direction; consciousness, but not self-consciousness; inherited instinct, but not conceptual reasoning. Such intelligences are trained, through processes of associative memory, but not educated, through the pursuit of rational ends self-consciously conceived. The dividing line between training and education is uncertain but real. In the field of animal intelligence least of all is the modern psychologist permitted to dogmatize. He only finds man with a history, literature, science, and the arts of civilization which the lower animal lacks. He knows man's works are due to his powers of symbolic thinking. He must suspect then that this is the distinguishing characteristic of man, differentiating him from the lower animals. All his observations go to confirm, and nothing to contradict, this position.

To quote Professor James: "One total object suggests another total object, and the lower mammals find themselves acting with propriety, they know not why. The great, the fundamental, defect of their minds seems to be the inability of their groups of ideas to break across in unaccustomed places. They are enslaved to routine, to cut-and-dried thinking; and if the most prosaic of human beings could be transported into his dog's soul, he would be appalled at the utter absence of fancy which there reigns. Thoughts would not be found to call up their similars, but only their habitual successors. Sunsets would not suggest heroes' deaths, but supper-time. This is why man is the only metaphysical animal."[2] If these things be true, and they have not been gainsaid, it is only a humorous exaggeration to speak of educated animals. The lower creation seems to lack that power of self-directed pursuit of consciously conceived ends which makes education possible. This power we have already named, in brief, self-activity. Man is the only educable being because only he has a sufficient measure of self-activity to attain by effort rational ends.

"The nature of education is determined by the nature of mind—that it can develop what is in itself only by its own activity. . . . Education is the influencing of man by man, and it has for its end to lead him to actualize himself through his own efforts. . . . Man, therefore, is the only fit subject for education. We often speak, it is true, of the education of plants and animals; but, even when we do, we apply other expressions, as 'raising,' 'breaking,' 'breeding,' and 'training,' in order to distinguish it from the education of man. 'Training' consists in producing in an animal, either by pain or pleasure of the senses, an activity of which, it is true, he is capable, but which he never would have developed if left to himself."[3]

The education that has grown reflective as to its foundations asks concerning the source of this self-activity which man displays and which makes of him the only fit subject of educational endeavor. A sufficient cause of man's self-activity is in question. The cause of any phenomenon in the last analysis reduces itself to the statement of the relation in which that phenomenon stands to the whole of which it is a part. Nothing short of the whole absolute reality is the complete cause of the fall of a sparrow or the loss of a hair. The sole, invariable, and necessary antecedent of a phenomenon cannot be found this side the whole truth, the sum total of things that are. The reality of which man is a part, is a unity; to assert any division in reality is to imply the whole so divided; to assert any multiplicity of real principles is to imply a corresponding multiplicity of inter-relationships between them, like good and bad, light and darkness, idea and matter, etc., which thus reduce themselves to one system. Is the whole of which self-active man is a part itself self-active? It is to be noted that man is not absolutely self-active, but he is limited just in so far as he is a part and not the whole. His limits he becomes aware of in the forces of heredity and the influences of environment. But the whole of which man is a part is not limited, being itself inclusive of all that is. Within this whole a measure of self-activity is discovered in man. Here is a self-activity of a certain degree then going on within the whole,

[2] James *Briefer Psychology*, p. 369.
[3] Rosenkranz, *Philosophy of Education* (tr. Brackett), pp. 19–20.

which the whole itself, being the whole, could not have received from beyond. There is limited self-activity within the whole in man, the whole is thus self-active, and so absolutely self-active. If there is a movement within the whole, then the whole is responsible for the movement, and so the whole possesses the quality of self-movement. The sufficient source of that self-activity which education finds in man is reached thus only in an absolutely self-active whole. The ultimate reality, which education implies to be mental and actual, it also implies to be self-active.

If it be true, as education would seem to warrant us in supposing, that reality is one actualized self-active mind, then it would likewise appear that man, as the only educable being, a potential mind capable of actualization through its limited self-activity, is the highest manifestation in the temporal process of the true reality. The self-activity of man, conditioning his education, is the clearest expression in the limits of time of the immanent and transcendent self-activity of reality. It is as though in man realizing his destiny through self-activity, the Absolute beheld himself reflected. The Absolute is; the finite becomes.

The Origin of Man Is God. Putting together these matters we may say, education implies, in the first place, as the origin of man, a reality which is mental, realized, and self-active. In religious language this absolute reality is called God.

The Conception of God. The conception of God as herein reached is that of one absolute mind, complete and self-moving. Being absolute, there are no other gods; being mind, He is not less than personal, however far He transcends the human conception of personality; being complete in Himself, there is no change of time, neither increase nor decrease; time exists in Him as a part, but He does not exist in time and grow old with the centuries; being self-active, He is not the transmitter of an alien limiting force but is the infinite free being, the adequate explanation of all force, energy, and movement that appear in time. From the point of view of the speculative physicist, matter disappears into some form of energy, like electricity; from the point of view of the speculative philosopher, energy disappears into some form of consciousness, like attention.

The only energy whose nature man really knows through immediate experience is that which his own consciousness exerts when he voluntarily or involuntarily attends. Here is energy at first hand; other energy, like electricity, appears at second hand in what it does, not at first hand in what it is. The energy of the world thus in the last analysis may be held to be the attentive aspect of the consciousness of God.

Idealistic Theism. This conception of God is not that of the transcendent Jehovah of the ancient Hebrews, for God is in His world; neither is it that of the immanent *Deus sive Natura* of the great Jewish philosopher, Spinoza, for the world and we are in God, living and moving and having our being. Our conception is neither a transcendent dualism, nor an immanent pantheism, but an idealistic theism. God is the self-conscious unity of all reality. Within His life falls the life of nature and of man. We are the content of His consciousness, and not we only, but all that which is, whether the heavens above, or the earth beneath, or the waters under the earth,—all that we know is a part of the infinite fulness of the content of His consciousness.

The error of pantheism consists in saying, All is God, instead of saying, All is God's. The ultimate reality is not to be spoken about as It; but to be spoken to as Thou. The error of transcendent dualism consists in supposing the world is without, instead of considering it as within, the life of God. He is not far away from any one of us; it is not even enough to say, He is with us and within us, and within the world; but we must go the whole way with St. Paul and say, we live and move and have our being in Him. The true doctrine of immanence is not that God is in nature and man, but that man and nature are in God. The truth is not an immanent God, but an immanent world; the world dwells in God, not God in the world. God is the including consciousness; the world is a part of the included content. God is the infinite Person in the unity of whose consciousness all things exist; the widening stream of time with its natural and human developments is a significant process in His consciousness, in which He is interested from before the foundation of the world as the fulfilment of one of His own meanings, and which is interested in Him as rapidly as it becomes conscious of its own explanation. Matter is the objective thought of the infinite consciousness, no less real, substantial, and solid on that account than it shows itself in man's experience, but nevertheless ultimately a process of thought in the consciousness of God. This is the doctrine of idealistic theism to which education brings us as the only adequate interpretation of its own implications concerning the origin of man.

The Environment of Man Is God. A great new light is thus thrown upon the final nature of the environment of man, hitherto described as intellectual, emotional, and volitional, in adjustment to which consists the education of man. The environment of man is God. Science, reached by the intellect of man, is the thought of God in the world; Art, reached by the emotions of man, is the feeling of God in the world; and Volition, as expressed through the will of man, is the plan of God in the world. We work out our own science, art, and volition, the health of civilization, our salvation, with fear and trembling, for it is God that worketh in us both to will and to do of His good pleasure. Because the world is the product of the Logos, the thought, of God, it is intelligible to man; because it is the product of the feeling of God, it is beautiful to man; because it is the product of the will of God, it is good to man. The Word became the world and dwelt about us, before it became the flesh and dwelt among us. Without the Word was not anything made that was made. There is a material as there is a human manifestation of the mind of God in time.

Those impersonal ideals of education descriptive of man's environment, viz., truth, beauty, and goodness, become personalized in the one inclusive consciousness of God. The world is His, and the fulness thereof. The true, the beautiful, and the good are the ideals of man because they are the ideas of God. He thinks the truth, enjoys the perfect, and wills the good. Thus much is sure, as the temporal process reveals, and infinitely more, too, unexpressed in time and so not entered into the mind of man to conceive. This last it is necessary to say emphatically in order to avoid the errors, while enjoying the fruits, of necessary anthropomorphism. No doubt the infinite God has other ways of revealing Himself to man than through the temporal order, but this is the present plan. To us now He speaks only through an environment, world-old, containing its essential elements of knowing, feeling, and willing. This total temporal environment is one part of the content of His consciousness; it is as a unit His temporal manifestation, His Son, which came to consciousness of itself as one with Him in the unique Person of all time, His greatest Son, Jesus of Nazareth, the Christ.

The Trinity. God is the self-conscious unity of all reality; nothing falls beyond His providential care. In this complete unity of self-consciousness, one can make abstractions of thought that do not exist in reality. There is the infinite Subject, the thinker, the I, the Father, who does not exist apart from the infinite Object, the thought, the Me, the Son, a portion of which is the temporal order, rising into clear consciousness of itself in Jesus, and there is the concrete unity of both aspects in one Being, the Spirit. God is Spirit. And the whole is one Person, as any self-conscious individual, himself a subject-object, is one. This is the true Trinity indeed, showing forth the social nature of God. This counting of the phases of the Absolute Self-consciousness, to which we are brought through the recognition of the environment of man as a manifestation of the ideas of God, is as important as it is interesting because of its historic and controversial bearings.

Summary. The sum of our discussion of the origin of man as suggested by the implications of his education is, that the adequate explanation of man as an educable being is an actualized, self-active, Mind, namely, God, made manifest to man through his temporal environment.

The Nature of Man. Second, as to the nature of man. Following our now familiar and characteristic method of philosophy, we have to point out three factual considerations upon which rest the implications of education concerning the nature of man. These considerations are not novel to us after ploughing through the preceding pages, only we have not as yet seen their deeper meaning. Philosophy is always thus adding the meaning of things to their seeming.

The Response of the Pupil. (a) Education is the product of the mind's effort. The development of mind is from within out, not from without in. No teacher and no curriculum can educate the youth who will not respond. The teacher may lead the pupil to the founts of learning, but he cannot make him drink. The teacher's art, as someone has said, consists in making the pupil so thirsty that he will want to drink. Teaching is not so much the cause of learning, which is so frequently asserted, as it is the occasion or condition of learning. The cause of learning is the pupil himself and his effort. The teacher, the curriculum, the apparatus, the school buildings,—these all are but the stimulating environment of the pupil. The teacher is like the gardener who digs about and nourishes the plant which grows of its own impulse. The pupil is like the plant so stimulated in so far as his response is his own, but he is unlike the plant in that his response may be withheld. There is a possible wilful obstinacy in pupils that does not appear in plants. If they do not become educated in the day of their visitation from the teacher, it is because they would not. The ultimate responsibility for winning an education rests with the will of the pupil. We try to teach, train, instruct, and discipline him, but we cannot educate him; he must educate himself. Every educated man is self-educated; the only difference is that in some cases the stimulating and nourishing environment was lacking, unfortunately so for both the man and his self-education, while in the other cases the man had good assistance. The pupil's ultimate power to make himself work must be acknowledged by teachers. Their function is not to make pupils learn but to make learning so attractive and compelling in interest that pupils will want to learn; not theirs to hector over and be-lecture pupils, but to provide a happy occupation for their free individualities. Not in me, not in me, sayeth the teacher, but the kingdom of education is within you. Education, all this means to say, is the result of the effort of the self-active mind to assimilate the incoming stimuli from the school; is free individuality expressing itself.

Results Proportionate to Effort.   (b) Education presents us with results proportionate to effort expended. The degree of effort put forth by the pupil in response to his educative environment, determines his educational attainment. The same school stimuli receive different responses from different individuals; the educational process is not so much the stimulus shaping the individual, as the individual responding to the stimulus. The same school sends forth pupils with a diversity of attainments, because the same stimuli have received individual responses. Just as the natural world, though one, has produced a variety of organisms through their individual reactions upon its stimuli, so the unitary environment of the school produces a variety of achievements through the individual responses of the pupils. The greater the effort expended, within the natural limits of health, the greater the amount of knowledge and the degree of development secured. One pupil puts forth more effort than another, he thereby secures a greater return. This is indisputable. It may even appear that the same pupil in successive periods of time gains in proportion as he expends. Strenuous one term, slack the next, his developed efficiency is correspondingly more and less. It is as though the degree of effort of the individual were variable in amount. Not simply the prior question of whether he will work or not, but also the present question of how much he will work, seems subject to the free decision of his own personality. Will I give attention at all? How much attention will I give? These two ultimate questions are answerable only by the individual pupil himself, and upon their momentous answers hang the weight of his present and future education. Every pupil is the keeper of his own educational results.

Partial Self-Realization Attained.   (c) Through the energy of effortful attention man becomes in his education what he is intended to be; he realizes his nature; develops his natural potentialities; attains his mental majority; declares his intellectual independence; is emancipated from the slavery of ignorance, superstition, fear, and evil; becomes a free being. That which is cramped, dwarfed, and hidden within the chambered recesses of his own personal nature is manifested in full fruition in the light. The word of educational development, "I become," is partially exchanged for the word of real existence, "I am."

The Nature of Man Is Freedom.   Putting these matters together concerning the nature of man, we may say that education means that through his own effort, helped by an invigorating environment, man becomes what he is intended to be; but to become through one's own effort, through response to stimuli, what one is intended to be is to be free. The nature of man is freedom.

The Nature of Freedom.   Education does not imply a freedom of acting with an unmotivated will, the so-called liberty of indifference, for the stimulating educational environment is present, presenting motives to consciousness to which to respond; neither does it imply a freedom of will to respond to the strongest motive, which is determinism, for education observes the inequality of response of different pupils to the same stimuli, and of the same pupil at different times. These observations do not prove, but they are indicative of, the presence of an independent variable in the conscious response of the pupil to educational motives. But in contrast to the liberty of indifference and determinism, education implies the freedom of consciousness to realize in some measure, through effort of attention, its own selected ends. Such freedom alone is the adequate possibility of education, for only such a free being has a rational end to be self-actively attained; only such freedom permits the self-realization of one's rational destiny. This is not an absolute freedom to do anything at any time; it is a limited freedom to do something at some time. It permits man to utilize his world to attain his own rational ends; it prevents his being the puppet of circumstances, the creature of environment, and the slave of the strongest impulse. It is a freedom, not of the will as a part of consciousness, but of consciousness itself to direct its own thoughts, to attend to selected ideas, thereby inhibiting others, and so to enact its own purposes in conduct. The will is free because the consciousness is free. My ability to direct my thoughts is my ability to act as I will. As a man thinketh in his mind, so is he in his life.

The Freedom of Mind.   Since the mind is a unity, though its operations are many, the question concerning the freedom of the will is really a question concerning the freedom of mind. The failure to recognize this fact has confused much of the controversy on this old question. Since the days of Augustine, even until now, the old notion of the mind as divided into so many separate and distinct faculties has most conveniently served the purposes of polemics. On this old basis the free-will question is threshed out, as Leslie Stephen has somewhere observed. But once it is recognized that the mind is a unity with a diversity of functions, then the question of freedom is reopened in a new way. On this basis it is no longer possible to say that the will is not free if it follows the strongest motive; for the strongest motive itself is a product of the energetic, or attentive, aspect of consciousness. Through attending to an idea the mind makes its motive, and through attending to one idea to the exclusion of others, it makes the strongest motive. The strength of motives is not a given datum, like color or noise; it is the repelling or appealing quality of an idea generated under the lens of attention. A casual glance of the mind over its present ideas reveals a series of strengths quite different from a studied scrutiny with a view to selection among them. To dwell upon a forbidden line of conduct may enhance its appealing power; to wait and listen for the still small voice of right may magnify its volume till it seems to drown all other sounds. Thus it may not infrequently happen that a motive weakest at the start is strongest at the finish. To follow such a mind-made motive is not to be determined, but to be self-determined, that is, to be free. If the mind in its selection of ends of action makes us free, then are we free indeed. The act of choice between conflicting motives, so frequently identified with the question of freedom, and so frequently, too, an apparently fated affair in view of the final strength of the motive to which we yield, is itself but the culmination of the free mental process of attention.

Often indeed in unimportant matters there is the conscious sense of dual possibility at the very moment of choice, which is by no means illusory, but signifies the mind's ability to shift its attention, and so its choice. But in important matters, when the mind is finally fixed upon one course of action to the exclusion of others, there is also the conscious sense that this is the only thing to be done under the circumstances, in which case the apparently determined decision is itself due to the preceding free and voluntary process of attending to all the possibilities, under the general purpose of following the best. No fact of introspection is more certain than my ability to direct my thoughts. But, through the recognized principle of ideo-motor action, to direct my thoughts is to direct my acts. Once a present idea is exclusively attended to, the nervous system takes care of its execution. It is not in man that walketh to direct his steps, for his nervous system may refuse its service, but it is in man that thinketh to direct his thoughts, and with an unimpaired nervous system, the deeds follow accordingly.

On the pivot of attention the question of freedom turns, as Professor James has shown. He writes, "*The question of fact in the free-will controversy is thus extremely simple.* It relates solely to the amount of effort or consent which we can at any time put forth. Are the duration and intensity of this effort fixed functions of the object, or are they not? Now, as I just said, it *seems* as if the effort were an independent variable, as if we might exert more or less of it in any given case."[4] To this introspec-

[4] James, *Principles of Psychology*, Vol. II, p. 571.

tive evidence, based on the unity of mental procedure, is added the weight of the implications of education. Without the freedom to realize one's chosen end through effort, man, like the lower animals, is a creature of heredity and environment, the fit subject of training with physical penalties and pleasures, but not of education as the self-realization of one's rational destiny.

Being a wholly temporal process, education implies a real present freedom and is silent concerning a transcendental freedom.

The Destiny of Man. Third, the destiny of man. There are two notable things about education that bear on this far-reaching question, and that go together. (*a*) Man's education as an empirical process is never completed; (*b*) the possibility of man's development seems infinite.

The Finiteness of Man's Grasp. No man is ever all he can be. At any point in his development he has a growing future. His purposes are not ended with his life, nor does he live in a spent world. Neither does the race in its development discover any waning intellectual possibilities; rather a growth in attainment, if not in capacity. Age does not wither, nor custom stale, the philosopher's love of truth, the artist's love of beauty, or the saint's love of virtue. These ideals of the human reason flee us as we pursue them in time. There is always more to know, and to love, and to do. With these fundamental demands on the universe from the great deeps of man's nature, the incident in life called death seems apparently to have nothing to do. Man does not limit his will to know, to enjoy, and to achieve, to his life's unknown term of years. His plans bridge the chasm of death; they call for an unending time in which their execution may be effected.

The Infiniteness of Man's Reach. Truth is as infinite as the thought of God, but it is waiting to be revealed to man's growing intellect. Beauty is as limitless as God's passion for the perfect, but it is waiting to be appreciated by man's developing emotions. Goodness is as eternal as the will of God, but it is waiting to be realized through the finite will of man. These infinite ideals are the unattainable objects of man's legitimate endeavor; they represent the goal of his development; they are the prophets of his present nature and future progress. Man's development is an infinite process; he is embarked on an unending voyage; he has matriculated in the University of the Universe, whence there is no graduation. The essence of eternity never gets itself fully expressed in the temporal order; time never completely includes the eternal meaning. Eternity possesses what time increasingly suggests. The true self of man he presses on to attain; his present incomplete growing self is but the intimation of what he really is. As the most philosophic of the poets of the last century has said:—

> Man partly is, and wholly hopes to be.

The Rationality of the World-Order.   Given this unlimited demand by man upon his world, what of it? Man has a nature to realize to which any amount of time assignable is inadequate. What follows? Either the universe is irrational, with a good work begun which could not be continued, or man has the power of an endless life. But the temporal order as so far forth developed discovers reason at its core. The world is intelligible, appreciable, and conformable, to the mind of man. The development of science, of art, and of history, presupposes a rational, passionate, and purposeful world-order. A caprice in nature indicative of an inherent irrationality has never appeared to the wondering and scrutinizing intelligence of man. If there be an unintelligible, unlovely, and wilful element in the eternal constitution of things, not once in historic time has it unmistakably declared itself. The error, the ugly, the evil, of the temporal order do not certainly declare the irrationality of the eternal; they may signify only the inadequacy of the temporal to express the whole meaning of the eternal. In the very inability of the infinite to get into the finite, as shown perhaps by these failures of the real to reach the ideal, may ultimately appear the very seal itself of the rationality of the eternal and temporal order. For, these very failures should we reasonably expect, in case the infinite and realized truth were the limit of temporal development.

As Professor Royce[5] has pointed out that the very possibility of error implies the actual existence of an inclusive experience which recognizes and corrects the error, so the argument may be extended to show that the very possibility of the ugly or the sinful implies an absolute experience within which they fall, are comprehended, and overcome. This present object is ugly because the critic's experience is large enough to include it and also a standard to which it should conform. This present act is sinful because my insight is large enough to tell me I ought not to do it in the very moment of its committal. Without such insight there had been no sin. To generalize, the ugly and sinful temporal order are such, if so at all, only because an eternal order includes them and judges them so to be. If the very appearances of irrationality in the world turn thus under inspection into evidence of its larger rationality, then do we return to the thought of what education demands of a rational world-order.

[5] *The Religious Aspect of Philosophy,* pp. 384 ff.

The Destiny of Man Is Immortality.   Education apparently reveals in man a capacity for infinite growth. Will the education of man, which is never completed at any chosen moment in time, and for the eternal continuance of which man seems fit, go on unendingly? It would be an irrational universe, one in which the part did not manifest the whole, if a process with so much human significance in it as education has, and crying out so for an unending time, were to be cut short without conclusion, like a refreshing river in desert sands. If all the evidences are trustworthy and our world is rational; if the finite really manifests, though darkly, the infinite; if the fragmentary suggests, though imperfectly, the complete; if the part reveals, though in a riddle, the meaning of the whole; if, finally, all temporal values get their ultimate recognition; then there is for man an opportunity, guaranteed by his universe, and unabridged by the transitional incident in life named death, to finish his education, to achieve his destiny, and to grow unceasingly into the likeness of the Infinite Being. This is the hope of immortality.

Being a temporal process, and implying an infinite continuance wherein self-conscious personalities approach their goal, education is silent concerning a Spinozistic immortality of having aimed at the eternal while living.

And since all minds with good brains respond more or less to educational endeavor, education has nothing to say concerning a conditional immortality.

And, like morality, education discovers after its best appeals certain characters that prefer the darkness of evil to the way of light. It also recognizes the dependence of real happiness or misery upon the quality of the character, whether good or bad. Wherefore it cannot but assert the possibility of permanently choosing the evil as against the good, whereby men place themselves in the position of the dragon under St. Michael's foot, while the victory is eternally to the good.

Summary of the Philosophy of Education.   Reviewing now the philosophical implications of education as a world-process in time, it would appear that education means that the origin of man is God, the nature of man is freedom, and the destiny of man is immortality. Thus does philosophy, from the implications of education as well as from the Kantian intellectual agnosticism and moral ladder, though baking no bread, as Novalis observed, still procure for us, not by proofs but by plausible implications,—God, Freedom, and Immortality.

It now remains for us only to incorporate these philosophical elements with our preceding empirical conception of education, in order that finally may appear in as complete a fashion as we can frame it our definition of the real and true nature of education. Philosophy has taught us to think that the adjustment to environment upon which biology insisted as the essence of education is really an endless process. The flow of time brings man momentarily and unendingly into a new and changing environment requiring a continual adjustment thereto. Concerning that physical body upon whose proper treatment physiology could not too strongly insist, philosophy reminds us that it is the temporary vesture of the mind to be utilized while it lasts and then laid aside. As for that development of mind which psychology stressed as the natural fruitage of the educational process, philosophy reminds us that the mind of man is fashioned for a growth that is unceasing. Concerning that environment to which education adjusts man, and which sociology defined for us as the achievement of humanity in the world as it attempted to know, to appreciate, and to do, philosophy has said that it is God, manifesting Himself in the temporal order, through man's ideals of Truth, Beauty, and Goodness. And of the conscious human being who all along has been our worthy object of educational endeavor, philosophy teaches us to think as free, capable of fashioning to some extent his own future according to his own plan.

Fifth Definition of Education. Putting all these matters together and summarizing our preceding total inquiry concerning the nature of education, we reach the following last conception: *Education is the eternal process of superior adjustment of the physically and mentally developed, free, conscious, human being to God, as manifested in the intellectual, emotional, and volitional environment of man.*

Herman Harrell Horne (November 22, 1874–August 16, 1946) earned the A.B. degree from the University of North Carolina in 1895, and the A.M. and Ph.D. from Harvard University, the latter in 1899. He later studied at the University of Berlin. He began his teaching career as instructor in Modern Languages at North Carolina during his senior year there, and served as instructor in Philosophy at Dartmouth College after receiving his doctorate. The following year he was appointed assistant professor of Philosophy and Pedagogy and was promoted to professor of Philosophy five years later. In 1909 he accepted the position of professor of History of Education and History of Philosophy at New York University, a post he held until his retirement as professor emeritus in 1942. He was a member of a number of professional societies, including the Religious Education Association, the American Philosophical Association, and the

American Academy of Political and Social Science. He lectured widely throughout the country on philosophy, pedagogy, and religion.

Horne demonstrated a wide interest in questions of religion and education and this interest was reflected in the more than twenty publications bearing his name. Among his better-known works in education are Idealism in Education, The Philosophy of Education, *and* The Democratic Philosophy of Education—Companion to Dewey's Democracy and Education. *He is remembered also for his article, "An Idealistic Philosophy of Education," which appeared in the* Forty-first Yearbook of the National Society for the Study of Education *(Part I). In his writings Horne outlined his idealistic point of view, and at times carried on a running battle with John Dewey.*

11

Liberal Education Reconsidered*

THEODORE MEYER GREENE

WHAT IN THE WORLD can I hope to say about liberal education that is fresh and illuminating? It will not surprise some of you that I have turned to John Dewey for help—not, as you will see, to his familiar doctrines which are today the basic articles of faith of so many Teacher's Colleges and Departments of Education, but rather to his characteristic approach to the problem of education. How, I have asked myself, did he succeed so amazingly in his efforts to revitalize and remold education in this country? How did he manage to precipitate such radical and widespread criticism of traditional educational attitudes and practices? What was the secret of his revolutionary impact upon American education?

The answer to these questions is, I think, readily found. Dewey's peculiar strength was his capacity for *basic* analysis of *basic* human problems. It was the creative philosopher in him who was able to formulate the great ideas or concepts for which he has justly become famous—such powerful concepts as those of human nature, institutionalized society, and the world of nature in dynamic interrelation, or the concepts of the great polarities of thought and action, fact and value, end and means. It was the practical statesman in him who was ready and able to apply these great ideas so fruitfully to many major areas of human activity— to art and politics, religion, science and education. But above all, it was

* Reprinted by permission of the publishers from Theodore Greene, *Liberal Education Reconsidered*, pp. 2–11, 24–45. Cambridge, Mass.: Harvard University Press, Copyright, 1953, by The President and Fellows of Harvard College.

his Socratic spirit of unremitting critical inquiry which impelled him to reexamine again and again not only the traditional beliefs and mores in his society but his own criticism of these beliefs and mores and his own constructive principles as well. Dewey would surely be the first to condemn the rigidification of his own philosophical doctrines into a new orthodoxy. He would wish us, above all, to embrace not his specific conclusions in any area of human endeavor, however valiantly he may have fought for these conclusions during his lifetime, but rather that spirit and method of critical inquiry which constitutes, he believed, the genius of modern science and the hope of the future, and which he himself so notably exemplified in his own lifetime.

Here lies, I am convinced with Dewey, the most promising approach to our subject. If we would see education in a fresh and illuminating way we must reëxamine it as profoundly, that is, as philosophically, as possible. We must try to formulate certain concepts—a very few will suffice —which are so basic and so powerful that, with their aid, we can see education in a new light. But it is no less essential, if we would take all the great germinal thinkers from Socrates to Dewey as our guides, that we embark on this venture in the experimental spirit of critical inquiry, ever on our guard against both traditionalism and irresponsible iconoclasm, ever responsive to genuine insights, old and new.

I cannot, of course, hope to emulate Dewey in the formulation of such fruitful and dynamic concepts, for these are the product of a first-rate creative philosophical imagination, and philosophers like Dewey and Whitehead, with creative imaginations of the first order, are very rare. These philosophical giants and those who have preceded them in our Western tradition would all agree, however, that it is the privilege and the duty of everyone who presumes to philosophize at all to do his best, borrowing and adapting where he must, and inventing where he can. They would insist on only one general requirement: that he deal with his subject as honestly and basically as possible. It is in this spirit, then, and with this challenging objective in mind, that I want to offer you experimentally, for your critical consideration, a trilogy of concepts which may perhaps help us to reëxamine liberal education in a manner basic enough to be genuinely illuminating.

If my approach to the problem of education is to be truly philosophical I must first list my fundamental presuppositions, which constitute my frame of reference. The first three of these presuppositions I take directly from Dewey, though they are of course not original with him and though I shall formulate them in my own words rather than in his. My fourth presupposition is highly controversial but it is crucial for my argument. I shall try to formulate it in such a way as to make it as acceptable as possible to all concerned.

These four presuppositions, which I must here offer you as unproved postulates because I cannot support them with evidence or argument in this lecture, relate to the human individual, to his society with its mores and institutions, to the world of nature which constitutes our spatio-temporal environment, and to whatever ultimate Reality may underlie both man and nature as their final ground. I introduce them at this point because I cannot see how we can really come to grips with liberal education unless we conceive of it in terms of the basic capacities and needs of the individual, in the society in which he finds himself and in our world of nature with its mysterious depths.

My first presupposition is that the individual human being is infinitely complex and valuable. His complexity is evidenced by the fact that he is, simultaneously, a psycho-physical organism, a social or "political" animal, a creator of artifacts, both utilitarian and artistic, a self-conscious thinker and critic, a carrier of culture, a responsible moral agent, and (many would add) an immortal soul. Although each of these generic characteristics of his has been recognized and studied for many centuries, their nature still is, and doubtless will continue to be, a subject of lively dispute. That each human individual is a being of infinite value is an article of faith to which all sincere humanists and theists subscribe, however much they may differ in their accounts of what this infinite value means and implies. Man's innate dignity and value is also basic to our democratic creed. It must, therefore, be a major presupposition of all theories of education in our Western democratic tradition.

My second presupposition is the enormous influence of society, with all its overlapping and interlocking institutions, upon each individual. Each of us has been profoundly affected since birth by the multiple impacts of his family, his local community, and his nation. Each of us reflects in countless ways the ideologies and mores—economic, political, and social—of our society. Each of us, in his own way, is the product of our complex Greco-Roman, Hebraic-Christian, scientific, democratic Western culture which differs so significantly from the no less complex cultures of India and China.

This culture and these social institutions themselves are, of course, the product of countless individual men and women. They are, as Dewey has so clearly pointed out, simultaneously the product of individual thought and effort and powerful conditioning factors in the life of each individual. We are very largely what our society and culture have made us; but we, in turn, can change the mores and beliefs of our society and culture more or less radically and thus control, at least in some measure, the social and cultural "conditioning" of future generations. A rounded education must therefore include a study of our society and culture. They constitute our all-important molding and malleable social environment.

My third presupposition is man's dependence upon, and his increasing control of, that larger environment which we call the world of nature. This physical world, of which we are a part by virtue of our physical nature, is the source of all our physical necessities and comforts and the object of all our scientific inquiries. Into this world are we born; in it we live our lives, battling for security and leisure; to it our bodies return at death. Its orderliness makes possible our growing scientific understanding and our every expanding technological power. Its beauties of form and color elicit our breathless admiration. Its fecundities, inanimate and animate, invite our explorations and exploitations. Its droughts and floods, diseases and violences, threaten our lives. Omnipresent, both benign and destructive, both stubborn and tractable, this world of nature affects our lives so continuously and profoundly that we live and live well only in proportion as we learn its ways and learn to "control" it by adapting ourselves to it. Such learning, which gratifies our innate curiosity and conditions our survival and our welfare, is a third essential component of a realistic education.

My final major presupposition is, as I have said, more controversial. It is that man and nature do not comprise the whole of reality but that both are rooted or grounded in an ultimate Reality that transcends space and time and all finite existence. This ultimate Reality has been the object of endless metaphysical speculation, East and West, through the centuries; it has also been identified with, or significantly related to, the God of man's religious aspirations. Men's metaphysical accounts of this Reality have differed as radically as have the descriptions of God in the great world religions, and there have always been intelligent and high-minded men who have, for a variety of reasons, repudiated all such metaphysical flights as irresponsible and all religious faith as unfounded. Yet the most convinced naturalist, if he is a man of intellectual integrity and humility, will at least acknowledge, with John Dewey, the unfathomable mystery of Nature, the finitude of all human knowledge, and the value of man's spiritual aspirations. Such naturalists will join with the sincere metaphysical idealist and the enlightened man of religious faith in condemning all moral cynicism and spiritual iconoclasm. In his own way he too will insist that the ultimate reaches of Reality remain shrouded in mystery and that man's knowledge must remain forever fallible—that all he can hope for, at his triumphant best, are, in T. S.

Eliot's words, "hints followed by guesses." No education is truly liberal and humane which fails to cultivate the attitudes of humility and reverence in the face of ultimate cosmic mystery.

These four presuppositions can be drawn together in a single sentence. I am presupposing the great complexity and the intrinsic value of every human being; his continual interaction with his society and culture; the ubiquity of nature as man's physical base of operations; and, finally, those depths of ultimate being and ultimate value which some philosophers entitle Reality with a capital R and toward which the man of religion turns in his search for God. I have stressed these presuppositions because no pattern of education can be really effective and useful if it is not realistically oriented to the person as both unique and social, and to man's environment as both spatio-temporal and eternal. This must be our frame of reference in our search for basic concepts with which to reexamine the education of free men in a free society.

A searching reconsideration of liberal education must concern itself with at least three major issues. What is its proper goal? What educational process will most effectively enable it progressively to realize this goal? In what kind of an academic community can this process best be initiated and sustained? These questions can be answered in a very general way in terms of the basic presuppositions which we enumerated earlier in this lecture. We can say that the goal of education is to prepare each individual, so far as his native endowment permits, to live well in his society and in the universe in which he finds himself; that that educational process is best which advances us most efficiently toward this goal; and that that academic community is best which best initiates and sustains this educational process. No one, I fancy, will quarrel with these generalizations. They fail, however, to answer such pressing questions as: What does it mean to "live well" in our society and our universe? How might education promote this good life? How should a school be constituted to assure this kind of education? Our basic concepts of structure, texture, and vitality will, I think, help us to answer these more specific questions.

Let us start with our goal—the fullest development of each individual in the context of his society and his total cosmic environment. Whatever else such development may entail, it must certainly include the development of man's mind. And our minds are well developed in proportion as they are well disciplined or well structured, individualized or well textured, and, above all, active and lively. Let us see what this might mean in more concrete academic terms.

A well-disciplined mind is one which is well equipped with the basic tools of thought and communication. These tools are, in part, "linguistic" in the broadest sense. We can think, express ourselves, and communicate with others effectively only with the aid of one or more of the languages —verbal and mathematical, symbolic and artistic—which mankind has devised for this very purpose. Most important for each of us is his mother tongue, but there are other languages which are also essential: foreign languages, for a true appreciation of the nuances of other nations and cultures; the languages of mathematics, for participation in man's most abstract and most precise thinking; the languages of the several arts, for the understanding and enjoyment of art in the various media; and, last but not least, the many specialized languages of science and history, philosophy and theology, for the comprehension of mankind's profoundest reflections about nature, man, and God.

Mastery of these "linguistic" tools, however, will not suffice. For the mind must also be trained to function powerfully and precisely with their aid—to observe and remember accurately and discriminatingly, to think clearly, to criticize judiciously. Only as we cultivate our native mental capacities do we become able to make effective uses of the complex "linguistic" apparatus available to us.

But linguistic and mental equipment are not enough. A well-developed mind is not only well equipped and well trained but also well informed. If we are to live well we must learn a great many facts about ourselves and about the physical, social, and spiritual actualities which daily confront us. And since we keep encountering new situations and new problems we must learn the techniques of fact-finding and fact-testing. Above all, we must acquire a lifelong passionate respect for fact and a deep hatred of illusion and error.

But a mind however well equipped and trained and however well stocked with factual knowledge and skilled in discovering new facts can, as we know, easily run amuck. If our minds are to serve us well in our society and our world we must also learn how to evaluate sensitively and judiciously. We must learn how to respond generously and wisely to every type of beauty in nature and in art, to truth in every area of human concern, to goodness wherever it appears or should appear, and to all holiness worthy of our reverence. It is this cultivated capacity for evaluation—this sensitivity to all the values which enrich human life and this ability to assess them judiciously whenever they compete for our loyalty —that distinguishes wisdom from mere knowledge and maturity from adolescent irresponsibility.

These, then, are some of the attributes of a well-structured mind. But why call it well-structured? Because these attributes are equally valuable for all men, because they are our cultural heritage, and because they can all be taught. They constitute, in sum, the so-called academic "disciplines," and it is these "disciplines," in turn, which constitute the basic structure of the educational process. Traditional education has excelled in precisely this area—it has concerned itself primarily with these (or at least some of these) basic "disciplines." Why, then, has "progressive" education so violently protested and rebelled against them? Because traditional education has tended to ignore the second essential component of a well-developed mind, namely, the component of texture.

Texture, we have said, signifies the factor of uniqueness and originality. A well-textured mind is a mind that has learned how to realize and express its own individuality, to be itself and not merely a stereotype. The only educational goal worthy of man's precious uniqueness is a mind which, in becoming well equipped and trained, well informed, sensitive, and mature, achieves the richest and fullest self-realization. Our pedagogical task must therefore be to help each of our students to be himself as completely as possible, to think and explore, learn and evaluate, as effectively as he is able in his own distinctive way.

That the components of structure and texture do indeed complement one another in the field of education is clearly demonstrated by the fact that a one-sided emphasis on either component produces grave mental frustrations and unbalance. The "progressivists" in education were quite right in insisting that mere discipline, for its own sake, stifles initiative, interest, and originality. The traditionalists have been equally right in pointing out that an undisciplined mind is not free but enslaved to every passing whim and impulse, incapable of significant originality and doomed to idiosyncratic triviality. Worthwhile originality, whether it be the masterpiece or world-shaking discovery of genius, or the ingenious inventiveness of a lesser talent, or even the run-of-the-mill freshness of personality and outlook of a person of average ability who is completely himself, is always the product of discipline *and* spontaneity, mental structure *and* texture. What education should aim at, therefore, is a mind able to put the disciplines to its own uses—to express correctly and felicitously its own ideas, to gather and interpret facts in its own way, to encounter and judge values on its own matured responsibility.

But we have still not completed our account of the well-educated mind. For what we value above all else in ourselves and others is a lively mind, a mind in ferment—insatiably curious and critical, imaginative and creative. A mind that is passive rather than active, regurgitative rather than fresh and critical, lacks the vital spark, however well disciplined it may be. So is, paradoxically, an undisciplined mind, however free from social restraints, since, without discipline, it lacks the tools and stamina, the knowledge and the mature perspective, requisite for significant originality. Our ultimate educational objective is a self-starting, self-criticizing, and self-nourishing mind—a mind that can function powerfully, creatively, and wisely under its own steam.

Such intellectual vitality cannot, however, be engendered by a frontal pedagogical attack, even by the most inspiring teacher. All that the inspiration of a teacher can do is to awaken in his students a temporary excitement which quickly dies away. We can promote the mental vitality of our students only by teaching them the disciplines in a spirit of profound respect for the individuality of each student. Here, as elsewhere, vitality is a function or by-product of structure and texture in happy combination. But it is also a prerequisite to the acquisition of mental structure and texture. What teacher has not failed in his attempt to help his student to learn the basic disciplines and to make them serve his own interests and needs because the student has lacked the requisite initial mental vitality? And what teacher has not experienced the profound satisfaction of watching a lively but untutored youth gradually become· able, with the help of acquired disciplines, to take charge of his own education and thus progressively to realize his own individual capabilities? Once again, the factor of vitality manifests itself simultaneously as the product of structure and texture and as a directive and vitalizing force.

It is appropriate that the goal of education be defined with major emphasis on the development of the mind, since this is the very special responsibility of the school. Our task as teachers is not to condition animals but to educate human beings, and the only education worthy of man must be focused primarily on that which so signally distinguishes him from all other living beings. We must beware, however, of an intellectualism which tries to divorce the mind from the total personality and which values mental achievement for its own sake. Mental development is valued in our Western culture precisely because the unfolding of our entire personality depends so greatly upon the proper education of the mind. We will do well, then, to restate the goal of education in the more inclusive terms of personality development. What kind of person should we seek to develop in our schools?

Once again our three basic concepts will stand us in good stead. The personality we would cultivate in ourselves and in others is, first of all, a well-disciplined and well-integrated one, with useful habits well coördinated and with mind and body, reason and emotion, instinct and will in harmonious structural relation. Lack of discipline can only result in loss of integration, and an unintegrated person is a person at war with himself, frustrated and miserable. Mere discipline, however, creates not persons but human robots, as totalitarian regimentation has so tragically demonstrated in recent years. Our Western ideal of a developed personality reflects our profound respect for each man's conscience and each man's inalienable right to freedom of thought, worship, and action. Yet the freedom which we cherish is not mere license or freakishness, nor is the spontaneity we wish to encourage an individual initiative harmful to others. Our hope is rather that all men may, so far as possible, learn how to be self-creative rather than self-destructive, and how to promote human welfare rather than human misery. Only such a personality will possess, we believe, the creative vitality worthy of man's highest capacities.

Our concern for each individual's total personality dictates a corresponding concern for the humane community. For personality and community are correlative concepts; each implies the other. Only in a genuine community can personality ripen into maturity, and only through the coöperative efforts of mature persons can a community come into being and maintain itself. If its individual members lack this maturity the social group will tend either to dissolve into a state of anarchy or to rigidify into a regimented human hive. Neither an anarchistic nor a monolithic society is propitious to the development of integrated, interesting, and creative personalities.

We must therefore redefine the goal of education once again to take into account man's social necessities and obligations. The social purpose of education must be to prepare young men and women for responsible and coöperative participation in all the overlapping social groups which constitute the structure of our complex society—in the family, in a business or profession, in the local community, in the nation, and in what is now hopefully called the family of nations. All men's generic rights and duties are the same in each of these institutional groupings—all men crave family affection and all can and should help to make the family a haven of tenderness and love; all men have civil rights and civic duties; all men need economic security and all save the incapacitated can contribute something to our corporate economic welfare. A well-rounded education should therefore include the study of our complex social structure and should prepare our youth so far as possible for a lifetime of informed and enthusiastic social activity. If such activity is to be worthy of free men in a free society, moreover, each individual must learn how, within the framework of common rights and duties, to make his own unique contributions to each social group to which he belongs. For only thus can he hope to realize his special capacities to the full, and only thus can he make his richest contribution to the social texture of his community. The more successfully education assists the men and women of our nation to participate in these various social activities in this spirit, the more will it contribute to the vitality not only of the individual but of the several social groups which claim his allegiance.

Our trilogy of concepts has, I believe, helped us to define our educational goal. This goal is, first and foremost, the cultivation of the well-disciplined, highly individualized, and lively mind—of a mind strong in structure, rich in texture, dynamic and creative. But our goal is also the nurture of man's total personality through structural integration and textural individuation, the development of persons able and eager to enjoy life to the full. And it is also, and no less urgently, a preparation for life in a community, a life of conformity to social order and of responsible deviation and revolt, a life of joyful coöperation with others in common enterprises for the common good.

If our thinking thus far has been sound, it should not be difficult to determine the basic pattern of the educational process best designed to achieve this objective. Our perennial questions as teachers and school administrators are: What shall we teach? and, How shall we teach it? Both of these questions can be answered unambiguously in the light of the preceding analysis. We should teach the only thing that really can be taught, that is, transmitted through formal instruction—not "subject-matter" and not "attitudes," but the basic "disciplines." They and they alone are what we should teach. And how should we teach them? With unremitting concern for the individuality of each student. How else can our students acquire the linguistic, factual, and normative training they need to live well and to contribute what they can to their society? And how else can the school avoid regimentation and do full justice to the uniqueness of every human individual?

There is, unfortunately, a good deal of confusion as to which of the academic disciplines are really basic. Academic divisions and departments have multiplied as scholars have staked out new fields of inquiry and as our competitive society has encouraged more and more specialized vocational training. Is there any way in which the really basic disciplines can be rediscovered and redefined? I believe there is.

First of all, only those disciplines are basic which equip men with *general* skills which are adaptable to a variety of situations, in contrast to the particularized skills for very specific activities. For example, training in "pure" science is a prerequisite for many different types of specific technological training and is clearly more adaptive to new problems as they arise. It is in this sense that a really liberal education is more basic than any form of vocational or, indeed, professional training. This fact is recognized by the professional schools which require an adequate liberal education as a prerequisite for admission to graduate study. Those "professions" which make no such requirement are not really "professions" at all; they are more or less specialized vocations.

These distinctions are not intended to be invidious but are merely intended to clarify the situation. Our society obviously needs not only professional men and women but countless men and women skilled in the many vocations essential to our economy. Indeed, the soundest liberal education must be supplemented by further professional or vocational training precisely because it is a general education for life and not a specific training for a specific job. We therefore reflect no discredit on professional and vocational training when we give priority to liberal education, any more than we discredit a man's profession or vocation when we insist that he is, above all else, a human being. We can therefore acknowledge without embarrassment that we are under heavy obligation to make available to all our young people as much liberal education as their native endowment enables them to assimilate with profit. In general, the more *effectively* a person is liberally educated, the richer will be his own personal life, the further will he be able to develop in his profession or vocation, and the more significant will be his total contribution to society.

If this is true, it is all the more important that the list of the basic liberal disciplines be determined. There are, I believe, only four such disciplines, though each is in fact a family of more or less self-contained inquiries. They are the disciplines of linguistic proficiency, factual discovery, normative evaluation, and synoptic interpretation. That this is not an arbitrary list will be evident if we but remind ourselves of the basic equipment which a man must have in order to live well.

Without language he can neither think his own thoughts nor communicate with others; and the more languages he knows, the better. It is particularly urgent that he learn at least one of each of the several generic types of languages—at least one foreign language in addition to his mother tongue, at least some mathematics, and the linguistic idiom of at least one of the fine arts.

Without a minimum of factual information about himself and his physical and social environment a man cannot even survive, let alone live well in security and comfort. And since new facts and new challenging situations are continually intruding themselves upon him, he needs to have at his command at least some of man's fact-finding and fact-testing techniques. Hence the value of basic training in at least one of the natural sciences and one of the social sciences. If such training is effective (as it seldom is), it will have "transfer value"; he will be able to use it the rest of his life in his continuing explorations of nature and society.

Without training in responsible evaluation—aesthetic, moral, and religious—man is condemned to blind dogmatic belief and is precluded from enriching experiences in the realms of art, of human relations, and of enlightened religious worship. This is the special domain of the "humanities," that family of disciplines designed to help men to learn how to be aesthetically, morally, and religiously sensitive and informed.

Finally, without the skills of synoptic interpretation man is doomed to cultural and sectarian myopia, to provincialism and prejudice. He can hope to transcend regional provincialism only by achieving wider national and global perspectives. He can understand the present only in the perspective of the past, his own culture only in relation to other cultures, his own religious sect only as part of a world religion which, in turn, is but one of several world religions. Religion takes on meaning, moreover, only in the context of the secular; science only in its relation to the moral and the artistic. In short, man is among other things a being capable of reflection, and reflection always involves seeing things in ever wider contexts. It is the special responsibility of the ancient disciplines of history and philosophy to promote this larger vision, to help man to escape from his provincialisms and to see all things—past and present, man and nature, finite and infinite—in their relation to one another.

I need hardly add that all four of these great disciplines are essential and irreplaceable in an education worthy of being called liberal. Though expertness in any variant of any one of them may indeed require a lifetime of specialized study, no one can honestly be said to be liberally educated who is completely untrained and unequipped linquistically, factually, normatively, and synoptically.

So much, then, for the basic liberal disciplines. They constitute in liberal or general education, *what* can be taught and should be taught from grade school through college. *How* they are taught must depend upon the age and background of the student and, no less, upon the individual talents of each teacher and the unique personality of each boy and girl. The educational process is well structured in proportion as it teaches the basic disciplines not as dead facts to be memorized but as vital tools to be mastered and put to use. It is richly textured in proportion as each participating teacher and student is encouraged to explore and use these disciplines in his own distinctive way. Teaching with this attitude is indeed an art and not a science. Much can be learned from example and experience, but no pedagogical formulae can ever take the place of authentic teaching talent. The true teacher is born, not made; all the rules and procedures in the world cannot, of themselves, make teaching and learning the vital personal experiences they actually become in a dynamic educational process.

This brings us, in conclusion, to the school as an academic community. Such a community should be, ideally, a free and coöperative society of older and younger inquirers dedicated to a common search for truth. This ideal is, of course, never perfectly realized but it is more closely approximated in some schools and on some college and university campuses than others.

It is partially realized in proportion as the teacher continues his own intellectual growth, that is, insofar as he is, in this fundamental sense, a scholar. Scholarship, so conceived, is essential to good teaching and not in conflict with it. It is partially realized in proportion as the student, of whatever age, exhibits the maturity of individual initiative and responsibility. Teachers thus dedicated to scholarship and students who are mature in this sense will inevitably stimulate one another and generate a school ethos or spirit of responsible coöperative inquiry. This ethos will function as a powerful directive and vitalizing force which will make itself felt in administrative policy, classroom discussion, and solitary study and reflection. Such a school, in short, will possess the institutional structure, texture, and vitality necessary to sustain the process of liberal education.

The ideal academic community will not be bedeviled by the "iron curtains" which so seriously threaten or impair the educational process in many of our schools and colleges today. The administration will not be out of touch with the faculty, as so often happens, nor will it "run" its faculty in a spirit of patronizing aloofness. Teachers and scholars in the several disciplines will not live and work in complacent provincial isolation. Teachers will not "teach down" to their students and insult them by demanding mechanical blue-book regurgitation. Students, in turn, will not be afraid of their teachers or afraid that intellectual interest and study will make their fellow students brand them as "apple-polishers" and social outcasts. The student will, moreover, not be doomed to the schizophrenia of two unrelated lives, one academic and one extracurricular, as he is at present so very frequently. His education will be a total education of his entire personality, continuous throughout his working hours and in all his varied activities.

Such a community, moreover, will in no sense be an ivory tower of utopian academic withdrawal from the concerns and problems of our society. For in proportion as it is truly liberal and vital, all its members, as younger and older scholars, will be intensely concerned with the most urgent problems of mankind—with scientific and technological advance, with political power and social justice, with the multiple threats of war and the conditions of peace, with art past and present, with man's moral rights and duties, and with the challenges of religious aspiration and belief. All the scholarship and all the teaching in such an academic community will be oriented, directly or indirectly, to man's perennial and current achievements and problems. The mature scholar will be not less but more alive to the tensions of his time than are thoughtful adults in any community. The student will not be idling away the precious years of youth in a mood of prolonged childishness, waiting to "start his life" until he has left school; he will be living, in school, as rich and responsible a life as after graduation.

The ideal academic community, in short, will reflect in its organization and curriculum the structure of the educational process and, in its administrators, faculty, and students, that texture of individuality and freedom which is no less essential for a liberal and liberating education. It will be vital in its scholarship because this scholarship will take live cognizance of the structured and textured vitality of everything that man encounters and seeks to understand—of nature, of human society, of human artifacts, and of ultimate Reality itself. It will be vital in its teaching because it will do justice to man's need for structured discipline and for the texture of spontaneous initiative and creation. Its impact, both upon the individual and upon society, will be profound because it is itself realistically oriented and intensely alive as a corporate on-going venture.

Such a community, moreover, would provide the strongest institutional safeguards against those tendencies which today most seriously threaten our cultural vitality and our personal well-being. It would be a living answer to the loneliness of being lost in an impersonal crowd—isolated in an unfriendly apartment house, or functioning as a cog in a huge industrial machine, or confused and perplexed as a solitary voter. But the answer it would give by precept and example would also be a rebuke to all forms of fascism or regimentation, whether secular or religious, because it is in essence a free community of responsible persons. It would show men how to avoid both nihilistic doubt and smug bigotry and how at least to make progress in the direction of mature reflective commitment. It would be opposed to all revolutionary thought and action which, in repudiating the cumulative wisdom of the past, invites a violent return to barbarism, and it would be opposed, no less resolutely, to all reactionism that seeks to arrest or turn back the clock and to eternalize an ancient order. It would combat an egalitarianism jealous of all special endowment and capacity and, simultaneously, the snobbish aristocracy of those who scorn and exploit the common man. It would, in short, be a mighty bulwark against all threats to a liberal progressive Jeffersonian democracy, and it would be our strongest secular institutional tutor of responsible free men.

Theodore Meyer Greene (January 25, 1897—) received the A.B. degree from Amherst College in 1918 and the Ph.D. from the University of Edinburgh in 1924. He began his teaching career in 1919 as instructor at Forman Christian College, the University of Punjab, India, and remained there for two years. He entered the Department of Philosophy at Princeton University as instructor in 1923; by 1938 he had risen to the rank of professor. From 1941 he served as chairman of the Division of Humanities. He left Princeton in 1945 for a year as visiting professor in Humanities at Leland Stanford University. In 1946 he was called to Yale University, where he became professor of Philosophy. Following a short period as visiting professor at Rice Institute, he took the chair of Henry Burr Alexander Professor in Humanities at Scripps College in 1955.

Greene's published works include Liberal Education Reconsidered, *and "A Liberal Christian Idealist Philosophy of Education" in the* Fifty-fourth Yearbook of the National Society for the Study of Education. *He wrote* The Arts and The Art of Criticism *while at Princeton. His most recent books are* Our Cultural Heritage, Liberalism—Its Theory and Practice, *and* Moral, Aesthetic, and Religious Insight.

Greene is an idealist in the sense that his point of view is essentially sympathetic with the long tradition of objective idealism that stems from Socrates, Plato, and Aristotle. He prefers, however, to call himself a Christian neo-Kantian.

12

The Outline of a Philosophy*

J. DONALD BUTLER

Our Knowledge Situation

THE METHOD OF KNOWLEDGE and the content of knowledge are necessarily related. The one implies the other, and vice versa. But this is to plunge into theory of knowledge itself, and to affirm one of the most general principles of idealism, namely, that knowledge as such, in addition to and apart from specific items of knowledge, implies the nature of that which is known.

Now the specific discoveries which the various sciences yield are of course important as specifics, especially in the time immediate to their discovery and as stepping stones to discoveries for which they may open the way. But they are not truth. They are descriptions; and as such their significance wanes, and they may even be supplanted by rather remarkably different descriptions.

While I do not wish to encourage an egocentric frame of mind nor a self-centered morality, I must assert my belief in the immediacy and priority of the self. From the individual and finite standpoint, this supplies what is lacking in the pragmatic description of the life process. The dynamic pulsating movement of experience is a process in which living individual souls participate, and who by their power of initiating, change the course of events from experience to experience.

* J. Donald Butler, *Four Philosophies and Their Practice in Education and Religion,* rev. ed. New York: Harper & Brothers, 1957, pp. 534–584. Copyright 1957 by Harper & Brothers. Used by permission.

Two evidences of the existence of the self are its continuing identity from experience to experience, and its awareness of a boundary which marks off a vast area which is not self from that subjective realm which is immediate.

Moving on from the knowledge of the self to more extensive knowledge of the order which is beyond self, we came to the most significant question as to whether the order other than self is foreign to selfhood as each man knows it in himself, or is similar to self and of the same character and substance.

I find that I agree, therefore, with the very general idealist principle, formerly stated, and already implied at the outset of this discussion of our knowledge situation, which is to the effect that the self is the interpreter in an interpretable world. By this I do not mean to argue that man sustains a totally harmonious relation with reality, or to imply that the moral and social problems of man are anything less than acute. I do mean to say, however, that there is that minimum in harmony of relation between individual man and the cosmos which is necessary to the basic well-being of selves as selves. Otherwise selfhood could not exist and thrive, as it is not uncommon for it to do. For this to be so is for the cosmos to follow some of the patterns of organization which selfhood also follows. While these patterns may not be summed up totally in the idea of interpretation, nevertheless the act of interpreting, i.e., of discerning, enjoying, and acting upon meanings, is close to a total characterization of the genius of selfhood. And since the world is not completely out of harmony with this, it is interpretable. Over all, for man to be an interpreter in an interpretable world, the implication is that in essence the cosmos partakes of the nature of selfhood, or an essence in harmony with it, and does not partake of some nature which is entirely foreign to and different from selfhood.

With the critical realists and the idealists, I believe in an epistemological dualism, but a more limited dualism than in the case of the critical realists. As is the case in both of these philosophies, I believe that there are two objects in every knowledge situation: the object which has a history in the space-time world and happens to confront me in a particular knowledge situation, and the object which is in my own consciousness when the transaction occurs. But the object in consciousness is not a copy of the object "out there"; strictly speaking there is not a direct correspondence between the two. The object "out there" provides, as it were, the raw material upon which the mind goes to work, but it is the unifying and interrelating activities of perception which yield the qualitative and meaningful object of consciousness.

There are two famous arguments for the existence of God in which I find weight and which I feel deserve the serious attention of all earnest seekers after truth. These, as all arguments, are no more than appeals to reason, and cannot therefore take the place of acts of faith; furthermore, they are not demonstrations or proofs, as one of them is considered to be by Neo-Scholasticism.

First in order of weight and significance is the ontological argument.

I also find weight in the cosmological argument as advanced by Neo-Scholastics.

The critical question, then, is this: Has God so spoken to man, and does He continue to communicate with men? For my answer to this consummately decisive question I turn to the Christian faith, in which I believe is to be found a cosmic movement which is equivalent to the coming of God to man. The truth communicated in this movement is not so much explicit as it is implicit truth for which persons and events are media, and which must be discerned in the response of faith.

And only a God who in essence is Spirit or Person could be a world ground for the specific psychological, spiritual, and personal events we confront as actualities in our world. This, I believe, is to say that existence, in this more precise use of the word, can be equated only with God, as the abiding, enduring, and changeless One, beside whom there is no other. It is even to say more: that God qualifies existence and that existence does not qualify God, as this discussion so far might imply. The root question of metaphysics is not, Does God exist? but What does existence mean? And my answer is that existence means God; that existence is a synonym, as it were, for God.

God, at the least, is Person; the best figure we have within our human experience which can represent Him is personality of selfhood.

He is, within His Being, a community; there is individuality within God, although the Godhead is not limited and is not finite. There is the One who is, and who is the foundation of all being, the Creator, whom we know as Father. There is the One who has incarnated Himself in our individual-social life process, who emptied Himself, who voluntarily gave Himself to be severed apart for us, who are many, that we might partake of the existence which is God's and thereby become members of the One. Him we have known historically, and we speak of Him as the Son. And then there is the One who makes himself immanent in the believer and in the community of believers, whom we know as the Holy Spirit. Yet the Three are not separate; they all partake of the One existence and essence, yet are individual, three Personalities in the One.

The community which is within God, shared by Father, Son, and

Holy Spirit, is a community which is to be extended, as it were, to include eventually all finite souls who respond commensurately to the Son's giving of Himself.

Primarily each individual man is a soul. He is a personality, if the word *personality* is used as having a spiritual context in addition to its psychological and sociological connotations.

This is not to imply any slight to the rational nature of man.

The biological aspect of selfhood, no more "real" than the rational, emotional, volitional, or social, finds its true understanding and function when it is seen as a part of the whole man, and not all of man.

The goodness which God intends for man is such a high achievement that he cannot realize it apart from God's help. Man needs the fellowship of God for its own sake, as an end in itself; but within a somewhat limited ethical view alone, he is unable to realize the end which is written in his nature as a norm without also having the fellowship of God as a means.

The ontological status of evil is much the same as the status of all values in the axiology of pragmatism. Evil is necessarily tied to the individual-social life process and has its existence within this process. Since the One who alone is, who alone has ultimate being, is good, how can evil have ultimate being?

Nature is itself a derived order which is rooted in Him who alone exists. It is best understood, therefore, as the created order; not an order comprised of indestructible order, nor of energy, not a mechanism of laws and relations, but an order designed to be the matrix in which souls can be given birth and nurtured into divine sonship.

Four major presuppositions will be stated and made quite explicit.

1. The first of these has to do with the ontology of values. It is that some values have the status of ultimate existence. Such values have this status not because they are independent realities, but because they are in and of the nature of God, who alone has ultimate and absolute existence. Of course, there is almost an infinite number and variety of values which do not have this status but are relative to the human scene alone and have the same kind of transiency that human experience has.

Ultimate values are real basic existences which have an ontology; their ontology is that they are rooted in God.

If you ask me if love is an ultimate value, I must say "yes"; but I must also say, "the love which we know because of what God is."

2. The second presupposition has to do with the need for effort in the possession of value. It is that all values, whether ultimate or temporal, are enjoyed and possessed only as the human subject, individual or social, participates or becomes engaged in active efforts or relations by

which he (or society, as the case may be) moves from present actual fact to a new situation in which the old fact is replaced by newly realized value. Values are what they are in essence largely because there are individual persons to possess and enjoy them. This is the subjective side of value. The presupposition that ultimate values have their existence in and of God does not imply that our possession of them is automatic and without effort.

3. The third presupposition supplies a criterion as a guide in the realization of value. It is that values are realized in the great majority of value situations by relating parts and wholes, if not exclusively in this manner. Aesthetic values are possessed when a work of art is understood and appreciated as a differentiated whole.

I have contended so far that men can partake of ultimate value only by being related to God and being in Him and of Him. I would like to contend further that the only way in which we can be in and of God is for Him to be broken. How can those who are created, as it were outside of God, at least separate and distinct from Him, who are creatures and not God, and who have in a measure their own autonomy, their own privacy, and their own individuality—how can they partake of that which God is unless God chooses to share that which He is, in and of Himself?

4. We cannot view value theory, it seems to me, as though we ourselves are objective spectators who can think with complete and full impartiality about our value problems. As problems they involve us, and because the problems have to do with values, we are predisposed toward the solution. One way in which we are predisposed is to desire a solution which is advantageous to ourselves or to our group. Another more basic way in which we are predisposed is that not only are we concerned about the means by which a good life is lived, but we are concerned about the ends which constitute a good life.

There are four theoretical connections between axiology and education which are very clear to me.

I maintain, that, whatever the ontology of a value is, persons or societies must be actively engaged in its actualization or they cannot possess it and enjoy it for themselves.

The uniqueness of the educational institution of society looked at in the light of value theory is that it is more especially a value-realizing institution than is any other institution with the exception of religion.

A third aspect of the theoretical connection between axiology and education is the necessary relationship between educational objectives and value theory.

A fourth consideration concerning the relation of axiology and education is the significance for children and youth of their value problems and decisions.

Value problems are the first reflective steps of maturing youth. They provide the first occasion for reflective decisions; therefore, value concerns in education are of unique importance, with all children, but especially with adolescents because in their struggles and tensions are the early occasions for genuinely reflective decision.

In addition to decisions which have just been described respecting the evaluation of specific values, there are other decisions having to do with the whole of value experience which have to be made in the process of maturing. These are judgements concerning the foundations of and nature of value. It seems to me that any education would be superficial which did not make some provision for judgement concerning such fundamental considerations however fully it makes provision for specific value judgements.

The truly educative acts are those which go on within the private experience of the learner and are comprised of the student's own self-activity, never of the artifices of the clever teacher.

There must be an abundance of subject matter fitted into its place in the educative process, constituting the raw stuff on which to "try the soul's strength." But it has its place as a part in the whole, and not as the whole, an important caution to be remembered.

At any rate such an education will need to be provided by a composite of institutions rather than one single institution.

J. Donald Butler (April 8, 1908—) studied at the Municipal University of Omaha, Nebraska, earning his A.B. degree there in 1929. In 1933 he completed the work for his Master of Religious Education degree at the Biblical Seminary, New York City. Four lears later he finished work for the Ph.D. at New York University, where he studied under his fellow idealist Herman H. Horne.

Butler's professional experience has been in both education and religion. He was superintendent of schools in McLean, Nebraska, for one year (1929–1930). From 1933 through 1939 he served as assistant minister in the Second United Presbyterian Church, Jersey City, New Jersey. For five years (1937–1942), he was part-time instructor in Education at New York University. During World War II, from 1942 through 1943, he served as Community Organization Adviser in the Office of Civil Defense. He was a member of the faculty of the Princeton Theological Seminary from 1944 to 1958, holding the ranks of associate professor (1944–1954) and professor of the History and Philosophy of Education (1954–1958). *He served as acting dean of the Princeton Theological Seminary during two six-months periods, one in the academic year 1954–1955 and the other in 1955. From 1958 to 1961 he was professor of Christian Education, Austin Presbyterian Theological Seminary, Austin, Texas. In 1961 he became James Wallace Professor of Religion and chairman of the Department of Religion, Macalester College.*

Butler has contributed several articles to the Twentieth Century Encyclopedia of Religious Knowledge (*Schaff-Herzog*), *as well as numerous definitions to Good's* Dictionary of Education. *He was consultant to Theodore Greene when the latter prepared his chapter for the* Fifty-fourth Yearbook of the National Society for the Study of Education. *But Butler is best known for his* Four Philosophies and Their Practice in Education and Religion. *It is from the second edition of this book that the selection quoted has been taken.*

Recommended Readings for Part Three

Students are urged to consult the annotated bibliography at the end of this volume for information on the books cited here.

The following books in philosophy and philosophy of education should be especially useful.

A. PHILOSOPHY:

RICHARD BRANDT, *Ethical Theory*

PAUL EDWARDS and ARTHUR PAP (eds.), *A Modern Introduction to Philosophy*

ALFRED CYRIL EWING, *The Idealist Tradition*

JOHN PASSMORE, *A Hundred Years of Philosophy*

PLATO, *The Republic*

HERBERT W. SCHNEIDER, *A History of American Philosophy*

MARY WARNOCK, *Ethics Since 1900*

B. PHILOSOPHY OF EDUCATION:

J. DONALD BUTLER, *Idealism and Education*

NELSON B. HENRY, *Modern Philosophies and Education*

IMMANUEL KANT, *Education*

LOUIS A. REID, *Philosophy and Education*

ROBERT R. RUSK, *The Philosophical Bases of Education*

Realism

Introduction to Part Four

So FAR in these readings we have seen that pragmatism is a philosophy that stresses the context in which experience takes place. Human nature is conceived to be the product of experience, and human intelligence is accepted as the best means available for man to solve his numerous problems and to achieve his many values. The scientific method is prized and extended even into the realm of moral decisions. Pragmatists are inclined to believe that the educative task is best achieved in a democratic atmosphere, where intelligence can work freely.

Idealism, on the other hand, holds that man and nature do not comprise the sum of reality, but that both are grounded in an ultimate reality that transcends time and space and all finite existence. Unfortunately man will never know the full boundaries of reality, for his knowledge appears destined to remain in the realm of "hints and guesses." The findings of science are taken as "descriptions" rather than truth, and the essence of man is his personality, or his "spiritual self," which is a finite expression of the Infinite Spirit. The stress upon human personality and the conviction that the human being is intimately related to other beings in a social and spiritual community are important ingredients in this philosophy of education.

The third philosophical position we shall study is realism. The modern interpretation of the term "realism" is the doctrine that there is an objective reality apart from that which is presented to the consciousness. The realist believes that the cosmos is composed of tiny, yet complex, particles of energy called atoms, which are in turn built up from protons, neutrons, and electrons. An object is but the particular form that a combination of these atoms takes. Our senses receive stimuli from these particular objects—the eye receives light waves reflected from a house—and we are said to perceive. Perceptions are thought to be true to the extent that they are found to correspond to the actual facts of reality. Nature contains laws and principles that man can know, and it is the discovery of these laws and principles by scientific investigation that is the final object of knowledge. Likewise, there are moral laws that are believed to be at work in the universe, and these can be uncovered by close observation of nature.

One may surmise that all realists are in agreement. Such is not the case, however, for there are many different kinds of realists; neo-realists, critical realists, classical realists, etc. They do not agree on all matters, and when they do agree it is for quite different reasons.

So far as education is concerned, realists have emphasized different things, but in the main they have thought of the process of education as the acquiring of verified facts that enable the learner to adjust to the realities of the external world. The realistic outlook has been carried over into American education by such men as Ross L. Finney, the sociologist; Frederick S. Breed, the philosopher; Edward L. Thorndike, the psychologist; and William Chandler Bagley, the "essentialist."

Among the most able realists concerning themselves with education today are Harry S. Broudy and Robert M. Hutchins. Selections from their writings are included here. In addition, two chapters are taken from the writings of Alfred North Whitehead.

Alfred North Whitehead's philosophy is tightly written and quite abstruse. In part, at least, this may account for the failure of educators who find interest in his "organic philosophy" to produce a satisfactory "organic philosophy of education." Yet, in order to understand Whitehead's writings on education, it is necessary to see that he believes that neither physical nature nor life can be understood unless they are seen as essential factors in the composition of what he calls "really real things," whose individual characters and interconnectedness constitute the universe. His notion of life implies a "certain absoluteness of self-enjoyment," that is to say, a "complex process of appropriating into a unity of existence the many data presented as relevant by the physical processes of nature." Each individual act of self-enjoyment he labels as an occasion of experience, and he holds that these occasions are the "really real things which in their collective unity compose the evolving universe, ever plunging into the creative advance. . . ." He views life as a process that involves the notion of ". . . a creative activity belonging to the very essence of each occasion." He goes on to describe the process of self-creation as the "transformation of the potential into the actual." Thus, to conceive of the proper function of life, "we must discriminate actualized data presented by the antecedent world, the non-actualized potentialities which lie ready to promote their fusion into a unity of experience, and the immediacy of self-enjoyment which belongs to the creative fusion of these data with those potentialities." He calls this the "doctrine of the creative advance." Finally, Whitehead adds the characteristic of aim, which he defines as the "exclusion of the boundless wealth of alternative potentialities, and the inclusion of that definite factor of novelty" that serves to select the way to entertain those data in the process of unification. Education is the process of self-development, and Whitehead's aims for education are his guidelines for the selection of data for occasions of experience.

Whitehead says that, in order to achieve the maximum self-development in each individual, education should be aimed at producing men who possess both culture and expert knowledge in some special direction.

Harry S. Broudy calls himself a classical realist—classical because his basic ideas about personality, its destiny, and its goals are drawn in large part from the theories of Plato and Aristotle; realist because he accepts the notion of truth being independent of the knower, and "the idea of structures in the universe, man, and society that are normative for man's striving toward the good life and for the education that will help him achieve it." Broudy emphasizes the role of the school in the cultivation of intellectual values, but he admits his indebtedness to modern psychology, the science of education, and some of what he calls "the more basic contributions of Dewey's instrumentalism." The new problem of which he speaks in the article found in these readings is, "How can I live a life of well-being with the maximum of social usefulness?" He answers his question by suggesting that he can achieve his goal through self-cultivation, which means, so far as education is concerned, the appropriation of "the best and noblest of the cultural resources. . . ."

The classical humanists, while they have much in common with Broudy, have been interested in reorganizing liberal education in American secondary schools and colleges along the lines of the liberal-arts curriculum of the medieval university. They have been bitter critics of the watered-down curriculum, the doctrine of pupil interest and needs, vocational training, and the neglect of the humanities. Inspired by John Erskine of Columbia, Mortimer J. Adler has prepared a list of the "Great Books of the Western World," which he suggests be made the heart of the liberal-arts curriculum. Because it is unlikely that most colleges will follow the lead of St. Johns of Annapolis, Maryland, and because of the shortage of able teachers, Adler and Robert M. Hutchins have provided a means whereby most can secure a liberal education after college by reading the great books that Adler has described as "enduring best-sellers, civilizing forces, enlightening," etc. These books will become our great teachers, and we shall learn to think by rethinking the conclusions of the "great thinkers."

Robert Hutchins is less the pure philosopher and more the practical educator. His account of Locksley Hall is an interesting description of what a college might be like if it were cut along the lines of the Hutchins and Adler ideal.

13

The Aims of Education*

ALFRED NORTH WHITEHEAD

CULTURE IS ACTIVITY OF THOUGHT, and receptiveness to beauty and humane feeling. Scraps of information have nothing to do with it. A merely well-informed man is the most useless bore on God's earth. What we should aim at producing is men who possess both culture and expert knowledge in some special direction. Their expert knowledge will give them the ground to start from, and their culture will lead them as deep as philosophy and as high as art. We have to remember that the valuable intellectual development is self-development, and that it mostly takes place between the ages of sixteen and thirty. As to training, the most important part is given by mothers before the age of twelve. A saying due to Archbishop Temple illustrates my meaning. Surprise was expressed at the success in after-life of a man, who as a boy at Rugby had been somewhat undistinguished. He answered, "It is not what they are at eighteen, it is what they become afterwards that matters."

In training a child to activity of thought, above all things we must beware of what I will call "inert ideas"—that is to say, ideas that are merely received into the mind without being utilised, or tested, or thrown into fresh combinations.

In the history of education, the most striking phenomenon is that schools of learning, which at one epoch are alive with a ferment of genius, in a succeeding generation exhibit merely pedantry and routine. The reason is, that they are overladen with inert ideas. Education with inert ideas is not only useless: it is, above all things, harmful—*Corruptio optimi, pessima.* Except at rare intervals of intellectual ferment, education

* Alfred N. Whitehead, *The Aims of Education and Other Essays.* New York: New American Library, 1949, pp. 13–26. Copyright 1929 by The Macmillan Company. Used by permission of The Macmillan Company.

in the past has been radically infected with inert ideas. That is the reason why uneducated clever women, who have seen much of the world, are in middle life so much the most cultured part of the community. They have been saved from this horrible burden of inert ideas. Every intellectual revolution which has ever stirred humanity into greatness has been a passionate protest against inert ideas. Then, alas, with pathetic ignorance of human psychology, it has proceeded by some educational scheme to bind humanity afresh with inert ideas of its own fashioning.

Let us now ask how in our system of education we are to guard against this mental dryrot. We enunciate two educational commandments, "Do not teach too many subjects," and again, "What you teach, teach thoroughly."

The result of teaching small parts of a large number of subjects is the passive reception of disconnected ideas, not illumined with any spark of vitality. Let the main ideas which are introduced into a child's education be few and important, and let them be thrown into every combination possible. The child should make them his own, and should understand their application here and now in the circumstances of his actual life. From the very beginning of his education, the child should experience the joy of discovery. The discovery which he has to make, is that general ideas give an understanding of that stream of events which pours through his life, which is his life. By understanding I mean more than a mere logical analysis, though that is included. I mean "understanding" in the sense in which it is used in the French proverb, "To understand all, is to forgive all." Pedants sneer at an education which is useful. But if education is not useful, what is it? Is it a talent, to be hidden away in a napkin? Of course, education should be useful, whatever your aim in life. It was useful to Saint Augustine and it was useful to Napoleon. It is useful, because understanding is useful.

I pass lightly over that understanding which should be given by the literary side of education. Nor do I wish to be supposed to pronounce on the relative merits of a classical or a modern curriculum. I would only remark that the understanding which we want is an understanding of an insistent present. The only use of a knowledge of the past is to equip us for the present. No more deadly harm can be done to young minds than by depreciation of the present. The present contains all that there is. It is holy ground; for it is the past, and it is the future. At the same time it must be observed that an age is no less past if it existed two hundred years ago than if it existed two thousand years ago. Do not be deceived by the pedantry of dates. The ages of Shakespeare and of Molière are no less past than are the ages of Sophocles and of Virgil. The communion of saints is a great and inspiring assemblage, but it has only one possible hall of meeting, and that is, the present; and the mere lapse of time through which any particular group of saints must travel to reach that meeting-place, makes very little difference.

Passing now to the scientific and logical side of education, we remember that here also ideas which are not utilised are positively harmful. By utilising an idea, I mean relating it to that stream, compounded of sense perceptions, feelings, hopes, desires, and of mental activities adjusting thought to thought, which forms our life. I can imagine a set of beings which might fortify their souls by passively reviewing disconnected ideas. Humanity is not built that way—except perhaps some editors of newspapers.

In scientific training, the first thing to do with an idea is to prove it. But allow me for one moment to extend the meaning of "prove"; I mean —to prove its worth. Now an idea is not worth much unless the propositions in which it is embodied are true. Accordingly an essential part of the proof of an idea is the proof, either by experiment or by logic, of the truth of the propositions. But it is not essential that this proof of the truth should constitute the first introduction to the idea. After all, its assertion by the authority of respectable teachers is sufficient evidence to begin with. In our first contact with a set of propositions, we commence by appreciating their importance. That is what we all do in after-life. We do not attempt, in the strict sense, to prove or to disprove anything, unless its importance makes it worthy of that honour. These two processes of proof, in the narrow sense, and of appreciation, do not require a rigid separation in time. Both can be proceeded with nearly concurrently. But in so far as either process must have the priority, it should be that of appreciation by use.

Furthermore, we should not endeavour to use propositions in isolation. Emphatically I do not mean, a neat little set of experiments to illustrate Proposition I and then the proof of Proposition I, a neat little set of experiments to illustrate Proposition II and then the proof of Proposition II, and so on to the end of the book. Nothing could be more boring. Interrelated truths are utilised *en bloc*, and the various propositions are employed in any order, and with any reiteration. Choose some important applications of your theoretical subject; and study them concurrently with the systematic theoretical exposition. Keep the theoretical exposition short and simple, but let it be strict and rigid so far as it goes. It should not be too long for it to be easily known with thoroughness and accuracy. The consequences of a plethora of half-digested theoretical knowledge are deplorable. Also the theory should not be muddled up with the practice. The child should have no doubt when it is proving and when it is utilising. My point is that what is proved should be utilised, and that what is utilised should—so far as is practicable—be proved. I am far from asserting that proof and utilisation are the same thing.

At this point of my discourse, I can most directly carry forward my argument in the outward form of a digression. We are only just realising that the art and science of education require a genius and a study of their own; and that this genius and this science are more than a bare knowledge of some branch of science or of literature. This truth was partially perceived in the past generation; and headmasters, somewhat crudely, were apt to supersede learning in their colleagues by requiring left-hand bowling and a taste for football. But culture is more than cricket, and more than football, and more than extent of knowledge.

Education is the acquisition of the art of the utilisation of knowledge. This is an art very difficult to impart. Whenever a text-book is written of real educational worth, you may be quite certain that some reviewer will say that it will be difficult to teach from it. Of course it will be difficult to teach from it. If it were easy, the book ought to be burned; for it cannot be educational. In education, as elsewhere, the broad primrose path leads to a nasty place. This evil path is represented by a book or a set of lectures which will practically enable the student to learn by heart all the questions likely to be asked at the next external examination. And I may say in passing that no educational system is possible unless every question directly asked of a pupil at any examination is either framed or modified by the actual teacher of that pupil in that subject. The external assessor may report on the curriculum or on the performance of the pupils, but never should be allowed to ask the pupil a question which has not been strictly supervised by the actual teacher, or at least inspired by a long conference with him. There are a few exceptions to this rule, but they are exceptions, and could easily be allowed for under the general rule.

We now return to my previous point, that theoretical ideas should always find important applications within the pupil's curriculum. This is not an easy doctrine to apply, but a very hard one. It contains within itself the problem of keeping knowledge alive, of preventing it from becoming inert, which is the central problem of all education.

The best procedure will depend on several factors, none of which can be neglected, namely, the genius of the teacher, the intellectual type of the pupils, their prospects in life, the opportunities offered by the immediate surroundings of the school, and allied factors of this sort. It is for this reason that the uniform external examination is so deadly. We do not denounce it because we are cranks, and like denouncing established things. We are not so childish. Also, of course, such examinations have their use in testing slackness. Our reason of dislike is very definite and very practical. It kills the best part of culture. When you analyse in the light of experience the central task of education, you find that its successful accomplishment depends on a delicate adjustment of many variable factors. The reason is that we are dealing with human minds, and not with dead matter. The evocation of curiosity, of judgment, of the power of mastering a complicated tangle of circumstances, the use of theory in giving foresight in special cases—all these powers are not to be imparted by a set rule embodied in one schedule of examination subjects.

I appeal to you, as practical teachers. With good discipline, it is always possible to pump into the minds of a class a certain quantity of inert knowledge. You take a text-book and make them learn it. So far, so good. The child then knows how to solve a quadratic equation. But what is the point of teaching a child to solve a quadratic equation? There is a traditional answer to this question. It runs thus: The mind is an instrument, you first sharpen it, and then use it; the acquisition of the power of solving a quadratic equation is part of the process of sharpening the mind. Now there is just enough truth in this answer to have made it live through the ages. But for all its half-truth, it embodies a radical error which bids fair to stifle the genius of the modern world. I do not know who was first responsible for this analogy of the mind to a dead instrument. For aught I know, it may have been one of the seven wise men of Greece, or a committee of the whole lot of them. Whoever was the originator, there can be no doubt of the authority which it has acquired by the continuous approval bestowed upon it by eminent persons. But whatever its weight of authority, whatever the high approval which it can quote, I have no hesitation in denouncing it as one of the most fatal, erroneous, and dangerous conceptions ever introduced into the theory of education. The mind is never passive; it is a perpetual activity, delicate, receptive, responsive to stimulus. You cannot postpone its life until you have sharpened it. Whatever interest attaches to your subject-matter must be evoked here and now; whatever powers you are strengthening in the pupil, must be exercised here and now; whatever possibilities of mental life your teaching should impart, must be exhibited here and now. That is the golden rule of education, and a very difficult rule to follow.

The difficulty is just this: the apprehension of general ideas, intellectual habits of mind, and pleasurable interest in mental achievement can be evoked by no form of words, however accurately adjusted. All practical teachers know that education is a patient process of the mastery of details, minute by minute, hour by hour, day by day. There is no royal road to learning through an airy path of brilliant generalisations. There is a proverb about the difficulty of seeing the wood because of the trees. That difficulty is exactly the point which I am enforcing. The problem of education is to make the pupil see the wood by means of the trees.

The solution which I am urging, is to eradicate the fatal disconnection of subjects which kills the vitality of our modern curriculum. There is only one subject-matter for education, and that is Life in all its manifestations. Instead of this single unity, we offer children—Algebra, from which nothing follows; Geometry, from which nothing follows; Science, from which nothing follows; History, from which nothing follows; a Couple of Languages, never mastered; and lastly, most dreary of all, Literature, represented by plays of Shakespeare, with philological notes and short analyses of plot and character to be in substance committed to memory. Can such a list be said to represent Life, as it is known in the midst of the living of it? The best that can be said of it is, that it is a rapid table of contents which a deity might run over in his mind while he was thinking of creating a world, and had not yet determined how to put it together.

Let us now return to quadratic equations. We still have on hand the unanswered question. Why should children be taught their solution? Unless quadratic equations fit into a connected curriculum, of course there is no reason to teach anything about them. Furthermore, extensive as should be the place of mathematics in a complete culture, I am a little doubtful whether for many types of boys algebraic solutions of quadratic equations do not lie on the specialist side of mathematics. I may here remind you that as yet I have not said anything of the psychology or the content of the specialism, which is so necessary a part of an ideal education. But all that is an evasion of our real question, I merely state it in order to avoid being misunderstood in my answer.

Quadratic equations are part of algebra, and algebra is the intellectual instrument which has been created for rendering clear the quantitative aspects of the world. There is no getting out of it. Through and through the world is infected with quantity. To talk sense, is to talk in quantities. It is no use saying that the nation is large,—How large? It is no use saying that radium is scarce,—How scarce? You cannot evade quantity. You may fly to poetry and to music, and quantity and number will face you in your rhythms and your octaves. Elegant intellects which despise the theory of quantity, are but half developed. They are more to be pitied than blamed. The scraps of gibberish, which in their school-days were taught to them in the name of algebra, deserve some contempt.

This question of the degeneration of algebra into gibberish, both in word and in fact, affords a pathetic instance of the uselessness of reforming educational schedules without a clear conception of the attributes which you wish to evoke in the living minds of the children. A few years ago there was an outcry that school algebra was in need of reform, but there was a general agreement that graphs would put everything right. So all sorts of things were extruded, and graphs were introduced. So far as I can see, with no sort of idea behind them, but just graphs. Now every examination paper has one or two questions on graphs. Personally, I am an enthusiastic adherent of graphs. But I wonder whether as yet we have gained very much. You cannot put life into any schedule of general education unless you succeed in exhibiting its relation to some essential characteristic of all intelligent or emotional perception. It is a hard saying, but it is true; and I do not see how to make it any easier. In making these little formal alterations you are beaten by the very nature of things. You are pitted against too skilful an adversary, who will see to it that the pea is always under the other thimble.

Reformation must begin at the other end. First, you must make up your mind as to those quantitative aspects of the world which are simple enough to be introduced into general education; then a schedule of algebra should be framed which will about find its exemplification in these applications. We need not fear for our pet graphs, they will be there in plenty when we once begin to treat algebra as a serious means of studying the world. Some of the simplest applications will be found in the quantities which occur in the simplest study of society. The curves of history are more vivid and more informing than the dry catalogues of names and dates which comprise the greater part of that arid school study. What purpose is effected by a catalogue of undistinguished kings and queens? Tom, Dick, or Harry, they are all dead. General resurrections are failures, and are better postponed. The quantitative flux of the forces of modern society is capable of very simple exhibition. Meanwhile, the ideas of the variable, of the function, of rate of change, of equations and their solution, of elimination, are being studied as an abstract science for their own sake. Not, of course, in the pompous phrases with which I am alluding to them, here, but with that iteration of simple special cases proper to teaching.

If this course be followed, the route from Chaucer to the Black Death, from the Black Death to modern Labour troubles, will connect the tales of the mediæval pilgrims with the abstract science of algebra, both yielding diverse aspects of that single theme, Life. I know what most of you are thinking at this point. It is that the exact course which I have sketched out is not the particular one which you would have chosen, or even see how to work. I quite agree. I am not claiming that I could do it myself. But your objection is the precise reason why a common external examination system is fatal to education. The process of exhibiting the applications of knowledge must, for its success, essentially depend on the character of the pupils and the genius of the teacher. Of course I have left out the easiest applications with which most of us are more at home. I mean the quantitative sides of sciences, such as mechanics and physics.

Again, in the same connection we plot the statistics of social phenomena against the time. We then eliminate the time between suitable pairs. We can speculate how far we have exhibited a real causal connection, or how far a mere temporal coincidence. We notice that we might have plotted against the time one set of statistics for one country and another set for another country, and thus, with suitable choice of subjects, have obtained graphs which certainly exhibited mere coincidence. Also other graphs exhibit obvious causal connections. We wonder how to discriminate. And so are drawn on as far as we will.

But in considering this description, I must beg you to remember what I have been insisting on above. In the first place, one train of thought will not suit all groups of children. For example, I should expect that artisan children will want something more concrete and, in a sense, swifter than I have set down here. Perhaps I am wrong, but that is what I should guess. In the second place, I am not contemplating one beautiful lecture stimulating, once and for all, an admiring class. That is not the way in which education proceeds. No; all the time the pupils are hard at work solving examples, drawing graphs, and making experiments, until they have a thorough hold on the whole subject. I am describing the interspersed explanations, the directions which should be given to their thoughts. The pupils have got to be made to feel that they are studying something, and are not merely executing intellectual minuets.

Finally, if you are teaching pupils for some general examination, the problem of sound teaching is greatly complicated. Have you ever noticed the zig-zag moulding round a Norman arch? The ancient work is beautiful, the modern work is hideous. The reason is, that the modern work is done to exact measure, the ancient work is varied according to the idiosyncrasy of the workman. Here it is crowded, and there it is expanded. Now the essence of getting pupils through examinations is to give equal weight to all parts of the schedule. But mankind is naturally specialist. One man sees a whole subject, where another can find only a few detached examples. I know that it seems contradictory to allow for specialism in a curriculum especially designed for a broad culture. Without contradictions the world would be simpler, and perhaps duller. But I am certain that in education wherever you exclude specialism you destroy life.

We now come to the other great branch of a general mathematical education, namely Geometry. The same principles apply. The theoretical part should be clear-cut, rigid, short, and important. Every proposition not absolutely necessary to exhibit the main connection of ideas should be cut out, but the great fundamental ideas should be all there. No omission of concepts, such as those of Similarity and Proportion. We must remember that, owing to the aid rendered by the visual presence of a figure, Geometry is a field of unequalled excellence for the exercise of the deductive faculties of reasoning. Then, of course, there follows Geometrical Drawing, with its training for the hand and eye.

But, like Algebra, Geometry and Geometrical Drawing must be extended beyond the mere circle of geometrical ideas. In an industrial neighbourhood, machinery and workshop practice from the appropriate extension. For example, in the London Polytechnics this has been achieved with conspicuous success. For many secondary schools I suggest that surveying and maps are the natural applications. In particular, plane-table surveying should lead pupils to a vivid apprehension of the immediate application of geometric truths. Simple drawing apparatus, a surveyor's chain, and a surveyor's compass, should enable the pupils to rise from the survey and mensuration of a field to the construction of the map of a small district. The best education is to be found in gaining the utmost information from the simplest apparatus. The provision of elaborate instruments is greatly to be deprecated. To have constructed the map of a small district, to have considered its roads, its contours, its geology, its climate, its relation to other districts, the effects on the status of its inhabitants, will teach more history and geography than any knowledge of Perkin Warbeck or of Behren's Straits. I mean not a nebulous lecture on the subject, but a serious investigation in which the real facts are definitely ascertained by the aid of accurate theoretical knowledge. A typical mathematical problem should be: Survey such and such a field, draw a plan of it to such and such a scale, and find the area. It would be quite a good procedure to impart the necessary geometrical propositions without their proofs. Then, concurrently in the same term, the proofs of the propositions would be learnt while the survey was being made.

Fortunately, the specialist side of education presents an easier problem than does the provision of a general culture. For this there are many reasons. One is that many of the principles of procedure to be observed are the same in both cases, and it is unnecessary to recapitulate. Another reason is that specialist training takes place—or should take place—at a more advanced stage of the pupil's course, and thus there is easier material to work upon. But undoubtedly the chief reason is that the specialist study is normally a study of peculiar interest to the student. He is studying it because, for some reason, he wants to know it. This makes all the difference. The general culture is designed to foster an activity of mind; the specialist course utilises this activity. But it does not do to lay too much stress on these neat antitheses. As we have already seen, in the general course foci of special interest will arise; and similarly in the special study, the external connections of the subject drag thought outwards.

Again, there is not one course of study which merely gives general culture, and another which gives special knowledge. The subjects pursued for the sake of a general education are special subjects specially studied; and, on the other hand, one of the ways of encouraging general mental activity is to foster a special devotion. You may not divide the seamless coat of learning. What education has to impart is an intimate sense for the power of ideas, for the beauty of ideas, and for the structure of ideas, together with a particular body of knowledge which has peculiar reference to the life of the being possessing it.

The appreciation of the structure of ideas is that side of a cultured mind which can only grow under the influence of a special study. I mean that eye for the whole chessboard, for the bearing of one set of ideas on another. Nothing but a special study can give any appreciation for the exact formulation of general ideas, for their relations when formulated, for their service in the comprehension of life. A mind so disciplined should be both more abstract and more concrete. It has been trained in the comprehension of abstract thought and in the analysis of facts.

Finally, there should grow the most austere of all mental qualities; I mean the sense for style. It is an æsthetic sense, based on admiration for the direct attainment of a foreseen end, simply and without waste. Style in art, style in literature, style in science, style in logic, style in practical execution have fundamentally the same æsthetic qualities, namely, attainment and restraint. The love of a subject in itself and for itself, where it is not the sleepy pleasure of pacing a mental quarterdeck, is the love of style as manifested in that study.

Here we are brought back to the position from which we started, the utility of education. Style, in its finest sense, is the last acquirement of the educated mind; it is also the most useful. It pervades the whole being. The administrator with a sense for style hates waste; the engineer with a sense for style economises his material; the artisan with a sense for style prefers good work. Style is the ultimate morality of mind.

But above style, and above knowledge, there is something, a vague shape like fate above the Greek gods. That something is Power. Style is the fashioning of power, the restraining of power. But, after all, the power of attainment of the desired end is fundamental. The first thing is to get there. Do not bother about your style, but solve your problem, justify the ways of God to man, administer your province, or do whatever else is set before you.

Where, then, does style help? In this, with style the end is attained without side issues, without raising undesirable inflammations. With style you attain your end and nothing but your end. With style the effect of your activity is calculable, and foresight is the last gift of gods to men. With style your power is increased, for your mind is not distracted with irrelevancies, and you are more likely to attain your object. Now style is the exclusive privilege of the expert. Whoever heard of the style of an amateur painter, of the style of an amateur poet? Style is always the product of specialist study, the peculiar contribution of specialism to culture.

English education in its present phase suffers from a lack of definite aim, and from an external machinery which kills its vitality. Hitherto in this address I have been considering the aims which should govern education. In this respect England halts between two opinions. It has not decided whether to produce amateurs or experts. The profound change in the world which the nineteenth century has produced is that the growth of knowledge has given foresight. The amateur is essentially a man with appreciation and with immense versatility in mastering a given routine. But he lacks the foresight which comes from special knowledge. The object of this address is to suggest how to produce the expert without loss of the essential virtues of the amateur. The machinery of our secondary education is rigid where it should be yielding, and lax where it should be rigid. Every school is bound on pain of extinction to train its boys for a small set of definite examinations. No headmaster has a free hand to develop his general education or his specialist studies in accordance with the opportunities of his school, which are created by its staff, its environment, its class of boys, and its endowments. I suggest that no system of external tests which aims primarily at examining individual scholars can result in anything but educational waste.

Primarily it is the schools and not the scholars which should be inspected. Each school should grant its own leaving certificates, based on its own curriculum. The standards of these schools should be sampled and corrected. But the first requisite for educational reform is the school as a unit, with its approved curriculum based on its own needs, and evolved by its own staff. If we fail to secure that, we simply fall from one formalism into another, from one dung-hill of inert ideas into another.

In stating that the school is the true educational unit in any national system for the safeguarding of efficiency, I have conceived the alternative system as being the external examination of the individual scholar. But every Scylla is faced by its Charybdis—or, in more homely language, there is a ditch on both sides of the road. It will be equally fatal to education if we fall into the hands of a supervising department which is under the impression that it can divide all schools into two or three rigid categories, each type being forced to adopt a rigid curriculum. When I say that the school is the educational unit, I mean exactly what I say, no larger unit, no smaller unit. Each school must have the claim to be considered in relation to its special circumstances. The classifying of schools for some purposes is necessary. But no absolutely rigid curriculum, not modified by its own staff, should be permissible. Exactly the same principles apply, with the proper modifications, to universities and to technical colleges.

When one considers in its length and in its breadth the importance of this question of the education of a nation's young, the broken lives, the defeated hopes, the national failures, which result from the frivolous inertia with which it is treated, it is difficult to restrain within oneself a savage rage. In the conditions of modern life the rule is absolute, the race which does not value trained intelligence is doomed. Not all your heroism, not all your social charm, not all your wit, not all your victories on land or at sea, can move back the finger of fate. To-day we maintain ourselves. To-morrow science will have moved forward yet one more step, and there will be no appeal from the judgment which will then be pronounced on the uneducated.

We can be content with no less than the old summary of educational ideal which has been current at any time from the dawn of our civilization. The essence of education is that it be religious.

Pray, what is religious education?

A religious education is an education which inculcates duty and reverence. Duty arises from our potential control over the course of events. Where attainable knowledge could have changed the issue, ignorance has the guilt of vice. And the foundation of reverence is this perception, that the present holds within itself the complete sum of existence, backwards and forwards, that whole amplitude of time, which is eternity.

—Presidential address to the Mathematical Association of England, 1916.

Alfred North Whitehead (February 15, 1861–December 30, 1947), son of an Anglican clergyman, is remembered as an educator, philosopher, and mathematician. His formal education at Sherborne School and Trinity College, Cambridge, was in such fields as political philosophy, liberal theology, and the classics. His first position was that of lecturer in Applied Mathematics and Mechanics at Trinity College. He served from 1911 to 1914 as reader in Geometry at the University of London, but he left this position in 1914 to become professor of Applied Mathematics in the university's Imperial College of Science and Technology. In 1924 he was appointed professor of Philosophy at Harvard, a position he held until 1937 when he became emeritus.

With Bertrand Russell, his most famous student, Whitehead wrote during his stay at Trinity College and the Imperial College Principles of Mathematics, *recognized as a great treatise on logic. After arriving at Harvard, he wrote* Science and the Modern World, *probably the best known and most frequently read of all his many writings. In 1927 he returned to Europe, where he gave a series of lectures that were published as* Process and Reality, an Essay in Cosmology. *In this book, judged by some to be his greatest, he developed his "philosophy of organism."*

His published works also include Treatise on Universal Algebra, Adventures of Ideas, Nature and Life, Modes of Thought, Religion in the Making *and* Aims of Education.

14

The Rhythm of Education[*]

ALFRED NORTH WHITEHEAD

By the Rhythm of Education I denote a certain principle which in its practical application is well known to everyone with educational experience. Accordingly, when I remember that I am speaking to an audience of some of the leading educationalists in England, I have no expectation that I shall be saying anything that is new to you. I do think, however, that the principle has not been subjected to an adequate discussion taking account of all the factors which should guide its application.

I first seek for the baldest statement of what I mean by the Rhythm of Education, a statement so bald as to exhibit the point of this address in its utter obviousness. The principle is merely this—that different subjects and modes of study should be undertaken by pupils at fitting times when they have reached the proper stage of mental development. You will agree with me that this is a truism, never doubted and known to all. I am really anxious to emphasize the obvious character of the foundational idea of my address; for one reason, because this audience will certainly find it out for itself. But the other reason, the reason why I choose this subject for discourse, is that I do not think that this obvious truth has been handled in educational practice with due attention to the psychology of the pupils.

[*] Alfred N. Whitehead, *The Aims of Education and Other Essays*. New York: New American Library, 1949, pp. 27–40. Copyright 1929 by The Macmillan Company. Used by permission of The Macmillan Company.

The Tasks of Infancy

I commence by challenging the adequacy of some principles by which the subjects for study are often classified in order. By this I mean that these principles can only be accepted as correct if they are so explained as to be explained away. Consider first the criterion of difficulty. It is not true that the easier subjects should precede the harder. On the contrary, some of the hardest must come first because nature so dictates, and because they are essential to life. The first intellectual task which confronts an infant is the acquirement of spoken language. What an appalling task, the correlation of meanings with sounds! It requires an analysis of ideas and an analysis of sounds. We all know that the infant does it, and that the miracle of his achievement is explicable. But so are all miracles, and yet to the wise they remain miracles. All I ask is that with this example staring us in the face we should cease talking nonsense about postponing the harder subjects.

What is the next subject in the education of the infant minds? The acquirement of written language; that is to say, the correlation of sounds with shapes. Great heavens! Have our educationists gone mad? They are setting babbling mites of six years old to tasks which might daunt a sage after life-long toil. Again, the hardest task in mathematics is the study of the elements of algebra, and yet this stage must precede the comparative simplicity of the differential calculus.

I will not elaborate my point further; I merely restate it in the form, that the postponement of difficulty is no safe clue for the maze of educational practice.

The alternative principle of order among subjects is that of necessary antecedence. There we are obviously on firmer ground. It is impossible to read *Hamlet* until you can read; and the study of integers must precede the study of fractions. And yet even this firm principle dissolves under scrutiny. It is certainly true, but it is only true if you give an artificial limitation to the concept of a subject for study. The danger of the principle is that it is accepted in one sense, for which it is almost a necessary truth, and that it is applied in another sense for which it is false. You cannot read Homer before you can read; but many a child, and in ages past many a man, has sailed with Odysseus over the seas of Romance by the help of the spoken word of a mother, or of some wandering bard. The uncritical application of the principle of the necessary antecedence of some subjects to others has, in the hands of dull people with a turn for organisation, produced in education the dryness of the Sahara.

Stages of Mental Growth

The reason for the title which I have chosen for this address, the Rhythm of Education, is derived from yet another criticism of current ideas. The pupil's progress is often conceived as a uniform steady advance undifferentiated by change of type or alteration in pace; for example, a boy may be conceived as starting Latin at ten years of age and by a uniform progression steadily developing into a classical scholar at the age of eighteen or twenty. I hold that this conception of education is based upon a false psychology of the process of mental development which has gravely hindered the effectiveness of our methods. Life is essentially periodic. It comprises daily periods, with their alternations of work and play, of activity and of sleep, and seasonal periods, which dictate our terms and our holidays; and also it is composed of well-marked yearly periods. These are the gross obvious periods which no one can overlook. There are also subtler periods of mental growth, with their cyclic recurrences, yet always different as we pass from cycle to cycle, though the subordinate stages are reproduced in each cycle. That is why I have chosen the term "rhythmic," as meaning essentially the conveyance of difference within a framework of repetition. Lack of attention to the rhythm and character of mental growth is a main source of wooden futility in education. I think that Hegel was right when he analysed progress into three stages, which he called Thesis, Antithesis, and Synthesis; though for the purpose of the application of his idea to educational theory I do not think that the names he gave are very happily suggestive. In relation to intellectual progress I would term them, the stage of romance, the stage of precision, and the stage of generalisation.

The Stage of Romance

The stage of romance is the stage of first apprehension. The subject-matter has the vividness of novelty; it holds within itself unexplored connexions with possibilities half-disclosed by glimpses and half-concealed by the wealth of material. In this stage knowledge is not dominated by systematic procedure. Such system as there must be is created piecemeal *ad hoc*. We are in the presence of immediate cognisance of fact, only intermittently subjecting fact to systematic dissection. Romantic emotion is essentially the excitement consequent on the transition from the bare facts to the first realisations of the import of their unexplored relationships. For example, Crusoe was a mere man, the sand was mere sand, the footprint was a mere footprint, and the island a mere island, and Europe was the busy world of men. But the sudden perception of the half-disclosed and half-hidden possibilities relating Crusoe and the sand and the footprint and the lonely island secluded from Europe constitutes romance. I have had to take an extreme case for illustration in order to make my meaning perfectly plain. But construe it as an allegory representing the first stage in a cycle of progress. Education must essentially be a setting in order of a ferment already stirring in the mind: you cannot educate mind *in vacuo*. In our conception of education we tend to confine it to the second stage of the cycle; namely, to the stage of precision. But we cannot so limit our task without misconceiving the whole problem. We are concerned alike with the ferment, with the acquirement of precision, and with the subsequent fruition.

The Stage of Precision

The stage of precision also represents an addition to knowledge. In this stage, width of relationship is subordinated to exactness of formulation. It is the stage of grammar, the grammar of language and the grammar of science. It proceeds by forcing on the students' acceptance a given way of analysing the facts, bit by bit. New facts are added, but they are the facts which fit into the analysis.

It is evident that a stage of precision is barren without a previous stage of romance: unless there are facts which have already been vaguely apprehended in their broad generality, the previous analysis is an analysis of nothing. It is simply a series of meaningless statements about bare facts, produced artificially and without any further relevance. I repeat that in this stage we do not merely remain within the circle of the facts elicited in the romantic epoch. The facts of romance have disclosed ideas with possibilities of wide significance, and in the stage of precise progress we acquire other facts in a systematic order, which thereby form both a disclosure and an analysis of the general subject-matter of the romance.

The Stage of Generalisation

The final stage of generalization is Hegel's synthesis. It is a return to romanticism with added advantage of classified ideas and relevant technique. It is the fruition which has been the goal of the precise training. It is the final success. I am afraid that I have had to give a dry analysis of somewhat obvious ideas. It has been necessary to do so because my subsequent remarks presuppose that we have clearly in our minds the essential character of this three-fold cycle.

The Cyclic Processes

Education should consist in a continual repetition of such cycles. Each lesson in its minor way should form an eddy cycle issuing in its own subordinate process. Longer periods should issue in definite attainments, which then form the starting-grounds for fresh cycles. We should banish the idea of a mythical, far-off end of education. The pupils must be continually enjoying some fruition and starting afresh—if the teacher is stimulating in exact proportion to his success in satisfying the rhythmic cravings of his pupils.

An infant's first romance is its awakening to the apprehension of objects and to the appreciation of their connexions. Its growth in mentality takes the exterior form of occupying itself in the co-ordination of its perceptions with its bodily activities. Its first stage of precision is mastering spoken language as an instrument for classifying its contemplation of objects and for strengthening its apprehension of emotional relations with other beings. Its first stage of generalisation is the use of language for a classified and enlarged enjoyment of objects.

This first cycle of intellectual progress from the achievement of perception to the acquirement of language, and from the acquirement of language to classified thought and keener perception, will bear more careful study. It is the only cycle of progress which we can observe in its purely natural state. The later cycles are necessarily tinged by the procedure of the current mode of education. There is a characteristic of it which is often sadly lacking in subsequent education; I mean, that it achieves complete success. At the end of it the child *can* speak, its ideas *are* classified, and its perceptions *are* sharpened. The cycle achieves its object. This is a great deal more than can be said for most systems of education as applied to most pupils. But why should this be so? Certainly, a new-born baby looks a most unpromising subject for intellectual progress when we remember the difficulty of the task before it. I suppose it is because nature, in the form of surrounding circumstances, sets it a task for which the normal development of its brain is exactly fitted. I do not think that there is any particular mystery about the fact of a child learning to speak and in consequence thinking all the better; but it does offer food for reflection.

In the subsequent education we have not sought for cyclic processes which in a finite time run their course and within their own limited sphere achieve a complete success. This completion is one outstanding character in the natural cycle for infants. Later on we start a child on some subject, say Latin, at the age of ten, and hope by a uniform system of formal training to achieve success at the age of twenty. The natural result is failure, both in interest and in acquirement. When I speak of failure, I am comparing our results with the brilliant success of the first natural cycle. I do not think that it is because our tasks are intrinsically too hard, when I remember that the infant's cycle is the hardest of all. It is because our tasks are set in an unnatural way, without rhythm and without the stimulus of intermediate successes and without concentration.

I have not yet spoken of this character of concentration which so conspicuously attaches to the infant's progress. The whole being of the infant is absorbed in the practice of its cycle. It has nothing else to divert its mental development. In this respect there is a striking difference between this natural cycle and the subsequent history of the student's development. It is perfectly obvious that life is very various and that the mind and brain naturally develop so as to adapt themselves to the many-hued world in which their lot is cast. Still, after making allowance for this consideration, we will be wise to preserve some measure of concentration for each of the subsequent cycles. In particular, we should avoid a competition of diverse subjects in the same stage of their cycles. The fault of the older education was unrhythmic concentration on a single undifferentiated subject. Our modern system, with its insistence on a preliminary general education, and with its easy toleration of the analysis of knowledge into distinct subjects, is an equally unrhythmic collection of distracting scraps. I am pleading that we shall endeavour to weave in the learner's mind a harmony of patterns, by co-ordinating the various elements of instruction into subordinate cycles each of intrinsic worth for the immediate apprehension of the pupil. We must garner our crops each in its due season.

The Romance of Adolescence

We will now pass to some concrete applications of the ideas which have been developed in the former part of my address.

The first cycle of infancy is succeeded by the cycle of adolescence, which opens with by far the greatest stage of romance which we ever experience. It is in this stage that the lines of character are graven. How the child emerges from the romantic stage of adolescence is how the subsequent life will be moulded by ideals and coloured by imagination. It rapidly follows on the generalisation of capacity produced by the acquirement of spoken language and of reading. The stage of generalisation belonging to the infantile cycle is comparatively short because the romantic material of infancy is so scanty. The initial knowledge of the world in any developed sense of the word "knowledge" really commences after the achievement of the first cycle, and thus issues in the tremendous age of romance. Ideas, facts, relationships, stories, histories, possibilities, artistry in words, in sounds, in form and in colour, crowd into the child's life, stir his feelings, excite his appreciation, and incite his impulses to kindred activities. It is a saddening thought that on this golden age there falls so often the shadow of the crammer. I am thinking of a period of about four years of the child's life, roughly, in ordinary cases, falling between the age of eight and twelve or thirteen. It is the first great period of the utilisation of the native language, and of developed powers of observation and of manipulation. The infant cannot manipulate, the child can; the infant cannot observe, the child can; the infant cannot retain thoughts by the recollection of words, the child can. The child thus enters upon a new world.

Of course, the stage of precision prolongs itself as recurring in minor cycles which form eddies in the great romance. The perfecting of writing, of spelling, of the elements of arithmetic, and of lists of simple facts, such as the Kings of England, are all elements of precision, very necessary both as training in concentration and as useful acquirements. However, these are essentially fragmentary in character, whereas the great romance is the flood which bears on the child towards the life of the spirit.

The success of the Montessori system is due to its recognition of the dominance of romance at this period of growth. If this be the explanation, it also points to the limitations in the usefulness of that method. It is the system which in some measure is essential for every romantic stage. Its essence is browsing and the encouragement of vivid freshness. But it lacks the restraint which is necessary for the great stages of precision.

The Mastery of Language

As he nears the end of the great romance the cyclic course of growth is swinging the child over towards an aptitude for exact knowledge. Language is now the natural subject-matter for concentrated attack. It is the mode of expression with which he is thoroughly familiar. He is acquainted with stories, histories, and poems illustrating the lives of other people and of other civilisations. Accordingly, from the age of eleven onwards there is wanted a gradually increasing concentration towards precise knowledge of language. Finally, the three years from twelve to fifteen should be dominated by a mass attack upon language, so planned that a definite result, in itself worth having, is thereby achieved. I should guess that within these limits of time, and given adequate concentration, we might ask that at the end of that period the children should have command of English, should be able to read fluently fairly simple French, and should have completed the elementary stage of Latin; I mean, a precise knowledge of the more straightforward parts of Latin grammar, the knowledge of the construction of Latin sentences, and the reading of some parts of appropriate Latin authors, perhaps simplified and largely supplemented by the aid of the best literary translations so that their reading of the original, plus translation, gives them a grip of the book as a literary whole. I conceive that such a measure of attainment in these three languages is well within the reach of the ordinary child, provided that he has not been distracted by the effort at precision in a multiplicity of other subjects. Also some more gifted children could go further. The Latin would come to them easily, so that it would be possible to start Greek before the end of the period, always provided that their bent is literary and that they mean later to pursue that study at least for some years. Other subjects will occupy a subordinate place in the time-table and will be undertaken in a different spirit. In the first place, it must be remembered that the semi-literary subjects, such as history, will largely have been provided in the study of the languages. It will be hardly possible to read some English, French, and Latin literature without imparting some knowledge of European history. I do not mean that all special history teaching should be abandoned. I do, however, suggest that the subject should be exhibited in what I have termed the romantic spirit, and that the pupils should not be subjected to the test of precise recollection of details on any large systematic scale.

At this period of growth science should be in its stage of romance. The pupils should see for themselves, and experiment for themselves, with only fragmentary precision of thought. The essence of the importance of science, both for interest in theory or for technological purposes, lies in its application to concrete detail, and every such application evokes a novel problem for research. Accordingly, all training in science should begin as well as end in research, and in getting hold of the subject-matter as it occurs in nature. The exact form of guidance suitable to this age and the exact limitations of experiment are matters depending on experiments. But I plead that this period is the true age for the romance of science.

Concentration on Science

Towards the age of fifteen the age of precision in language and of romance in science draws to its close, to be succeeded by a period of generalisation in language and of precision in science. This should be a short period, but one of vital importance. I am thinking of about one year's work, and I suggest that it would be well decisively to alter the balance of the preceding curriculum. There should be a concentration on science and a decided diminution of the linguistic work. A year's work on science, coming on the top of the previous romantic study, should make everyone understand the main principles, which govern the development of mechanics, physics, chemistry, algebra and geometry. Understand that they are not beginning these subjects, but they are putting together a previous discursive study by an exact formulation of their main ideas. For example, take algebra and geometry, which I single out as being subjects with which I have some slight familiarity. In the previous three years there has been work on the applications of the simplest algebraic formulæ and geometrical propositions to problems of surveying, or of some other scientific work involving calculations. In this way arithmetic has been carefully strengthened by the insistence on definite numerical results, and familiarity with the ideas of literal formulæ and of geometrical properties has been gained; also some minor methods of manipulation have been inculcated. There is thus no long time to be wasted in getting used to the ideas of the sciences. The pupils are ready for the small body of algebraic and geometrical truths which they ought to know thoroughly. Furthermore, in the previous period some boys will have shown an aptitude for mathematics and will have pushed on a little more, besides in the final year somewhat emphasising their mathematics at the expense of some of the other subjects. I am simply taking mathematics as an illustration.

Meanwhile, the cycle of language is in its stage of generalisation. In this stage the precise study of grammar and composition is discontinued, and the language study is confined to reading the literature with emphasised attention to its ideas and to the general history in which it is embedded; also the time allotted to history will pass into the precise study of a short definite period, chosen to illustrate exactly what does happen at an important epoch and also to show how to pass the simpler types of judgments on men and policies.

I have now sketched in outline the course of education from baby-hood to about sixteen and a half, arranged with some attention to the rhythmic pulses of life. In some such way a general education is possible in which the pupil throughout has the advantage of concentration and of freshness. Thus precision will always illustrate subject-matter already apprehended and crying out for drastic treatment. Every pupil will have concentrated in turn on a variety of different subjects, and will know where his strong points lie. Finally—and this of all the objects to be attained is the most dear to my heart—the science students will have obtained both an invaluable literary education and also at the most impressionable age an early initiation into habits of thinking for them-selves in the region of science.

After the age of sixteen new problems arise. For literary students science passes into the stage of generalisation, largely in the form of lectures on its main results and general ideas. New cycles of linguistic, literary, and historical study commence. But further detail is now un-necessary. For the scientists the preceding stage of precision maintains itself to the close of the school period with an increasing apprehension of wider general ideas.

However, at this period of education the problem is too individual, or at least breaks up into too many cases, to be susceptible of broad general treatment. I do suggest, nevertheless, that all scientists should now keep up their French, and initiate the study of German if they have not already acquired it.

University Education

I should now like, if you will bear with me, to make some remarks respecting the import of these ideas for a University education.

The whole period of growth from infancy to manhood forms one grand cycle. Its stage of romance stretches across the first dozen years of its life, its stage of precision comprises the whole school period of second-ary education, and its stage of generalisation is the period of entrance into manhood. For those whose formal education is prolonged beyond the school age, the University course or its equivalent is the great period of generalisation. The spirit of generalisation should dominate a Univer-sity. The lectures should be addressed to those to whom details and procedure are familiar; that is to say, familiar at least in the sense of being so congruous to pre-existing training as to be easily acquirable. During the school period the student has been mentally bending over his desk; at the University he should stand up and look around. For this reason it is fatal if the first year at the University be frittered away in going over the old work in the old spirit. At school the boy painfully rises from the particular towards glimpses at general ideas; at the University he should start from general ideas and study their applications to concrete cases. A well-planned University course is a study of the wide sweep of generality. I do not mean that it should be abstract in the sense of divorce from concrete fact, but that concrete fact should be studied as illustrating the scope of general ideas.

Cultivation of Mental Power

This is the aspect of University training in which theoretical interest and practical utility coincide. Whatever be the detail with which you cram your student, the chance of his meeting in after-life exactly that detail is almost infinitesimal; and if he does meet it, he will probably have forgotten what you taught him about it. The really useful training yields a comprehension of a few general principles with a thorough grounding in the way they apply to a variety of concrete details. In subsequent practice the men will have forgotten your particular details; but they will remember by an unconscious common sense how to apply principles to immediate circumstances. Your learning is useless to you till you have lost your textbooks, burnt your lecture notes, and forgotten the minutiæ which you learnt by heart for the examination. What, in the way of detail, you continually require will stick in your memory as obvious facts like the sun and moon; and what you casually require can be looked up in any work of reference. The function of a University is to enable you to shed details in favour of principles. When I speak of principles I am hardly even thinking of verbal formulations. A principle which has thoroughly soaked into you is rather a mental habit than a formal statement. It becomes the way the mind reacts to the appropriate stimulus in the form of illustrative circumstances. Nobody goes about with his knowledge clearly and consciously before him. Mental cultivation is nothing else than the satisfactory way in which the mind will function when it is poked up into activity. Learning is often spoken of as if we are watching the open pages of all the books which we have ever read, and then, when occasion arises, we select the right page to read aloud to the universe.

Luckily, the truth is far otherwise from this crude idea; and for this reason the antagonism between the claims of pure knowledge and professional acquirement should be much less acute than a faulty view of education would lead us to anticipate. I can put my point otherwise by saying that the ideal of a University is not so much knowledge, as power. Its business is to convert the knowledge of a boy into the power of a man.

The Rhythmic Character of Growth

I will conclude with two remarks which I wish to make by way of caution in the interpretation of my meaning. The point of this address is the rhythmic character of growth. The interior spiritual life of man is a web of many strands. They do not all grow together by uniform extension. I have tried to illustrate this truth by considering the normal unfolding of the capacities of a child in somewhat favourable circumstances but otherwise with fair average capacities. Perhaps I have misconstrued the usual phenomena. It is very likely that I have so failed, for the evidence is complex and difficult. But do not let any failure in this respect prejudice the main point which I am here to enforce. It is that the development of mentality exhibits itself as a rhythm involving an interweaving of cycles, the whole process being dominated by a greater cycle of the same general character as its minor eddies. Furthermore, this rhythm exhibits certain ascertainable general laws which are valid for most pupils, and the quality of our teaching should be so adapted as to suit the stage in the rhythm to which our pupils have advanced. The problem of a curriculum is not so much the succession of subjects; for all subjects should in essence be begun with the dawn of mentality. The truly important order is the order of quality which the educational procedure should assume.

My second caution is to ask you not to exaggerate into sharpness the distinction between the three stages of a cycle. I strongly suspect that many of you when you heard me detail the three stages in each cycle, said to yourselves—How like a mathematician to make such formal divisions! I assure you that it is not mathematics but literary incompetence that may have led me into the error against which I am warning you. Of course, I mean throughout a distinction of emphasis, of pervasive quality—romance, precision, generalisation, are all present throughout. But there is an alternation of dominance, and it is this alternation which constitutes the cycles.

—Address to the Training College Association of London, 1922.

15

New Problems and
Old Solutions[*]

HARRY S. BROUDY

Is THERE ANY POINT to announcing that the world is undergoing rapid change and that the problems of the sons are not the problems of their fathers and that the solutions of the fathers cannot be the solutions for the sons?

In our own country this fact of change has been made the theme of our most popular philosophy of education. So much so that for many educational workers to dub a proposition or a proposal as old-fashioned is equivalent to proving it false. Accordingly, for anyone to assert that the philosophy of Plato and Aristotle may still have something worthwhile to say to educators is to invite doubt as to his sobriety, sanity, sincerity, or all three.

Yet the Classical Realist, who can be fairly sure of his sobriety and quite sure of his sincerity, does assert this. If he is not insane, he does so because he believes that human nature has an invariant structure and that the truth about that structure is an invariant truth. This means that generically, for man as man, certain types of problems grow out of his nature and not out of his times and circumstances. Fiji Islanders and New Yorkers, in this generic sense, strive for the same satisfactions and are exposed to the same hazards, and if they achieve happiness or misery, it is for the same sort of reasons.

Life is judged good to the degree that we recognize it as resulting

* Harry S. Broudy, "New Problems and Old Solutions," *Studies in Contemporary Educational Thought,* Vol. 40, No. 11. Bulletin of Information, The Kansas State Teachers College of Emporia, November, 1960, pp. 9–24. Used by permission of the author's *Building a Philosophy of Education,* Prentice-Hall, Inc., 2nd edition, 1961.

from our own choice and striving; to the degree that it stretches our powers, and to the extent that it unifies us as persons. To achieve the good life every man has to make his peace with the world of nature by knowing the ways of things, with society by knowing the ways of men, and with himself by knowing what is true, good, and beautiful. Finally, he must know what is really important and commit his whole life to it.

Classical Realism believes that one can meaningfully make statements of this sort about all men at all times, and that in this generic sense, they describe the problems of men and point to the kind of education needed to solve them.

What Classical Realism does not assert is that the individual forms these generic problems assume are the same. These issue from the times and circumstances and not from the nature of man as such. Both the South Sea Islander and the Eskimo strive for self-determination, but what an Eskimo seeks to achieve might be of little use to the South Sea Islander. And if this sounds odd, it may seem less so if we note that if the South Sea Islanders and Eskimos were to study physics, it would be the same physics they would learn even though the applications for the Eskimo would not involve clearing the jungle nor would the South Sea Islander be concerned with the stresses and strains in igloos.

Pragmatic and Experimentalist philosophies of education are fascinated by the great difference between the problems of the Eskimo and South Sea Islander; the Classical Realist sees this difference as real enough but as intelligible only if understood as species or instances of generic similarities in the human lot. He therefore is concerned in *general* education with what South Sea Islander, Eskimo, and New Yorker need to learn as human beings and he leaves to *special* education what people need to learn to become efficient Eskimos, South Sea Islanders, or New Yorkers.

Freedoms of Classical Liberalism

If we face new problems, they are new because they grow out of conditions peculiar to our times, our culture, and our relations with other people who are likewise caught in their own peculiar predicaments. Can we understand these problems as instances of the generic problems of men, of the good life and its hazards?

I think we can say that our problem is still that of achieving self-determination, self-realization, and self-integration, but we are called upon to achieve them in a social order dominated by large scale machine industry. These are not the conditions of agricultural America, or of small business America, or of pioneering-days America, or of small town America of the period between 1860 to 1925.

The word "Self" in the three dimensions of the good life mentioned above is at least one-half of the problem; the nature of large scale machine industry is the other half. Selfhood has to do with individuality; with human beings who regard themselves and would like to be regarded by others as the ultimate units of reality and meaning. Each human being perceives himself as the center of a universe from whom stream purposes and actions and into whom stream the effects of the actions of men and the forces of nature.

Each human being is, in the words of Immanuel Kant, a moral legislator because he can make decisions in terms of whether an action would be "right" and not merely in terms of whether it would be pleasant or expedient. Each human being is a potential creator of new visions of what the world might be, although only a minute fraction of them ever got beyond the state of sporadic dreaming. Each human being is a potential appreciator of beauty, goodness, and truth and a potential sufferer of pain, frustration, tragedy and evil.

Because of these potentialities, it is the individual human being, the person, who stages the drama of life. Values may not originate entirely or even in great part within him, but they cannot be realized apart from him.

In addition, Christianity, Judaism, and their numerous variants relate man to God by an individual relation. Sin, guilt, and salvation once the early tribal forms of religion are transcended, are individual experiences and not collective ones.

Modern democracy made the individual a political unit giving him a voice in community decisions. Modern science and technology provided the community with the means for increasing the potentialities of the individual a thousand fold, especially by relieving him from grinding toil, fear of poverty, and at least some diseases.

Certainly up to very recent times, the notion of the human individual becoming more effective, more free, more cultivated, more humane, more dignified, and indeed even more noble, made sense. It made sense in the Western World in general, but particularly in the United States, where opportunity to grow was greatest and the resulting growth achieved a breath-taking rapidity.

It made sense to talk of free men coming together to decide what they should do about their common concerns. It made sense to say that each man "made up his mind" about political problems and then voted as his conscience and knowledge dictated.

It also made some sense to speak of men as *economically* free. To be sure, some of this was illusory, because what a man chose to do by way of earning a living, and how he prospered at it were never wholly within his control. Nevertheless, there were genuine alternatives open to anyone willing to work hard, willing to take risks, and willing to pull up stakes and strike out in new directions.

It made sense to talk about the human individual being *morally* free. Man perceived the arena of human action as peopled by heroes, villains, and innocent bystanders. He believed that men were to be held responsible for what they did and blamed or praised according to their intentions and their success. If matters turned out well, he sought a hero to reward; if matters turned out otherwise, he grimly looked for a villain to punish, and whether the action was of a private individual or a public official made no difference.

To sum it up, the 19th century and perhaps the first few decades of the 20th century found us thinking in terms of what might be called Classical Liberalism. Men were thought of as free individuals working out their destiny in a society they agreed to form for the sake of their own individual welfare. For the average middle-class American boy—even up to the First World War—the plenitude of Horatio Alger books expressed simply but effectively this life-style and life ideal. Poor but honest; unschooled but intelligent; untrained but industrious; underdog but unafraid; given this combination of traits, fortune would more often than not elevate the hero into a successful middle-class career in the counting house or store of his grateful employer.

It is perhaps a symptom of our times that the Horatio Alger hero would today be forbidden to escape the blessings of schooling, guidance, and vocational training. He would be regarded as a maladjusted truant and his widowed mother, instead of serving as a tragic inspiration, would be reduced to precisely that degree of poverty by mothers' aid and welfare relief which would make both mother and son drably depressed rather than moderately heroic. Perhaps an even more important symptom of these times is that it is difficult to name any set of books that depicts a life-style so clearly recognizable and so widely accepted as was that of the Horatio Alger hero.

Interdependence Vs. Freedom

What has happened to this ideal of free individuals working out their political, economic, and moral destiny in a democratic society?

As an ideal it is still very much with us. To put more and more of man's destiny into his own hands, to make institutions more and more democratic is still the dominant goal of the free world.

However, science and technology have begun to pay the rich dividends of mass production so that the average American has more creature comforts than had the nobles of the Middle Ages and all this by working fewer and fewer hours per week. The great dream of the Enlightenment, viz., that the rational powers of men could be used to pull them from the depths of misery, disease, and poverty were not dreams after all.

There was, however, a price for all this: on the surface a small price, but a price, nevertheless. It was that men should specialize their efforts and then coordinate them. If the work of constructing a motor car could be subdivided into 1000 operations with one man performing each, if the parts were made interchangeable, and if each part could be fitted into the whole at the right time, the cost of automobiles would come down to the point where even the workers could have one—at least. This had been impossible so long as an individual craftsman fashioned the component parts by hand and assembled them himself.

This certainly seemed like a small price to pay for universal automobile ownership. The worker performed an indispensable service, but he himself was no longer indispensable. To be sure, he could bargain with his employer through his union, but as a bargainer he himself amounted to virtually nothing. To be sure, he was well paid and the work was neither exhausting nor uncommonly dangerous, but he needed little skill to perform it; what he needed more was patience to endure it. What came off the line was in a sense his, but not in a very significant sense.

But let us extend this development of the Machine Age a bit further. To make automobiles by mass production one needs large and certain supplies of steel, glass, rubber, cloth, and many other items. The industries making these have to coordinate their efforts so that the right materials and fabricated parts are at the assembly plant at the right time and in the right quantities. For this to happen there have to be elaborate transportation systems that use enormous amounts of power and operate over vast distances. This in turn means roads, rails, and landing fields. Automobiles, moreover, change the clothing, housing, and eating habits of people. For example, people no longer plan overnight housing for visitors because the automobile can carry the visitors away as fast as it brings them in.

The upshot of the matter is an ever tightening interdependence. A network of relations has been woven into which every phase of our life has been enmeshed. For not only has the way we earn a living been caught up in the web, our moral, political, social, and even our aesthetic life have not escaped.

Our moral life, for example, consists of making choices in accordance with what we think is the right thing to do. But the choice is meaningful only for a free man facing genuine alternatives. In the moral life, praise and blame are appropriate categories. We praise him who has done what he should, i.e., what is considered to be right and blame him who has not. But in what sense can we blame a corporation or a nation? If one tries to place the blame for a poor product on a large organization, one soon finds out that each person can show that he had done his part. The fault lies in the whole enterprise or in some anonymous error often slight, taken by itself, that almost never can be traced.

Accordingly, fewer and fewer of the transactions of daily life can appropriately be blamed or praised. These moral labels no longer seem to fit them. And even in our personal life, so much of what we are called upon to decide involves factors over which we have very imperfect control, that we cannot always honestly assume the responsibility for the decision or the consequences.

And so we have reached the point where the criminal, if he is knowledgeable, can claim that his crimes were the results of bad environment and no fault of his own, while the judge can retort that it is the system not he that is responsible for the 10-year sentence about to be imposed.

Heroes and villains are retained in stories and movies albeit not in those making some claim to being serious literature. The new generations are either "Beat" or "Angry," if we are to believe current writers, but for neither condition does the individual hold himself responsible. What is worse, he can find no villain whom he can honestly blame.

Politically, the helplessness of the individual is even more marked. The worker can protect himself only by combining with others in unions. Manufacturers, lawyers, doctors, teachers, and every group with a common interest organized to consolidate tiny fragments of power. Alone they would achieve nothing, but together they may represent enough votes to persuade or intimidate some legislator.

What, for example, is the individual to do about atomic bombs and the threats they pose? The individual feels and to a large extent is helpless. In the last war nothing was more pathetic than the revelation that the individual soldier's skill and courage meant little in the eventual outcome. The individual rebel with or without cause is perceived as a fool not a hero. "Be an intelligent citizen!" we exhort ourselves and others.

"Do your duty, vote, discuss, be active!" But it all comes to nothing unless we organize, submerge ourselves in a cause, become anonymous atoms of power to be used for the common goal, against or with the pressures of other groups. Everywhere power means mass effort and mass effort means Man, not you, not I, not Mr. Jones.

Not even our aesthetic life escapes. Motion picture producers, television officials, book and newspaper publishers cannot afford to cater to small publics. To cater to the big publics means finding what the largest numbers will like and patronize. That which is not so standardized is expensive, hard to get, or requires a refinement of taste and knowledge that only a few possess.

In addition, and this is no small matter, it requires courage to deviate appreciably from what the run of our friends and associates enjoy.

The Self and Its Freedom

It may be asked just why the integration of us all into vast organizations of work, government, and indeed even of play should make life a problem for us. Should it not, it may be asked, simplify matters? To be "other-directed," to use an expression of David Riesman, author of *The Lonely Crowd*, is to relieve us of the need for making decisions at every turn. There is a warm feeling of security in knowing that we are doing what everyone else is doing, and after all, 50 million Frenchmen and 170 million Americans can't be wrong.

Maybe this should be so, but it is not. The loss of control over our decisions is literally a destruction of the Self, for there is less and less that *I* do and think, and more and more of thinking and action that is performed through me. We are all familiar by now with the admonitions of the anthropologists that we are only what our society makes us: that what we think and feel and do is a response to social pressures and demands not of our own making; that the Self as an originator of thought and action is probably an illusion occasioned by our ignorance of the forces that really are moving us.

All of this probably is true, although it is hard to see how this could be established, but even if it were so established, our problems would still be the same: why should people be unhappy over the loss of Selfhood if there is no genuine Selfhood to lose?

The answer to this may well be that the Self which is shaped by social forces, is not the whole Self. We assimilate food to form a body with a unique pattern of fingerprints, hair, and eyes. So may it be that although society provides us with a standard set of drives and means to its satisfaction and even a standard set of molds whereby all of our experience is conceived and named, nevertheless, they result in a unique individual Self.

Each Self has the power to free itself from the sources of its stimuli insofar as it can deal with the symbols of these stimuli rather than the sources themselves. Sticks and stones, the children chant, will break my bones, but names will never hurt me—no, not even the names of sticks and stones. From the concepts of hero, green grass, gridiron, football, and Saturday, I can conjure up an image of myself the hero of a football game lying on the green grass of the gridiron on a Saturday afternoon.

In imagination, in dream and in thought, the shuffling of what has come into our experience from the culture goes on incessantly. When it is guided by the rules of logic, we call it thought; by the rules of aesthetics we call it art; by the rules of usefulness we call it invention, by the rules of wish and desire we call it dreaming or wishful thinking.

Yet these evanescent, symbolic creations can become the goals and aspirations of the person and accordingly he can act upon the world and his culture in a way that would have been impossible had he not lived.

To be, for a human being, is first of all to be a source of decision, a source of commitment. It is to be a source of action as well as a source of reaction. In a tightly integrated world, human life is indeed possible and can even be enticingly comfortable, but to the extent that we merely react to the demands of our social milieu in our average socially-conditioned way, we are not truly individual Selves, but rather a social Self— an instrument of the social order. This mode of life is a threat to the personal, individual, creative Self whose autonomy of imagination and thought is frustrated and nullified by a social order in which he cannot act in any really important way; where his free choices are among the trivia of life rather than among the essentials. There are for him, in the words of William James, no "momentous options."

When frustrated the Self becomes unhappy, uneasy, bored and seeks to escape its *malaise* by whatever routes its imagination can devise. He joins lodges, goes in for hobbies, becomes as eccentric as he dares. Free floating anxiety increases, and he worries about the future instead of planning for it. He exaggerates his grievances over minutiae inasmuch as he can do little about his grievances over the major matters. In a word, his mental health is impaired.

If genuine Selfhood is indispensable to human happiness, and if our social order is heading toward a form where this Selfhood is threatened, we have a problem indeed. And it is new because at no time in history has the threat to individuality taken precisely this form. It is not simply the threat of another tyrant who wished to rule our lives; this we understand. It is not simply the threat of a natural catastrophe such as an Ice Age that will reduce our life to that of struggling physical organisms. It is not even the threat of atomic war and destruction. It is new because the threat is garbed in the gifts of material well-being. These we cannot even consider giving up, and yet the price of these gifts may be Selfhood itself.

Solutions New and Old

The conflict between the individual and the social order is hardly new, and social philosophy has always been concerned with resolving it. We can, I believe, sort out three types of solutions. Each has a more or less modern version developed to meet the current edition of recurrent problems.

1. The first group I would call corporate identification. Historically, it is represented first by tribalism in which the group is regarded as a single person; in which every man is responsible for the action of the group and the group for the action of each individual. Even divinities were identified with separate tribes.

A philosophical version of this solution is the Absolute Idealism of Hegel, Bosanquet, and Royce. These philosophers argue that the individual can realize himself only through the social institutions and cultural resources provided by his society. He can be self-determining only if he can utilize the power of these institutions, and he can integrate his life only by identifying his goals with the goals of the group. Without arguing that totalitarian governments derive their *methods* from Absolute Idealism, it nevertheless remains true that the submission of the individual to the State—joyfully or otherwise—receives no little support from this kind of conception.

Advocates of democratic methods also want to secure corporate identification, i.e., to have the individual identify his good with that of the group. However, the responsibility for deciding both what is good for himself and for the community is placed upon the individual. Democratic deliberation and discussion should result ideally in a community of persuasion.

Even since the depression of the Thirties, educational philosophers in our country have been torn between their desire to preserve the rights of the individual, to determine the common good and the rights of the group, to coerce recalcitrant members who through stupidity, stubborn-ness or some emotional block cannot or will not see that their own ulti-mate welfare coincides with the welfare of the group. We find this conflict in the writings of John Dewey, and W. H. Kilpatrick of the Ex-perimentalist School, but we also find it in writings of Robert M. Hutchins of the conservative school.

Not a little of the ingenuity of modern educators has gone into ex-ploring *methods of persuading individuals* to uncoerced consensus.[1] Role playing, group therapy, and group dynamics in general are devoted to producing corporate identification with a minimum of psychical dam-age to the individual ego.

An educational program that places all of its eggs in this basket will stress the skills of group living, of getting along, of communication, of democratic leadership. These social learnings will have high priority. The learning of standard subject matter will be relegated to means, and not always the most important means, of reaching human relation goals. Because this philosophy is so violently opposed to absolute principles and rules, every phase of life is, theoretically at least, to be regulated by what the group after due deliberation finds it advisable to do.

That this approach evades the evils of despotic totalitarianism can be granted; that it tries to preserve the dignity and meaning of the individual is undeniable. But what kind of individuality is preserved? It is the social Self that is built and nurtured in this way. A sensitive "other-directed" personality is what this approach to life is most likely to produce. The deviate is treated with less harshness and arbitrariness than in an absolutistic system; he is treated as sick or maladjusted to be rehabilitated not punished.

Life on this approach achieves a high level of social accommodation. The quality of life imposed upon us by our aloneness is shunned as slightly pathological. Yet the great literature, religion, and art of a people often rise from this well of solitude; from personalities who in suffering create new patterns of value possibility. Such new visions are not the product of committees, bureaus, and conferences. They are created by individuals of great capacity who transcend for a while their social Selves, i.e., the demands and pressures of communal life.

It may well be that in a democratic society the educator must devote the major part of his time and resources to the average person in his communal life, i.e., to the social Self, but if the democratic society is to

[1] *The Improvement of Practical Intelligence,* by R. Bruce Raup *et al.* New York: Harper & Brothers, 1950.

prosper and progress, it will need the kind of individual to whom the educator is likely to pay little attention. Much of the current wave of resentment against public education stems from the feeling that it has neglected these highly gifted individuals and that we have consequently suffered a loss of leadership *vis à vis* the Soviet Union. This criticism may be misguided in the form in which it is usually presented, but it is hard to deny that the group approach to learning, if carried too far, will cancel out individual variations, and possibly those luck shots that revolutionize thought and action.

Equally serious is the possibility that even in the case of the ordinary individual, the level of value realization will be lowered by an over-zealous group approach. Will the individual be permitted or persuaded to seek higher levels of intellectual, moral, and aesthetic experience than the group, at any given time, demands?

2. A quite different solution to the problem of the individual and the social order might be called *solution by revolt*. This can take one of two forms: revolt by defiance and/or revolt by flight, physical or psychical.

The revolt by flight is really a retreat from the demands of group life into the mountains or desert as a hermit, or into a more simple stage of life, as when a gifted artist or engineer retires to the lonely seaside and spends his days whittling at the country store. These are dramatic flights. Day-dreaming, escapes into fiction and fantasy are not so drastic but no less escapes. A sudden abandonment of the world for the life of a religious recluse may be another form of this revolt. One could list many more.

Revolt by defiance has a different mood. Here the individual acknowledges that he cannot destroy the social order and that he cannot really free himself from it. He sees no rational way of asserting his Selfhood, for rationally the more he surveys the world, the less essential he as an individual is to it. Very well, he will assert his freedom and individuality in spite of all the reasons against it and the lack of reasons for it. He will act, become engaged in the fight for something or other with all his vigor despite all obstacles. He will make himself felt, even though he perish in the process.

This sort of defiance, associated with the Existentialist philosophy of *Jean-Paul Sartre*,[2] has a strong appeal to the post-war generations who have trouble in finding any sense in any pattern of social life. Sometimes it takes the form of criminal attacks on the social order; at others, it may be dramatically courageous action in behalf of some social cause. Inas-

[2] *Existentialism*, tr. by Bernard Frechtman, New York: The Philosophical Library, 1947.

much as it is not a rational justification that the defiant one seeks, it is impossible to predict what form the self-assertion will take, except that it will be vigorous, persistent, and difficult to ignore.

3. A third form of the revolt is somewhere between outright attack and retreat. It is a division of the Self into a group member for part of the time and into an escapee from it at another. In this form one stays on his job, performs one's social duties acceptably. He reserves, however, a secret part of his life, like the famous Walter Mitty, for solitary adventures in the aesthetic life, climbing mountains, in romance, or in any one of a thousand activities that may distinguish him from the crowd or release him from its expectations.

About the solutions by revolt one may observe that they do not accomplish what they promise, viz., to restore the individual's freedom, self-realization, and integrity. In flight, the individual may achieve a freedom from the restraints of social life, but not freedom for anything that he really values. The values he can realize apart from the social context are meager and what sort of integration can he achieve if he cannot forget that he has achieved serenity by surrender? And forget completely he cannot.

The solution by defiance, despite its heroic aspects, comes to no more than a pathetic gesture, unless the cause in behalf of which he dares all is itself an heroic cause. But once our actor has admitted that not all causes are necessarily heroic, the strength of his position evaporates. His assertion of the Self is an assertion of freedom, but he is forthwith a slave to whatever project he has committed himself, inasmuch as only loyal devotion to it makes sense of his gesture. And yet given a cause large enough and a personality sufficiently cultivated one can conceive a life pattern with a high order of freedom, self-realization, and self-integration. Perhaps the real attractiveness of this solution lies in the courage it demands and manifests for it is difficult not to admire courage whatever form it takes.

4. I come now to what I regard as on old solution to the new problem of our time.

Our task is to find a formula for life that will provide the maximum of subjective happiness or sense of well-being with the maximum of social usefulness. How can I live a life that in the long run will be felt as satisfactory and which at the same time meets the demands of my social order? Nay, even exceeds these demands and leaves it a better social order for my having lived in it? How can my life be both subjectively and objectively good?

The answer of Classical Realism is self-cultivation. Cultivation of the individual's capacity to achieve value in the intellectual, moral, and aesthetic departments of experience. For education it has always meant the appropriation by the individual of the best and noblest of the cultural resources of his time. It has meant to become a connoisseur in every area of human life, so that the individual not only lives, but lives well.

This conception of life and education assumes that there are levels of value experience. The social Self tends to experience these at the average level of group approval and competence. This is a necessary minimum in order to provide a flywheel for social life in which similarity of attitude and knowledge assures efficiency in action and uniformity in feeling. Intellectually, this is the level represented academically by the grade of C. Morally, it is represented by the stage in which custom and law define behavior. Aesthetically, it is represented by popular literature, music, and art. The social Self when healthy reaches this level, but does not need to rise above it.

To go beyond the good-enough requires a high degree of self-cultivation, or a degree of education that goes well beyond the aspirations of most men. Indeed, one wonders whether any man without special stimulation would ever get started on the arduous road beyond the mediocre and good-enough.

The first stage of self-cultivation is mastery of the arts of learning. Among these we include the skills of acquiring knowledge. They include the symbolic skills such as reading and mathematics, the skills of thinking, communicating, and studying. For the well-educated man these arts are perfected to the point of effortless use; to the point where he enjoys the use of them. With Aristotle this view holds that pleasure is the *natural accompaniment of good* functioning.[3]

Beyond the arts of learning the road of cultivation penetrates the knowledge and art selected by the best minds of every epoch. Here are the Sciences and the Humanities; what men of training, experience, knowledge, and life-long devotion to study have judged to be true, good, and beautiful. There is perhaps no end to this road, but each step along the way makes of the traveler a finer instrument of discrimination, action, and thought.

Subjectively, therefore, a high order of cultivation opens to us the heights and depths of value experience, closed to those unwilling to perfect their capacities for it. But it means even more. It means greater freedom for the individual, because the greater his knowledge, the more his power is increased over the potentialities of technological civilization. Technology can make it possible for the cultivated man to own more

[3] *Nicomachean Ethics,* 1175a 21–22.

great books than did the kings of Medieval days, but for the man without cultivation technology can do little. Technology can make available to millions our greatest dramas, but it cannot give these millions the cultivation they need to enjoy them.

For the cultivated man, therefore, the opportunities for highly individualized forms of self-determination, self-realization, and self-integration are made possible by the technical resources afforded by the new Machine Age. And, it may be added, as this Age works itself out to its technological conclusion, more time should be available to the individual both for self-cultivation and the fruits thereof.

However, if subjective happiness were the only result of cultivation, it could hardly be defensible as a solution, because too much of this happiness would be purchased by the individual at the cost of the group whose institutions and efforts made his happiness possible. Self-cultivation, if it is to be defended as a mode of life and education, must also be socially good.

If we ask ourselves what it takes in the way of character and knowledge to maintain and guide a highly developed technological society, I think the case for self-cultivation is not hard to make out.

Political freedom is still possible in our time, but only if we can achieve understanding in political science, economics, sociology, social psychology, and kindred subjects. The day when such complex issues as taxation, foreign policy, and foreign trade can be intelligently decided around the cracker barrel or through reading the editorials of the local newspapers is probably gone forever.

Intellectual freedom is still possible and indeed it is what makes all the other freedoms possible in our time. However, to be intellectually free means to know much more about more subjects than was necessary for our forebears. A simple grounding in the three r's is no longer sufficient to enable the individual to form rationally defensible opinions.

Finally, even moral freedom is still possible, if we meet the terms imposed by new conditions. True, the heroes and villains are no longer so easily discernible as they once were. But this does not so much release us from our obligations to choose wisely as it increases the amount of knowledge needed to make a wise and just decision. The examination of the consequences of our acts is now a complicated and sophisticated procedure. Simple goodness of heart, while still a necessary condition for morality, is no longer a sufficient condition.

We could go into the problems of aesthetic freedom, religious freedom, and freedom in all areas of life. But the analysis would be more or less the same, viz., the cultivation of our powers through the best knowledge available alone frees us from the web of interdependence of the Machine Age. It frees us not by escape or flight, nor by indiscriminate immersion into group enterprises. It frees us by giving us a chance to envision a type of behavior and life that expresses us as individuals and not merely as members of a class. And all this with the possibility that our own individuality may enrich the character of the social Self that registers the progress of the social order.

It may be objected that the cult of excellence or the cult of self-cultivation is after all an aristocratic ideal valid only for the gifted few with the leisure and the brains to undertake it. Much of the antagonism to the Classical Realistic position comes from sincere educators who fear that the goal of self-cultivation is incompatible with a democratic society.

But if our argument means anything it is that the democratic social order in a Machine Age is impossible unless the members undertake self-cultivation on a large scale. Can this be done? Differences in brains and talent cannot be denied, and fortunately do not have to be. Individuality and excellence do not prescribe in advance any one particular combination of talents. All they ask for is the full exploitation of the capacities the person happens to have. Highly intelligent mediocrity is less individual, less interesting, and less fruitful for the social life of the community than the authentic life-style of a person with a more modest native inheritance.

The great sin is not lack of brains, but lack of cultivation is a principle and a promise that the science of education is obligated to redeem, and there is reason to believe that it can redeem it.

If we were to restate this long elaboration of the old answer to the new problem it might be that we ought to become connoisseurs in as many areas of value experience as circumstances permit and that general education in school should set us well on the road to doing so.

So viewed the new age need hold no terror for us, and the work of previous ages need not be thrown away in despair. Man is still man and the dyamics of his happiness and the requirements for the good life and good society are generically the same. There is a sense in which problems and answers are neither old nor new; it is the sense in which they are timeless structures revealed in a timeless insight in the form of universal truths.

Harry Samuel Broudy (July 27, 1905—) was born in Filipowa, Poland, but he received his higher education in American institutions. He earned the A.B. at Boston University in 1929, and the M.A. (1933) and Ph.D. (1935) at Harvard. He began his professional career in 1935 as an assistant in Philosophy at Harvard. The next year he served as a supervisor in the Division University extension, Massachusetts State Department of Education. In 1937 he became director of graduate study for the Massachusetts State Teachers Colleges. In 1938–39 he was in charge of tabulation and interpretation of the Rural School Survey in Massachusetts.

Professor Broudy was appointed professor of Philosophy and Education at Massachusetts State Teachers College, North Adams, in 1937. Two years later he took a similar position in the Massachusetts State Teachers College, Framingham. Since 1957 he has been professor of Education in the College of Education, University of Illinois. In addition, he was visiting lecturer at Boston University in 1951 and 1956, and taught during summers at New York University (1950), the University of Southern California (1949 and 1956), and the University of Florida (1955 and 1957).

Professor Broudy's best-known work is Building a Philosophy of Education. *He co-authored* Massachusetts Youth Study, Psychology for General Education, Exemplars of Teaching Method, Democracy and Excellence in American Secondary Education, *and has contributed articles to a number of journals in education and philosophy. Professor Broudy calls himself a classical realist.*

16

Locksley Hall:
A College of the Future[*]

ROBERT MAYNARD HUTCHINS

I HAVE THOUGHT that instead of presenting an article of my own, I might offer here the annual report of the Chairman of the Faculty of Locksley Hall for the year 1988–89.

The report begins:

To the Board of Visitors of Locksley Hall:

As the elected representative of the faculty, I have the honor to submit its report for the year 1988–89. At this time, which marks the expiration of my five-year term and the end of the first 25 years of the College, it seems appropriate to review the history of the College since its foundation. This will necessarily involve some account of the origins and progress of the state of Rancho del Rey.

As is well known, the state of Rancho del Rey originated in the gift to the public by the owners of the King Ranch in Texas of 100,000 square miles. The reason for the gift was that the owners of the ranch had become convinced that the development of people was more important than that of animals. They therefore determined to provide a refuge for those who could not face the prospect of having their children go through the American educational system, but who did not wish to secede from the Union. Two conditions were attached to the gift. First, the land was to be organized into a state in accordance with the provisions of the

[*] Robert M. Hutchins, "Locksley Hall: A College for the Future," *School and Society*, Vol. 87, September 12, 1959, pp. 334–338. Used by permission.

Address to the Conference on the Shape of a College for the Future, Miami University, Oxford, Ohio, April 18, 1959.

treaty between the Republic of Texas and the United States. Second, American women of child-bearing age who had children under 12 were to have priority in gaining entrance to and owning land in the new state. Those who were married were permitted to bring their husbands with them if they wished.

The financial resources of the donors were such that they easily persuaded the legislature of Texas to see the merits of their plan, and since both houses of Congress had for many years been controlled by residents of Texas, no difficulty was experienced in Washington. President Stevenson signed the measure on Christmas Day, 1964, and Rancho del Rey was admitted to the Union on January 1, 1965. Immigration began at dawn the next day, and our state, which was formerly occupied by a few cowboys and a couple of million cattle, is now the most densely populated in the Union, having passed Rhode Island in 1975. As loyal Americans we hope that the depopulation that has taken place in other states will prove to be only temporary.

It cannot be too often emphasized that Locksley Hall is only one unit in the educational system of Rancho del Rey and that its dependence on the other units in the system is complete. For example, the average student at Locksley Hall finishes his formal liberal education at the age of 18. This would not be possible in the three years ordinarily spent here if it were not for the organization of the six-year elementary schools and three-year high schools of this state. On the other hand, 50% of our graduates go on to the University, and this would not be possible if it were not for the recognition by the University that liberal education is the best preparation for professional study and research. If I may be pardoned a personal word, I may say that one of the most moving experiences of my life was that day 1967 on which the Cosmological Faculty of the University, at the insistence of the sub-faculty in medicine, voted down special requirements in mathematics and science for entrance to medical work and decided to admit applicants on the basis of their fulfillment of the requirements of Locksley Hall in liberal education.

First, then, Locksley Hall has flourished because of the excellence of the educational system of which it is a part. A second reason for its success is that there never has been any doubt about its own role in the system. It is devoted solely to liberal education, the education that every citizen ought to have. In the schools and colleges of Rancho del Rey vocational training is unknown. The constant acceleration of technology since the '50's and the steady reduction in the working week to the present 20 hours have made direct preparation for earning a living in the educational system an obvious absurdity. In this state young people are trained for jobs on the job. The object of the educational system is to teach them what they cannot learn on the job—how to be citizens and human beings. As the Commanding Officer of the United Nations Police Force, Chief John Eisenhower, has nobly said, "The one certain calling is citizenship; the one certain destiny is manhood."

Locksley Hall has no departments. All members of the faculty are expected to be able to give instruction in all the subjects studied in the College. It has, however, three divisions. In addition to the division devoted to the instruction of youth, it has a division for the preparation of teachers and one for the education of adults.

Among the many blessings conferred upon us by the Founding Fathers of Rancho del Rey, the constitutional prohibition against academic degrees must come high on the list. The statutory prohibition of schools of education has proved equally valuable. The two together have meant that in this state it has been possible to educate teachers. In the early days there were fears of a teacher shortage; but they did not materialize. Every intelligent man and woman teaching in the United States started for Rancho del Rey as soon as the state was opened up to settlement. In the effort to establish their priority, many of these teachers adopted children under 12, and I regret to say that one distinguished male scholar from Columbia was detected at the border disguised as a pregnant woman. Candor compels me to add that teachers' salaries in Rancho del Rey have always been somewhat higher than elsewhere. This is because of the constitutional provision known as the General Motors Index, which stipulates that the compensation of teachers must always be equal to that of junior executives in that great corporation.

A powerful inducement to teachers to join the faculty of Locksley Hall is the complete independence and freedom that we enjoy. Locksley Hall has no president and no board of trustees. The Board of Visitors has no power; the faculty of the College has the legal as well as the moral responsibility for its management. The faculty is aware, however, that all bodies of privileged persons inevitably tend to deteriorate and therefore welcomes the public and private criticism that the Board has lavished upon it in the last 25 years. The faculty knows that its rejection of many of the recommendations of the Board would have provoked, in lesser men, some feelings of resentment. The principle that management is the function of the faculty and criticism the function of the Board is now established, and all parties are agreed that it must remain forever inviolate.

It must be added that the freedom we enjoy is accompanied by a responsibility we did not expect. It is very convenient to have somebody else to blame. Here at Locksley Hall we of the faculty can blame nobody but ourselves. We cannot evade the consequences of our weakness and self-seeking by relying on the President or the Trustees to save us from them, and we are denied the consolation of attributing whatever anybody in or out of the College does not like about it to the arrogance of the administration and the stupidity of the Board. In the early years of the College some of my older brethren, who had been brought up under a different system, felt so uncomfortable when called upon to cast votes for which they would be held responsible that they echoed the cry of the ancient Israelites, "Give us a King to rule over us." Fortunately, wiser counsels prevailed. We have been much assisted by the fact that we have no departments and no academic ranks. These fruitful sources of group bickering and individual animosity being absent, we have been able to think for an increasing part of the time when we are together about what is good for the College and for the community. But it is no use denying that the path has been a hard one. We record again our gratitude to the Board of Visitors for helping us to be better than we otherwise would have been.

The number of teachers required in Rancho del Rey was small in proportion to the population because the number of subjects taught was somewhat less than a third of the number taught in other states. My great predecessor, the first Chairman of the Faculty, had emblazoned on the walls of the senior common room as a constant reminder to us all the words of Sir Richard Livingstone: "The good schoolmaster is known by the number of valuable subjects he declines to teach." The excellence of the elementary and secondary schools and the fact that students do not come to us until they have passed the examinations in these schools mean that Locksley Hall never has had to offer remedial work in Greek or Latin, to say nothing of mathematics or English. The students arrive at our gates prepared to go on with these subjects and to add to them the exploration of the world of ideas, which is, of course, their main business with us. These limitations on the number of subjects taught have made possible the level of teachers' salaries that the General Motors Index requires.

Of course, a good deal of re-training was necessary to permit our educational system to absorb the teaching immigrants to whom I have referred. Most of them never had had any liberal education. By the use of films, television (open and closed circuit), and the teaching machines invented by B. F. Skinner, we were able to expedite this process.

Today prospective teachers at Locksley Hall get a liberal education. They then go on to the University to study one or more of the three fields to which the University confines itself—theology, cosmology, and law.

Thereafter, they work here as apprentice teachers with the more experienced members of the staff. Every seminar and discussion group at Locksley Hall has two teachers—a senior and a junior member of the faculty. The teachers learn to teach by teaching.

The constitutional prohibition of academic degrees has had one incidental benefit: commencement exercises are unknown in Rancho del Rey. At no time, therefore, is a citizen of this state given the impression that he has completed his education. The state is a community learning together, and the citizen is expected to keep on learning throughout his life. This is why the curriculum of Locksley Hall could remain simple and clear: the College has been under no pressure to teach every young student everything that he might need to know at later stages of his career. The aim of the College is to teach the student what he needs to know in order to keep on learning, to awaken his interest in continued learning, and to train him in the habits that will help him to learn whatever he wants to learn.

Locksley Hall is the realization of the ambition that Woodrow Wilson expressed just 80 years ago. He said, "Here is the key to the whole matter: the object of the college . . . is not scholarship . . . but the intellectual and spiritual life. Its life and discipline are meant to be a process of preparation, not a process of information. By the intellectual and spiritual life I mean the life which enables the mind to comprehend and make proper use of the modern world and all its opportunities. The object of a liberal training is not learning, but discipline and the enlightenment of the mind. . . . What we should seek to impart in our colleges, therefore, is not so much learning as the spirit of learning. You can impart that to young men; and you can impart it to them in the three or four years at your disposal." Having acquired this spirit, the 50% of our graduates who do not go on to the University are expected, like the other citizens of this state, to enroll in discussion groups in which their intellectual interests and capacities may develop. The faculty of Locksley Hall organizes such groups for adults of this community who wish to continue their liberal education.

In the educational system of Rancho del Rey, time-serving and the accumulation of credits are unknown. Goals are set up for the students to reach. The examinations determine whether or not he has reached them. The student may present himself for the examinations whenever he is ready to do so. If he fails, he may take them again. The chronological age of students and what used to be called their "adjustment to the group" are matters of supreme indifference to everybody, including the student himself and his contemporaries. I have said that in Rancho del

Rey the elementary school takes six years and the high school and the college three years each. But these are statements of averages. The goals having been set by the teaching staff, it was found that in the ordinary case six years of instruction prepared the pupil for the examinations of the elementary school, three years for the high school, and three years more for the college. As far as Locksley Hall is concerned, 10% of our students graduate in less than three years, and 10% in more. Eighty per cent take the average time.

The goal that was set for the students of Locksley Hall was the acquisition of that education which in the opinion of the faculty was necessary for a free man in a free society. It cannot be too strongly insisted that the educational program of Locksley Hall was designed for everybody and that experience has shown that it can be mastered by everybody, though at different rates of speed. If there is one thing that the history of Locksley Hall demonstrates, it is that the ancient American doctrine that the course of study must be trivial and the life of the student frivolous because most young people cannot be interested in anything important is as fallacious as it was popular. The Latin motto of the Students' Association of Locksley Hall is *sero sed serio*—we may be young, but we are in earnest.

All citizens of Rancho del Rey are expected to achieve the education that is offered by Locksley Hall. Although the intellectual attainments of the people of this state are clearly higher than those of any other, there is no evidence that their native capacities exceed those of persons born elsewhere. Since the founding of this country, experience everywhere has shown that the young American will respond to the best that can be offered him. The reason he has been offered in some places less than the best is that his elders do not want to take the trouble to find out what the best is or to find out how it may be effectively offered. We have known, moreover, since the time of Plato that what is honored in a country will be cultivated there. The state of Rancho del Rey was established in honor of the human mind. It was to be a community learning together. The culture of this state, therefore, supports at every point the serious intellectual purpose of the educational system of this state.

To descend to a more practical level, consider, if you will, the effect upon the interests and, hence, upon the development of the young of a system in which everybody has studied or is studying the same things and has a common language and a common stock of ideas. At Locksley Hall, for example, the faculty and all the students have followed or are following the same prescribed curriculum and are discussing the issues it raises throughout their waking hours. The multiplication of the power of the individual through the support of the academic community is added to the multiplication of this power that comes from the support of the larger community outside. We are perfectly prepared to believe that students who have succeeded with us would have failed elsewhere. We suggest, as Edward Gibbon did long ago, that like conditions produce like effects.

The conditions obtaining in Rancho del Rey have made it, as everybody knows, the cultural center of the world. The head of the Chinese delegation to the United Nations remarked last year that Peking even today had not achieved the beauty, serenity, and vitality of our capital, and the President of Greece has applied to our state the words in which Pericles described his native city. The principal newspapers, publishing houses, magazines, dramatic groups, film studios, and television networks now have their headquarters here. The leading artists, writers, musicians, scientists and scholars of the world now reside among us.

But it would be selfish of us to be concerned only with the happiness of our own state. In every walk of life the citizens of Rancho del Rey and the graduates of Locksley Hall—the oldest of whom are now about 40—are making a world-wide contribution. It often has been remarked that it is fortunate the graduates of Locksley Hall are not much interested in making money, because their equipment is such that if they wanted to, they would make all the money there was. In the professions, in politics, and in business they have distinguished themselves, earning the affection of their alma mater and the admiration of their fellow citizens.

The period through which we lived in the '40's, '50's, and early '60's of this century is now commonly called the Age of Illusion. It was a period in which things were not what they seemed, or at least not what we said they were. At this epoch Americans were in the habit of saying one thing and believing another and thinking one thing and doing another. Numerous efforts were made to repeal the Law of Contradiction. The fact was that our situation had changed too fast for our ideas. The result was that we could offer no rational explanation for much that we did. For example, we had an economic theory built on the mindless mechanism of the market and a political theory based on the conception of the night watchman state. When these theories appeared inapplicable and unworkable in an advanced industrial society, we had no guide to intelligent action. The educational system of those days was suitable to the production of consumers, jobholders, objects of propaganda, and statistical units. The universities were not centers of independent thought. They appeared designed for vocational certification and highly specialized research. In their never-ending quest for money, they felt compelled to sell themselves to the highest bidder. Instead of enlightening the society, particularly about its own shortcomings, they flattered it. Hence, they flattered and perpetuated its illusions.

The era that now seems to be dawning will be called, we hope, the Age of Reason. The change began with the end of the Cold War and the transfer of all weapons to the United Nations 15 years ago. That made it possible for us to begin to think what we were doing and to reflect at last in a rational way about how we might use our resources for the benefit of our fellow citizens in America and throughout the world. The change has been accelerated by the example of the State of Rancho del Rey and by the work of its people. In this change, Locksley Hall is proud to have played a modest part.

Robert Maynard Hutchins (January 17, 1899—) began his higher education at Oberlin College at the age of sixteen. He interrupted his studies during World War I to enter ambulance service with the American and Italian armies. The war over, he entered Yale University, where he received the A.B. degree in 1921, an honorary A.M. in 1922, and the L.L.B. in 1925. Many universities both here and abroad have honored him with the L.L.D.

Hutchins' teaching career began in 1921 with his appointment as master of English and History at the Lake Placid School in New York. He next went to Yale in 1923 as secretary of that institution, where he rose to lecturer in the Law School in 1925, acting dean in 1927, and dean in 1928. He also served as professor of Law at Yale from 1927 to 1929. He left that position to accept the presidency of the University of Chicago, where he served as chancellor from 1945 to 1951. From 1951 to 1954 he was associate director of the Ford Foundation. He has served as president of the Fund for the Republic since 1954.

Hutchins' work in higher education is widely known. As a classical humanist he has advocated a return to the liberal-arts curriculum of the medieval university. Partly influenced by Adler, he recommended basing the undergraduate curriculum on the great books of Western civilization—the works of approximately one hundred writers from Homer to the present—and supplementing this program with additional reading. His theory is that as the student reads these books he learns how the great thinkers reasoned, thus learning to think independently. More than a dozen books based on Hutchins' lectures have been published.

Recommended Readings for Part Four

Students are urged to consult the annotated bibliography at the end of this volume for information on the books cited here.

The following books in philosophy and philosophy of education should be especially useful.

A. PHILOSOPHY:

PAUL EDWARDS and ARTHUR PAP (eds.), *A Modern Introduction to Philosophy*

EDWIN HOLT, *The New Realism: Cooperative Study in Philosophy*

RALPH BARTON PERRY, *Realms of Value*

BERTRAND RUSSELL, *The Problems of Philosophy*

PAUL ARTHUR SCHILPP, *The Philosophy of Alfred North Whitehead*

HERBERT W. SCHNEIDER, *A History of American Philosophy*

ROY WOOD SELLARS, *The Philosophy of Physical Realism*

MORTON WHITE, *The Age of Analysis*

A. N. WHITEHEAD, *Science and the Modern World*

B. PHILOSOPHY OF EDUCATION:

ARISTOTLE, *Politics*

HAROLD DUNKEL, *Whitehead on Education*

NELSON B. HENRY, *Modern Philosophies and Education*

A. N. WHITEHEAD, *Aims of Education*

Religious Thought and Philosophy of Education

Introduction to Part Five

THE NEXT PART of these readings will be devoted to a discussion of some of the philosophies underlying parochial education in this country.

While there is no one Catholic philosophy of education, there is considerable agreement among Catholic educators concerning the philosophical bases of education, and these common convictions find application in the largest number of parochial schools controlled by any religious group in this nation. By the beginning of this century there were more than 850,000 students enrolled in Catholic elementary and secondary schools. By the 1958–59 school year the number had increased to nearly 5,000,000, and by 1965–66, it had increased to over 5,500,000. Thus, when we consider Catholic education, we are not concerned with a minute part of the total scene of this country.

The Catholics felt themselves forced to build and maintain separate schools. During the colonial period, the Catholics lived outside the cultural and political activities for the most part. And although some of the more onerous disabilities and penalties placed upon Catholics by a predominately Protestant nation were lifted at the start of the national period, only four states in their constitutional conventions gave Catholics political rights that were equal to those granted Protestants. Moreover, Catholics considered their situation intolerable when they found their youth attending schools where Protestant hymns were sung and prayers said, and where the textbooks contained statements that they found objectionable. Even the Catholic-founded state of Maryland passed "An Act to Prevent the Growth of Popery." The Catholics, therefore, turned to the establishing of their own schools, a practice which, as we have seen, has been continued.

The first Catholic school in the British colonies was established about 1640 by the Jesuits in Maryland at a place called St. Mary's City. The next two schools to be founded were likewise in Maryland: at Newton in 1673, and at Bohemia Manor in 1744. In the nineteenth century the number of Catholics migrating to America greatly increased. This increase, the continued insistence upon the reading of the Protestant Bible in the state schools, and what the Catholics themselves came to recognize as a serious leakage from the Church led certain bishops to hold a series of seven "Provincial Councils" between the years of 1829 and 1949.

In 1829 the seven bishops who attended the first Provincial Council in Baltimore urged the necessity for Catholic schools. They insisted that the grave loss of faith on the part of Catholic boys and girls, particularly those from poor families, required the establishment of schools free from the defects that marred available schools. By 1840 the situation was thought not to have improved, and again the bishops assembled in Baltimore to urge their priests to protest current practice in the non-Catholic schools. The fifth Provincial Council of 1843, likewise held in Baltimore, observed that the same objectionable practices were being continued in the available schools. As the direct result of the exhortations of the Provincial Council individuals, bishops, and regional councils of bishops began to order priests to establish parochial schools and to require Catholic parents to send their children to them. It was in the Midwest that this movement found its greatest support, especially in the action of the second Provincial Council of Cincinnati, which ordered all pastors of souls to provide a school in each parish or congregation to be under the direction of the congregation and the priest. In the fall of 1884 the third Plenary Council of Baltimore ordered that within two years a parochial school be built near the church and maintained "in perpetuum." It was in this way that Catholic schools came to be founded in this nation, and it accounts for their continued growth as the Catholic population grew.

In one of the most important pronouncements on Catholic education, "The Christian Education of Youth" (*Divini Illius Magistri*), Pope Pius XI explained the nature of education; the division of rights in education between the Church, the family, and the state; the environment and subject of education; and the proper end of education. Some of the presuppositions, stated or implied in the encyclical letter, concern the natural order, while certain others pertain to what the Catholics would call the supernatural order. Together these presuppositions form "a perennial unchanging charter" which, from the beginning of the Christian era, has served as the solid core of its philosophy. This core consists of a belief in a personal God whose existence can be proved by reason. Man is by nature a rational free being whose perfection consists in knowing and possessing goodness, truth, and beauty. Man has both a spiritual soul and a material body; the former enables him to transcend the material, while the latter enables him to have a continuity with nature. God placed man upon this earth and endowed him with a supernature by which he can eventually share in a divine life after a period of trial. Adam, the first man, fell from God's favor and thus lost for the entire human race the conditionally promised supernatural life. But the Eternal Son of God was sent to redeem man and to restore to him God's grace and the supernatural life. The educated person, then, is formed in the example and teaching of Christ, who has been called the perfect man. A more recent statement on Christian education came from the Second Vatican Council and is reproduced in full in Chapter 17.

Chapter 18 from Cunningham's *Pivotal Problems of Education,* discusses the fourfold development of man and the educative process

Chapter 19 explains some of the principles and practices of Lutheran education (Missouri Synod), while Chapter 20 presents what one Jewish scholar believes to be the reorientation necessary for Jewish education in an age of science.

The Lutheran religion was brought to America by Swedish and German colonists. And, though they were Protestants, they soon felt the lash of civil government and some of the same religious restrictions of which the Catholics complained. As a result they began to establish separate schools. Among the Protestants, the Lutherans have been the most active in founding schools, and, among the Lutherans, it has been the Missouri Synod that has built the most schools and enrolled the most pupils. The Missouri Synod, established in 1847, is one of several associations of Lutheran congregations that are called synods and that were organized to aid the clergy, extend missionary efforts, promote education, etc. This particular synod is composed of congregations from almost every continent. In North America alone, the Synod's 1,374 elementary schools enroll over 161,000 pupils, while approximately thirty secondary schools have more than 13,750 students.

Mr. Allan Hart Jahsmann's recent book, *What's Lutheran in Education?* is the most extensive statement on Lutheran philosophy of education yet produced. In the selections taken from his book, Jahsmann raises the question whether there is a *philosophy* of Luthern education or whether there is just a *theology* of Lutheran education, as some Lutherans have been prone to believe. He comes to the conclusion that there is a Lutheran philosophy of education and that it represents Biblical theology and Lutheran thinking applied to education. To say that there is no Lutheran philosophy of education, writes Jahsmann, is to suggest that theology does not influence educational programs. Having established this, Jahsmann turns to a consideration of sixteen theological principles that determine objectives, seven observations on the implications of doctrine for objectives of Lutheran education, and some principles of curriculum that flow from the Lutheran doctrine of the scriptures and Lutheran philosophy of education.

Few Jews migrated to America before the nineteenth century, and those who did, in spite of their objections to the Protestant bias and some of the observances found in the common schools, sent their children to these schools but supplemented the schoolwork with programs of religious instruction offered during non-school hours. During the nineteenth century, however, the migration of German and Eastern European peoples brought to these shores an increasing number of Jews in whom the tradition of Jewish education as a responsibility of the Jewish community was strong. Nevertheless, the Jews were much slower than the Lutherans and the Catholics about founding a system of schools. Indeed, it was not until 1910 that the American Jewish school system, as a supplement to the public schools, received its "first real creative impulse" in New York City. As the number of Jewish communities has continued to increase, the number and variety of Jewish schools has increased, until now almost every well-organized Jewish community has a system of one-day-a-week schools, weekday-afternoon schools, and all-day schools. The first is similar to the Protestant Sunday school, after which it was patterned. The weekday-afternoon school serves the purposes of those who wish their children to receive a more extensive education in the Jewish tradition. And although some parents send their children to one or the other of these schools, they still may be staunch advocates of the public schools, which their children also attend. The all-day schools, designed to completely replace the public school, is usually patronized by the children of Orthodox Jews. Some have incorrectly referred to these all-day schools as parochial schools, because they, like their Protestant and Catholic counterparts, offer both secular and religious subjects. Most Jews would argue that they should be called private schools, since they are not a parish or church school and are not controlled by a central "church," such as is the case with the Catholic or the Missouri Synod schools.

It is difficult to find a spokesman with whom all Jews would agree. Nevertheless, Doctor Meir Ben-Horin, a very well-known Jewish scholar, has been chosen for inclusion in these readings. According to him, the age of science has not yet arrived, although it is coming. In order to hasten its coming, he suggests that Jewish education must be relentless in its pursuit of truth, proclaim the unity of science and love, foster the Jewish peoples' quest for new relevance of Judaism to the human situation, and participate in the effort to express the meaning of God and the essence of Jewish faith. In the second selection from Ben-Horin we find him pleading for Jewish education to deal with "genuine problematic life situations," inculcate the spirit of transcultural sympathy, develop skills and understandings necessary for cooperative planning in communal affairs, promote fearless scientific inquiry, and judge the results of Jewish education by its fruits.

So far, we have seen that the Catholic Church and the Missouri Synod of the Lutheran Church have established separate schools to perpetuate their religious convictions as well as to instruct their children in the conventional subjects of reading, writing, science, etc., and that the Orthodox Jews have built all-day schools to preserve the Jewish culture and to teach religious beliefs.

At a time when these kinds of schools have been increasing in number, there are those who have been busy developing other means of fostering religious instruction. The Sunday school has been extensively employed, particularly by the Protestants. Provisions have been made to release children during public-school hours for religious instruction. More recently shared time programs have been arranged between public and parochial schools. Some people have insisted that the public school should teach a body of principles that are common to all religions, while others have campaigned for the history and literature of religion to be taught as part of the social sciences and humanities without any attempt to develop a religious commitment.

17

Declaration on Christian Education*

POPE PAUL VI

Introduction

THE SACRED ECUMENICAL COUNCIL has considered with care how extremely important education is in the life of man and how its influence ever grows in the social progress of this age (1).

Indeed, the circumstances of our time have made it easier and at once more urgent to educate young people and, what is more, to continue the education of adults. Men are more aware of their own dignity and position; more and more they want to take an active part in social and especially in economic and political life (2). Enjoying more leisure, as they sometimes do, men find that the remarkable development of technology and scientific investigation and the new means of communication offer them an opportunity of attaining more easily their cultural and spiritual inheritance and of fulfilling one another in the closer ties between groups and even between peoples.

Consequently, attempts are being made everywhere to promote more education. The rights of men to an education, particularly the primary rights of children and parents, are being proclaimed and recognized in public documents (3). As the number of pupils rapidly increases, schools

* The translation of the "Declaration on Christian Education" is taken from *The Documents of Vatican II*, published by Guild Press, The American Press, and Associated Press and copyrighted 1966 by The American Press. Used by permission of the National Catholic Welfare Conference and Guild Press, Inc.

are multiplied and expanded far and wide and other educational institutions are established. New experiments are conducted in methods of education and teaching. Mighty attempts are being made to obtain education for all, even though vast numbers of children and young people are still deprived of even rudimentary training and so many others lack a suitable education in which truth and love are developed together.

To fulfill the mandate she has received from her divine founder of proclaiming the mystery of salvation to all men and of restoring all things in Christ, Holy Mother the Church must be concerned with the whole of man's life, even the secular part of it insofar as it has a bearing on his heavenly calling (4). Therefore, she has a role in the progress and development of education. Hence this sacred synod declares certain fundamental principles of Christian education especially in schools. These principles will have to be developed at greater length by a special post-conciliar commission and applied by Episcopal conferences to varying local situations.

The Meaning of the Universal Right to Education

All men of every race, condition and age, since they enjoy the dignity of a human being, have an inalienable right to an education (5) that is in keeping with their ultimate goal (6), their ability, their sex, and the culture and tradition of their country, and also in harmony with their fraternal association with other peoples in the fostering of true unity and peace on earth. For a true education aims at the formation of the human person in the pursuit of his ultimate end and of the good of the societies of which, as man, he is a member, and in whose obligations, as an adult, he will share.

Therefore, children and young people must be helped, with the aid of the latest advances in psychology and the arts and science of teaching, to develop harmoniously their physical, moral, and intellectual endowments so that they may gradually acquire a mature sense of responsibility in striving endlessly to form their own lives properly and in pursuing true freedom as they surmount the vicissitudes of life with courage and constancy. Let them be given also, as they advance in years, a positive and prudent sexual education. Moreover they should be so trained to take their part in social life that properly instructed in the necessary and opportune skills they can become actively involved in various community organizations, open to discourse with others and willing to do their best to promote the common good.

This sacred synod likewise declares that children and young people have a right to be motivated to appraise moral values with a right conscience, to embrace them with a personal adherence, together with a deeper knowledge and love of God. Consequently it earnestly entreats all those who hold a position of public authority or who are in charge of education to see to it that youth is never deprived of this sacred right. It further exhorts the sons of the Church to give their attention with generosity to the entire field of education, having especially in mind the need of extending very soon the benefits of a suitable education and training to everyone in all parts of the world (7).

2. Christian Education

Since all Christians have become by rebirth of water and the Holy Spirit a new creature (8) so that they should be called and should be children of God, they have a right to a Christian education. A Christian education does not merely strive for the maturing of a human person as just now described, but has as its principal purpose this goal: That the baptized, while they are gradually introduced to the knowledge of the mystery of salvation, become ever more aware of the gift of faith they have received, and that they learn in addition how to worship God the Father in spirit and truth (cf. John 4:23) especially in liturgical action, and be conformed in their personal lives according to the new man created in justice and holiness of truth (Eph. 4:22–24); also that they develop into perfect manhood, to the mature measure of the fulness of Christ (cf. Eph. 4:13) and strive for the growth of the Mystical Body; moreover, that, aware of their calling, they learn not only how to bear witness to the hope that is in them (cf. Peter 3:15) but also how to help in the Christian formation of the world that takes place when natural powers viewed in the full consideration of man redeemed by Christ contribute to the good of the whole of society (9). Wherefore, this sacred synod recalls to pastors of souls their most serious obligation to see to it that all the faithful, but especially the youth who are the hope of the Church, enjoy this Christian education (10).

3. Authors of Education

Since parents have given children their life, they are bound by the most serious obligation to educate their offspring and, therefore, must be recognized as the primary and principal educators (11). This role in education is so important that only with difficulty can it be supplied where it is lacking. Parents are the ones who must create a family atmosphere animated by love and respect for God and man, in which the well-rounded personal and social education of children is fostered. Hence the family is the first school of the social virtues that every society needs. It is particularly in the Christian family, enriched by the grace and office of the sacrament of matrimony, that children should be taught from their early years to have a knowledge of God according to the faith received in Baptism, to worship Him, and to love their neighbor. Here too they find their first experience of a wholesome human society and of the Church. Finally, it is through the family that they are gradually led to a companionship with their fellowmen and with the people of God. Let parents, then, recognize the inestimable importance a truly Christian family has for the life and progress of God's own people (12).

The family which has the primary duty of imparting education needs the help of the whole community. In addition, therefore, to the rights of parents and others to whom the parents entrust a share in the work of education, certain rights and duties belong indeed to civil society, whose role is to direct what is required for the common temporary good. Its function is to promote the education of youth in many ways, namely: To protect the duties and rights of parents and others who share in education and to give them aid; according to the principle of subsidiarity, when the endeavors of parents and other societies are lacking, to carry out the work of education in accordance with the wishes of the parents; and, moreover, as the common good demands, to build schools and institutions (13).

Finally, in a special way, the duty of educating belongs to the Church, not merely because it must be recognized as a human society capable of educating, but especially because it has the responsibility of announcing the way of salvation to all men, of communicating the life of Christ to those who believe, and, in her unfailing solicitude, of assisting men to be able to come to the fulness of this life (14). The Church is bound as a mother to give to these children of hers an education by which their whole life can be imbued with the spirit of Christ and at the same time do all she can to promote for all peoples the complete perfection of the human person, the good of earthly society, and the building of a world that is more human (15).

3b. Various Aids to Education

In fulfilling its educational role, the Church eager to employ all suitable aids, is concerned especially about those who are her very own.

Foremost among these is catechetical instruction (16), which enlightens and strengthens the faith, nourishes life according to the spirit of Christ, leads to intelligent and active participation in the liturgical mystery (17) and gives motivation for apostolic activity. The Church esteems highly and seeks to penetrate and ennoble with her own spirit also other aids which belong to the general heritage of man and which are of great influence in forming souls and molding men, such as the media of communication (18), various groups for mental and physical development, youth associations, and, in particular, schools.

4. Importance of Schools

Among all educational instruments the school has a special importance (19). It is designed not only to develop with special care the intellectual faculties but also to form the ability to judge rightly, to hand on the cultural legacy of previous generations, to foster a sense of values, to prepare for professional life. Between pupils of different talents and backgrounds it promotes friendly relations and fosters a spirit of mutual understanding; and it establishes as it were a center whose work and progress must be shared together by families, teachers, associations of various types that foster cultural, civic, and religious life, as well as by civil society and the entire human community.

Beautiful indeed and of great importance is the vocation of all those who aid parents in fulfilling their duties and who, as representatives of the human community, undertake the task of education in schools. This vocation demands special qualities of mind and heart, very careful preparation, and continuing readiness to renew and to adapt.

5. Duties and Rights of Parents

Parents who have the primary and inalienable right and duty to educate their children must enjoy true liberty in their choice of schools. Consequently, the public power, which has the obligation to protect and defend the rights of citizens, must see to it, in its concern for distributive justice, that public subsidies are paid out in such a way that parents are truly free to choose according to their conscience the schools they want for their children (20).

In addition it is the task of the state to see to it that all citizens are able to come to a suitable share in culture and are properly prepared to exercise their civic duties and rights. Therefore, the state must protect the right of children to an adequate school education, check on the ability of teachers and the excellence of their training, look after the health of the pupils, and, in general, promote the whole school project. But it must always keep in mind the principle of subsidiarity so that there is no kind of school monopoly, for this is opposed to the native rights of the human person, to the development and spread of culture, to the peaceful association of citizens, and to the pluralism that exists today in ever so many societies (21).

Therefore, this sacred synod exhorts the faithful to assist to their utmost in finding suitable methods of education and programs of study and in forming teachers who can give youth a true education. Through the associations of parents in particular they should further with their assistance all the work of the school but especially the moral education it must impart (22).

6. Moral and Religious Education in All Schools

Feeling very keenly the weighty responsibility of diligently caring for the moral and religious education of all her children, the Church must be present with her own special affection and help for the great number who are being trained in schools that are not Catholic. This is possible by the witness of the lives of those who teach and direct them, by the apostolic action of their fellow-students (23), but especially by the ministry of priests and laymen who give them the doctrine of salvation in a way suited to their age and circumstances and provide spiritual aid in every way the times and conditions allow.

The Church reminds parents of the duty that is theirs to arrange and even demand that their childdren be able to enjoy these aids and advance in their Christian formation to a degree that is abreast of their development in secular subjects. Therefore, the Church esteems highly those civil authorities and societies which, bearing in mind the pluralism of contemporary society and respecting religious freedom, assist families so that the education of their children can be imparted in all schools according to the individual moral and religious principles of the families (24).

7. Catholic Schools

The influence of the Church in the field of education is shown in a special manner by the Catholic school. No less than other schools does the

Catholic school pursue cultural goals and the human formation of youth. But its proper function is to create for the school community a special atmosphere animated by the Gospel spirit of freedom and charity, to help youth grow according to the new creatures they were made through Baptism as they develop their own personalities, and finally to order the whole of human culture to the news of salvation so that the knowledge the students gradually acquire of the world, life, and man is illumined by faith (24). So indeed the Catholic school, while it is open, as it must be, to the situation of the contemporary world, leads its students to promote efficaciously the good of the earthly city and also prepares them for service in the spread of the Kingdom of God, so that by leading an exemplary apostolic life they become, as it were, a saving leaven in the human community.

Since, therefore, the Catholic school can be such an aid to the fulfillment of the mission of the People of God and to the fostering of the dialogue between the Church and mankind, to the benefit of both, it retains even in our present circumstances the utmost importance. Consequently this sacred synod proclaims anew what has already been taught in several documents of the magisterium (26), namely: The right of the Church freely to establish and to conduct schools of every type and level. And the Council calls to mind that the exercise of a right of this kind contributes in the highest degree to the protection of freedom of conscience, the rights of parents, as well as to the betterment of culture itself.

But let teachers recognize that the Catholic school depends upon them almost entirely for the accomplishment of its goals and programs (27). They should, therefore, be very carefully prepared so that both in secular and religious knowledge they are equipped with suitable qualifications and also with a pedagogical skill that is in keeping with the findings of the contemporary world. Intimately linked in charity to one another and to their students and endowed with an apostolic spirit, may teachers by their life as much as by their instruction bear witness to Christ the unique Teacher. Let them work as partners with parents and together with them in every phase of education give due consideration to the difference of sex and the proper ends Divine Providence assigns to each sex in the family and in society. Let them do all they can to stimulate their students to act for themselves and even after graduation to continue to assist them with advice, friendship, and by establishing special associations imbued with the true spirit of the Church. The work of these teachers, this sacred synod declares, is in the real sense of the word an apostolate most suited to and necessary for our times and at once a true service offered to society. The Council also reminds Catholic parents of the duty of entrusting their children to Catholic schools wherever and whenever it is possible and of supporting these schools to the best of their ability and of cooperating with them for the education of their children (28).

8. Different Types of Catholic Schools

To this concept of a Catholic school all schools that are in any way dependent on the Church must conform as far as possible, though the Catholic school is to take on different forms in keeping with local circumstances (29). Thus the Church considers very dear to her heart those Catholic schools, found especially in the areas of the new churches, which are attended also by students who are not Catholics.

Attention should be paid to the needs of today in establishing and directing Catholic schools. Therefore, though primary and secondary schools, the foundation of education, must still be fostered, great importance is to be attached to those which are required in a particular way by contemporary conditions, such as: Professional (30) and technical schools, centers for educating adults and promoting social welfare, or for the retarded in need of special care, and also schools for preparing teachers for religious instruction and other types of education.

This sacred Council of the Church earnestly entreats pastors and all the faithful to spare no sacrifice in helping Catholic schools fulfill their function in a continually more perfect way, and especially in caring for the needs of those who are poor in the goods of this world or who are deprived of the assistance and affection of a family or who are strangers to the gift of faith.

9. Catholic Colleges and Universities

The Church is concerned also with schools of a higher level, especially colleges and universities. In those schools dependent on her she intends that by their very constitution individual subjects be pursued according to their own principles, method, and liberty of scientific inquiry, in such a way that an ever deeper understanding in these fields will be obtained and that, as questions that are new and current are raised and investigations carefully made according to the example of the doctors of the Church and especially of St. Thomas Aquinas, there may be a deeper realization of the harmony of faith and science. Thus there is accomplished a public, enduring, and pervasive influence of the Christian mind in the furtherance of culture, and the students of these institutions are molded into men truly outstanding in their training, ready to undertake weighty responsibilities in society and witness to the faith in the world (31).

In Catholic universities where there is no faculty of sacred theology there should be established an institute or chair of sacred theology in which there should be lectures suited to lay students. Since science advances by means of the investigations peculiar to higher scientific studies, special attention should be given in Catholic universities and colleges to institutes that serve primarily the development of scientific research.

The sacred synod heartily recommends that Catholic colleges and universities be conveniently located in different parts of the world, but in such a way that they are outstanding not for their numbers but for their pursuit of knowledge. Matriculation should be readily available to students of real promise, even though they be of slender means, especially to students from the newly emerging nations.

Since the destiny of society and of the Church itself is intimately linked with the progress of young people pursuing higher studies (32), the pastors of the Church are to expend their energies not only on the spiritual life of students who attend Catholic universities, but, solicitous for the spiritual formation of all their children, they must see to it, after consultations between Bishops, that even at universities that are not Catholic there should be associations and university centers under Catholic auspices in which priests, religious, and laity, carefully selected and prepared should give abiding spiritual and intellectual assistance to the youth of the university. Whether in Catholic universities or others, young people of greater ability who seem suited for teaching or research should be specially helped and encouraged to undertake a teaching career.

10. Faculties of Sacred Sciences

The Church expects much from the zealous endeavors of the faculties of the sacred sciences (33). For to them she entrusts the very serious responsibility of preparing her own students not only for the priestly ministry, but especially for teaching in the seats of higher ecclesiastical studies or for promoting learning on their own or for undertaking the work of a more rigorous intellectual apostolate. Likewise it is the role of these very faculties to make more penetrating inquiry into the various aspects of the sacred sciences so that an ever-deepening understanding of sacred Revelation is obtained, the legacy of Christian wisdom handed down by our forefathers is more fully developed, the dialogue with our separated brethren and with non-Christians is fostered, and answers are given to questions arising from the development of doctrine (34).

Therefore, ecclesiastical faculties should reappraise their own laws so that they can better promote the sacred sciences and those linked with them and, by employing up-to-date methods and aids, lead their students to more penetrating inquiry.

11. Coordination to Be Fostered in Scholastic Matters

Cooperation is the order of the day. It increases more and more to supply the demand on a diocesan, national, and international level. Since it is altogether necessary in scholastic matters, every means should be employed to foster suitable cooperation between Catholic schools, and between these and other schools that collaboration should be developed which the good of all mankind requires (35).

From greater coordination and cooperative endeavor greater fruits will be derived particularly in the area of academic institutions. Therefore, in every university let the various faculties work mutually to this end, insofar as their goal will permit. In addition, let the universities also endeavor to work together by promoting international gatherings, by sharing scientific inquiries with one another, by communicating their discoveries to one another, by having exchange of professors for a time and by promoting all else that is conducive to greater assistance.

The sacred synod earnestly entreats young people themselves to become aware of the importance of the work of education and to prepare themselves to take it up, especially where because of a shortage of teachers the education of youth is in jeopardy.

This same sacred synod, while professing its gratitude to the priests, religious men and women, and the laity who by their evangelical self-dedication are devoted to the noble work of education and of schools of every type and level, exhorts them to persevere generously in the work they have undertaken, and, imbuing their students with the spirit of Christ, to strive to excel in pedagogy and the pursuit of knowledge in such a way that they not merely advance the internal renewal of the Church but preserve and enhance its beneficent influence upon to day's world, especially the intellectual world.

Paul VI, Giovanni Battista Montini (September 26, 1897—), the son of a wealthy newspaper editor and member of parliament, was born near

Brescia, Italy. He attended the Istituto Arici, Brescia, Lombard Seminary, Pontifical Ecclesiastical Academy, and Gregorian University, Rome. He was ordained a priest on May 29, 1920 and eventually entered the Vatican Secretariat of State, where, except for a brief appointment in 1923 in the Apostolic Nuncio's Office in Warsaw, he remained until he was 57 years of age. During this period he also served as National Ecclesiastical Assistant to the Italian Federation of Catholic University Students and as professor of History of Pontifical Diplomacy. He went on to become head of a department in the Secretariat of State in 1937, sub-secretary of state in 1944, and pro-secretary of state for ordinary affairs in 1952. Pius XI made him Archbishop of Milan in 1954 and in December 1958 Pope John XXIII made him a cardinal. He was elected Pope after five ballots on June 21, 1963 and selected as his name Paul VI. He was crowned on June 30, 1963. In the autumn of the same year he reconvened the Ecumenical Council initiated by Pope John in 1962. During the Council the document reproduced here in full was prepared and approved.

18

The Fourfold
Development of Man[*]

WILLIAM FRANCIS CUNNINGHAM

WE HAVE NOW CONSIDERED in some detail the four phases of the educative process that must be included in any treatment that merits the appellation "philosophical"; the problem of ends (pupil nature and needs) and the three means within the school for the achievement of these ends, (1) the curriculum, (2) the teacher and (3) the institution. It now remains for us to summarize briefly the point of view we have been stressing throughout this presentation, the philosophy of Supernaturalism as interpreted by the Catholic Church divinely commissioned to carry forward the work of Christian education: "Going therefore, teach ye all nations." (Matt. XXVIII, 19).

1. The Fourfold Development of Man

Education concerns the whole man, a body-mind organism, living in a material environment (the physical universe), a social environment (fellowman) and, for the humanist as we have defined him as well as for the supernaturalist, an environment which is spiritual (God's providence). In this larger meaning of the term "education," the school is by no means the only educative agency. Every experience the individual lives through is educative if he passes through it with mind awake. If he sees the mistakes he made in any experience and in the light of that knowledge learns how to avoid those mistakes, he is better prepared to meet similar experi-

* William F. Cunningham, *The Pivotal Problems of Education*. New York: The Macmillan Company, 1940, pp. 551–561, 563–567. Copyright 1940 by William F. Cunningham. Used by permission of the publisher.

ences with the prospect of more adequate adjustment in those problematic situations with which life will inevitably confront him. There are, in addition to the school three important agencies which, in a very special way, have educational functions to perform.

(A) PHYSICAL DEVELOPMENT

There is first of all the home. The child begins his life in the home. Commonly, he spends his entire childhood and the greater part of the period of adolescence under the same influence. The physical development of the child is determined primarily by heredity, and this factor is settled at birth in the family. With the advance of medical science, the health-conserving agencies are playing a larger and larger part in safeguarding, promoting, and when lost, restoring health. But all these influences together can never equal the factor of heredity in determining the health that any individual enjoys through life.

(B) SOCIAL DEVELOPMENT

The second agency that early plays a part in the development of the individual is the community. Here the factor of environment is supreme. The home, of course, is the first environment that influences the development of the child, but early in life the neighborhood begins to exert its influence. This influence first comes through play groups, but as the individual grows older, the larger community of which he forms a part, whether urban or rural, and later government in all its forms, local, state and national, all play their part in influencing the development of the individual. As adolescence passes into maturity, vocational calling becomes an outstanding influence. Professional men, the doctor, the lawyer, the clergyman, all have their distinctive traits that mark them as a group. So too with those who labor with their hands, the farmer and the factory worker. Leisure time also plays its part. The congeries of traits we call "personality" is to a great extent determined by the influences which the community in all its forms brings to bear on the developing individual beginning with birth and continuing all through life, since to be alive is to be undergoing the process of change.

(C) RELIGIOUS DEVELOPMENT

The third agency which plays a part in determining the kind of individual the child develops into—is an influence that operates in the realm of the spirit, the Church. Here is the distinctive feature that marks off the philosophy of Supernaturalism from all other philosophies giving naturalistic answers, to the threefold inquiry into the origin, nature, and destiny of man. With regard to origin, Supernaturalism says that man came from God (the fact of creation); with regard to nature, he is made to the image and likeness of God ("And God created man to his own image." Gen. I, 27.); and in destiny, man's chief object in life is to return to God from whom he came. The Church is ever at hand all through life to guide him and, through the administration of the sacraments, strengthen him in living a life about the natural. In this way only can he attain the supernatural destiny to which he is called, life with God hereafter.

(D) MENTAL DEVELOPMENT

The school, as the formal agency of education, has a most important part to play in all phases of this development. In the matter of physical development (health) too often in the past have the ministrations of the school been harmful rather than helpful. But with the advance of knowledge in the fields of physical and mental hygiene all this has been radically changed for the better. The school today often substituting for the failure of the home, develops within its pupils health knowledge, health habits, and health attitudes that should play a great part in reducing the incidence of sickness and prolonging life. The striking difference in this field between a Catholic school informed by the philosophy of Supernaturalism and a school conducting a purely naturalistic program will be in the matter of attitudes. For the naturalist, loss of health is the greatest calamity that can befall an individual. Not so, for the supernaturalist. Rather, it is the loss of health of soul, not health of body, which is the great calamity of life. Sin not sickness is the great evil. In fact, often it is a siege of sickness that awakens the sinner to the evils of a misspent life and puts him again on the road of virtue which alone can lead him to his true destiny, life with God. Developing this attitude in the mind of the pupil is one of the great contributions the Catholic school should make in forming the true Christian.

Similarly in the social development of the pupil, the school has an important part to play. From the family and the play group of the neighborhood the child passes into the larger school group, the kindergarten or the primary grade. As he grows older this school group continually increases in size, and the part the individual pupil plays in its activities grows in importance. Characterized by teacher control in the early years the social life of the school gradually comes more and more under the control of the students themselves, until, during the later years devoted to general education, the function of the school administrator is primarily that of guidance. The one thing youths lack in directing their social life is experience, and this must be substituted for by the experience of those responsible for the administration of the school as a community of scholars. The ideal to be aimed at is *companionship in the pursuit of knowledge.* Students privileged to pass their years of later adolescences in such a community have the best promise of developing the personality traits of kindness, courtesy, and coöperation which characterize the ideal citizen.

Again, in the religious development of its pupils the school is an important factor. Through the curriculum the ideal Catholic school gives the pupil a knowledge of his faith of deepening intensity as the pupil climbs the educational ladder, so that at the end of his period of general education one may be confident that he *knows* his faith and, if necessary, is prepared to defend it against assault and misinterpretations. Through the reception of the sacraments and participation in common worship, the community of scholars that is the school, shares in the effects of divine grace. They feel themselves lifted up to a level of devotion and deep appreciation of their faith, and it may truthfully be said of them—they *love* it. Finally throughout the social life of the school—through the example of inspiring teachers, through personal guidance and disciplinary regulations drawn up for their welfare, and through a system of rewards and punishment truly social in nature—they receive training in the moral virtues. In any community with a feeling of solidarity the severest punishment for an antisocial offense is exclusion from that community. The school should be slow to use this severe penalty but it is the most effective of all penalties and in extreme situations must be applied. The ideal to be striven for is that a discipline superimposed from above down in the early years is gradually transformed into a discipline self-imposed from within out. Virtues are habits. Every habit is set in action by some stimulus. In the case of the moral virtues this stimulus must be from within the individual in the form of attitudes that will put these habits into action in those situations which call for them. When this is achieved, then students *live* their faith.

The Specific Function of the School. The school will play a part in all these phases of pupil development, but the question arises, is there not one area in which it is supreme? Is there not *one specific function* for which the school, as one of the great social agencies, is to be held accountable? The Church throughout its history has carried on many educational functions, even using the term "education" in its narrower significance. For centuries the monasteries carried on whatever schooling there was for the great mass of mankind in Western Europe. There agriculture was developed as a science and an art and taught to the tillers of the soil. There and there alone was the lamp of learning kept burning when the dark cloud of the barbaric invasions settled over Europe in the fifth century and following. During the Middle Ages the universities owed their origin and development to the Church as the patron of learning. Many of her greatest saints like Albertus Magnus and Thomas Aquinas were the intellectual lights of this period and they taught within the universities. But no one would claim that mental development, the education of students in the liberal arts and sciences, or in the practical arts such as agriculture, is the specific function of the Church. Rather is it the religious development of mankind for which it was divinely commissioned and in all its activities this must take precedence.

Similarly, the school has one specific function for which it has been brought into being by society and this is the mental development of youth privileged to share its ministrations. With Newman we may call this "intellectual education" but since all knowledge begins in the senses, the word "intellectual" when used in this phrase has a wide connotation embracing the whole of our mental life. In this sense the school is an intellectual agency. This does not mean the school ignores the body. Just the contrary. Man as a somato-psychic organism functions as a whole in all life activities, and this is particularly true in that life activity which is the school's particular concern, learning. But in the philosophy we are presenting the thing that makes man man, is mind. The distinctions implied in speaking of physical, mental, social and religious development are *logical* distinctions made for clarifying thought so that with clear thinking behind it the practical procedures of the school may be carried on intelligently. With these distinctions clearly in mind, we say that the specific function of the school on all levels of general education is the making of minds. It is an intellectual agency. Cloudy thinking among American educators during the past several decades has brought forth what is called the "residual theory" of the school. The school is to take care of the "residue" after it has been determined what functions are adequately provided for by the other social agencies. With the breakdown of the American home through divorce and the urbanization of our population; with the community failing to do its part in developing within its members those qualities of character that are the test of responsible citizenship; and with the church ceasing to play a dominant role in the life of individuals and the community as it did in the founding of the nation and throughout its early history, the claim is now made that the school must take over all of these functions. Courses in cooking are introduced on the lower levels and in "Choosing a Mate" on the higher levels, as if this is the way to restore the American home to its former status. So many so-called "practical" courses heve been introduced, that rare indeed is a school found now where a few first-line subjects are studied intensely and continuously over a number of years. Yet such study is the only procedure that insures mastery of the fundamentals in the early years and mastery of that part of the social inheritance adapted to assimilation through formal study in the later years. "Enrichment of the curriculum" has brought about impoverishment of the student with debilitation of the best in the American educational tradition. And all this we can lay at the door of those administrators who have unintelligently advocated this "residual theory."

We realize that this emphasis on the school as an intellectual agency may easily lead to a misunderstanding of our position. This was the experience of Newman. In spite of the clarity with which he presented his thesis in the great educational classic *The Idea of a University*[1] the distinction which he makes between the "instrumental" function of the university and its one "essential" function has not been grasped by many of his readers. Our contention here is that this same distinction applies on all levels of the educational ladder devoted to general education. The school is not a hospital or health center, though it will not be indifferent to the health of its students; it is not a parish church, though it will not neglect their moral and spiritual formation; it is not the home, though it acknowledges that it stands *in loco parentis* and will not neglect giving its students training in the social amenities of community living; it is not a country club, though it will recognize its obligation to furnish recreational facilities for its students under sympathetic supervision; it is not a training school for gladiators though when dealing with later adolescents it may have an extensive athletic program of intramural and intercollegiate athletics; and finally, it is not a community center as that term is ordinarily understood, though school life will furnish many opportunities for the practice of the social virtues of loyalty and coöperation. The school will do all of these things, but if intelligently administered it will recognize that these are instrumental functions; efforts on its part to help other agencies, the hospital, the home, the church, etc., achieve their functions. But again, if intelligently administered, it will never let the performance of any one or all of these functions interfere with the effective performance of its own *essential* function, intellectual education.

The insistence with which Newman returns again and again to this point has led one writer to label Newman's idea "the philosophy of severance."[2] Yet separation of the intellectual and religious elements in educa-

---

[1] See quotation, page 163, in Chapter VI, "The Universal Human Needs," Section 1, "The School."

[2] T. Corcoran, S.J., "Liberal Education and Moral Aims," *Thought*, June, 1926.

tion was farthest from Newman's mind. True enough, in his great work on the university he does not treat of religious training. But the title of the book explains why. He is treating of the university in its "bare idea," not as an "instrument of the Church" helping the Church achieve its functions. If we wish to know Newman's attitude with regard to how the university should combine these two functions, we must go to his sermons, notably the first sermon delivered before the newly founded university, entitled "Intellect, the Instrument of Religious Training," which we have quoted at length in Chapter VII, "The Fourth Factor in Man Making" (pp. 260–261). In that sermon he says:

It will not satisfy me, what satisfies so many, to have two independent systems, intellectual and religious, going at once side by side, by a sort of division of labour, and accidentally brought together. It will not satisfy me, if religion is here, and science there, and young men converse with science all day, and lodge with religion in the evening. It is not touching the evil, to which these remarks have been directed, if the young men eat and drink and sleep in one place, and think in another; I want the *same roof* to contain *both the intellectual and moral discipline* . . . *I want the intellectual layman to be religious, and the devout ecclesiastic to be intellectual.*[3]

STATEMENT OF PURPOSE

The Catholic School

concerned with general education whether elementary school, high school or liberal college of arts and sciences, has as its aim the education of youth in a manner that will promote

The Fourfold Development of Man.

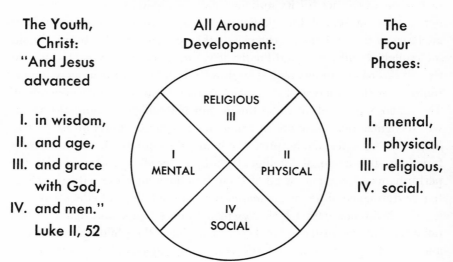

The Youth, Christ: "And Jesus advanced	All Around Development:	The Four Phases:
I. in wisdom,		I. mental,
II. and age,		II. physical,
III. and grace with God,		III. religious,
IV. and men." Luke II, 52		IV. social.

[3] *Sermons on Various Occasions.*

I. The Catholic school recognizes that its *specific function* is the preservation and propagation of the intellectual tradition of Catholic culture and that the means to this end is the development in students of the intellectual virtues that they may "advance in wisdom."

II. But it realizes that an educational program truly Catholic gives due attention to their physical development (health)

IV. and to their social development as good neighbors in community living and as loyal citizens of the state.

III. Finally, the Catholic school as a social agency serving the Church, gives special attention to the religious development of its students

    (1) through instruction truly intellectual that they may *know* their faith,

    (2) through participation in divine worship that they may *love* it,

    (3) and through training in the moral virtues that they may *live* it.

St. Luke in his statement concerning the youth, Christ, suggests the analysis we have made here of the school's three instrumental functions on the one hand, and its one specific function on the other: "And Jesus advanced in wisdom, and age, and grace with God and men." (See Figure 29, "Statement of Purpose.") Wisdom is one of the intellectual virtues as analyzed by St. Thomas following Aristotle, with knowledge and understanding as the other two in the speculative order. Prudence, knowing what to do, and art, knowing how to do it, are the two in the practical order.[4] It is, of course, the liberal arts and sciences the school is chiefly concerned with. Their development is particularly the work of the school. The instructional activities of the classroom, lecture hall, library, and laboratory are those that develop the intellectual virtues. In school as in life we must place first things first. This means the specific function of the school must take precedence over all supplementary instrumental functions. No matter how important they may be in life, *e.g.*, the moral virtues, they cannot be first in the school, for the simple reason that the instructional activities of the school are aimed at the development of the intellectual virtue. Insofar as the school is successful in this endeavor its students will "advance in wisdom," and with their growth in knowledge and understanding basic to wisdom, the school has made its primary contribution to the other three phases of development, physical, social and religious. We have emphasized this point in Figure 29, "Statement of Purpose," underlining the word "*specific*" in statement I. "The Catholic school recognizes that its *specific* function is the preservation and propagation of the intellectual tradition of Catholic culture."

[4] St. Thomas Aquinas, *Summa Theologica*, 1, 2, Q. LVII.

2. The Educative Process in Catholic Education

On the level of brute creation, instinct is the dominant characteristic of animal life; on the human level, reason is supreme; but for the Catholic, the final arbiter in all problems with which life is continually confronting us is not instinct; nor is it reason; it is *faith*. St. Augustine's "Credo ut intelligam," "I believe that I may understand," is an expression of this attitude towards the riddles of the universe. Reason alone could never give the great philosophers of all time, Plato, Aristotle, etc., any concept of the promise that revelation brings to the Christian, the beatific vision of God hereafter. Nor could it bring a conscious realization of the supernatural life to be lived here and now.

In the same way does faith bring to the Catholic an insight into the process of education that makes the realization of these ultimate objectives possible, an insight denied to the unbelieving. For the Catholic seeking an understanding of the nature of man which will explain his behavior in all its contradictions, the depths of degradation to which he falls and the heights of sanctity to which he climbs, the doctrine of *original sin* on the one hand and that of *divine grace* on the other are the solutions of these mysteries. In regard to the first Pascal has well stated the attitude of the Catholic:

It is an astonishing thing that the mystery most removed from our knowledge, that of original sin, should be something without which we cannot have knowledge of ourselves. For it is certain that nothing so shocks our reason as saying that the sin of the first man rendered those culpable, who, being so distinct from the source, seem incapable of participation in it. . . . Certainly nothing shocks us more rudely than this doctrine, and yet without this mystery, the most incomprehensible of all, we are incomprehensible to ourselves.[5]

When we inquire, "What are the educational implications of this doctrine of original sin?", we can state the answer in this brief phrase *the necessity of discipline.* Here is the sharp contrast in educational procedures that characterize an education truly Catholic in contrast with the naturalistic theories parading today under such high sounding names as "progressive education," in which the true concept of liberty, that is, *liberty under the law,* is confounded with a liberty that runs to license.

When we analyze the concept "discipline," intelligently interpreted,

[5] Quoted by Matthias Laros, *Confirmation in the Modern World,* Sheed & Ward, 1938, pp. 165–166.

we see that it admits of two varieties, both of which must characterize the "bringing forth" of the child (*educare*, to bring forth) if the process is to be education. In the first place chronologically, there is a discipline that must be superimposed. Even the ultramoderns admit this in the case of the infant. Habits of feeding, sleeping, etc., and other vital activities intimately associated with the customs of the society in which the infant is to take his place one day as an adult, must be imposed upon him. Similarly during childhood and adolescence the same process must be continued. In school this is the very meaning of the curriculum, a series of selected activities that are graded to meet the developing capacities of youth, through the learning of which he becomes capable of taking his place in civilized society. Even the adult does not escape from this discipline from without. It touches him in the many forms that we call "social control," *e.g.*, custom and law.

But early in the life of the child this discipline which we may call "social discipline" imposed, as it is, by society, must be replaced in any system of education intelligently administered, by a discipline which is self-imposed. In the school these two aspects of mental discipline, the social and the individual (which is self-discipline) are in inverse ratio as the child matures and mounts higher and higher on the educational ladder until, on the university level, the student is on his own and a high degree of self-discipline is his only safeguard against wasted hours and dissipated opportunities.

In life in general when wounded human nature is contending against what Newman calls "those giants, the passions and the pride of man," the question arises whether human nature alone can win the battle. Here is where faith once more brings insight to the Catholic along with assurance that victory is possible. Redemption by Christ means help to reestablish our fallen human nature. "My grace is sufficient for thee" were the assuring words to St. Paul. And grace means that we have it within our power not merely to conquer the animal within us but to rise above it and lead a life truly supernatural, that is, a life above nature. But the price of this help we call "grace" is effort on our part to overcome the disordered inclinations within us. God helps those who help themselves.

In the intellectual life many are the mysteries that confront us. Here again the Catholic has an advantage. The grace of divine faith illumines his intellect, and his belief enables him to understand, where the unbeliever finds nothing but discouragement and despair. In the *Divine Comedy*, Virgil, symbolizing reason, could lead Dante only so far. Then it remained for Beatrice, symbolizing revelation, to lead him on. In

Virgil's words: "So far as reason sees here, I can tell thee; from beyond that point, ever await Beatrice, for 'tis a matter of faith."[6] St. Thomas received his greatest help in writing his masterpiece, the *Summa,* at the foot of the crucifix. Through the influence of divine grace we are made "adopted sons of God" in St. Paul's words, and through this adoption as members of the mystical Body we share the life of Christ, Our Brother, a life that is above nature because it is with God. As Pope Pius XI has expressed it in his *The Christian Education of Youth:*

The true Christian, product of Christian Education, is the supernatural man who thinks, judges, and acts constantly and consistently in accordance with right reason illumined by the supernatural light of the example and teaching of Christ.

That the channels of grace might always be open to the faithful, Christ established His Church. And in its establishment He made it a teaching institution. "Going therefore teach ye all nations."[7] In the light of this fact we are prepared now to formulate our definition of Catholic education. It is: the process of growth and development whereby the natural man baptized in Christ, *under the guidance of the teaching Church* (1) assimilates a body of knowledge derived from human effort and divine revelation, (2) makes his life ideal the person of Jesus Christ, and (3) develops the ability, with the aid of divine grace, to use that knowledge in pursuit of this ideal.

It is education so defined and so interpreted that must ever be the concern of the Catholic school for all pupils at all levels of maturity, in all countries, at all times. To the Catholic school throughout the world, therefore, we address the words of the Psalmist:

Specie tue et pulchritudine tua, intende, prospere procede, et regna.
With thy comeliness and thy beauty, set out, proceed prosperously, and reign.[8]

William Francis Cunningham (May 18, 1885–January 20, 1961) was graduated from the University of Notre Dame in 1907 with an A.B. degree. After graduation he attended the seminary at Holy Cross College, Washington, D.C., until ordained a priest of the Roman Catholic Church in June, 1911. The following year he received his Ph.D. from the Catholic

---

[6] *Purgatorio,* Canto XVIII, 46.
[7] Matthew XXVIII, 19.
[8] Psalm XL, 5.

University of America. Father Cunningham began his teaching career as professor of Philosophy at Portland University in 1912, and in 1917 he was appointed vice president and director of studies of that institution. He went to Notre Dame in 1919 as professor of Education and served as director of the School of Education from 1924 to 1928. From 1928 to 1933 he was dean, head of the department, and professor of Education at the College of St. Thomas, St. Paul, Minnesota. He returned to Notre Dame in 1933 as professor of Education, a position he held until his death.

Father Cunningham was an active member of the board of review of the North Central Association (1926–1946), the executive committee of the Association of American Colleges (1923–1946), the national educational committee of the Boy Scouts of America, and is a past officer of the National Catholic Education Association and the National Conference of the Church Related College.

He is the author of The Pivotal Problems of Education *and a more recent work entitled* General Education and the Liberal College.

19

What's Lutheran in Education?*

ALLAN HART JAHSMANN

EVERY HUMAN BEING has a philosophy, a basic outlook, a *Weltanschauung*, a point of view, through which he sees his world and finds its meanings and purposes and values.

As Aristotle said long ago: "Whether we want to philosophize or whether we do not want to philosophize, we must philosophize." To the extent to which the human mind functions, to that extent it forms some notions, hypotheses, theories, ideas, and judgments of the world and what goes on in it, especially insofar as the individual himself is involved in it.

And even though most people make no systematic effort to gain a true and unified picture of the world and their part in it, and are often inconsistent "split" personalities in that they do not apply their philosophy to life, yet a man adds content to his philosophy and becomes an organized, integrated human being to the extent to which he applies his philosophy to the issues and problems of life and living.

What is a philosophy of education? In the light of what has just been said, it is one's philosophy, one's world view, and one's way of thinking, applied to education. Strictly speaking, there are as many philosophies as there are individuals, and if you don't think Mrs. Schmidt has a philosophy of education, just ask her what her idea of education is or how *she* thinks school ought to be conducted and why.

* Allan Hart Jahsmann, *What's Lutheran in Education?* St. Louis: Concordia Publishing House, 1961, pp. ix–xii, 2–10, 48–50. Used by permission of the author and publisher.

What is a Lutheran philosophy? There are some men in the Lutheran Church who deny that one can properly speak of a *Lutheran* philosophy of life and of education. Because a Lutheran takes as his basic assumptions the doctrines of Holy Scripture, and because his primary or first principles are established by revelation instead of by reason, they say that one can speak only of a Lutheran *theology* and not of a Lutheran *philosophy*.

In considering this position we readily acknowledge the following: In the measure that theology determines a person's point of view, to that extent it is a part of his philosophy. And when a Lutheran applies Lutheran theology to the questions of education or systematizes his educational thinking in harmony with his theological principles, to that extent his theology is the *basis* of his educational philosophy, the foundation on which he builds his structure of thinking.

But the very nature of philosophy suggests that there is a Lutheran philosophy and, from one point of view, *many* Lutheran philosophies, for though Lutherans accept the doctrines of Holy Scripture as inspired divine truth and their standard of faith, yet this does not mean that they must cease to think. Rather, they have the philosophic task of thinking consistently in harmony with their theology and of critically evaluating their educational theories and practices in the light of their philosophy or, as we might call it, historical Lutheran faith.

Again the question: What is a *Lutheran* philosophy? When is a point of view, an approach, an idea, a system, a product, a person, truly and distinctly Lutheran? The answer isn't simple, and will be elaborated throughout the book, but this much can be said at the outset: *One* of the distinguishing features of a genuine Lutheran is that he accepts the Bible as the primary source and basis of his faith, hence, truly Lutheran thinking flows from, or is in harmony with, Biblical theology.

Krauth sums up the nature of Lutheran theology and thereby also identifies and describes a basic essential of anything intrinsically Lutheran when he says in his classic book, *The Conservative Reformation and Its Theology*, "It is a fundamental principle of the Reformation that God's Word is the sole and absolute authority and rule of faith and life, a principle without accepting which no man can be truly Evangelical, Protestant, or Lutheran."[1] This is called the formal principle of Lutheranism.

There are, of course, other principles, factors, qualities, and charac-

[1] Charles P. Krauth, *The Conservative Reformation and Its Theology*. Philadelphia: General Council Publication Board, 1899, p. 17.

teristics that are essential to Lutheranism and typical of anything classifiable as Lutheran. For example, Lutherans emphasize that Christ is the focus of the Scriptures and that justification by faith in Him is the central doctrine.[2] This is called the material principle. The effect of this material principle on the nature of Lutheran thinking and practice will be indicated.

Here let it simply be said that truly Lutheran *educational* philosophy is Biblical theology and Lutheran thinking applied to education. To say (as it has been said) that Lutherans do not have a philosophy (or theory) of education is to maintain that their theology does not influence their educational program. This certainly is not true. One should also recognize, furthermore, that some educational questions are strictly in the category of education. These approach theology only when they involve ultimate meanings.

Much thinking about educational implications of Lutheran theology has appeared in the past, and Lutheran pastors and teachers have talked a great deal about educational purposes, responsibilities, methods, and problems. All of this can be called Lutheran educational theory or philosophy.

However, to date no thorough systematic theoretical study of Lutheran education has been published, either from a theological, philosophical, or from an educational point of view. That a comprehensive, integrated statement of the Lutheran point of view in education is needed will be admitted by all who know the need of clear and consistent thinking. Without such studies much educational work will continue to be haphazard, self-contradictory, and inefficient.

The Board of Parish Education of The Lutheran Church—Missouri Synod has a committee working on the Lutheran philosophy of education. Its task is to publish, as soon as possible, a thorough systematic study of Lutheran principles of education. The project deserves the prayers of the church.

The present book is being published because it contains material that others have said would contribute to the educational training of Lutheran pastors, teachers, and lay leaders. It is not an official statement of the Lutheran philosophy of education. It is a personal study of what Lutheran theologians and educators have thought about basic concerns in a philosophy of education. It is an attempt to get a clearer understanding of the Lutheran way in education, but it is only preliminary to the integrated statement of Lutheran educational theory so urgently needed.

[2] Article IV of the Augsburg Confession.

Theological Principles that Determine Objectives

What, then, are some of the theological principles or doctrines that function as presuppositions, premises, or postulates in Lutheran education? Obviously, they can only be mentioned here, even though there is a distinct need for what Fitzpatrick calls a theology of education—a thorough study of the educational significance of all theological doctrines.[3]

Lutheran theology holds that

1. There is a personal God who is triune, three Persons in one divine essence, Father, Son, and Holy Spirit. This God has revealed His glory and power in His works of creation (in the designs of nature). He has also put His Law into the hearts of all men, so that all can know Him as a holy and righteous God, who requires and rewards the good and condemns and punishes the evil. In other words, all human beings have a natural knowledge of God and a moral sense, though the extent of it varies. (Rom. 1–2)

2. The only sure norm of religious knowledge and truth is the Bible, because man's natural knowledge is highly imperfect and because the Holy Scriptures are God's inspired revelation of Himself, His nature, His intents and purposes, His will, and His dealings with His people and the world. Lutheran theology distinguishes between the Law and the Gospel in the Scriptures and emphasizes that it is only through the Gospel, the message of God's plan of salvation in Christ, that anyone can truly know God as Father. (2 Peter 1:19–21; Rom. 1:16; 10:17)

3. God created all things, heaven and earth and all creatures, also man (Gen. 1—3; Rev. 4:11). As He Himself declares in Genesis, He made all things "very good." Man, too, was created "very good." "Very good" in the judgment of God is perfection.

4. According to the Bible, man's body was fashioned by God and made into a living soul by His breath of life. The Bible sometimes speaks of man as consisting of body and soul, but uses the term soul interchangeably or together with such terms as mind, heart, spirit, strength, inner being, and others.

5. Man was created in the image of God, in His likeness. In this state of perfection, man was holy and possessed immortality.

6. Through the sin of disobedience man lost the image of God and

[3] Edward A. Fitzpatrick, *Exploring a Theology of Education*. Milwaukee: The Bruce Publishing Co., 1950.

became corrupt in spirit and body, so that by nature he is now spiritually blind, dead, and no longer in fellowship with God; in fact, natural man is at enmity with God and under His judgment of condemnation.

7. God in love has provided a way of reconciliation, a way of restoring man to peace and life with Him. In Biblical and Lutheran theology, salvation is by way of God's grace and forgiveness. This way involved a plan of redemption according to which God sent His only Son Jesus Christ to make atonement for the sins of the world. He did so by living a perfect life and dying on the cross as man's Substitute. The message of God's forgiveness through faith in the vicarious atonement by Jesus Christ is called the Gospel.

8. The focus of God's revelation of Himself is to be found in Jesus Christ. He is the Word Incarnate, the embodiment of the Gospel. "The Word was made flesh and dwelt among us," says the Evangelist St. John, "and we beheld His glory, the glory as of the Only-Begotten of the Father, full of grace and truth" (John 1:14). In Him God was reconciling the world to Himself. "God commended His love toward us in that . . . Christ died for us," says St. Paul (Rom. 5:8).

9. Lutheran theology declares the Biblical doctrine of justification, according to which every human being is justified, has forgiveness of all sins and peace with God on account of the vicarious life and death and resurrection of Jesus Christ, the Son of God, for the sins of the whole human race. However, the peace and salvation which God offers to all because it has been procured by Christ for all must be appropriated individually. Lutherans therefore hold that salvation is completed as far as the acquisition and intention on the part of God are concerned, but not as regards its appropriation by man.[4] It still needs to be appropriated by man.

10. For the individual appropriation of the forgiveness of sins earned for all, personal faith is necessary; and by faith is meant faith in Jesus Christ as the divine Savior from sin.[5] The Formula of Concord defines the righteousness of faith, or justification by faith, as follows:

We believe, teach, and confess that faith alone is the means and instrument whereby we lay hold of Christ, and thus, in Christ, of that righteousness which avails before God, for whose sake this faith is imputed to us for righteousness, Rom. 4:5.[6]

[4] John Theodore Mueller, *Christian Dogmatics: A Handbook of Doctrinal Theology*. St. Louis: Concordia Publishing House, 1934, p. 311.
[5] Article IV of the Augsburg Confession.
[6] *Book of Concord*, ed. F. [G. Friedrich] Bente. St. Louis: Concordia Publishing House, 1922, p. 220.

The nature of this faith will be described more fully later. A classic definition of saving faith is the following statement from the Apology of the Augsburg Confession:

That faith which justifies is not merely a knowledge of history . . . but it is the certainty, or the firm, strong confidence in the heart, when, with my whole heart, I regard the promises of God as *certain and true*, through which there are offered to me, without my merit, the forgiveness of sins, grace and salvation, through Christ the Mediator.[7]

11. But it is impossible for man in an unconverted state to believe the Gospel and to put his trust in Christ. The Scriptures deny to the intellect, heart, and will of natural man any capacity to will, to begin, to concur, to act in this matter of faith.[8] A power which will produce in man a change of heart and mind, or saving faith in Christ and His way of life, is necessary. This power is the Holy Spirit operating in and through the Word of God and producing repentance and faith in Christ and His redemptive work.

12. When a person feels contrition, or true sorrow over sin, and puts his trust in Christ as Savior from sin, he is born again spiritually. This beginning of spiritual life in the Biblical sense of the term takes place, then, not in a mere feeling or moment of "decision," or in the turning over of a new leaf in a moral determination, but in dependence on Jesus Christ and His way of salvation.

13. The new birth, or regeneration, is the beginning of what is called renewal or sanctification. As a person is spiritually born again and thus becomes a child of God, the Triune God begins not only to live in him but also to restore in him the image of God. Genuine faith in Christ is a "faith which worketh by love" (Gal. 5:6). Article VI of the Augsburg Confession begins: "Also they [the Lutherans] teach that this faith [that God forgives sins freely for Christ's sake] is bound to bring forth good fruits." As Walter Bartling has pointed out in a study of the Pauline "in Christ" concept, the Bible represents "being in Christ" as being dead to sin and alive to God. Being alive to God involves sharing in the life of Christ and living a Christlike life by the power of His Spirit.[9]

14. The work of the Holy Spirit in the heart of a person, the renewal

[7] *Ibid.*, p. 36.
[8] The Formula of Concord, Thorough Declaration, II.
[9] Walter Bartling, "The New Creation in Christ," *Concordia Theological Monthly*, XXI, June, 1950, 404.

of the image of God in man, takes place within fallen human beings having a sinful, corrupt nature. The process of growing in grace, of putting off the so-called old man and putting on the new, is a lifelong struggle. In Lutheran theology the righteousness of faith (the imputed righteousness of Christ) is always complete and perfect. The righteousness of life (the inherent righteousness of the believer) is always very imperfect in the life on earth and is acceptable to God only because the believer in Christ is clothed in the perfect righteousness of Christ (Is. 61:10; Rev. 7:9–17).[10]

15. But though sanctification is held to remain imperfect in this life, maturity and perfection remain a goal, an aim, an objective of the Christian life. "Be ye therefore perfect, even as your Father in heaven is perfect," is the will of Jesus (Matt. 5:48). And in Lutheran Biblical theology the final end and destiny of all believers in Christ is the beatific vision, which connotes the perfection that the believers in Christ will have when they are completely restored to the image of God in eternal life and bliss in heaven.[11] Added to the hope of a new body in the resurrection from the dead is also the hope of a new and perfect world to be established at the second coming of Jesus Christ.[12]

16. All those who truly believe the Gospel and trust in Jesus Christ as their Savior from sin and its consequences are called the body of Christ, the church, of which He is the Head. Until the return of Jesus Christ the church continues to have certain functions to fulfill on earth, among which are worship, witnessing, teaching and preaching, the practice of Christian charity, and fellowship.[13]

Of course, for the non-Lutheran or the doubting Lutheran all these doctrines or propositions need to be substantiated. They are elaborated in Lutheran exegetical and systematic theology. The concern of this present study is the educational implications of these doctrines or theological principles.

[10] Formula of Concord, Thorough Declaration, II.

[11] E. L. Wilson, "Faith," *The Abiding Word*, ed. Theodore Laetsch. St. Louis: Concordia Publishing House, 1946, I, 220.

[12] Martin H. Franzmann, "Christ the Hope of Glory," *Concordia Theological Monthly*, XXIV, December 1953, 896.

[13] The Apology of the Augsburg Confession defines the church as follows: The Church is not only the fellowship of outward objects and rites, as other governments, but it is originally a fellowship of faith and of the Holy Ghost in hearts. . . . And this Church alone is called the body of Christ, which Christ renews and sanctifies and governs by His Spirit, as Paul testifies, Eph. 1:22, when he says: "And gave Him to be the Head over all things to the Church, which is His body, the fullness of Him that filleth all in all. . . ." (*Book of Concord*, p. 71)

Implications of Doctrines Related to Educational Objectives

It would be easy to make many applications of Lutheran theology to educational theory. This is the task of a theology of education. The following paragraphs point to educational objectives.

1. Because man is a creation of God, children belong first of all to God—not to parents, not to the organized church, not to the state—and it is for God to say what the purposes of man's education ought to be.

2. Since God's purpose in creating heaven and earth, and man, was that He might be glorified, the first and final purpose of all education, and certainly of Lutheran education, ought to be the glorifying of God. Some people prefer to call this the ultimate end of man on the part of God, and insist that it must not be called the ultimate objective or aim. They say objectives are that at which human beings aim. But the question might be asked, "Ought not God's and man's objectives be identical?"

Regardless of the objections or the replies, those who make the glory of God the ultimate or final end of Lutheran education are in harmony with the doctrine that the ultimate purpose of all of God's works is His glory. An educational program designed to serve this purpose will teach children, youth, and adults that their purpose, too, is to glorify God in all that they are and do and may become. The Biblical principle of life is: "Whether, therefore, ye eat, or drink, or whatsoever ye do, do all to the glory of God" (1 Cor. 10:31).

3. The Scriptures indicate that when Adam and Eve came from their Creator's hand, they bore a likeness to God in their total being. They were perfect in their physical as well as mental and emotional make-up and behavior. In His image man pleased God and reflected His glory in all that he was and did. And no doubt it was God's intent and purpose that all men should continue to live in a happy, intimate communion with Him.

But the Biblical doctrine of man clearly spells out that sin changed man's original condition and relationship with God. Because all human beings have inherited sin ever since the fall of man, the first great need of man is the removal of sin and the restoration of fellowship with God. Only in this way can the image of God be restored in man, and only in a restored condition is man able to glorify God.

Since Jesus and the forgiveness of sins earned by His redemptive work are the only Way back to life with God, the first concern of Lutheran education must always be the leading of people to a conviction of sin and a personal faith in Jesus Christ as the Lamb of God who takes away the sin of the world (John 1:29). Those who come to Christian faith need to grow through daily repentance, a continuing awareness of sin and a maturing faith in the promises of God through Jesus Christ.

4. Inasmuch as this saving faith is held to be a creation of the Spirit of God, operating through the Gospel, it becomes necessary that Lutheran education have as a primary purpose and function the preaching and teaching of the Gospel. Of course, man must be confronted with the demands of God's Law in order to grow in an awareness of his sin and his need of the Savior; hence the Law of God must also be taught in connection with the Gospel. But from a Pauline, Lutheran, and evangelical point of view the Law is "our schoolmaster to bring us to Christ that we might be justified by faith, but after faith is come, we are no longer under a schoolmaster" (Gal. 3:24, 25). Legalism, the attempt to develop spiritual children of God through rules, demands, threats, force, and a righteousness of works, is always false, futile, and destructive of faith and spirit, as St. Paul so clearly demonstrates in Gal. 3. In Christian education the concern must always be faith in Jesus Christ, which comes only by the personal experience of the Spirit of God, operating through the promises of God's grace in Jesus Christ.

5. Nevertheless, as previously indicated, God's purpose in redeeming mankind, in making His plan of salvation known through His Word and church, in creating faith in Jesus Christ, extends beyond faith. Godliness —Christlikeness "unto the measure of the stature of the fullness of Christ" —Christian maturity and completeness in Christ—is what God wants in people.[14] The goal is full-grown completeness of perfection of the total human being. Christian perfection and maturity involves all aspects of spiritual life—the physical, mental, emotional, social, moral, as well as religious sides of a total self. Since the life of man is a unit, he cannot be truly moral and religious apart from his physical, mental, emotional, social, vocational, or recreational life. He is spiritual, he is moral, he is religious *in* the various other aspects of his life. Hence complete sanctification, the total Christianizing of the individual, is the goal of Christian education.

6. The power to live a Christian life (which, incidentally, is a life of love because God is Love) is in the very nature of true Christian faith. This faith, through its grateful reliance on God's forgiving love in Christ

[14] See such passages as Lev. 19:2; Titus 2:11–14; Tim. 3:16, 17; and Eph. 4:11–13. These will be discussed later.

and His atoning work, is active in love. It expresses itself in love of God and fellow man because it is the workings of the Holy Spirit, "who proceeds from the Father and the Son."

So the goal of sanctification involves faith in Jesus Christ and justification and fellowship with God and a growing up into Christ in all things through the power of His Spirit in the inner man. And in this faith and fellowship, whereby God restores His image in man partially already on earth, there is the promise and hope also of complete sanctification in heaven. There man will again have a perfect knowledge of God's will and a readiness to fulfill it perfectly, thereby glorifying God in all things.

7. One more observation. The Scriptures indicate that the believers in Christ on earth are not only to be "filled with the knowledge of Christ's will" that they might "walk worthy of the Lord unto all pleasing" (Col. 1:9, 10), but they are also to fulfill specific services for Christ as members of His church. A great Lutheran educator has emphasized that the training of the young for participation in the life and work of the church is a major aim of Christian education.[15] This part of the task of Lutheran education will also be noted in the following statements of ends and objectives.

Secular education concerns itself with the development and preparation of man for life on this earth only. Its concern is therefore largely materialistic, and its content tends to be temporal and pragmatic in quality. Even humanism uses almost exclusively the ideals and content of life on earth.

Though Lutheran education is also interested in the development of man for a useful and good life on earth, it approaches this concern through the primary goal of eternal life with God. To realize the I-God relationship, Lutheran education uses chiefly what it calls the means of grace—the Word of God. This Word is properly identified in Lutheran theology as *The Gospel of God's forgiving love in Christ*. It is the divine plan of salvation revealed in the Holy Scriptures and in the Sacraments of Holy Baptism and the Lord's Supper. In its broadest sense the term Word of God includes the whole Bible, because in the last analysis the entire Scriptures are the inspired revelation of God's will for His people as manifested by His "mighty acts" (cf. Psalm 78), the Hebrew *dabhar* here meaning both word and work.

Lutherans believe that the Word of God is efficacious; that it is the means by which God creates, strengthens, and sustains the faith in Christ which produces the Christian life. Says Rein:

[15] M. [J. M.] Reu, *Catechetics* (Chicago: Wartburg Publishing House, 1931), p. 275.

It is only through this Word, which is Spirit and life, that man can be spiritually reborn so that he becomes a new creature in Christ. This Word alone can enlighten his mind and heart so that he not only has a proper concept of life and the universe, but also strives to glorify God and to serve his fellow men in all that he does.[16]

Because the Scriptures (the canonical books of the Old and New Testaments) are the Word of God in a very special sense, and are the source and norm of Christian faith and life, it follows that the Lutheran principle of *sola Scriptura* determines the essential nature of the *Stoff* of the educational program.[17]

This Word of God, revealed by the Scriptures, appears, of course, also in secondary or derived forms, not only in the original inspired Hebrew and Greek texts. It appears, for example, in sermons, hymns, pictures, prayers, human lives (living epistles—2 Cor. 3:3), historical events, experiences—even in afflictions. But all these find their truly Christian meanings in "the more sure Word" of the Scriptures (1 Peter 1:19–21).

Many Lutheran principles of curriculum content are derived from the Lutheran doctrine of the Scriptures. Without further elaborating this doctrine, let it be noted that it demands:

1. That the Bible be given first place in any curriculum for Christian education.

2. That the Bible be dominant not only as basic subject matter but also as a dynamic frame of reference and an orienting force which Christianizes every other subject in a curriculum.

3. That the Bible be seen as theology, as the inspired revelation of God, as divine truth and doctrine, as essentially Gospel manifested by the acts of God in past history; not mere stories, history, wise sayings, moral instruction, or the recorded religious experience of others.

4. That Jesus Christ be acknowledged as the Word of God incarnate, the Logos, to whom all of Scripture must be related in order to be interpreted properly.

5. That the Law and the Gospel be distinguished in Biblical content, and that both be taught in proper relationship to each other, according to the purpose and function of each.

---

[16] R. C. Rein, "A Lutheran Philosophy of Christian Education," *Lutheran Education,* LXXXIV, April 1949, 470.

[17] For official statements on Lutheran acceptance of the canonical books of the Bible as the only source and norm of Christian doctrine, see *Doctrinal Declarations,* St. Louis: Concordia Publishing House, 1957, p. 3 et passim.

6. That the Law of God be used to serve the Gospel (a) by developing an awareness of sin and the need for a Savior and God's forgiveness; (b) by revealing the paths of righteousness for those who desire to follow Christ because they have been made righteous through faith in Him.

7. That the Gospel of God's forgiveness of sins through faith in Jesus Christ be the dominant note in Lutheran education, since it is the means for the development of Christian faith and the motivation for Christian living.

8. That the Bible text itself be given to the learner to the extent possible, in the original languages on the highest level.

9. That the Bible be taught in its totality, because "*all* Scripture is inspired by God and is profitable for teaching, for reproof, for correction, and for training in righteousness, that the man of God may be complete, equipped for every good work" (2 Tim. 3:16, 17 RSV).

Allan Hart Jahsmann (November 3, 1916—) earned his B.S. degree in Social Science at St. Louis University in 1939. In 1943 he completed the A.B. degree at Concordia Seminary, St. Louis, where two years later he received the B.D. His A.M. and Ph.D. degrees were earned at St. Louis University in 1952 and in 1956 respectively. In addition, he has done graduate work at Northwestern University, Iowa State University, and Washington University.

Dr. Jahsmann has held a number of important positions in the Lutheran Church—Missouri Synod. He was a parish pastor in Warren, Ohio, from 1945 to 1948. Then he joined the St. Louis office of his church as assistant editor of Sunday-school literature. He became associate editor in 1956 and continued in that capacity until 1959. At present he is general secretary of Sunday schools. Throughout this period with the Missouri Synod he had served on various committees, including the Committee on the Lutheran Philosophy of Education. In 1957 and 1958 he was visiting professor of education at Concordia Teachers College, River Forest, Illinois, and periodically is a visiting professor of practical theology in the graduate school at Concordia Seminary, St. Louis, Mo. In 1961 and 1962 he held a post-doctoral fellowship in religion and psychiatric theory at the Menninger Foundation in Topeka, Kansas.

Dr. Jahsmann has authored a number of books for children and several textbooks on the teaching of religion as well as "What's Lutheran in Education?" In addition he edits a national magazine for church school teachers titled Interaction.

20

Jewish Education

MEIR BEN-HORIN

Jewish Education in an Age of Science[*][†]

IS OURS THE CENTURY or the age of science? There is much support for the view that science has come and has conquered. "The starry heavens above, the moral law within" are still taken by many as proof almost beyond question for the truths they accept "on faith." Not smaller, perhaps, is the number of those who concede that "science ruleth" because of *the gleaming engines about, the perceptive mind within.*

Yet the case for the view that science has come, but not conquered, is not without merit. Like the image of a Rorschach inkblot, our century has been "seen" as the age of fascism, of national socialism, of bolshevism, of the common man, of capitalism, of "the rising tide of color." Because of the rapidity of social change in our time, "ages" come and go like book "months" and music "weeks" and fire prevention "days." This is true of the "age" of the *fascio* and the *Hakenkreuz.* Some "ages" exist side by side, such as say, the age of Gandhi's *ahimsa* (non-violence) and Lenin's age of violent revolution. Other "ages" are really ages-in-the-making rather than actual, past or present. To these belong both the age of democracy and the age of science.

[*] Meir Ben-Horin, "Jewish Education in an Age of Science," *Judaism.* New York: American Jewish Congress, Vol. 9, No. 4, Fall, 1960, pp. 339–45. Used by permission of the author and publisher.

[†] Far from constituting an Age of Science, Dr. Ben-Horin maintains that our age, as judged by a large number of egregious manifestations in politics as well as ideology, is actually pre-scientific. However, the inevitability of the latter poses a number of basic questions as to both the goals and methods of Jewish education. Here, the author essays to outline the reorientation required of Jewish education, if it is to function effectively in the coming Age of Science.

Do the world wars, the cold war, the local wars, the Kassem, Castro, Nasser, Mao Tse-tung revolutions bespeak the age of science? Do the suppression of Hungary and Tibet? Is it truly an age of science in which consumer goods reach the public before they have attained acceptable standards of health and safety? Dishonest management and corrupt labor unions, scholars of deceit, best-selling music by verdict of "the syndicate," rages of fashion, the vogue of revivalists, magic healers, mystics and "beat" philosophers—are these the sign of science? Disease, deception, poverty, honorless profiteering, rugged politics and trading in human destinies—do they not rather describe and define pre-scientific times?

It may be wiser to acknowledge that we live in pre-historic times and that human history worth the name has not yet begun. By the same token, neither a mature era of democracy nor a full-fledged epoch of science has thus far dawned upon mankind. Only those who are bent on besmirching the good name and high prestige of science will affix the scientific label to pre-scientific and essentially anti-scientific manifestations of man's nature.[1]

The age of science needs to be created. It is not here nor is its coming an inevitable decree of nature. But if we survive our pre-scientific superstitions, animosities, absolutisms, fanaticisms, it may be brought into being.

To hasten its coming and to prepare for the age of science, Jewish education needs to become serious about the following four interrelated propositions.

First, Jewish education *as education* must be relentless in the pursuit of truth. This is to say that its commitment to Judaism and its commitment to truth based on evidence must never be viewed as incompatible.

Truth, as far as education is concerned, is greater than nationalism, greater than victory on election day, greater than winning prizes on television and elsewhere, greater than amassing fortunes, honors, favors of the mighty and of the beautiful. Truth is the seal of the Eternal.

Bertrand Russell has said, "Be scrupulously truthful, even when truth is inconvenient, for it is more inconvenient when you try to conceal it." And he has warned, "Do you think it worth while to produce belief by concealing evidence, for the evidence is sure to come to light."

In 1924, the American Historical Association, upon the recommendation of its Committee on History Teaching in the schools and of its

[1] See Meir Ben-Horin, "Communism and the Faith in Man," *The Reconstructionist*, Vol. 20, No. 1, February 26, 1954. Also *idem*, "Toward the Dawn of History," Joseph L. Blau *et al.*, editor, *Essays on Jewish Life and Thought* (presented in honor of Professor Salo W. Baron). New York: Columbia University Press, 1959, pp. 39–54.

executive council, resolved that "genuine and intelligent patriotism, no less than the requirements of honesty and sound scholarship, demand that textbook writers and teachers should strive to present a truthful picture of past and present, with due regard to the different purposes and possibilities of elementary, secondary, and advanced instruction; that criticism of history textbooks should therefore be based not upon grounds of patriotism, but only upon grounds of faithfulness to fact as determined by specialists or tested by consideration of the evidence; that cultivation in pupils of scientific temper in history and in the related social sciences, of a spirit of inquiry and a willingness to face unpleasant facts, are far more important objectives than the teaching of special interpretation of particular events; and that attempts, however well meant, to foster national arrogance and boastfulness and indiscriminate worship of national 'heroes' can only tend to promote a harmful pseudo-patriotism."

The crux of the matter is concealment of evidence. Whether we teach the age of the earth or the origins of the human species; whether we teach the story of the oil that kept the lamp burning on the first Hanukkah; or whether it is the story of the donkey who spoke to Balaam; or whether our subject is the difference between Conservative, Orthodox, and Reform Judaism or its naturalistic versions; whether we teach the contributions made to Zionist realization by Max Nordau or by his opponent Chaim Weizmann, or Ben-Gurion or his opponent Vladimir Jabotinsky; whether we teach the virtues of science and the sins of religion or *vice versa*—in all events, the truth and all relevant evidence, whether pleasant or not, "dangerous" or not, the truth is what we must strive to attain, the truth or the search for it, the passion for it, the relentless pursuit of it.

If science embodies such relentless pursuit of truth, Jewish education must in this sense be scientific. Legend must be understood as legend, poetry as poetry, older belief as older belief, palpable error as such, verified claim as such. Jewish education must be an adventure in the pursuit of truth about Jews and Judaism, ancient, medieval, modern.

Jewish education as a guided and encouraged quest for truth about Jewish existence implies the centrality of the intelligent process in its methods. Truth is not handed down but is arrived at through inquiry. Jewish education, therefore, is inquiry into the nature, the meaning, and the direction of Jewish development. Is is free inquiry, not inquiry with preordained conclusions or with prescribed official doctrines of schools, seminaries, national organizations, parent congregations, or individual authorities. It is free inquiry, proceeding from real problems to relevant data to warranted conclusions.

Consider, for example, the proposition that archaeology confirms the Bible. Herman Wouk in *This Is My God* (p. 24) writes: "Archaeologists have known for some time that the history of Eastern Mediterranean civilization in the Bible is accurate; that we have in hand substantial corroboration of the main points of the Jewish national narrative; that in fact—setting aside the miraculous details which the scientific mind demurs from—it all happened." Here is a real problem for Jewish education: What does archaeology really affirm about the Bible and what does it not? Wouk's statement is not so dishonest as to slur over the obvious fact that archaeology does not confirm claims of divine intervention in, say, the genesis of the earth or the standstill of the sun during Joshua's battle with the five kings or the Revelation on Mount Sinai or the ten plagues or the splitting of the Red Sea or the Heavenly fire that on Mount Carmel consumed Elijah's burnt-offering and wood and stones and dust and water and thus demonstrated that Elijah's and not the Baal priests' god is the true God. Yet Wouk puts these unconfirmed reports of the Bible side by side with confirmed ones such as the existence of Abraham and Moses. Says Wouk: "Archaeologists have known . . . that in fact—setting aside the miraculous details which the scientific mind in principle demurs from—it all happened." What "all happened"? The reader's attention is not directed to the exceptions mentioned parenthetically and with implied derision of the "scientific mind." His attention is directed to the primary assertion to the effect that according to archaeology "it all happened."

For Jewish education we must claim canons of truthfulness that are far more stringent than those which make for some best-selling novels or biographies. In the age of science in-the-making, to be Jewishly educated means to have acquired an understanding of Judaism in the light of the best available evidence and understanding of the rise of a civilization, its lasting accomplishments, and its unresolved problems. To be an educated Jew is to have at least an inkling, based on prolonged inquiry, of Israel's historic struggle to emancipate itself from its own older myths and to emerge from ongoing encounters with reality carrying a purer faith and a more humane vision of God.

Whitehead wrote: "In the conditions of modern life the rule is absolute, the race which does not value trained intelligence is doomed." To this it may be added that there is no future for the uneducated peoples in the coming ages of science, and those who do not live by the truth and by the pursuit of truth, will not live at all.

In the second place, Jewish education in the age of science, which is to come, must do its share in proclaiming, teaching, and demonstrating the unity of science and of love. The age of science which is not, at the same time, the age of love is not likely to be an age at all. Science is not viable without love.

Traditionally, Jewish religion has proclaimed that "God is truth, his Torah is truth, his prophets are truth and He abounds in doing goodness and truth." Yet God is also love. He shows mercy to thousands, forgiving iniquity and granting acquittal. He loves us with everlasting love, has drawn us with love and blesses us with love. In Him, truth and love are inseparable.

Science has often been alleged to be dispassionate, neutral, beyond passion and compassion.

Yet precisely in an age of science the common recognition of the essential unity of intelligence and compassion or mind and love may save the age. Judaism as a religio-ethical civilization may undergo a renewal of relevance if it can demonstrate, in thought, in action, and in education, that in the fusion of human intelligence and human love, mankind may have a force that is stronger than that released by atomic fission. For Jewish education it would follow that compassionate love should join the process of intelligence in its methodological center. Neither suffices without the other. Science without love may destroy itself and the world. Love without science tends to be forgetful of actual conditions to be effective. Love leads intelligence to transcend conditions; intelligence leads love to fasten upon transcendence within immanence, upon ideals within the realm of fulfillment. Science may be understood as the method of love; love as the engine of science. Consummation of both is human salvation.

Jewish education as the education of, by, and for a religious civilization must pioneer in developing the fuller meaning of the unity and identity of mind and love, and must come to regard the release and development of these twin powers in human beings as among its central obligations.

Third, Jewish education for the age of science must address itself to the question and the quest of Jewish relevance.

By relevance is meant availability to furnish guidance for the solution of basic human problems of the modern world.

One such problem is the population explosion. By 1975, it has been estimated, 77 million human beings will be added to the human race each year and by 2000 it will be 126 million new humans each year. Six billion men, women, and children may greet the year 2000, as against the 2½ billion that walk the earth today. In this development, the central fact is that population growth will tend to be greatest where people are poorest. This means that the nations concerned are likely to resort to desperate means in order to get their share of the world's resources.

Another problem is the attainment of an economy of plenty and at the same time a political structure of individual liberty, a social order in which social planning goes hand in hand with personal and group initiative.

A third problem is the achievement of full independence of nations together with unitedness of mankind.

A fourth problem is the achievement not of the UN but of the UR, the United Religions, and the US, the United Sciences, and the UE, the United Educations, the UA, the United Arts.

Israel has been exporting technicians to a number of countries in the Far East and in Africa. It has exported actresses, dancers, women's fashions and models. Citrus fruits and cars and public relations personnel as well as political personalities have gone forth from its shores. Admiration for its military victories, for the spirit of the Ingathering of the Exiled has been generated widely. All these are remarkable accomplishments which may be belittled only by an ungenerous spirit. And then there is Yael Dayan's book and there are paintings and musicians and composers and more serious novelists.

But Torah in a new, not ordinary, sense. Torah with a new relevance to modern industrial society, to the struggle between democracy and totalitarianism, to the ongoing conflict between the sciences and the humanities and the theologies. Torah with a new relevance to the human situation has not gone forth from Zion. Nor should it be expected in the early decades of Jewish statehood.

American Jewry has been exporting Leonard Bernstein and Aaron Copland and UNRRA's Herbert Lehman and Doctor Salk and J. Robert Oppenheimer and Golda Meir and the heroic Colonel David Marcus who is buried at the cemetery of the West Point Military Academy. But Torah, in the sense of a new design for civilization, has not gone forth from American Jewry except, perhaps, in embryonic form.

For the preparation of our people for the creation of new relevance is not a political problem nor a military problem nor an economic problem, important as these are. It is essentially an educational problem.

Science producing new forms of human association across the continents increases the degree of irrelevance that older forms of human association have for us. The distance between us and the intellectual victories of the past grows more rapidly than the flight of chronological time permits us to believe. As Professor Baron has it, the concept of national sovereignty is more and more obsolete. Adolf A. Berle, Jr. taught us that the concept of private property is undergoing basic change in an age of corporations and labor unions and governmental responsibility for public welfare. Where "the show is rigged," whether in industry, in sports, in literature, free competition is a myth. Nor are we entirely sure of the age-old bit of common sense that there are definite limits to what the human mind can do. Herbert Spencer, we are reminded by Viscount Samuel, made a division between the known, the unknown, and the unknowable. "But whether there is an unknowable is itself among the unknown."[2] More recently, Professor John Herman Randall, Jr., suggested that "the world for science knows no limits—it is co-extensive with the world of vision, with everything man finds in the world."[3] Said Professor Philippe LeCorbeiller of Harvard recently in discussing "The Crisis in Science Education": "Science is Power: the power of doing things that have never been done before. No one can set limits to what science might achieve."[4]

Similarly, science producing new forms of understanding of natural events increasingly relegates to remoter recesses of antiquity pre-scientific interpretations of the universe. Today, notions of a superhuman will intervening to originate cosmic energy rapidly seem to join notions of the divinity of mountains, stars, emperors, selected messengers and prescriptions of medieval physicians: they sound almost equally dated and outdated. The idea that godhood attaches to an Absolute or an Ultimate, although enjoying a current vogue, strikes many as not less antiquated idolatry than cruder and earlier modes of idol worship.

In the realm of human associations and in the realm of beliefs about the cosmos, renewed Jewish relevance is a condition of continued Jewish existence. In ages of science, to be is to be in the lead, or at least with the lead group. To attain such renewal, a sustained educational effort is required—an effort that embraces the Jewish people as a whole, from the kindergarten to the graduate school and to life-long educational pursuits.

Jewish education in a scientific age in-the-making signifies a sustained search for new relevance. It signifies the enrollment of our people as a whole in the inquiry into the fundamentals of Judaism in the remote and

[2] *Belief and Action*, Indianapolis-New York: The Bobbs-Merrill Co., 1937, p. 37. See also his *In Search of Reality*, New York: Philosophical Library, 1957, p. 135.

[3] *Nature and Historical Experience*, New Cork: Columbia University Press, 1958, p. 306.

[4] Philippe LeCorbeiller, "The Crisis in Science Education," in Brand Blanshard, editor, *Education in the Age of Science*. New York: Basic Books, 1959, p. 230. *See also* Sir Julian Huxley's brilliant essay, "The Future of Man," *Bulletin of the Atomic Scientists*, Vol. xv, No. 10, December 1959, pp. 402–404, 409.

recent past, into the impost of science and democratic principles upon these fundamentals, and in the application of its creative thought to fruitful innovation which, in the spirit and with the forms of Israel's traditional culture, may produce a new golden age of culture under science.

Finally, as the education of a religious civilization, Jewish education is duty-bound to concern itself with the core concept of Jewish religion—the belief in God and the meaning of God.

The age of science-to-come is not likely to be a monolithic one, and existing versions of Judaism may be expected to continue functioning and creating their institutions, including their institutions of education. Their attitudes toward science will range, as now, from opposition to co-existence to wholehearted self-identification. The meaning of God presents not much of a problem to the anti-scientists and the co-existentialists. They will persist in adhering to traditional or near-traditional meanings. But those who adopt the scientific frame of mind and cannot withhold assent to the evolving pictures of the universe presented by the sciences, will have to reconstruct their religious outlook so that it may complement science in the manner proposed for love so that unified science, love, and faith may come to be "our life and the length of our days."

Professor Robert Ulich of Harvard has defined faith as the "consciousness of everything seeable being in the embrace of the unseen."[5]

But what is the nature of "the unseen"? It may be suggested that faith in the age of science may come to be identified as the consciousness of everything seeable or given, seeable or present, being in the embrace of the ungiven, the unpresent, the as-yet-ungiven, the as-yet-unpresent but present-to-be or simply *consciousness of everything present being in the embrace of promise, the promise of existence.* Faith is consciousness of the reality and the realiability of the promise inherent in existence. Judaism under science may come to be the religion of the promise. *Matter*, after all, is derived from *mater*, mother, or that which holds the promise of productivity and new life. Nature is derived from *natura* meaning she who gives birth.[6] God may come to be worshipped not simply as cosmic process but as the cosmic process by which the promise of existence turns into reality. God may come to be conceived as the universe acting on the level of its highest potentialities, as what the

[5] *The Human Career, A Philosophy of Transcendence.* New York: Harper & Brothers, 1955, p. 53.

[6] *Cf.* Herbert W. Schneider, 'The Unnatural" in *Naturalism and the Human Spirit*, edited by Y. H. Krikorian. New York: Columbia University Press, 1944, p. 125.

cosmos does with its potentiality for salvation, as the *Gestalt* of the cosmic promise.

These formulations, in all their tentativeness, are offered as indications of what kinds of reconstruction may be required in order to carry faith in God forward into the age of science.

In sum, Jewish education in an age of science and functioning within the framework of Jewish civilization must meet the scientific challenge by

(1) activating human intelligence in the pursuit of truth;
(2) striving to unite scientific method to compassionate love;
(3) fostering the Jewish people's quest for new relevance of Judaism to the human situation in the modern world;
(4) participating in the efforts of Jewish philosophy, theology, scholarship, the arts, and of the Jewish community, as a whole, to express the meaning of God and the essence of Jewish faith in the language of men and women who see the world through the eyes of science.

The Jewish past was built on three foundations: Learning or *Torah;* worship or *abodah;* charity or *gemiluth hasadim.*

The Jewish future seems to require a four-sided base: the relentless pursuit of truth; the search for relevance; the coalescence of science and love; the re-reading of the book of nature for the evidence of its promise.

Loyalties in Jewish Education[7]

IN THE FIRST PLACE, Judaism, as the evolving religious civilization of the Jewish People, by virtue of its participation in contemporary technological civilization, is involved in the science-induced rapid social change which characterizes our time. Judaism shares in the opportunities of the age, suffers its tensions, undergoes the terrors of its still rampant irrationalisms and mysticisms, and contributes to its trials and its triumphs.

It follows that merely to habituate our young in ancient and medieval outlooks, assumptions, beliefs, and loyalties is to prepare the coming generations for life in the past, for practices expressing historically significant, but no longer vitally applicable meanings. It is to equip them with knowledge of an obsolete cosmology, physiology, anthropology and history, and with a morality, a theology, and a philosophy no longer acceptable without serious reservations.

[7] Meir Ben-Horin, "Loyalties in Jewish Education," *Reconstructionist*, Vol. 22, No. 3, March 23, 1956, pp. 17–21. Used by permission of the author and publisher.

Education for Judaism as the *creatively involved* civilization of our Peoples requires a basic reorientation in which the traditional texts, concepts, value-judgments and value-commitments are regarded, not as exclusive ends-in-view, but rather as instrumentalities for the ends of a reawakened Jewish creativity. In conjunction with the non-Jewish value-systems which we share and create as members of the broader community, the historical *sancta* or symbols of self-consecration and the historic *civilia* or ways of common conduct and common thought of "catholic Israel" ought to function as means for securing both continuous safety and safe continuity in the transition from past to future experience. For, if the proper study of man is no longer simply man, but, in Dewey's language, "the continuous reconstruction" of man's experience, then the proper study of man as Jew is the progressive reinterpretation, reformulation, and reconstruction of Jewish experience.

A Jewish education of this kind dealing with "genuine problematic life-situations," and aiming at their cooperative solution, is no longer just supplementary in nature as is most present-day Jewish schooling. Education for the reconstruction of Jewish experience is not simply an addition of certain courses of study or of a number of credit-hours to an already crowded curriculum of public education. Being reconstructive rather than additive in nature, it is concerned with activities and educative experiences related to the core questions of life, and, especially of Jewish life, in our time. Its province is not to provide ancient and medieval answers to queries to which general education furnishes modern scientific answers. Rather its office is to grapple with problems which never can be of equal concern to the general American school: the *Jewish problems* of our time arising from our very will to continued Jewish existence. These include the problems of how to express Jewishness, personally and collectively, in twentieth-century America and in the twentieth-century world; problems of the nature and function of religion in scientific-technological society; problems of changing Jewish communal and congregational organization, authority, and sanction; problems of proximity and distance in relation to the State of Israel; problems relating to the direction and the contents of Jewish education itself.

Second, Jewish education must wholeheartedly and earnestly strive to inculcate the spirit of trans-cultural empathy. While fostering loyalty to Judaism as the distinctive civilization of Jewry throughout the world and the ages; while never minimizing the reality and the enormity of anti-Semitism and anti-Israelism, social, racial, and religious; while creating a sense of responsibility for the welfare and the freedom of the

Jewish state and Jewish communities the world over; Jewish education must at the same time help to combat feelings of animosity *vis-à-vis* the non-Jewish world in general and democratic society in particular. It is, according to this view, the function of Jewish education to teach the rising generations of our people that independence may mean utter isolation and that interdependence is not a step toward assimilation and eventual disappearance. Love for Judaism is either compatible with love for all ethical civilizations and for the humanity of our species, or it is in itself incompatible with Judaism. "Chosenness" is an immoral principle, if it refers to anything but the superiority of human intelligence and love over the pre-humanities of nature and the inhumanities, ancient and modern, of ecstatic terror. The individuality of all things is a more accurate description of reality than "the unity of all things," but, on the human level, this individuality need not spell captious pugnacity. Rather it should imply the capacity for what Schopenhauer called *Mitleid* and *Mitfreude* or, roughly, sympathy and sym-pathos, compassion and comfort.

Third, in theory and in practice, Jewish education ought to make its contribution to the development of the understandings and the skills necessary for cooperative planning in communal affairs. Active citizenship in a free society, both internal and external to Jewish life, will make such personality structure perhaps the primary goal of all education. The Jewish school on all levels, fortified by the power of a millennia-old religious tradition in mutual responsibility of group and individual, should become an active force in this vital area of education. Far from being concerned mainly with attitudes appropriate to "naturalization" or "super-naturalization" in otherworldly spheres of "being," the modern Jewish educator ought to give increasing attention to the means of teaching the qualities of public-minded citizenry, combining idealistic vision with this-worldly skill and intelligence in decisive social action.

Fourth, in the area of science and religion Jewish education should take its place in the forefront of fearless inquiry and broader understanding. Jewish teachers, perhaps for the first time in their lives, become aware of the pressing need for convincing answers when confronted by a class of children or adolescents. Since parents and students continue to regard the Jewish school as a school of religion, the teachers' responsibility in this context touches upon some of the deepest sensibilities of the community. If Jewish religion is to live, not only by virtue of the synagogue and the home, but also because of what the school does for it and with it, Jewish educational leadership must be asserted in this crucial sector of life for which no single institution can hold an exclusive monopoly.

The Jewish School Is more than an Annex to the Synagogue

It is the duty of the Jewish school to be more than an annex to the synagogue. The school is neither the junior congregation nor, on the high school and college levels, is it the senior congregation. The school ought to promote, encourage, and teach participation in public worship and observances, just as it ought to teach understanding of and participation in other public activities, such as the United Jewish Appeal, organized Zionism, Hebrew arts, and Jewish research. Yet the specific function of education *qua* education with respect to religion is not just practice but thought, not just participation but inquiry, not just observance but reflection. If the continuing shift from revelationary to communal authority requires the application of reflective intelligence to the problem of Jewish religion and religiosity, the school ought to observe and to practice loyalty to the standards and modes of untrammeled investigation and, transcending congregational commitments to doctrine, ought to liberate the powers of religious creativity.

For, finally, institutions will be judged by what they do to liberate human intelligence for the creation of richer meanings and more adequate ways of achieving the fulfillment of the human promise. Jewish education, to the extent that it emerges from its pre-professional stage of mere subject-matter transmission and dogmatic indoctrination, will cease habituating our young to routine behaviors and ideas and adjusting them to a fixed social and intellectual situation which, as one may put it, is *preparing them for what is known not to be and is not preparing them for the unknown that is to be.* To the degree that Jewish education seriously and sincerely dedicates itself to the shaping of consummate Jewish personalities whose free minds and compassionate hearts rise to the challenge of the "new age" in the spirit of the citizen-soldiers of Gaza and of the citizen-soldiers of Concord and Lexington—to that degree will Jewish education itself become an object of loyalty to those who can do and those who can teach, those who can think and those who can love.

Meir Ben-Horin (December 31, 1918—) was born in Konigsberg, the capital of East Prussia. He received a classic-humanistic education at the

Städtisches Gymnasium und Realgymnasium *in the Free City of Danzig and studied modern Hebrew literature, Greek and Roman literature, Jewish philosophy, Jewish mysticism, and archaeology of the Middle East at the Hebrew University in Jerusalem. He holds the degree of Bachelor of Jewish Pedagogy,* cum laude, *from the Teachers Institute of the Jewish Theological Seminary of America, and the M.A. and Ph.D. from Columbia University.*

Ben-Horin served in the U.S. Army during World War II in Italy, Germany, and Austria. He is a member of the U.S. Army Reserve and holds the rank of Major in Civil Affairs.

In 1957 Ben-Horin published his Max Nordau—Philosopher of Human Solidarity, *a first attempt to present in a systematic and comprehensive manner the philosophy of one of the founding fathers of the State of Israel. The philosophy of human solidarity, or solidaritarianism, upholds the faith in man conceived not as* homo faber *but as* homo faber domus, *not as builder in general but essentially as home-builder on the personal and local, the tribal and national, the global and the cosmic levels. Solidarity, in Ben-Horin's interpretation of Nordau, denotes the unity of democracy and science, of compassion and intelligence, of mind and love. It stands, in Ben-Horin's view, as the free world's answer and challenge to the totalitarian creeds of our time.*

As a solidaritarian, Ben-Horin seeks to formulate a program and a philosophy of education in which the mind-love continuum stands at the center and functions as both goal and method. He adheres to the reconstructionist, rather than the progressivist, interpretations of Deweyan pragmatism.

Ben-Horin's writings have appeared in The Educational Forum, School and Society, Saturday Review, Reconstructionist, Jewish Quarterly Review, American Jewish Year Book, Essays in Jewish Life and Thought. *He is co-editor of essays and studies, presented in honor of Abraham A. Neuman, president of Dropsie College, Philadelphia, and managing editor of* Jewish Social Studies, *New York.*

He serves as professor of Education and chairman of the School of Education at the Dropsie College for Hebrew and Cognate Learning in Philadelphia.

Recommended Readings for Part Five

Students are urged to consult the annotated bibliography at the end of this volume for information on the books cited here.

The following books in philosophy and philosophy of education should be especially useful.

A. PHILOSOPHY:

HERBERT W. SCHNEIDER, *A History of American Philosophy*

B. PHILOSOPHY OF EDUCATION:

Encyclical Letter, Divini Illius Magistri of His Holiness Pope Pius XI
ALLAN JAHSMANN, *What's Lutheran in Education?*
A. H. JOHNSTON, *A Philosophy of Education*
A. V. JUDGES, *Education and the Philosophic Mind*
PHILIP H. PHENIX, *Education and The Common Good*
ROBERT ULICH, *Crisis and Hope in American Education*
H. P. VAN DUSEN, *God in Education*.....

Existentialism

Introduction to Part Six

EXISTENTIALISM is a name for a philosophical tendency rather than for a philosophy. It began to manifest itself in Western Europe after World War I, but it did not become influential in philosophical circles until after World War II. Existentialism is a shift in emphasis from an all-consuming concern for essence to an increased concern for existence. Essence is said to follow from existence, and what a man *becomes* constitutes his essence. Existentialists deny that we human beings are held helplessly in the grasp of historical and natural forces. They insist on the importance of human freedom, personality, and will. They call our attention to the irrational and unconscious elements in human nature and remind us of the adverse effects our technical advances may have upon our freedom. Existentialists tend to be staunch supporters of education, for they believe it to be the foundation of human progress.

Soren Kierkegaard (1813–1855) is frequently called the originator of modern existentialism. He was a Danish philosopher who studied theology at the University of Copenhagen, graduating in 1840. He was a studious man whose life was marked by physical suffering and mental torture, for he was a hunchback. He carried out a feverish attack upon the theology and practices of the state of Denmark, maintaining that religion was for the individual and not entirely the province of the church. One writer has called Kierkegaard's position a protest against any sort of action that would "exalt society at the price of submerging the individual." Philosophically Kierkegaard objected to Hegel's idea of the rational world ("The real is the rational and the rational is the real"). He thought it presumptuous and ridiculous, for the belief rested upon the assumption that a particular part of the yet incomplete world, namely Hegel, could know what its completed form must be. Only God himself, if anyone—and certainly not Hegel—could know this. Thus, no human being could know his place in the universe from the beginning, but would have to exercise his intelligence to prove himself as he lived his own particular life in a world of anguish, surrounded by loneliness and faced with the prospects of death.

Other well-known existentialists are Karl Jaspers (1883—), Martin

Heidegger (1889—), and Jean Paul Sartre (1905—). Jaspers is recognized as the man who worked out the most satisfactory statement of existentialism in the twentieth century. Heidegger, a follower of the phenomenology of Husser, has described what he believes to be the fundamental experiences that lie behind everyday scientific knowledge, while Sartre, the atheistic existentialist, is perhaps best known for his literary efforts, in which he has shown that man is "condemned to be free," that people make their own hell, and that life is a rather ineffective passion. He delights in pointing out that some people exist only *in* themselves, while others exist *for* themselves.

The two American educators who have written most extensively on Existentialism and education are Van Cleve Morris, of the University of Illinois, Circle Campus, and George Kneller, of the University of California at Los Angeles. One cannot begin to summarize all these men have had to say about education. One can gain some insight into what they are thinking if he will note with Morris that education may be defined as *"awakened awareness* in the learner—existential awareness of himself as a single subjectivity present in the world." The task of education which falls chiefly on the secondary schools, as Morris sees it, is "to provide the occasions and circumstances for the awakening and intensification of awareness." Morris tries to show that there are three constituent awarenesses which make up what he calls the "psychological content of the self": These are (1) *choosing* agent, unable to avoid making choices throughout life, (2) *free* agent, absolutely (sic) free to set the goals of his life, and (3) *responsible* agent, personally accountable for his freely selected choices. The teacher's task is "to arrange the learning situations in such a way as to bring home the truth of these propositions to every individual."[1]

Criticisms have arisen with respect to Existentialism. Two of the current criticisms, and perhaps the most telling ones are that existentialists, as well as certain other philosophical positions, erroneously attempt to infer ends and practices for education for general philosophical statements; and, that these same existentialists have not understood what academic philosophers writing on Existentialism are doing or saying.

In the readings that follow Professor Van Cleve Morris attempts to state the substance of the existentialist's position and he suggests certain implications for education. Professor George Kneller gives in greater detail what he believes is implied for education. Professor Bruce Baker,

[1] Van Cleve Morris, *Existentialism in Education.* New York: Harper & Row, Publishers, 1966.

on the other hand, critically reviews the writings of certain noted existentialists on education, criticizes the altogether too prevalent practice of inferring educational guidelines and practices from general writings on existentialism, and calls for greater attention to the I-Thou philosophy of Martin Buber.

21

An Overview: Existentialism and Education [*]

VAN CLEVE MORRIS

AMERICAN EDUCATION continues in search of a guiding principle by which to order its affairs. Hardly a week passes but another statement of educational aims and purposes is run from the nation's presses.

Most of this debate swirls around the protagonistic head of Experimentalism which in a short half century has initiated truly remarkable changes in educational theory and practice. Platonic Idealists, Aristotelian Neo-Thomists, and even Rousseauian Naturalists almost daily in the public prints hurl themselves against the house of Experimentalism, hoping, if not to storm out and rout, at least to infilter and infect it with the germs of what to them is a more reasonable and truthful view of things. There are few signs that the struggle is likely to abate.

In fact, if portents are accurate, we are about to witness a new and vigorous assault, originating in this case not from one of the older, more conventional traditions but rather from a fresh and genuinely modern theory of man—Existentialism. The intellectual, to say nothing of the lay, world knows so precious little about this philosophical infant (or

[*] Van Cleve Morris, "Existentialism and Education," *Educational Theory*, Vol. 4, No. 4, October, 1954, pp. 247–258. Used by permission of the author and *Educational Theory*.

better, adolescent) that the full fury of the assault may be some years off. But the issue shall be joined sooner or later.

This paper is an effort (1) to state the substance of the Existentialist point of view, (2) to note points of contrast and comparison with Experimentalism, and (3) to suggest from our study of Existentialism some implications for education. Unfortunately, for this final section we have little to go on; Existentialist writers have not as yet systematically turned their attention to the education of man. At this point therefore we shall be on our own.

What Is Existentialism?

The casual reader has no doubt run across references to Existentialism with increasing frequency in recent years. It is said, as it is probably said of every new philosophy, that Existentialism is a philosophy of crisis, a theory of life and man particularly fitted for our anxious times. It is not clear what actually is meant by this; for if this means that Existentialism is the spiritual medicine which can quiet man's nerves and can steady and strengthen him for living in an era of peril, then it is certainly false. For, as we shall see, Existentialism is hardly a comforting analgesic. On the contrary, it leaves man more exposed than he has ever been to the pains and agonies of existence. It leaves him alone, completely alone, bereft of any shield whether it be of the grace of a supernatural God or the comforting company of men. Indeed, if Existentialism is a philosophy of crisis, then it certainly must be considered as a part *of* the crisis rather than a foil *against* it.[1]

The reader will also recall vague references to Existentialism which have suggested its apparent disinterest in morals. One hears that Existentialists are vulgar and obscene and that Existentialism means quite literally 'each one his own judge of right and wrong.' The implication is that there is no such thing as right and wrong, and therefore no need for personal responsibility for moral choices. This feeling has been the

---

[1] In a sense Existentialism may become man's bulwark. Absolutistic doctrines, promising safety and security, have revealed a nasty habit of disintegrating just when men needed them most. When these card houses collapse men find themselves with nothing left on which to build. Existentialism refuses to erect these marvelous but fragile edifices and therefore avoids deluding men into what can only be false security. Existentialists therefore consider their point of view an improvement if only because it is more trustworthy, because it is so radically realistic in describing the world men live in. A life without pretense, even if difficult and hazardous, is to be preferred to a life full of confident hopes for security and salvation which turn out to be mere illusions.

unfortunate result of the total misinterpretation of the writings of the French Existentialists, most notably Jean-Paul Sartre. Sartre is an accomplished novelist and playwright, as well as philosopher, and his non-philosophic works might be accused of vulgarity. And it is true that he considers each individual his own judge not only of right and wrong but of the criteria by which one judges right and wrong. But it is erroneous to construe this to mean that right and wrong do not exist and an outright inversion of actual fact to intimate that Sartre believes personal responsibility for ethical choices has become unnecessary. On the contrary, as we shall see, the radical necessity for individual responsibility in making moral decisions is practically the central principle in the Existentialist network of ideas.

Incidentally, the name of Sartre has gained such popularity in recent years on both sides of the Atlantic that people have begun to think of Sartre and Existentialism almost as synonymous. As a matter of actual fact, Sartre is only a late comer on the Existential stage, and is surprisingly enough, only partially representative of genuine Existentialism today.

Although the philosophical problem of existence has been touched on in classical and medieval writings, it never came to the fore as a central philosophical theme until Soren Kierkegaard (1813–1855) began its development about a century ago. This turbulent and complex Danish figure remained obscure for more than half a century, until early in the nineteen hundreds when his works began to appear in German translation. English translations did not begin to arrive until 1935. Most of the systematic elaboration of existential philosophies has therefore taken place quite recently and the major Existentialist figures are still living.

Of these men, Karl Jaspers (1883—) and Martin Heidegger (1889–) have been responsible for the German development and Gabriel Marcel (1889–) and the aforementioned Sartre (1905–) the French development of what has come to be known as the philosophy of Existence, or Existentialism. Generally speaking, Jaspers and Marcel, both Catholics, represent the Christian 'wing' and Heidegger and Sartre the secular and (in the case of Sartre) atheistic 'wing' of the movement.

As the philosophic sightseer circles 'round this complex chamber of wonders (or horrors)', he is assailed by doubt as to which of the few small doors he should most profitably enter first. For, in a sense, Existentialism is not merely a set of new answers to old metaphysical questions but instead a bold attempt to provide new kinds of answers by considering the questions in an entirely new setting.

Classical philosophy comes to an end in Hegel, because it has become folly to construct intellectual totalitarian systems in which everything is taken up, harmonized, rationalized, and justified. Such palaces are still marvelous, but nobody can live in them. The savour and reality of human existence, its perils and triumphs, its bitterness and sweetness, are outside in the street.[2]

To begin with, classical philosophy and in fact all philosophy from Plato to Hegel has traditionally centered its attention on the question of essence; philosophers have repeatedly felt that the main business of philosophy is to answer the question "What is reality?" Study of this central question is customarily carried on through study of other companion questions of essence: What is man?, What is God?, What is the Universe?, What is Knowledge, Truth, Beauty, Good, Evil?

Existentialism turns its attention elsewhere, relegating questions of essence to subordinate status. The Existentialists claim that the question "What is man?" must wait upon an answer to the problem of explaining what it means to say that man *is*. How can we search for essence before we have even explained the *existence* of the thing we seek the essence of?

Older philosophies have merely assumed existence or have engaged in flashy ratiocinations like the Cartesian 'Cogito ergo sum' to "prove" it. The Existentialist says this will not do, that a thorough study of existence must precede any intelligent attack on the problem of essence. This then becomes the primary *new kind* of question that Existentialism raises, i.e., What does it mean to say 'I am'?

Among some of the Existentialists, the argument goes even further, to the point of stating that existence should take priority over essence in philosophic study because in fact it precedes essence in terms of cosmic development. Sartre is most apt to use this thesis and he puts it in this wise: When an artisan makes a shoe, the idea (essence) of the shoe is in his mind before he makes it. Man considers God a king-sized artisan who had an idea of man before He made man. Hence, the popular notion that essence always precedes existence. But, says Sartre, there is no creator of man. Man discovered himself. His existence came first; he now is in the process of determining his essence. Man first is, then he defines himself.[3]

Else, say the Existentialists, we would have to assume a creator of man (God), and then to explain God, we must assume a creator of God, then a creator of God's creator, and so forth, ad infinitum. This of course is

[2] H. J. Blackham, *Six Existentialist Thinkers*. London: Routeledge and Kegan Paul, Ltd., 1952, p. 44.

[3] J. P. Sartre, *Existentialism*, translated by B. Frechtman. New York: Philosophical Library, 1947, pp. 16–17.

ridiculous and so likewise is the notion of an uncreated creator. We are left therefore with man who is mere existent, he *is* before he is any particular thing.

In like fashion goes the rebuttal to Descartes and his "I think, therefore I am." What a monstrous non sequitur this has been discovered to be! Why does it follow that I am merely because I am capable of thought? Moreover even to utter the first clause "I think" I must presuppose my existence and my ability to utter it. Unless I existed I certainly could not engage in thought. I therefore must exist *before* I think:

. . . it is the existence of my body in the world that constitutes me a subject before it is given to me as an object to a subject.[4]

Thus, it is more nearly correct to invert and modify Descartes: "I am, therefore I have one of the prerequisites for thought." We shall see later that Existentialism, in effect, uses neither of these but more nearly "I choose, therefore I am."

Thus we behold man, aboriginal man that is, as pure existent devoid of any essense whatsoever. He is not bound by any antecedent or a priori human nature but is completely free to determine his own nature. This freedom is total; man can choose what he shall be. It is this process of choosing and of becoming which describes, as accurately as one can, what the Existentialists believe is fundamental to human existence. If man has an essence, it is literally his freedom from essence and his consequent freedom to choose and become what he will.

Now the concept of freedom has always been a subject of much discussion and dispute among philosophers, and all of the older theories wavered between a position of complete determinism on the one hand and some kind of union of freedom within ultimate determinism on the other. Existentialism refuses to walk this tightrope, and flatly and clearly states the case for complete, undiluted, and absolute freedom. It insists that any attempt at joining or harmonizing the two is merely philosophical squirming, intellectual equivocation in the face of an uncomfortable decision. It is just this necessity for choosing between determinism and freedom which occasioned one of Kierkegaard's major works, *Either/Or*. In summary, his thesis is this:

Either: the life of the individual person, a microcosm as the image of God, capable of free, responsible action, and therefore . . . a life of toil and much suffering and many dangers; *or:* the life of an impersonal, unfree member of a

4 H. J. Blackman, *op. cit.*, p. 68.

collective, without the possibility of independent knowledge and responsible action, a life in the service of unknown forces—, and as compensation for the loss of freedom at best a false, illusory dream of material welfare in an earthly paradise which can never become a reality.[5]

Yes, indeed, "a life of toil and much suffering and many dangers." For to be free one must surrender the privilege of seeking comfort in a supernatural or superhuman authority. We cannot honestly insist on freedom in our successes and then in times of stress suddenly enter "a universe where we can just give up, fall on our father's neck, and be absorbed into the absolute life as a drop of water melts into the river or the sea."[6] If he is merely a pawn acting out the determined thoughts of God, then man's works are all second-hand. He has lost his creativity. He has lost his freedom. He is no longer man. On the contrary, the "essence" of man is that he is free. He can create. He can choose. And, whether he likes it or not, "toil, suffering, and danger" are his.

Indeed, history is one long episode of man's toilsome struggle to escape from this freedom.[7] In his anxiety and anguish,[8] he has tried the religious escape but been turned back. Now he attempts the cultural escape, the submersion of his humanity in the ocean of mass thinking and mass behavior. As Ortega y Gasset has put it, "modern man, afraid of the lonesomeness of his existence, has been trying to steal himself into the anonymity of the social collective."[9]

But this route is also blocked. For, as the Existentialist shows, we cannot claim freedom from responsibility for our acts by attributing them to the conditioning effects of the environment. It is of course true that men have been and are creatures of culture, and once buried in the social collective they find it almost impossible to get out:

To battle against princes and popes is easy compared with struggling against the masses, the tyranny of equality, against the grin of shallowness, nonsense, baseness, and bestiality.[10]

[5] Johannes Holenberg, *Soren Kierkegaard* (transl. by Maria Bachmann-Isler). Basel: Benno Schwabe and Co., 1949, p. 417 (quoted in K. F. Reinhardt, *The Existentialist Revolt*. Milwaukee: Bruce Publishing Co., 1952, p. 36).

[6] William James, *Pragmatism*. New York: Longmans, Green and Co., c. 1907. p. 292.

[7] See Eric Fromm, *Escape from Freedom*.

[8] This and "dread," "forlornness," and "despair" are favorite Existential words.

[9] K. F. Reinhardt, *op. cit.*, p. 114.

[10] S. Kierkegaard, The Journals, ed., A. Dru, p. 1317. (Quoted in F. H. Heinemann, *Existentialism and the Modern Predicament*. London: Adam and Charles Black, 1953, p. 35.)

But the irrevocable fact is that men do not *have* to follow environment's way. There is nothing in man that inevitably and inexorably drives him to accept one behavior pattern over another. However much the sociologist and anthropologist turn him into a cultural product, man can still oppose his culture. He cannot lay his faulty values, his barbaric politics, or even his personal psychoneurosis to his membership in a given human group—family, community, or national society—for he *could* have had it otherwise. Man can choose which way he will take; and this freedom to choose distinguishes him from all other phenomena in the universe. To be a man is to be undetermined, to be free.

No factor outside of a person's own will ever dooms him to follow a certain course. No external condition modifies his behavior in any way. Each person could have taken another course or have chosen another way to act.[11]

We see man, then, as the determiner of his own nature, definer of his own values. He is not the promiscuous and irresponsible scoundrel suggested by the phrase "every one his own judge of right and wrong." On the contrary, existential man feels the terrible burden of responsibility thrust on him by the withdrawal of all other supports. Sartre puts it this way:

My freedom is the unique foundation of values. And since I am the being by virtue of whom values exist, nothing—absolutely nothing—can justify me in adopting this or that value or scale of values. As the unique basis of the existence of values, I am totally unjustifiable. And my freedom is in anguish at finding that it is the baseless basis of values.[12]

Far from being carefree and irresponsible, existential man is continually in the presence of doubt and anguish as to what he should do, for he knows that when he chooses, he chooses for Man. His life and conduct become his definitions of Man. Each word, each deed, each choice, represents his responsible understanding of what man is, and therefore each becomes a tiny building block in the existential edifice of value. Certainly no reasonable head could call this ethical theory an invitation to rascality.

We have only to develop one additional concept to bring this overly brief sightseeing tour to an end, i.e., the concept of transcendence. This is not to be confused with either the transcendental or transcendentalism, for Existentialists have no outer world, no supersensory, supernatural,

---

[11] J. M. Spier, *Christianity and Existentialism,* transl. by D. H. Freeman. Philadelphia: The Presbyterian and Reformed Publishing Co., 1953, p. 71.
[12] H. J. Blackham, *op. cit.,* pp. 155–156.

transempirical region representing the "control booth" of the universe. Transcendence is the Existentialist name for the unique mode of human existence. Since man is indeterminate, since he is capable of choice, he is always seeking to realize himself. He constantly engages in reaching up, struggling for a new and higher definition of himself.

Now this process is, in effect, the process of becoming. In short, to exist is to be engaged in the process of becoming, and it is destined to go on as long as man is on the earth. There is no limit to what man can become. His *rate* of advance is of course always checked by the upper limits of his facility for making free choices, but that he shall advance and that there is no end point to his advance there is no question.

Man's existence is then marked by his reaching up beyond himself, in making himself over, in constantly reordering human nature:

> . . . human reality cannot be defined because it is not something given, it is in question. A man is possibility, he has the power to be. His existence is in his choice of the possibilities which are open to him, and since this choice is never final, once for all, his existence is indeterminate because not terminated.[13]

Sartre expresses it similarly:

> . . . man is constantly outside of himself; in projecting himself, in losing himself outside of himself, he makes for man's existing; and, on the other hand, it is by pursuing transcendent goals that he is able to exist; man, being, this state of passing-beyond, and seizing upon things only as they bear upon this passing-beyond is at the heart, at the center of this passing-beyond.[14]

Man is thus, unlike any other phenomenon in the cosmos, always oriented toward his possibilities, toward the transcendent notions of what he might be.

In a sense, the idea of transcendence boils down to man's gift of what might be termed dynamic self-consciousness. Not only can man think, but he can think about (and criticize and correct) his thinking; not only can man contemplate but he can contemplate his facility for contemplation; not only can man have feeling but he can have feeling about feeling. This no other organism, so far as we know, shares with us. Thus man is not only conscious, but he is also, and uniquely self-conscious. He can possess a certain quiddity at a given moment and at the same moment be conscious of, and criticize and seek to change, this quiddity. He is, in a sense,

[13] H. J. Blackham, *op. cit.*, p. 88.
[14] J. P. Sartre, *op. cit.*, p 59.

always standing outside himself (transcendent) and engaging in thought-ful plans about how to do himself over.

Existentialism and Education

We come now to a consideration of the role of education in an existential world. What does all this mean for the education of man?

At the outset, it seems probable that the existential school will be a place where man's non-rational, i.e., his aesthetic, moral, and emotional self will be much more in evidence than his scientific, rational self. Experimentalists have envisioned a school where youngsters learn by using the scientific method to solve real, genuine problems, by using their reflective intelligence to explore and test possible alternative solutions to the perplexities their environment poses. Existentialists, while no doubt providing room for this kind of teaching, will be more interested in developing the affective side of man, his capacity to love, to appreciate, to respond emotionally to the world about him.

This seems probable because of the Existentialist Imperative—the necessity for personal "involvement" in human situations and the consequent requirement for unguided, unjustifiable but nevertheless responsible choice on the part of the individual person. Existentialists are not so concerned about gathering factual evidence on a problem; science can do that. They are more concerned with what man does with the evidence. Science does not prescribe answers; it only gathers data. It is the individual who selects the answers, and he does so with no help from anyone. He is not compelled by nature to select any one answer; he can select any. His selection is therefore his alone, and he is responsible for it. He cannot justify it except in terms of himself. He may of course choose in a way in which the majority chooses. But the company of a majority does not make his choice right. He is condemned to live in constant anguish and doubt as to whether his choice was the right one.

Although there is no easy escape from this anguish, it is presumed that the development of the affective dimension of human personality would better prepare the individual for this kind of existence than would the development of his rational and scientific faculties which are after all supposed to be kept objective, neutral, and therefore free of personal preference.

For better or worse, therefore, the Existentialist educator would seem to be committed to the task of developing the choice-making power in the individual, and it seems probable that in working to this end, he will move away from the sciences, including the social sciences, and increasingly turn to the humanities and the arts. For it is here where man's aesthetic, emotional, and moral proclivities are exercised.[15]

By way of paradox, however, the opposite point of view might easily be developed. If the business of living is to be, at least in part, an effort to escape from this anguish, the *deadening* of the affective centers might emerge as a suitable educational objective. In this event, the more dull and insensitive a person became, the more satisfying and certain a life he would presumably lead. I take it however that Existentialists do not consider the amelioration of anguish as either possible or desirable. It is in the very nature of things that we are free; being free we are committed to live in anguish, and we must make the best of a very difficult situation.

As for pedagogy, it seems inevitable that the existential school will become more individual-centered. In a way, it will have to be, since its prime consideration is the individual living unattached in a friendless world. The "group method," so long a friend of democratic Experimentalism, will have to be discarded. You cannot teach the individual the true significance of his unique individualism with group dynamics; the very function of group dynamics is to illustrate the superiority of group decision over individual decision.

In fact, it would seem likely that all forms of cooperative endeavor would atrophy, at least all those in which decisions were sought (as distinguished from those in which factual information is shared). And we would likely find boys and girls working individually with their teachers, assessing the material before them and learning the necessity for making existential choices.

To an Experimentalist, this would of course be an intolerable kind of school, one in which the social and gregarious qualities of human experience would certainly atrophy and die. But the Existentialist does not value gregariousness. Gregariousness is only a transparent excuse for the loss of man's unique existential individuality, only a pretty word for explaining man's unhappy capitulation to the cosmic forces trying to make him a mass animal. If man is to regain that which makes him human, he must be willing once again to stand alone, willing to withstand the pressures of history and culture, and to chart the course of his own life, not only for himself but on behalf of Man.

This is surely a large order, particularly in an age when we cower before the awesome might of man-made instruments of power. To think

---

[15] For a similar analysis emphasizing "the culture of the emotions" as the future core of the curriculum, see R. Ulich, *Crisis and Hope in American Education.* Boston: Beacon Press, 1951, Ch. III.

that men can be expected to stand up to these twentieth-century behemoths may be only philosophic whistling in the dark; but stand up they must, say the Existentialists, if men are to cease being animals and start being men.

One can readily see from all this that Existentialists would hardly be expected to concern themselves, as have the Experimentalists and the Reconstructionists, with the problem of cultural change and social reconstruction. The way to the good life, according to the Existentialists, is not through social reform; that only tends to substitute one kind of social collectivity for another. In both, men are driven by tradition, custom, and public opinion. The way to the good life, or as the Existentialist would put it, the *authentic* life, is instead for each individual human being to begin realizing himself by asserting his individuality and making his own choices instead of being stampeded into the choices of the collectivity. In school, therefore, youngsters would not be encouraged to examine and criticize the cultural tradition they were inheriting with a view to its improvement and reform. They would instead be concerned with developing that integrity in themselves necessary to the task of making personal choices of action, taking personal responsibility for these choices, whether the culture smiles or frowns. Sociologists are always arguing about how to improve society—by improving social institutions or by improving individuals. Existentialists clearly choose the latter.

The problem, therefore, of democracy vs. authoritarianism seems rather irrelevant to the Existentialists. Democrats, they say, delude themselves with the myth that group decision is not authoritarian. But surely there can be tyranny in majority rule. We all live under the oppressive leveling influence of mass opinion, custom, and habit. Is this not tyranny? If democracy means group decision, let us have none of it.

If, however, democracy means individual choice, if the Fourth-of-July speeches concerning the freedom of the individual are to be taken literally and at face value, then we shall be on our way to an existential conception of socio-political life. For the individual is his own best (and *only*) judge of what he should do; any defection from his freedom, whether excused or justified by autocratic fiat, democratic law, or "the cake of custom," thereby subtracts from his intrinsic humanness. The only adequate socio-political order is one which recognizes and values the absolute freedom of the human person. The school in such an order shall be the instrument through which the individual learns how to use this freedom.

Here finally we come upon a most profound divergence of Existentialist and Experimentalist educational theory. We have said that the Existentialist school will not become involved in any particular choices but only in the choice-making process itself. If this be true, it would hardly claim to be a school at all in our modern sense. For schools, as they have been defined by contemporary students of culture, are places where specified values, skills, attitudes, and modes of response are presumably selected out of the multitude open to men as the particular cultural conditioners a given human group has chosen for itself. Civilizations invent and build schools because they have become self-conscious of their own experience and wish to perpetuate it; they support educational systems because they have made choices and wish these choices to become the working equipment of oncoming generations.

All this would become impossible in Existentialist theory. No choice is demonstrably better than any other because there are no external standards by which one may measure their validity. Each man, being radically free, is his own supreme court of value. He cannot look to culture or to history for any guidance whatsoever. His schooling therefore would become, in our modern understanding of the term, quite meaningless; indeed, if education means the selection and acquisition of certain modes of response over others, it seems most preposterous to believe that Existentialists could have schools at all. If, in short, education, as Childs and other Experimentalists have so forcibly stated, is primarily a *social* undertaking perpetuating and interpreting a social system to succeeding generations; and if, on the other hand, Existentialists view society only as a new mode of tyranny over the minds of men, then we might even conclude that Existentialism would have no traffic with education in any shape or form. Indeed, the case might even be developed that Existentialism is the very denial of education as we understand it today.

We have deliberately painted a much more radical picture than is perhaps warranted. Since the Existentialists have not addressed themselves to the problem of education,[16] it is precarious to make speculations —even "educated" ones—about what their ideas mean in educational terms.

It seems appropriate nonetheless to approach this interesting problem

[16] There have been some very interesting and provocative educational interpretations of Existentialist thought, two of which are especially recommended and are mentioned in the footnote on p. 312. As yet, however, formal students of Existentialism still seem largely preoccupied with the elaboration of their systematic thought on the philosophical level and have not yet translated its meaning into social, political, economic, or educational terms. This was remedied with the appearance of R. Ulich's book, *The Human Career: A Philosophy of Self-Transcendence.* This is a scholarly application of some Existentialist ideas (particularly transcendence) to education in America. More selective of Existentialist concepts, Ulich presents a much more optimistic outlook than that herein suggested. The Ulich book was published in 1955. See annotated bibliography on page 406.

if only to open it for discussion. There can be no doubt that Existentialism, to use the jargon of the times, is the "hottest thing" in philosophic "business." We are going to be hearing much more from it.

Van Cleve Morris (June 28, 1921—) was educated in the public schools of Kalamazoo, Michigan. He took his undergraduate work at Oberlin College, Oberlin, Ohio. Following World War II he attended Teachers College, Columbia University, where he received the M.A. degree in 1947 and the Ed.D. degree in 1949.

In September of 1951 he was appointed assistant professor of Education at the College of Education, University of Georgia, Athens, Georgia, where he served until 1955. During the academic year 1953–54 he received a faculty fellowship from the Fund for the Advancement of Education of the Ford Foundation. This fellowship took him on leave of absence from the University of Georgia for the post-doctoral study of comparative educational philosophy at Harvard University, The Catholic University of America in Washington, D.C., and New York University. His study program during this period centered on those educational theories that stand opposed to John Dewey's experimentalism.

In 1955 he was appointed to the staff of the Graduate School of Education, Rutgers University, where he was a professor of Education and coordinator of Teacher Education at Douglass College, the women's undergraduate division of Rutgers University. At present, he is Professor of Education, University of Illinois at Chicago Circle.

He has published in both professional and scholarly journals, such as The Educational Forum, The Catholic Educational Review, Teachers College Record, School and Society, *and the* Journal of Higher Education. *He is the author of* Philosophy and the American School, *and* Existentialism in Education.

22

Existentialism and Education*

GEORGE F. KNELLER

FOR THE EXISTENTIALIST, the real world (reality) is the world of the existing. We may describe carefully and scientifically the characteristics of a particular object or living thing—that "certain something" which constitutes its essence—but in order to know if it is genuinely alive or real, if it actually *is*, we must personally meet it, have an experience with it, become authentically involved with it.

The existentialist epistemology (if such it may be termed!) assumes that the individual is responsible for his own knowledge. Existentialist knowledge is "intuitive." It is "human." It originates in, and is composed of, what exists in the individual's consciousness and feelings as a result of his experiences and the projects he adopts in the course of his life. Likewise, the validity of knowledge is determined by its value to the individual. The teacher therefore should not limit himself to rational generalizations but should cultivate in himself the awareness that all human situations are different; these situations should be analyzed in terms of their irrational as well as rational components.

In contrast with the experimentalist approach to knowledge, which advocates the use of scientific methods for solving problems, the existentialist prefers solutions originating in the aesthetic, moral, and emotional self. The experimentalist utilizes reflective intelligence in exploring and

* George F. Kneller, *Existentialism and Education*. New York: Philosophical Library, 1958, pp. 3, 59, 61, 62–63, 64–66, 82, 83, 101–102, 111, 116–117, 122–123, 124 135–136, 139, 140, 153, 154–155. Used by permission of author and publisher.

testing possible solutions to problems posed by the environment; whereas the existentialist prefers to cultivate the affective side of man—his capacity to love, appreciate, become involved with, and respond emotionally to, the world around him. The existentialist is less concerned with gathering factual evidence because he knows the source of much of that evidence—resting as it does in universals. He is more concerned with what individual man *does* with the evidence, even if he is condemned to live in constant anguish and doubt as to whether his choice was the right one.

In fact, a good case could be made out by existentialists to show that the social humanism of instrumentalism saves it from completely subordinating the individual to elements of greater importance, namely, experience, nonhuman matter, and society, which the individual is born to serve and fit into as well as to improve.

The insistence in the classroom upon utilizing exclusively rational and empirical methods can serve only to inhibit the growth of independent thought and behavior because the student is necessarily influenced by the models which have been prefabricated for him. All he needs do is to fall in line with what is judged to be desirable conduct. The one who best conforms is the one who wins the prize.

One conclusion to be reached here is that the attainment of existentialist truth is similar to that of phenomenological reduction, in which one must forget all one knows *about* a problem in order to achieve a *unity with it*, and here discover the depth of one's obligation or the involvement incurred. Even a "purely scientific" analysis can be made to reveal the presence of a personal obligation and involvement; the only satisfactory way of handling a problem is to become one with it. One has to be a farmer, for example, to understand the real problems of farming.

The experimentalist would agree that to some extent human intelligence alone is capable of plotting the course of human development. But the existentialist sees this as a normative proposition. It presupposes norms which are achievable through human interaction and which in turn can create further norms, based on scientific experimentation. The existentialist's way is that of appropriation within the depths of the individual's subjective processes. There are no norms. Science is a tool; not a determinant. Experimentalism is a method; not a goal. Experience is an adverb; not a verb, or a noun.

Existentialists teach that values do not exist apart from the freely chosen acts of man. Action must not be predicated on abstract conceptions of value. Ideas of the good, the true, and the beautiful prevalent today are chiefly abstractions from empirical evidence or intellectual speculation; they cannot be accepted as authentic criteria for human behavior. The highest morality is a recognition of freedom; the lowest morality, as Jaspers clearly states, is the subjection of individual consciousness to standards or principles which have been preordained.

When the existentialist chooses values, he cannot choose evil as such. He must choose good, because, by his very act of voluntary, personal choice, he is affirming a worthwhile value. The good for the existentialist is always a positive affirmation of the self. Evil lies in following the crowd. However, the free choice of an act involves a personal responsibility for its commission. Thus the teacher must bring the student to realize the implications of his decisions. The student must not be shielded from the consequences of his choices. Nor must he blame his weaknesses or mistakes on the infirmity of his environment, on his family, on bad advice, or on human nature. Whether before himself or before God, he stands alone. The student must also recognize the inevitability of periods of intense frustration and loneliness; he must cultivate self-reliance as a key character trait. Existentialism thus provides no easy value criteria of a social or objective nature—no code or set of morals by which we may guide our actions. Man must look within himself for an understanding of the good, the true and the beautiful; and the cherished values of a teacher should never be foisted on students, lest these very values become a code or a pattern of conduct calling for uncritical acceptance.

All existentialists would likewise advocate a study of the world's religions as an academic matter, of comparative religion, to be specific, for the same reasons as those employed to defend other traditional subject matter in the curriculum. Existentialists would allow the religious attitude to develop freely within the student, if it were authentic. That is, the ideal school permits religious unfolding in accordance with whatever doctrine the student wishes to appropriate. Perhaps the most vital fact of all is the need for commitment; and this element of the doctrine alone assures the skeptic that the existentialist student does not wander aimlessly in a spiritual vacuum but comes to his own moral and religious convictions in the same way as he arrives at convictions on aesthetic, material, and other values.

Existentialists consider this transfer of educational responsibility as most unfortunate. Only in the home is a child free from mere enumeration among the masses of other children. Jaspers says that the home is "a symbol of the world which is the child's necessary historical environment"; it is more organic and deep-reaching in the education it imparts than the school can ever be. Of course, many homes are not ideal. But for that matter many schools are not ideal, either. Even so, classrooms and institutions always tend to levelize the child; he becomes simply one of many.

In contrast, it is in the home that the child finds the proper soil for cultivation of the authentic self. The genuine spirit of love and comradeship which develops in the family carries over into relations with the outside world, whether in school, factory, or public life.

The existentialist always asks: What genuine, self-determined expressions of love and comradeship can develop out of large groups or large classes? Only a rare teacher is capable of conducting a class in which all students enjoy a free play of ideas and behavior.

For the teacher in the classroom the implications are delicate indeed. On the one hand he must stress the values of life; on the other, the vital function of death. The problem becomes all the more complicated when we realize that for youth, death is really a paradox in time and place. As a natural phenomenon, it dwells too far in the future to be of serious momentary consideration; as an ever-present lure to live life to its full, it is accepted by many as the price one may have to pay for extracting the last measures of life's delight. Some youth, too, like to flirt with death— to conquer it, so to speak—and hence, laugh in derision at its seeming impotence.

To say that the teacher must incorporate these very real but delicate matters into his teachings is to demand that he revise his entire understanding of the life-death relationship. "*Sein zum Tode*" becomes, then, "*Erziehen zum Tode*," or "education-with-death-in-view." Perhaps what is needed more and more in these days of selfish living is an understanding, which could be brought to the attention of students, of the need to suffer death, in fact, to welcome it, if great wrongs and injustices may thereby be exposed and further prevented.

This means that the teacher is not an actor on a stage in front of an audience, performing so as to elicit applause and acclaim. He does not want imitators. Constructively, he seeks three goals: (1) the treatment of subject matter in such a way as to discover its truth in free association; (2) the achievement of what Harper calls the "autonomous functioning of the mind," in such a way as to produce in his charges a type of character that is "free, charitable, and self-moving" ("When one sees one's own ideas quoted verbatim, one's heart should sink"); and (3) evidence that his students hold something to be true because they have *convinced themselves* that it is true. This last ideal does not mean that truth is revealed, or instrumental, or discovered, but rather that it has been thought out afresh by every individual student, as if it had never before been conceived. The final test arises when the teacher has so educated his students that their minds have been effectively liberated and that as the personality develops, ideas that once were common between teacher and student may actually grow apart and never again have affinity for each other.

Since for the existentialist the truth is infinite, it follows that the curriculum cannot be prescribed. There is no denial of the integrity of subject matter; no denial that limits may be set on the extent to which at a certain point in human development certain material is appropriate; but far more essential, in fact indispensable, is the student's relation to the material studied. This relation differs from that advocated by the instrumentalist, for subject matter is not considered as exactly secondary to the individual; in fact, in the latter's free relation to content studied, he may lose himself; he may deny—even subjugate—himself. But in doing so, he retains his freedom to observe, inquire, explore, seek personal release—in sum, "appropriate" the curriculum.

Again, regarding the subject matter which historically has made up school curricula, the existentialist has misgivings, because the social sciences especially lead the student to feel that he is nothing more than an object about which conclusions have already been reached. . . .

The existentialist would give the humanities a central place in the curriculum—not, however, for purposes simply of analysis or appreciation but because of what Paul Tillich calls the human impact they exert in revealing man's inherent guilt, sin, suffering, tragedy, death, hate, and love.

Problem-centered methodology the existentialist would consider to be impersonal and unproductive, largely because the problems are usually socially oriented; they are of immediate concern to the individual only in his social obligations. Our educational system is much too preoccupied with immediate solutions—with helping young people solve only the most material of life's problems. Also, the solution of these problems seems to be intimately linked with universal reason and with a kind of generalized thought which establishes the conditions necessary for valid solutions. It then assumes that one investigator should be able to reach the same conclusion as another and the implications of their assumptions have universal validity. Problem solving is acceptable only if the problem originates in the life of the one who has to appropriate the solution. It is unacceptable if problems are derived from the needs of society or the "on-going situation."

The idea of play is thus united with ideas of art and science to become a valuable means of self-expression and a necessary adjunct for the appropriation to oneself of other forms of "being." Note here, however, that most varsity sports, parading such ideals as "fighting for dear old Alma Mater," have little place in the existential scheme of things because the hero of the day, who has scored the winning touchdown or knocked in the winning run, may well be a completely unauthentic person. His athletic values may have been prefabricated for him. His appropriation may have been artificial and non-creative.

. . . nothing should be excluded from the mind of a person, no matter how young, provided he is capable of understanding it.

The grave danger is not that students will be faced with problems of existence too early in life, for most teachers are now quite well aware of the need for psychological readiness; it is not that students cannot bear to understand themselves; but that the teacher will fail to look for the moment of receptivity and give his charges the *opportunity* to know themselves.

This, then, might be said to constitute existentialism's first weakness— that in a freedom-loving society its preachments are less poignant.

A second weakness lies in existentialism's attitude toward scientific inquiry. It makes short shrift of tests of verifiability. The existentialist says that science treats man as an object; it handles the human being as it does other natural phenomena, and consequently tends to destroy man's essential dignity. While it may be true that certain phases of materialism and scientific research tend to treat human beings in a dispassionate, detached fashion, it hardly follows that the objective findings of the laboratory are without relevance for man's improvement and ultimate fulfillment.

Existentialism's third weakness lies in its peculiar understanding of sound values and community relations. Without arguing the case for social determinism, we must recognize that human values and projects are fairly exclusively the result of an interaction of individual and community forces. Could absolute individual freedom in fact be tolerated by modern communities and cultures? Is it fair to grant the existentialist absolute freedom when the consequences of such freedom would by common consent become injurious to the body politic?

A fourth weakness, closely related to the above, derives from existentialism's very inwardness and subjectivity. For Kierkegaard, in fact, the only truth, the only absolute, lies in subjectivity. But introspection and self-analysis cannot take place in a vacuum, else it becomes solipsistic, self-flagellating, abortive.

George F. Kneller (August 30, 1908—) holds degrees from American and English universities. He received the B.A. from Clark, the M.A. from the University of London, and the Ph.D. from Yale. In addition, he took work at Grenoble, Heidelberg, Berlin, Paris, Oxford, and Southern California.

Professor Kneller has taught in the schools of Worcester, Massachusetts (1930–1935), Hamden, Connecticut (1935–1939), and in the Hotchkiss School, Lakeville, Connecticut (1940–1942). He has also served as a member of the faculty of the University of Kansas City (1943–1945), Yale University (1945–1950), University of London (1950–1953), and the University of California at Los Angeles (since 1953). His first appointment at U.C.L.A. was visiting associate professor (1953–1954). The next five years he held the rank of associate professor, becoming professor in 1960.

Professor Kneller's publications include The Educational Philosophy of National Socialism, Education in Mexico, Air Age Effects on Thinking, *and* Federal Aid to Private Schools. *His most recent works are* Higher Learning in Britain, Existentialism and Education, *the first formal treatise on the relation of existentialism and education,* Foundations of Education *and* Educational Anthropology.

Dr. Kneller also wrote the articles on "History of Higher Education" for the Encyclopedia Americana, *1960, "Educational Administration" for the* Encyclopedia Britannica, *1960, and "Comparative Education" for the* Encyclopedia of Educational Research, *1960. He has contributed several articles to professional journals in the field of educational philosophy.*

23

Existential Philosophers on Education[*]

BRUCE F. BAKER

AT THE CONCLUSION of his article "Existentialism and Education" Van Cleve Morris states that ". . . we might even conclude that Existentialism would have no traffic with education in any shape or form. Indeed the case might even be developed that Existentialism is the very denial of education as we understand it today."[1] Such a statement is by no means surprising when we consider the approach of Morris and others, such as George Kneller, to the problem of developing an Existentialist philosophy of education. For, although these authors usually mention the views of a number of Existentialists, there is an underlying tendency to identify Existentialism with the ideas of Sartre and attempt to relate his philosophy to education. Thus we find that Sartre's concept of pure freedom for man, his notion of the isolation and solitude of each person that results from the impossibility of authentic human relationships, and his probing descriptions of the basic motivations of human behavior, concluding with the statement that "man is a useless passion," are predominant factors in the attempts of Morris, Kneller, and others to relate Existentialism to education. For example, with regard to the concept of freedom, Kneller says:

Existentialism's third weakness lies in its peculiar understanding of sound values and community relations. . . . Is it fair to grant the existentialist absolute

* Bruce F. Baker, "Existential Philosophers on Education," *Educational Theory*, Vol. XVI, No. 3, July 1966, pp. 216–24. Used by permission of the author and *Educational Theory*.

[1] Van Cleve Morris, "Existentialism and Education," *Educational Theory*, Vol. 4, No. 4, October, 1954, appearing in Joe Park, ed., *Selected Readings in the Philosophy of Education*, second edition (New York: Macmillan, 1963), pp. 551, 552.

freedom when the consequences of such freedom would by common consent become injurious to the body politic? . . . Small wonder that anixety, nausea, absurdity, and nothingness become the chief categories of such a system![2]

Morris recognizes the danger of identifying Existentialism with Sartre.

. . . people have begun to think of Sartre and Existentialism almost as synonymous. As a matter of actual fact, Sartre is only a late comer on the Existential stage, and is surprisingly enough, only partially representive of genuine Existentialism today.[3]

But then he goes on to make the following statement:

Now the concept of freedom has always been a subject of much discussion and dispute among philosophers, and all of the older theories wavered between a position of complete determinism on the one hand and some kind of union of freedom within ultimate determinism on the other. Existentialism refuses to walk this tightrope, and flatly and clearly states the case for complete, undiluted, and absolute freedom.[4]

Such statements as these make plain the difficulty of any attempt to inject these notions into American public education as a whole, apart from the question of the desirability of doing so.

However, the point to be made here is that Sartre has written little, if anything, on the educational problems that these authors discuss. And this situation is not unique to Sartre among the Existential philosophers, for most of them have not been concerned with a philosophical examination of educational issues. As a result, Kneller and Morris have decided that the most profitable approach is to infer what Existentialists "would" say about education.[5] Yet, since Existentialists disagree sharply among themselves on so many vital issues, this approach is dangerous at best, especially when the extreme views of Sartre, the most popular figure of the movement, are so often taken as exemplary of the philosophy as a whole.

II

Another approach to the matter might be to examine what has actually been written by Existentialists on education. Even though, as we have noted, the material is for the most part meager, there is some literature by

[2] George F. Kneller, *Existentialism and Education* (New York: Philosophical Library, Inc., 1958), pp. 154, 155.
[3] Morris, "Existentialism and Education," p. 539.
[4] Morris, "Existentialism and Education," p. 542.
[5] See Kneller, pp. viii, ix, 122, and Van Cleve Morris, *Philosophy and the American School* (Boston: Houghton Mifflin Co., 1961), pp. 100, 393.

Existential philosophers on the subject. Three of the most significant examples will be briefly discussed in this section: Nietzsche's *On the Future of Our Educational Institutions*, Ortega y Gasset's *Mission of the University*, and Jaspers' *The Idea of the University*.

The first of these works consists of a series of lectures given by Nietzsche at the University of Basle during the first three months of 1872. By this time Nietzsche was a twenty-seven year old professor of classical philology at Basle and, although the seeds of later themes were being sown, especially in *The Birth of Tragedy*, he had not yet formulated his mature thought. As the title of his lectures indicates, Nietzsche is primarily concerned with German educational institutions. In his introduction he indicates two forces which he believes are undermining German schools: "These forces are: a striving to achieve the greatest possible *extension of education* on the one hand, and a tendency *to minimise and to weaken it on the other*."[6] Nietzsche thinks that the attempt to extend education to all reflects merely a concern for economic gain, and, although it is necessary for the masses, it weakens what he considers to be a "true educational institution."[7] This type of institution has as its goal the inculcation of "culture" through awakening in students a concern for classical art and literature, especially that of Hellenic Greece, after a thorough grounding in German language and literature. Nietzsche stresses that this cultural education must take place within a framework of strict discipline: "We recognize the fatal consequences of our present public schools, in that they are unable to inculcate severe and genuine culture, which should consist above all in obedience and habituation."[8] This education would be geared not to the common man but to a select group of persons:

I have long accustomed myself to look with caution upon those who are ardent in the cause of the so-called 'education of the people' in the common meaning of the phrase. . . . The education of the masses cannot, therefore, be our aim; but rather the education of a few picked men for great and lasting works.[9]

Thus, revealing the influence of Schopenhauer, Nietzsche concludes that the product of the "true educational institution" would be a few geniuses whose work is the "pure reflection of the eternal and immutable essence of things."[10]

This brief outline of the main points raised in *On the Future of Our*

[6] Friedrich Nietzsche, *On the Future of Our Educational Institutions*, trans. by J. M. Kennedy, *The Complete Works of Friedrich Nietzsche*, ed. by Oscar Levy, v. III (London: Allen and Unwin, 1909), p. 12.

[7] Nietzsche, p. 95.

[8] Nietzsche, p. 60.

[9] Nietzsche, pp. 74, 75.

[10] Nietzsche, p. 113.

Educational Institutions represents, in essence, an expression of the type of cultural education Nietzsche thought necessary for German institutions of learning as well as a critique of the educational situations he himself had experienced, both as student and teacher. From a certain point of view, these lectures may even be viewed as one instance of the constant battle, still raging, between a "progressive" type of education concerned with utilitarian results and a more conservative standpoint, seeking its roots in classical tradition. In many ways Nietzsche exemplifies an extreme example of the latter position: "I for my own part know of only two exact contraries: *institutions for teaching culture and institutions for teaching how to succeed in life.* All our present institutions belong to the second class; but I am speaking only of the first."[11] His infatuation with Hellenism, the influence of Schopenhauer, and the emphasis on obedience, harsh discipline, and fixed rules—these factors point out the conservative side of Nietzsche. But these views are the result of early influences that, for the most part, either later lose their appeal or are modified by his developing thought. For example, Nietzsche's stress on "obedience and habituation" contrasts with his later concern that each man obey his own conscience in order to become "what he is" (and also, incidentally, contrasts sharply with Morris' statement on "Existentialism's" concept of freedom in education).

As the titles of their works indicate, Ortega and Jaspers direct their attention primarily to the university, whereas Nietzsche speaks in terms of the broad spectrum of educational institutions. Nietzsche recognized that education is primarily geared toward providing a livelihood for the average person, even though he was trying to develop a different notion of education. Ortega agrees with Nietzsche on this point. He conceives of education in terms of an economic principle of supply and demand. All economic activity arises because of some form of scarcity, and this is the case with education:

Man is occupied and preoccupied with education for a reason which is simple, bold, and devoid of glamour: in order to live with assurance and freedom and efficiency, it is necessary to know an enormous number of things, and the child or youth has an extremely limited capacity for learning. . . . Scarcity of the capacity to learn is the cardinal principle of education. It is necessary to provide for teaching precisely in proportion as the learner is unable to learn.[12]

But rather than suppress the importance of this fact, Ortega sees the education of the common man for his role in life as the foundation of the

11 Nietzsche, p. 98.
12 José Ortega y Gasset, *Mission of the University*, trans. by Howard Lee Nostrand (Princeton: Princeton University Press, 1944), p. 68.

university: "The university, in the strict sense, is to mean that institution which teaches the ordinary student to be a cultured person and a good member of a profession."[13] He maintains that the university has three essential functions, ordered according to importance:

We come to the conclusion therefore that the university's teaching comprises these three functions:
  I. The transmission of culture.
 II. The teaching of the professions.
III. Scientific research and the training of new scientists.[14]

Like Nietzsche, Ortega considers the transmission of culture to be the fundamental aim, though by culture he means something quite different from Nietzsche's use of the term: "Culture is the system of vital ideas which each age possesses; better yet, it is the system *by* which the age lives."[15] Also, Ortega believes that the first two functions of the university must be set apart from the third; for, with his stress on the ordinary student, his position on the current controversy of "teaching vs. research" is that good teaching and productive research are incompatible:

I have lived close to a good number of the foremost scientists of our time, yet I have not found among them a single good teacher. . . . The selection of professors will depend not on their rank as investigators but on their talent for synthesis and their gift for teaching.[16]

The fact that the university's primary mission is to cultivate and enrich the ordinary man's awareness of the cultural ethos of his time implies, for Ortega, that there is an additional function of the university:

. . . the university must intervene, *as* the university, in current affairs, treating the great themes of the day from its own point of view: cultural, professional, and scientific. . . . the university must assert itself as a major 'spiritual power,' higher than the press, standing for serenity in the midst of frenzy, for seriousness and the grasp of intellect in the face of frivolity and unashamed stupidity.
Then the university, once again, will come to be what it was in its grand hour: an uplifting principle in the history of the western world.[17]

Now for Jaspers, "the university is a community of scholars and students engaged in the task of seeking truth."[18] On this basis he conceives

---

[13] Ortega, p. 93.
[14] Ortega, p. 62.
[15] Ortega, p. 81.
[16] Ortega, pp. 92, 93.
[17] Ortega, p. 99.
[18] Karl Jaspers, *The Idea of the University,* ed. by Karl W. Deutsch, trans. by H. A. T. Reiche and H. F. Vanderschmidt (Boston: Beacon Press, 1959), p. 1.

of three essential functions of the university by means of which its basic "idea" may be realized; and these bear striking resemblance to those of Ortega: "Three things are required at a university: professional training, education of the whole man, research. For the university is simultaneously a professional school, a cultural center and a research institute."[19] However, unlike Ortega's three functions of the university, these do not represent a hierarchy of goals:

In the idea of the university . . . these three are indissolubly united. One cannot be cut off from the others without destroying the intellectual substance of the university, and without at the same time crippling itself. All three are factors of a living whole. By isolating them, the spirit of the university perishes.[20]

And this "spirit of the university" is to be understood in terms of the "intellectual substance" Jaspers mentions. As he says while outlining his mode of approach in the introduction to *The Idea of the University*:

We shall, first, consider the nature of intellectual life in general, one of whose forms is realized in the university. Next, we shall turn to the responsibilities inherent in the corporate realization of intellectual life at the university. Lastly we shall consider the concrete foundations of the university and how these affect its functioning.[21]

Intellectual life is thus the "substance" of the university and is viewed by Jaspers as a life devoted to the relentless pursuit of knowledge: "Within the life of the university teachers and students are driven by a single motive, man's basic quest for knowledge."[22] Through this quest the ultimate goal of "truth" is to be realized. As a result of his understandable concern about the university's involvement in politics, Jaspers emphasizes that this realization must be limited to the theoretical level rather than enter the field of political action. Even so, since the university is the guardian of truth, it represents, for him as for Ortega, a kind of intellectual model: "The university is meant to function as the intellectual conscience of an era."[23]

On the other hand, Jaspers seems to reverse Ortega's ordering of the functions of the university. Instead of aiming primarily toward the cultivation of the common man, the university seeks knowledge and truth, i.e., research. Thus, in a tone somewhat reminiscent of Nietzsche, Jaspers believes that tight restrictions must be placed on the type of student allowed to enter the university:

[19] Jaspers, p. 40.
[20] Jaspers, p. 41.
[21] Jaspers, p. 3.
[22] Jaspers, p. 41.
[23] Jaspers, p. 121.

Equality of intellectual status cannot be decreed. . . . Nor must we be deceived by the dream that all people can achieve the noblest function of humanity. This is a utopian dream which is not realized simply by assuming that it exists already when, in fact, no one knows or is capable of knowing to what extent it can be realized. . . . The university must maintain its aristocratic principles if it is not to fall prey to a universal lowering of standards.[24]

Related to this is the fact that, whereas Ortega maintains that teaching, the primary function of the university, must be separated from research, Jaspers believes that the two must be connected and the functions of the university be seen as a unified whole:

Moreover, teaching itself is often—even most of the time—stimulating to research. Above all, teaching vitally needs the substance which only research can give it. Hence the combination of research and teaching is the lofty and inalienable basic principle of the university. . . . ideally the best research worker is also the best and only teacher.[25]

If the university is to bear the fruit of genius Jaspers recognizes that the mind must be free of constrictions and declares, in contrast to Nietzsche, that "no authority, no rules and regulations, no supervision of studies such as are found in high schools must be allowed to hamper the university student."[26]

These writings represent an interesting commentary on some important educational issues by three thinkers whose philosophical work has been termed "Existential" in character. There are points of significant agreement among them, but they disagree on so many basic issues that it would be difficult indeed to develop an Existentialist philosophy of education on the basis of these three works.

In addition, these views on education do not seem to be primarily "Existential" in nature. They appear to be written on a different level and for different purposes from their authors' philosophical writing—more from the point of view of the university professor than from that of the Existentialist who is attempting to include education within his particular philosophical position. Thus we find the overriding concern with issues that are of prime importance to the university professor: e.g., academic freedom, teaching vs. research, culture vs. technology, and the impact of the university on society and the state and vice versa. The opinions expressed by these philosophers are significant and vital contributions to this debate; but they do not solve the problem of relating Existentialism to education, for there is really no serious attempt to analyze the notion of

[24] Jaspers, p. 97.
[25] Jaspers, pp. 44, 45.
[26] Jaspers, p. 54.

education as a whole and to integrate this within the philosopher's own form of Existentialism. Jaspers, for example, mentions the importance of communication, especially Socratic-type discussion, in *The Idea of the University*, and the notion of communication is an important part of his philosophy. Yet in this work he never connects its educational significance to the basic concept of his philosophy, *Existenz*. (In fact, *Existenz* per se is mentioned only in a two-page chapter of the book, the purpose of which is to determine "the foundation of the scientific outlook."[27]) On the other hand, as we have seen, the severe restrictions Nietzsche places upon the student actually contradict the pure individuality of his mature thought.

III

Thus it would seem that the views of Nietzsche, Ortega, and Jaspers do not found a concrete basis upon which an Existentialist philosophy of education can be built. However, there has been one noticeable omission from the group of Existentialists who have written on education—Martin Buber. He, more than any other Existentialist, has, in the spirit of Dewey, treated education as a serious topic for philosophical inquiry, one which is an integral part of his I-Thou philosophy.

This is not the place to exposit in depth Buber's philosophy of education; the details of this subject have been well presented elsewhere.[28] What will be noted here are some of the key relationships between his philosophy of education and his philosophy as a whole. Buber's philosophy, as presented in his major work, *I and Thou*, is grounded on the two basic attitudes man may take toward the world, I-It and I-Thou. This delineation of fundamental attitudes is related to the distinction made in his essay "Education" between the two instincts which ground education, the originative or creative and that of communion. Just as he attempts to overcome the subjective-objective dichotomy at the heart of the I-It attitude, Buber is concerned to transcend this same persistent conflict in educational theory. The modern "subjective" emphasis on creativity, like the "objective" stress on the classical tradition, fails to touch the essence of education for Buber.

[27] Jaspers, p. 29. In the English translation cited, Jaspers' term *Existenz* is misleadingly rendered "human existence" rather than left in the original German; such a translation is more appropriate when Jaspers uses *Dasein*. See Karl Jaspers, *Die Idee der Universität* (Berlin: Springer-Verlag, 1946), pp. 31, 32.

[28] See especially Maurice S. Friedman, "Martin Buber's Philosophy of Education," *Educational Theory*, Vol. 6, No. 2, April, 1956, and Maurice S. Friedman, *Martin Buber, The Life of Dialogue* (New York: Harper and Brothers, 1960), Chap. 20.

Education is a form of the fundamental I-Thou relation, the specific embodiment of which in an educational framework is the teacher-student relation. Education is to be understood in terms of the communion between teacher and student because the development of the pupil as a person rests on the impact of one human being upon another: "The relation in education is one of pure dialogue."[29] This does not mean that subject matter is neglected, but that it is seen in proper perspective. Through mutuality the student develops an awareness of the meaning of what the teacher as a person and the author of a book as a Thou present before him. In this way subject matter is brought from the abstract impersonality of objective knowledge to a personally meaningful reality that is alive because it is grounded on that which is "between" man and man.

In order that true dialogue can transpire between teacher and student it is essential that the pupil have confidence in the teacher as a Thou who can be trusted, not a dominating symbol of power:

When the pupil's confidence has been won, his resistance against being educated gives way to a singular happening: he accepts the educator as a person. He feels he may trust this man, that this man is not making a business out of him, but is taking part in his life, accepting him before desiring to influence him.[30]

This imposes a heavy responsibility upon the teacher, who is in the position of selecting the "world" of reality and truth of the student. The teacher must attempt to understand the point of view of the student by "experiencing the other side," which Buber calls "inclusion." That is, the teacher must see the student as a Thou to be met in dialogue rather than an It, an object to be manipulated and used to his own advantage. The former alternative makes true education possible; the latter leads inevitably to propaganda. Buber does not believe that teachers can or should maintain a purely objective detachment from the developing attitudes of students, as some have recommended. Teachers, as human beings, cannot divorce themselves of their attitudes and value commitments without destroying themselves as persons. The real issue for Buber is whether the teacher should impose his values upon the student with a view toward domination and exploitation by propaganda or present himself to the student and allow the latter to develop his own self through this meeting with the "other." Thus the teacher must walk a "narrow ridge" between suppression of the student's individuality and the influence required by

[29] Martin Buber, *Between Man and Man*, trans. by Ronald Gregor Smith (Boston: Beacon Press, 1955), p. 98.
[30] Buber, *Between Man and Man*, p. 106.

the nature of the teaching situation, his only guidance being his "attitude" —I-It or I-Thou: "In education, then, there is a lofty asceticism: an asceticism which rejoices in the world, for the sake of the responsibility for a realm of life which is entrusted to us for our influence but not our interference—either by the will to power or by Eros."[31] The basic principle underlying this relation between teacher and student is the education of character—the willingness of the teacher to communicate his whole being or "character" to that of the student in order to help him develop an attitude of responsibility for his own life so that, in his own unique way, he may make an authentic unity of it.

But, to achieve authenticity, this "attitude" must lead the pupil beyond a concern with his own individual development: "He [the teacher] can bring before his pupils the image of a great character who denies no answer to life and the world, but accepts responsibility for everything essential that he meets."[32] By fulfilling his responsibility to the student, the teacher can awaken him to a similar responsibility for his fellow man, society, and the world. Buber's whole I-Thou philosophy can be looked at as a basis for social reconstruction, and his views on education can be seen as the building of the foundation for this reconstruction:

Today the great characters are still 'enemies of the people', they who love their society, yet wish not only to preserve it but to raise it to a higher level. Tomorrow they will be the architects of a new unity of mankind. It is the longing for personal unity, from which must be born a unity of mankind, which the educator should lay hold of and strengthen in his pupils. Faith in this unity and the will to achieve it is not a 'return' to individualism, but a step beyond all the dividedness of individualism and collectivism. A great and full relation between men and man can only exist between unified and responsible persons. . . . Genuine education of character is genuine education for community.[33]

Buber goes on to extend this idea of the education of character beyond the realm of youth and applies it to his notion of adult education. In the essay "The Demand of the Spirit and Historical Reality" he says:

If the new house that man hopes to erect is not to become his burial chamber, the essence of living together must undergo a change at the same time as the organization of living. . . . He must also *educate* sociologically, he must educate men in living together; he must educate man so he can live with man.[34]

---

[31] Buber, *Between Man and Man,* p. 95.
[32] Buber, *Between Man and Man,* p. 116.
[33] Buber, *Between Man and Man,* p. 116.
[34] Martin Buber, *Pointing the Way,* trans. by Maurice Friedman (New York: Harper and Brothers, 1957), p. 179.

With this goal in mind, Buber has actually implemented his idea of adult education in post-war Israel. The great need of Israel at this time was the unification into one whole of people of diverse backgrounds who were immigrating there. To help alleviate this problem, the Adult Education Centre of the Hebrew University established the School for Adult Education Teachers in 1949 with Buber in charge in order to produce men and women who would go into the immigration camps and attempt to bring the people into the fold of the community. Like the education of youth, this type of adult education is not to be understood merely in terms of an institutionalized activity or a formal transmission of knowledge:

Our aim goes considerably beyond that of imparting knowledge. We are not directly and especially interested in knowledge. We are interested in man. Man must have knowledge, too, but if knowledge becomes the center of the person, it is just the opposite of what we want. We want the wholeness of a person because only whole persons can influence others as we want to influence others. This particular conjunction of situation and person is Adult Education as I understand it.[35]

So both the education of youth and adult education can only be understood in terms of Buber's basic I-Thou philosophy; for the essence of education is the manifestation of the I-Thou relation through the authentic communication of one human being with another.

Thus Buber, in contrast with other major Existentialists, has developed a philosophy of education within his overall philosophy. This is not to say that Buber presents us with the "Existentialist" philosophy of education, but only that he has carried out a philosophical examination of education from the standpoint of his own particular brand of Existentialism. By limiting ourselves to this conclusion, we at least avoid, on the one hand, guessing what a variety of thinkers would say regarding this subject and, on the other, attempting to reconcile a number of diverging views on education that are not particularly Existential in nature in order to come up with an Existentialist philosophy of education. And in the end it may well be that Buber's philosophy, which avoids the negative extremes of Sartre and yet which is grounded on a particular conception of Existential authenticity, will prove to be one of the most significant and influential contributions to educational philosophy since Dewey.

Bruce F. Baker (June 23, 1939—) was born in Boston but went to public schools in Rhode Island. He attended Dartmouth College from 1957 to

[35] Martin Buber, "Adult Education in Israel," *The Torch*, the official publication of The National Federation of Jewish Men's Clubs, Inc. (Spring, 1952), p. 9.

1961, where he earned the B.A. degree, graduated Phi Beta Kappa, and received the Sam J. T. King Prize in philosophy. He took his graduate work at Northwestern University where he was awarded the M.A. in philosophy in 1963 and the Ph.D. in philosophy of education in 1964. From the time of the completion of the Ph.D. to 1966 he was stationed at the U.S. Army Adjutant General School, Fort Benjamin Harrison, Indiana. In September, 1966, he became Assistant Professor in both the Department of Philosophy and the Department of Education at Purdue University. Dr. Baker has contributed to Educational Theory *and assisted in the preparation of one book.*

Recommended Readings for Part Six

Students are urged to consult the annotated bibliography at the end of this book for further information on the books cited here.

The following books in philosophy and philosophy of education should be especially useful.

A. PHILOSOPHY:

WILLIAM BARRETT, *What is Existentialism?*
————, *Irrational Man*
MARTIN BUBER, *Between Man and Man*
————, *I and Thou*
JAMES EDIE, *What is Phenomenology?*
KARL JASPERS, *Reason and Existenz*
WALTER KAUFMAN, *Existentialism from Dostoevsky to Sartre*
GABRIEL MARCEL, *The Philosophy of Existentialism*
JEAN-PAUL SARTRE, *Existentialism and Human Emotions*
JOHN WILD, *The Challenge of Existentialism*

B. PHILOSOPHY OF EDUCATION:

GEORGE F. KNELLER, *Existentialism and Education*
VAN CLEVE MORRIS, *Existentialism in Education*
HUSTON SMITH, *Condemned to Meaning*
ROBERT ULICH, *The Human Career*

Philosophical Analysis

Introduction to Part Seven

THE *Principia Mathematica,* prepared by Bertrand Russell in collaboration with Alfred North Whitehead, more than any other work gave impetus to the analytic movement among philosophers in English-speaking countries. The supporters of this movement have not been united; instead they have broken into two groups: the formalists, represented by Russell, and the linguists, represented by Ludwig Wittgenstein.

The formalists set aside the metaphysical, introduced the scientific method into philosophy, advocated a carefully defined technical vocabulary, and devised a modern logical technique. Russell began to see each philosophical problem as a problem of analysis in which one begins with the results and works back toward the premises. On examination, data are found to be vague, complex, and largely interdependent logically. By analysis the philosopher reduces these data to propositions that are, as nearly as possible, simple and precise. He then arranges them into a deductive chain in which the number of initial propositions form the guarantee for the remainder. These initial propositions are different from the data because they are more precise, simpler, and supposedly less infected with logical redundancy. The discovery of premises, then, belong to philosophy, but the work of deducing the body of common knowledge from them belongs to mathematics.

A number of consequences stem from Russell's philosophy of analysis. Among these are: (1) The only decisive weapon of philosophical controversy is the demonstration that certain premises lead to contradiction; philosophical arguments may be said to disprove, but they can prove nothing. (2) Philosophical statements are looked upon as means for causing others to see what we believe we have seen. To put it another way, "If that way of putting my argument will not convince you, then perhaps this way will." (3) Science alone discovers new knowledge and confirms hypotheses. (4) Ordinary language is to be mistrusted. Instead we need to rely upon artificially contrived language (symbolic logic).

The linguistic branch of philosophical analysis owes its origin more to Wittgenstein than to any other person. Ludwig Wittgenstein (1889–1951), a student under Russell at Trinity College, Cambridge, claimed to have shown the hollowness of many of the philosophical problems usually taken up by philosophers, including some that the other branch of analysis takes quite seriously. He believed that philosophical puzzles arose from the nuances of language, and that these can be cleared up by a careful examination of language. In the *Tractatus* he explains that language is an activity in which we use part of our experience (our words, images, etc.) to represent other parts of our experience. Language and thought are thus inseparable, and the philosophical task becomes one of clarifying our language and thought. What can be said can be said clearly, and any discussion worthy of the name must be confined to making sense. The limits of our language mark the limits of our world. If there is a world beyond cognition, it is a mystical world that we do not know and that cannot, therefore, be a subject of our discourse.

The first educator to apply the methods of philosophical analysis to education was C. D. Hardie, an Englishman. In 1942 he published his *Truth and Fallacy in Educational Theory,** in which he analyzes the educational theory of Herbart and John Dewey.

Another English educator to apply analysis to education was D. J. O'Connor. In his *Introduction to the Philosophy of Education†* he explains what logical analysis can do for education, discussing value theory, and indicating the nature of educational theory. Over the past few years analysts have directed a torrent of criticism at philosophers in education. They have pointed up the deficiencies in the preparation of these philosophers. They have charged that certain educationalists have fostered social engineering, and have resorted to eclectic and synoptic efforts which have "spawned vagueness, ambiguity, pseudo-problems and pseudo-explanations, vacuous principles and impractical prescriptions." Moreover, it is claimed that most educational philosophers have used philosophy to give an aura of respectability to their efforts. They are prone to teach classical theories which they understand only superficially and generally oversimplify into "schools" and "typical positions." In contrast to these sorts of efforts, the analyst sees his task as much less ambitious and as one of making clear "the diverse factors that are involved in complex issues of major theoretical impact." This he proposed to do by means of logical and linguistic analysis.‡

* C. D. Hardie, *Truth and Fallacy in Educational Theory*. Cambridge: Cambridge University Press, 1942.

† D. J. O'Connor, *Introduction to the Philosophy of Education*. New York: Philosophical Library, 1957.

‡ Reginald D. Archambault, *Philosophical Analysis and Education*. New York: The Humanities Press, 1965.

The analysts have their critics, too. Some have called it a passing philosophical fad produced by an over-concern for academic respectability and prestige. Others have said that it was not as original as commonly supposed for was not Plato an analyst when he discussed the meaning of virtue and justice? Still others see its main purpose and achievement as antiseptic in character—clarifying our thought and language—but neglecting the synoptic aspects of the philosophical enterprise in education.

The three selections in these readings are intended to explain what the analyst is attempting to do, first by presenting a general description of his work by Professor Newsome and following this by two articles in which analysis is applied in education by Coombs and Komisar and Montefiore.

24

Analytic Philosophy and Theory of Education *

GEORGE L. NEWSOME, JR.

FOR BETTER OR WORSE, analysis, logical and linguistic, is being offered by some of its advocates as a theory of education, or possibly even as a theory of educational theories. What are some of the distinguishing features of analytic philosophy? What are the pitfalls in relating analysis to education? Is analytic philosophy a second order theory of education? How may analytic philosophy contribute to the development of theory in education? Can analytic philosophy adequately meet the demands of a practical discipline such as education? For the purposes of discussing and clarifying these kinds of questions, an analytic approach will be taken in this paper.

Distinguishing Features of Analytic Philosophy

Although analytic philosophy may be termed a "school of thought," it is not a system of philosophy. Indeed, from the analytic point of view, systems of philosophy are repudiated.[1] Within the school of analytic

---

* George L. Newsome, Jr., "Analytic Philosophy and Theory of Education," *Proceedings of the Sixteenth Annual Meeting of the Philosophy of Education Society,* published by the society, June, 1960. Used by permission of Ernest E. Bayles, editor of the *Proceedings, and* George L. Newsome, Jr.

[1] Herbert Feigl, "Aims of Education For Our Age of Science: Reflections of a Logical Empiricist" in *Modern Philosophies and Education.* Chicago: The University of Chicago Press, 1955, p. 304; Israel Scheffler (ed.), *Philosophy and Education.* Boston: Allyn and Bacon, Inc., 1958, p. 7; and Richard W. Dettering, "Philosophical Semantics and Education," *Educational Theory,* 7:143–149, July, 1958, p. 146.

philosophy there are numerous differences of opinion concerning matters philosophical. It seems to make little difference, however, whether one looks to the group stressing informal logic and common language or to the group emphasizing symbolic logic and philosophy of science, philosophical analysts seem to agree on one major function of philosophy: clarification. By and through philosophical analysis (logical and linguistic) what men say (statements, sentences, or propositions) can be clarified and made meaningful or exposed as nonsense.

The statements that men make are, of course, sometimes clear and meaningful, but because of the "open texture" of language, ambiguity, vagueness, and other linguistic difficulties, confusion arises. Furthermore, and probably even of greater concern, because of "improper" philosophical training, common sense notions, or just plain ignorance, emotive and metaphysical statements worm their way into discourse. Lest such emotional expressions and "nonsense" pass for statements of fact or "profound insights," language must be subjected to a thorough and dispassionate scrutiny loosely termed "analysis."

Just how one performs analysis, the particular methods and techniques by which language is analyzed, and the various tests or criteria of meaning are matters of major concern and debate among analytic philosophers. Although analytic philosophers disagree about many aspects of analysis, they do seem to be in general agreement concerning several ways in which analytic philosophy differs from the traditional philosophies of Western culture.

1. Analytic philosophers strongly contend that truths about human experience and the universe cannot be discovered by philosophical means.[2] Matters of empirical fact and truths about the world are discovered or established by science—not by philosophers.

2. Analytic philosophers seriously question (many completely reject) the idea of logical unity of truth, goodness, and beauty.[3] Many, if not most, analytic philosophers maintain that statements concerning matters of fact and statements of value are radically different kinds of statements which require entirely different means for verification.[4] Some analytic

[2] Alfred Jules Ayer, *Language, Truth and Logic*. New York: Dover Publications, Inc., n.d., pp. 71–72; Arthur Pap, *Elements of Analytic Philosophy*. New York: The Macmillan Company, 1949, p. 6 and p. 478; and D. J. O'Connor, *Introduction to The Philosophy of Education*. New York: Philosophical Library, 1957, pp. 5–6.

[3] Ayer, *op. cit.*, pp. 102–103; Dettering, *loc. cit.*, p. 147; and Charles L. Stevenson, *Ethics and Language*. New Haven, Conn.: Yale University Press, 1944, p. 173.

[4] Pap, *op. cit.*, pp. 23–26; Henry D. Aiken, "Moral Philosophy and Education," *Harvard Educational Review*, 25: 39–59, Winter, 1955, p. 51; and John Hospers, *An Introduction to Philosophical Analysis*. Englewood Cliffs, N.J.: Prentice-Hall, Inc., 1953, pp. 476–482.

philosophers seriously doubt that statements of value can have any meaning beyond that of personal preference.[5]

3. Analytic philosophers strongly maintain that language does not give us a true picture or copy of reality.[6] Verbal expressions have only such meanings as we give them, and hence do not derive their meanings from objects in the world. We relate words to the world, and the relationship is not a "one-to-one" relationship that makes language exactly correspond to reality.

4. Analytic philosophers prefer to deal with the problems of man one by one and strongly resist the urge to construct broad, general, and speculative theories.[7]

5. Analytic philosophers, since they construct no general and speculative theories, do not consider analytic philosophy to be composed of metaphysical, ethical, or epistemological theories. To them the subject matter or analytic philosophy is thought of as theories for the clarification of language, and such concepts, methods, and presuppositions as might be found in most sciences.[8]

6. Since analytic philosophy is concerned only with clarification of language, most often the language of science or some other discipline, one can philosophize about almost anything, because to philosophize is to analyze language.[9]

Analysis, both logical and linguistic, has always in some form or other characterized philosophy. It was the stock in trade of Socrates, Plato, and Aristotle.[10] From the time of Socrates to the present, analysis has frequently been employed as a means for ushering in synthesis and speculation, or philosophy in the "grand manner." Whatever analysis reduced, separated, or exposed, *a priori* metaphysics promptly restored, unified and justified as an ultimate reality, a transcendental entity, a state of mind, or as some kind of unobservable, unknowable reality beyond the corrupting influence of linguistic analysis and the positive verification of science. Furthermore, *a priori* philosophers have, in spite of Ockham's Razor or

[5] Reference here is made to those who view ethical statements as purely emotive expressions. For example, see Hospers, *op. cit.*, pp. 471–476 for discussion of this view, or Ayer, *op. cit.*, pp. 102–113 for a classic argument by one of the chief exponents of the emotive theory of ethics.

[6] Max Black, "Language and Reality," *Proceedings and Addresses of The American Philosophical Association*, 1958–59, Yellow Springs, Ohio: The Antioch Press, 1959, pp. 16–17; Ayer, *op. cit.*, p. 42; and O'Connor, *op. cit.*, pp. 39–40.

[7] Scheffler, *op. cit.*, pp. 6–7; and Dettering, *loc. cit.*, pp. 146–147.

[8] Pap, *op. cit.*, p. 1.

[9] *Ibid.*, p. 478, and O'Connor, *op. cit.*, p. 4.

[10] Pap, *op. cit.*, Preface vii.

the Principle of Parsimony, often multiplied entities beyond necessity. By assuming much, *a priori* philosophers sought to prove much, but their proof was no better than their assumptions, and frequently no more than the assumptions.[11] It is against this synthetic and speculative philosophy that analytic philosophers rebel.

Pitfalls in Relating Analysis to Educational Theory

Educators, when confronted with the problem of relating analytic philosophy to education, are likely to find analytic philosophy to be "strange" and different, and the usual ways of relating philosophy to education not very rewarding. Analytic philosophy seems to be lacking in the "systematic niceties," ideological, doctrinaire, and moralistic canons, and the more immediate practical applications to education to which educators seem to be accustomed. Analytic philosophy also confronts the educator with a new and strange terminology, with a "frightening calculus of language," with "distinctions too subtle for the practical minded," and with an alarming restriction upon treasured emotive and metaphysical statements. Moreover, in attempting to relate analytic philosophy to education, educators should be careful not to make one or more of the following mistakes: (1) Attempting to construct an analytic philosophy of education modeled after traditional systems and ideologies,[12] (2) Attempting to derive implications for education from analytic philosophy,[13] and (3) Becoming so fascinated with language games, logic, or philosophy of science that the relation of analysis to education becomes superficial.

The fact that philosophical analysis is analysis of language rather than analysis of feelings, mental states, or concrete situations, indicates that it is a second or third level order of analysis. Consideration of this fact suggests that instead of constructing an analytic philosophy of education or deriving educational implications from analytic philosophy, all one need do is employ analytic methods and techniques in analyzing statements about education.

[11] Philosophy is not a system for proving by axiomatic methods truth about the universe in a metaphysical fashion. Logic, of course, does contain methods for proving, but such proofs are logical not metaphysical. For further discussion, see O'Connor, *op. cit.*, pp. 29–35.

[12] Scheffler, *op. cit.*, p. 2.

[13] Feigl, *op. cit.*, pp. 304–305.

Analytic Philosophy as Second Order Theory of Education

Education as a practical activity is a process which should not be confused with education as a discipline and body of knowledge. Education as a discipline is related to the process of teaching and learning, but it differs from the process in that it is composed of statements, rules, directives, principles, and the like about various aspects of practice. The discipline of education then is verbal and linguistic; it is knowledge that purports to be in a considerable measure propositional and cognitive in character. Frequently this discipline of education is termed "theory of education" although it might more appropriately be termed "pedagogical knowledge."[14]

The body of pedagogical knowledge contains many statements which do have genuine philosophical connotations. They appear on their face to be propositions which assert something significant about education. For example, such statements as "real and life-like activities produce more learning than assign-study-recite procedures," and "education is the process of self-realization in which the self realizes and develops all of its potentialities," appear to be genuine and significant propositions about education. How may these statements be verified? What kind of evidence would be needed for verification? What cognitive meanings do the propositions have? What matters of fact do they assert? What do such terms as "real," "life-like," "self," and "potentialities" mean? What does it mean to say a self realizes itself? When is a self, self realized? Questions of this sort suggest that neither of the two statements is clear or cognitively meaningful. Suppose a teacher were asked to implement either or both statements, how could one determine empirically the result or consequence? Are these statements metaphysical (necessary and synthetic), purely analytic (tautologies), emotive; or are they commands, questions, or resolves?

It is precisely questions of this sort about statements, as ambiguous and meaningless as those just cited with which analytic philosophy deals. By and through analysis, both logical and linguistic, educational philosophy as a second order of analysis can clarify and make meaningful or expose as nonsense many statements about pedagogy. When one carefully

[14] Paul Komisar, *"Pedagogical Knowledge and Teacher Education," Proceedings of the Fifteenth Annual Meeting of the Philosophy of Education Society.* Lawrence: The University of Kansas Press, 1959, pp. 15–22.

explores the meaning, the means of verifying, the semantics, the structure, and the context of such statements, he is playing the role of analytic philosopher. Furthermore, he is dealing with education at the second level of abstraction; namely, the level of clarifying statements of pedagogy.

How May Analytic Philosophy Contribute to the Development of Theory in Education?

Those who deal with pedagogy and philosophy of education frequently feel considerable pressure to provide, if possible, and justify, if necessary, a theory of education.[15] Can criticism and analysis meet the more positive challenge of helping to construct an integrative theory of education? Does not the discipline of education, since it is a hodge podge of facts and theories derived from other disciplines, need a unifying theory? Is not the chief function of philosophy that of constructing generalized theories (philosophies), be they metaphysical or not, as a prerequisite to a critical and analytical approach to theory?[16] Or is it that philosophy only needs to be clear about the more general relations that exist between and among matters of fact; or what one philosopher has termed "synoptic clarity"?

If a synoptic clarity be admitted, then can analytic philosophy clarify statements concerning the more general relations of matters of fact, and can it clarify the more general features of a theory of education? In certain respects analytic philosophy, if it be conceived relative to the task, can meet this demand. Analytic philosophy need not be viewed merely as sentence editing, or as lexicography, or as literary censorship.[17] Analytic philosophy can help to develop a defensible theory of education in the sense that it can help analyze and clarify language, provide models of theory, state criteria for meaning and verification, and in general, help unsnarl the logical and linguistic tangles in pedagogical knowledge.[18] The degree to which analytic philosophy can actually bring about a unity of

---

[15] Example of such concern for a "defensible theory" of education are "Symposium: The Aims and Content of Philosophy of Education," *Harvard Educational Review*, Vol. 26, Spring, 1956, and "A Symposium: What Can Philosophy Contribute to Educational Theory," *Harvard Educational Review*, Vol. 28, Fall, 1958.

[16] For example, *see* Harry S. Broudy, *Building a Philosophy of Education* Englewood Cliffs, N.J.: Prentice-Hall, Inc., 1954, and J. Donald Butler, *Four Philosophies and Their Practice in Education and Religion*. New York: Harper and Brothers, 1957.

[17] Ayer, *op. cit.*, p. 59 ff.

[18] Probably with the exception of a few articles and O'Connor's little book, not much seems to have been done along this line.

knowledge in education similar to that undertaken by some logical empiricists in the unified sciences movement remains to be seen.

Some of the characteristics of pedagogical knowledge present genuine difficulties for analytic philosophers. Many of the so-called "principles and theories" of teaching, learning, and curriculum are merely descriptions of practices, summaries of case studies, matters of opinion, or application of certain concepts such as democracy, socialization, or creative expression to educational practice. Pedagogical knowledge contains very few, if any, general laws under which individual facts can be adequately subsumed and explained. The so-called theories and principles of pedagogy are not only descriptive, but they frequently are directive as well. Descriptions and directives (prescriptions)[19] point to consequences rather than to logical conclusions.[20] Yet, somewhere between description and prescription, dealers in pedagogical knowledge apparently make some kind of logical inference. Such inferences are not deductions because no conclusions follow necessarily from established premises. Similarly, the inference is neither a valid inductive causal inference, nor a statistic inference in terms of probabilities. The only alternative left is that it is a probable inference, in some cases an inference based on reasoning by analogy.[21]

Probable inferences and reasoning by analogy, though weak, are not always false or unproductive. The major problem is to be found in evaluating such arguments and explanations. Though such arguments and explanations can be logically evaluated in part, ultimately one must appeal to some more fundamental explanation such as one finds in the sciences.[22] But, probable inference cannot always be so tested and verified. The prescriptions which come from the inference might be rather significant, in the opinion of many competent judges. The problem-project method of teaching and the core curriculum, for example, are frequently thought to be more productive than more traditional methods of teaching and curricula designs, yet empirical testings have not shown them to be decidedly superior. Educators, however, must make decisions; they must choose methods and curricula designs in terms of the best evidence and logical arguments available. They cannot postpone action

[19] Technically speaking, directive and prescriptive language is not the same and do not have the same meanings. Directions are, however, frequently put in persuasive form. For example, see Bernard Rabin, "Teachers Use of Directive Language," *Educational Leadership*, 17:31–34, October, 1959, for various forms in which directive language appears.

[20] P. H. Nowell-Smith, *Ethics*, Penguin Books, Ltd., 1954, p. 149.

[21] See, Irving M. Copi, *Introduction to Logic*. New York: The Macmillan Company, 1953, Chapter 11, pp. 311–326.

[22] *Ibid.*, p. 322.

until some remote future when scientific inquiry will have confirmed some one particular method or curricula plan. If choice must be made in absence of decisive evidence, then the educator would at least like to know as clearly as possible the probable consequence of his choice. Analytic philosophy can help the educator clarify statements of probable inference and help him clearly and logically state the probable consequences of choosing one course of action over another.

Since pedagogical knowledge is often prescriptive, practical, and not logically precise, one of an analytic persuasion might be tempted to dismiss too quickly pedagogical statements as emotive, cognitively meaningless, unanswerable, or the like. This however, might be a serious mistake based upon an untenable separation of thought from action, language from language function, ends from means, and logical and linguistic clarity from empirical consequences. Many of the significant statements in pedagogical knowledge do not seem to fit into the neat classifications of logic and language.[23] Facts do appear to color values and values do apparently influence choice among facts. Actions have consequences and consequences of actions seem ultimately to relate back to the logic and language of inquiry and deliberation which led to choice.

Pedagogical prescriptions are not all as illogical or emotive as one might suspect. Some prescriptions are much like those of the physician who, for example, might prescribe certain medicines and a diet as a remedy for some particular physical condition. Surely the prescription and its predicted consequences are not emotive or unscientific. Similarly, when the educator prescribes: "to promote interest and facilitate learning, employ life-like activities that meet the felt needs of the learner and come within the learner's range of experience"—he is providing a prescription and predicting consequences of its employment. Such a prescription with its stated consequences is not beyond empirical confirmation. If the kinds of evidence needed for confirmation can be specified, then the statement has meaning and can be clarified.

Many pedagogical statements are not as logically and linguistically "pure" as the foregoing illustration. Some are rather moralistic in character and their consequences, if any, "intangible." For example, if one should prescribe that "students ought always be treated as ends and never as means only," then a moralistic imperative has been introduced, the consequences of which seem to defy empirical confirmation. What is an end? How does one treat a student as an end? What meaning, if any, does

---

[23] For example, see Gilbert Ryle, *Dilemmas*, Cambridge University Press, 1954, Chapter 8—"Formal and Informal Logic," 111–129.

the statement have? Similarly, many statements about educational aims and values and a wide variety of value judgments, when subjected to analysis reduce to statements of preference or emotive expressions of the form "I like such and such and so should you" or "hurrah for X."[24]

Mere preference, as a simple expression of desire or a "I like it," and intellectual preference based upon experience and anticipated consequences of action are quite different.[25] To be sure, some educational moralisms and value preferences are statements of simple preference which have little or no cognitive meaning. An intellectual preference, however, may be discussed in terms of experience, evidence, and probable consequences. Not only may it be intelligently discussed, but statements about it can be clarified.

Analytic philosophers who dismiss intellectual preference (moralistic or valuational) seem to hold to a rather narrow and truncated view of analysis. Such a narrow view might result from a confusion of substantive ethics with analytic ethics.[26] Substantive ethics deals with first-level problems of deliberation and choice. In pedagogical knowledge statements of substantive ethics serve as practical modes of communication, the main function of which is direction and control of conduct, not prediction of empirical fact.[27] Analytic ethics, on the other hand is a second-level analysis of the language of ethics and hence is concerned largely with problems of logic and meaning.

Can Analytic Philosophy Meet the Demands of a Practical Discipline?

So far, in the short history of modern analytic philosophy its major successes have been in the fields of science and mathematics.[28] It is rather paradoxical, however, that modern natural sciences achieved their preeminence without analytic philosophy, indeed, often in opposition to philosophy. A philosophical analysis of science is somewhat like a chemi-

[24] Many statements in educational discourse are purely statements of personal likes and dislikes. Arthur P. Coladarci and Jacob W. Getzels, *The Use of Theory in Educational Administration.* Stanford University Press, 1955, pp. 10–14, claim educators are afraid to theorize, have an inadequate professional language, and frequently tend to become emotionally identified with their own views.

[25] The distinction which is being made here is John Dewey's distinction between *desire* and *desirability. See,* John Dewey, *Democracy and Education.* New York: The Macmillan Company, 1916, p. 279.

[26] Aiken, *loc. cit.,* p. 42.

[27] *Ibid.,* p. 51.

[28] Pap, *op. cit.,* Preface viii.

cal analysis of a known solution, neat, easy, and according to the rules. Philosophical analysis of the newer applied and practical disciplines, on the other hand, is more like the chemical analysis of an unknown solution; very necessary, perhaps, but very difficult and uncertain. In natural sciences and mathematics a rather "firm" language has been developed along with precise methods, techniques, proofs, and verifications. Evidence counts for much more than opinion (even informed opinion), moralisms have been rooted out, and psychological factors reduced to a minimum. Furthermore, the particular things which are studied are frequently material things or abstractions. In either or both cases, statements about such things are much more easily adapted to analytic dichotomies such as synthetic or analytic than are statements about the things studied by the behavioral sciences and practical disciplines.[29]

Some of the particular distinctions, techniques and methodology of analysis, particularly of the logical empiricist kind, though apparently well suited to analysis of scientific language might not be equally appropriate for analysis of the language of pedagogy or social sciences. One might suspect then that the informal logic and common language approach might have more to offer.[30] On the other hand, the languages of education are not common languages, and the logic of educational discourse and argument is a practical logic rather than an informal logic. It may be suggested then that an analytic philosophy of the social sciences and practical disciplines is needed. There seems to be no reason why the logical and linguistic methods of analysis cannot be modified so as to be more applicable to the kind of logical and linguistic problems found in the social sciences and practical disciplines. To this end, educational philosophers of an analytic persuasion might well devote considerable attention.

George L. Newsome, Jr. (October 5, 1923—) earned both the B.S. and M.A. degrees at the University of Alabama in 1950. He earned his Ph.D. at Yale in 1956. From 1950 to 1953 he taught history and social studies in public secondary schools in Alabama. He served as guest instructor at Trinity College, Hartford, Connecticut, in the summer of 1954, lecturer at the University of Bridgeport, 1954–55, becoming assistant professor at the latter in 1955 and associated professor in 1957. He also served as guest professor at New Haven State Teachers College, New Haven, Connecti-

---

[29] *See,* Nowell-Smith, *op. cit.,* Chapter 7, pp. 95–104, for explanation of the functions of Practical Discourse and how the Analytic-synthetic dichotomy breaks down.
[30] Reference here is to the John Wisdom-Gilbert Ryle school of analysis.

cut, in the spring terms of 1955 and 1957. Since 1958 he has been professor of the Philosophy of Education Society. *He has also conducted research in both the Department of Philosophy and in the College of Education.*

Professor Newsome is the author of several articles on the philosophy of education; they have appeared in The Journal of Teacher Education, The Teacher Education Quarterly, Educational Theory, *and* Proceedings of the Philosophy of Education Society. *He has also conducted research studies, the results of which have been published in* The Journal of Psychology, Educational Administration and Supervision, *and in publications of various commissions and foundations. He is the author of one book in general philosophy,* Philosophical Perspectives.

25

Moral Philosophy and the Teaching of Morality[*]

ALAN MONTEFIORE

IT MAY VERY WELL be asked what moral philosophy has to do with teaching morality at all. What could a moral philosopher possibly have to say on the subject? Why should he *want* to say anything? Is it not true that many contemporary linguistic and analytic philosophers have gone out of their way to disclaim any special competence or professional interest in this field? They seem almost to have made it a matter of honor to have detached themselves from any direct contact with the practical issues of life. So all that one could reasonably expect from a contemporary moral philosopher writing under the above title is yet one more explanation of why the public is (or at any rate used to be) sadly mistaken in looking to him for any relevant contribution to the problems of moral teaching; and if older philosophers—or Continental philosophers—thought, or think, otherwise, this only goes to show how confused they were, or are, about the proper nature and objects of their trade.

Actually, this would not in general be a fair account of the position of even the most analytically inclined of contemporary philosophers. Many of them do, certainly, stoutly maintain that their job as philosophers is necessarily limited to explaining the nature of moral arguments (in the sense of showing what people are arguing about—or ought to be arguing

[*] Alan Montefiore, "Moral Philosophy and the Teaching of Morality," *Harvard Educational Review*, Vol. 35, No. 4, Fall, 1965. Pp. 435–449. Used by permission.

about, if only they were clear-headed enough) or the meaning of moral concepts, such as "right" and "wrong," "virtue" and "vice," "conscience" and "responsibility," and so on; and they maintain, too, that their explanation of what is at stake must always stop short of taking in the battle. (That is to say, that they cannot take sides *qua* philosophers—what they may do as citizens or men is, of course, another story.) But it is interesting to see how some of them—who may in fact be men of deep moral commitment—try to have it both ways, as it were, and to argue that just to be clear about the meaning of moral terms and about the nature of moral argument may after all have an inescapable impact on the moral positions that one can in practice take up. Moreover, there are now quite a number of analytically trained philosophers who are increasingly doubtful of this doctrine of the moral neutrality of moral philosophy. So it is, on one count or another, by now distinctly wide of the mark to suggest that contemporary analytic philosophers are all firmly united in insisting that moral philosophy has nothing to do with morals.

Still, it is not all that easy to say off the cuff just *exactly* what it may have to do with the teaching of morals. Nobody could reasonably pretend that moral philosophers bear any more distinguished moral characters than other men; nor that they have clearer or more definite opinions on what is right and what is wrong; nor, where they do have opinions, that these are, as the opinions of philosophers, any more likely to be right or generally acceptable. Moral philosophers are in general no better equipped as moral educators than anyone else: they have no special qualifications to tell people what they ought to do or how they ought to behave. So what *is* the relevance of what they may have to say?

One short answer to this question is that a moral philosopher might not unreasonably hope to be able to help people whose business it is to inculcate standards of morality and to train moral character, to understand more clearly the nature of what they are doing and to set in clearer perspective the aims which they may pursue. This may not sound very exciting; but clarity in such matters is, of course, no little or easy thing. Without it, it is hard to know what is worth attaining or how best to set about seeking to attain it. Moreover, though it may sometimes happen that a muddled teacher is a positive stimulus to his or her pupils, more often muddle simply reproduces muddle. Perhaps this may not always matter; and no doubt there is a sense in which it is true that an inarticulate example may be worth more than ten times as much as the most highly articulate precept. But one can only afford to rely on this when one is sure that the example is going to be understood as an example of what one wants to be understood. And it is important that some people should at least sometimes ask themselves what they think this is.

However, although I think that the short answer is right so far as it goes, I do not believe that it quite succeds in being a complete one. I do not think that there is in principle only one unrestrictedly "correct" clarification to be provided of many of the central issues that must face anyone who thinks about moral education. I think that the way in which one seeks to give or accept such clarification may itself have an important bearing on one's understanding of the proper aims of moral education. And although I do not believe that one's approach to clarification can have any *direct* implications for the kind of behavior that one may wish to recommend in particular situations, the approach may well, I think, have its implications as to the type of person that one may seek to produce.

What sort of thing is it that you are wanting to do to people, or to make of them, when you seek to educate them to a sense of moral values? I do not mean this question to be one about the detailed provisions of the moral code that you might wish to see them adopt: about whether, for example, you are trying to instill into them a spirit of patriotism or of pacifism; whether you want them to adopt strict rules of premarital and extramarital chastity; whether you feel that they should always place filial obedience near the head of their list of obligations, and so on. I mean to ask rather: Do you feel that a man or woman has reached full moral maturity only when he or she has learned to take full personal responsibility for every decision of principle, for every value by which he or she determines to live? Or do you think that there are certain authorities in matters of morals? Do you think that a central moral lesson— perhaps the basic one—is that of a certain obedience to something or someone other than the individual's own elective will? And if so, obedience to what sort of authority? To the needs of society? If so, to these needs as measured by whom or by what standards? Or to the teaching of a church? Or to some less personal but still objectively determinate principle, such as that famous Utilitarian demand for the Greatest Happiness of the Greatest Number?

It is clear that whichever sort of answer you give, all sorts of difficulties, both practical and theoretical, will remain. It is clear, too, that people with very different overall views of the ultimate purpose of moral education may nevertheless find a considerable overlap in the methods they hit upon to pursue their different ends. All the same, one's conception of the ultimate aims and nature of morality is almost bound to have some impact on the framework within which any form of practical moral education, formal or informal, may be undertaken. If you see morality as essentially the concern of the free, autonomous individual, that is one thing; if you see it as essentially a certain type of acceptance, that is very much another. And although everyone may have his own order of preferences, in the first case, as to what these moral individualists should in their freedom choose as their guiding standards, there remains a fundamental difference between teaching people that they must in the last resort take over the full responsibility of working out their own moral standards for themselves and, on the other hand, teaching them that they must in the last resort learn to accept some other authority as ultimate. To repeat: this may not in the short run lead to any differences in the practical exhortations to be given and in the practical examples to be set; differences may, but need not, come in the details of obligations and duties, of observances to be fulfilled and of behavior to be avoided. But there are bound to be wide differences of general attitude—differences of a sort that may in some situations be almost too general to be noticed and in others so pervasive as to color even practical agreements with a sort of overall haze of discord.

Where might philosophy come into this matter? For the sake of brevity, I propose by way of example to concentrate on one major division among these various ranges of opinion: the division between those who think that all true morality must in the last resort spring from the free and deliberate decisions of mature and responsible individuals and those, on the other hand, who see it as resting on whatever external norm or authority. (By "external" I mean roughly "going beyond the individual and in some way confronting him as a fact which he must discover and with which he must come to grips," whether such facts are thought to relate to the opinion or decision of some authoritative Being or institution or rather to some impersonal and universal standard implicit in human nature itself.) Many very important differences exist between people on either side of this fence. But for immediate purposes there is no need to go into these; for the moment, and for the further sake of convenience, it may be enough simply to take over the common labels by which those who argue as individualists may be called Autonomists, and their doctrine the Autonomy of Morals, while those who oppose them may be called Ethical Naturalists or Descriptivists. Philosophy may now be said to come into the matter as the systematic struggle between those who believe on either side that the case for Autonomy or for Naturalism (or Descriptivism) can be settled not just on the basis of one's own moral preferences, but on that of conclusive logical argument. Or to put it in a slightly different way: philosophy comes in either with the arguments of those who think that it is actually possible to prove as a result of clear-headed reasoning that morality in its true sense is necessarily a matter of individual decision, or with the arguments of those who think that it is possible to prove the reverse.

The Autonomist Argument

We will look first at the case for Autonomy. In brief, though perhaps not entirely clear and only semi-technical terms, it can be summed up as the doctrine that it is never possible validly to derive any genuine moral judgement from premises that do not themselves at least implicitly include a moral judgement among them. From this, and if one makes one further assumption, it follows that no matter what the facts may be, nor what definitions may be introduced, no one can be logically compelled by his acceptance of facts and definitions alone to adopt any particular moral position. The further assumption is simply that it makes no sense to talk of peculiarly moral facts with an independent status of their own. This is, of course, an important assumption and not everyone would make it. G. E. Moore, who was responsible for introducing the not very suitable term "naturalism" into this context of argument, was a convinced objectivist—at any rate, at the time when he wrote his main work on moral philosophy. But though he undoubtedly thought that values had their own independent status, he at the same time argued that since "good," the fundamental concept of ethics, is unanalyzable, any attempt to derive ethical conclusions from non-ethical premises must for that reason turn out to be fallacious. Moore originally thought that all other ethical concepts could be defined in terms of "goodness." Other objectivists have held that "goodness" and "obligation" were equally primitive and indefinable, and hence maintained a version of the "no-ought-from-an-is" doctrine within the framework of ethics itself. Objectivists such as Moore or, for example, Sir David Ross, would thus certainly have counted themselves as non-Naturalists or Autonomists in the sense that they would have denied the possibility of deriving genuine moral judgements from premises that do not themselves include a moral judgement among them; yet it is clearly part of their doctrine that he who has it in him to recognize the facts of morality for what they are must find his moral position effectively determined for him. I do not here wish to argue against this form of objectivism, but rather dogmatically to assume its unacceptability. And if all such talk of independently moral facts *is* ruled out as senseless

—as the great majority of philosophers would nowadays rule—it would indeed follow from the doctrine of Autonomy that no one can be logically compelled by his acceptance of facts and definitions alone to adopt any particular moral position.

Put like this, the doctrine of Autonomy may sound formal and somewhat remote. But it is, if correct, destructive of any idea of absolute moral authority. The reasons for this may be indicated as follows: Consider a problem of morals from the point of view of some particular individual. First of all, he must try to get clear about the exact nature of the problem situation; that is, he has to get clear as to the facts. Then, he may ask what most people, or his society, would say—or what would generally be regarded as his duty in his circumstances; but the answers to these questions lie likewise in the realm of facts—facts about society, facts about what others may think. Next, he is confronted with all sorts of urgent exhortation and advice; but other people's expressions of their views merely provide him with further facts about them and about what they want, hope, fear, approve or think. Even his own feelings are to be recognized by him as facts about himself. In short, there is nothing which people can say to him by way of making known to him their views or the views of whatever they take to be the most relevant authority, that cannot be represented as being among the facts of his situation. But from the recognition of the *facts* of his situation, nothing follows, according to the doctrine of Autonomy, by way of a genuinely moral judgement. For that he has to take responsibility in his own individual decision.

It would, actually, make very little difference to its effectively anti-authoritarian, individualist character if the doctrine of Autonomy *were* to be taken in one of its objectivist versions, according to which, among the facts of my situation there may lie my obligations and my duties—as independent of and as authoritative to my own personal will as any other impersonal fact. For even if it is admitted, for the sake of argument, that moral values might themselves be counted as constituting in some way independent facts, who is to say what these so-called moral facts are? The Party or the Church? One's parents or the village elder? After all, the fact that X (whichever would-be authority X may be) says that so-and-so is a moral fact is not itself a moral fact, but only a fact about what X says; and, according to any version of the Autonomist doctrine, from such non-moral factual premises as these, no moral conclusions can follow. Hence, even if there are moral facts, every man must in the end decide for himself by what or by whom they are to be known: which is to say that there can in the last resort be for him no other responsible authority than that of his own independent judgement. Until he recognizes this, any Autonomist may say, he has not yet understood the true nature of morality.

Thus, although the doctrine of Autonomy is presented, and understood by those who present it, as a doctrine about the possibilities and impossibilities of valid, logical argument, it is at the same time a doctrine of characteristically liberal and, in general, Protestant flavor. I do not want to exaggerate the Protestant side of this characterization, nor, indeed, to pretend that it is not possible to give a certain sense to the notion of moral authority within an Autonomist framework. But both flavors are, I think, pretty recognizably there.

It *is* possible to give a *certain* sense to the notion of moral authority within an Autonomist framework. For in the first place, few contemporary Autonomists at any rate would think that just any decision or preference on the part of an independent individual would count as a moral judgement. Moral judgements are on the contrary very special sorts of decisions. Naturally enough, Autonomists differ among themselves as to the proper characterization in detail of a moral judgement as distinct from any other kind of judgement; and some of these differences are very considerable. But one very widely accepted characterization of a genuinely evaluative moral judgement is that it should be universal in scope: that it should be applicable, and be meant as applying, to everybody alike —that is, to whoever might find himself in a certain repeatable type of situation. However, it is not always by any means easy to tell just what are the further implications of a universal moral judgement of this sort; sometimes the difficulties may be intellectual ones, but far more often they will arise from lack of experience, lack of imagination, or prejudice due to one's own naturally strong interests and emotions. In circumstances of this sort, it may be reasonable to defer to the "outside authority" of someone recognized to be of greater experience, wiser imagination, and disengaged impartiality. And though, of course, each individual must in the end take responsibility for his own choice of authority to be trusted—for his own judgement as to who is to be counted as sufficiently impartial, experienced and wise—still, so far as the more detailed judgements are concerned, he may be prepared to treat this authority as absolute.

Secondly, an Autonomist may quite coherently decide to give his whole faith and trust to some institutionalized or institutionally backed authority such as the Party or Church, priest or section commander, or whatever it might be. To do this is (from an Autonomist viewpoint) like giving a blank check to somebody else, already signed but needing to be filled in on one's behalf with whatever the authority may consider to be the appropriate moral judgements. But once again, the decision to adopt such an authority, as one's decision-maker by proxy or by power of attorney as it were, must be the individual's own. That something—say abortion—is wrong will still not follow from the fact that somebody else says that it is: it can follow only from this fact *together with my own overall decision* to accept what this somebody or institution says and to make it my own.

Thus, the Autonomist *can* give a sense to the notion of Authority; but only on the deeper understanding that Authority itself, if it is to be genuinely moral, must be founded on freely determined consent.

Whether this, as it seems to me, somewhat attenuated sense of "Authority" will still be sufficient for Catholic doctrine is not for me to say. Catholics themselves, of course, may take different views on the matter. In any case, whatever the force of traditional doctrines may be, their interpretation is always open to change; and certainly distinguished Catholic churchmen may on occasion be found to argue as full-blown Autonomists. Similarly, one can easily discover both Autonomists and non-Autonomists among Protestants. Still, I do not think it unfair to say that this doctrine of the moral supremacy of the enlightened individual conscience is of a more typically Protestant nature. Furthermore, the doctrine of Autonomy is hardly compatible with that of Natural Law, according to which certain values are embedded in the very nature of things, and are there to be recognized and discovered by whoever has the "eyes of reason" to see, but not to be modified in the light of so-called individual standards; and it may perhaps be rather more difficult for Catholics than for Protestants wholly to disentangle their beliefs from doctrines of this kind. (Still, even here one must say "hardly compatible" rather than "totally incompatible"; for there have been attempts to square this circle as well, and much could be made to depend on the exact way in which values are supposed to be embedded in nature.)

Still, however all this may be, my own view is that it is the political (in a wide sense) or social aspect of Autonomist ideology that is the more markedly significant. A society that believes that each man is in the last resort his own irreducibly independent source of moral values is a thorough-going individualistic and liberal society. Liberal with a small "l," of course; and not necessarily particularly humane or tolerant, though one may always hope that liberal society should be so. But certainly liberal in the classical individualist sense; and for better or worse—and it *could* in certain cases be worse—radically anti-totalitarian.

Can the Autonomist actually prove the correctness of his own point of view? To his own satisfaction at least I am inclined to think that he can.

The details of his case may vary and may involve considerable complications; it is no casual matter to determine in a sufficiently rigorous manner the proper criteria of logically valid derivation. But it is no part of my present concern actually to try to prove the Autonomist's case; and the main ideas behind his different arguments are perhaps simple enough. They are, to repeat (and disregarding Objectivist formulations), that there are clear distinctions to be made between moral and any sort of non-moral judgements; that logical argument can never validly conclude in any assertion that was not somehow or other already implicit in the premises of the argument; that since moral and non-moral are held to be thus distinct, the one can never be derived from the other, unless it was somehow already implicitly there in advance; and that from the non-moral alone, therefore, from the facts of nature or the facts of society, from the facts of one's own emotions or the facts about God and church, no moral judgement is to be derived. Thus, each and every man must decide for himself, whether he likes it or not. To learn to think morally is to accept the inescapable necessity of taking one's own responsibilities upon oneself.

So much, for the moment, for the Autonomist. His case may well seem a strong one; to himself it will seem invincible. But—it hardly needs saying—his opponent, the Naturalist, of whatever form or variety, may be equally convinced of the evident truth of *his* case and of the absurdity of that of the Autonomist. And the Naturalist, too, can find a good deal to say for himself.

The Case for Naturalism

The Naturalist's central contentions may be seen to conflict with those of the Autonomist at almost every point. The Naturalist may or may not think that a man has a certain limited area of independent moral decision —an area within which to decide what is right, not only in the fact-finding sense of "decide" in which I might try to decide whether it was going to rain or not, but also in the sense of "decide" in which I may decide what I am going to do. But he will certainly hold that this area is limited. For him, too, this can be represented as a matter of logic, though "logic" understood a little differently, no doubt. That is to say that there will be certain sorts of judgements which, in his view, could not *meaningfully* be presented as moral judgements: the judgement, for instance, that one had a moral obligation to dance a jig every morning or that it was morally permissible, or even admirable, to torture children on the third of each month. It is true, of course, that somebody might use the *word* "moral" in connection with judgements such as these; but this would simply be to show that such a man was using it in some entirely different way from that with which we are familiar, in some entirely different sense from that which is relevant here. The Autonomist may present his doctrine as founded on a point of logic; for the Naturalist, it is first and foremost on a point of logic (in a general sense) that the Autonomist is most evidently and profoundly mistaken. To take the Autonomist seriously is to regard him as committed to accepting, as at any rate meaningful, a whole range of allegedly moral assertions that no one in his right or reasonable senses, or with a proper understanding of the language, could regard as meaningful at all. If he claims (as he must) that the fact that a man is torturing a child is logically compatible with the judgement that the man's action is as such morally right, this to the Naturalist can only go to show that it is the Autonomist who has not as yet understood the true nature and meaning of morality.

I have said that the central contentions of the Naturalist may be seen to conflict with those of the Autonomist at almost every point. But it goes without saying that to talk as if there were, broadly speaking, but one type of anti-Autonomist doctrine involves the grossest of oversimplifications. It would be impossible to try here to go through all of the many importantly different forms which this doctrine or family of doctrines may take. However, there are perhaps two or three very broad distinctions that may usefully be indicated at this stage, the first two of which in fact cut across the Naturalist-Autonomist dichotomy and apply with equal force to both sides.

First, and maybe over-obviously, the differences between Autonomists and Naturalists need have nothing to do with the question of whether it is possible to explain on the basis of the natural or social sciences why people hold the moral views that they do hold. In general, to explain how it comes about that a man holds a given belief need be to imply nothing either about the truth of his belief or about the grounds on which its truth or falsity might be established. Many Autonomists certainly maintain the possibility of providing "natural" explanations of why men adopt the particular moral principles that they (freely) do; vice versa, some Naturalists—or Descriptivists, to give them their perhaps less misleading title—may differ from others in taking what is moral to be defined by reference to the sovereign will of God, and hence beyond natural explanation.

Second, the situation is complicated by the fact that while many Naturalists may concentrate on the notion of morality and on its definition (as they see it) partly or wholly by reference to some other factor than that of the individual's own elective will, others prefer to concentrate on the notion of evaluation in general. Thus Naturalists of this latter variety may see the crucial distinction to lie between individual preferences, purposes, desires, etc. on the one hand and genuine values on the other hand, where the values have to be based on something that confronts the individual as being beyond and outside him. From this standpoint, the non-Autonomy of moral values may be seen as springing not so much from their status as moral as from their status as values; and one may even be allowed to talk of individual (and to that extent non-evaluative) moral preferences or whims. In just the same way, while there are some Autonomists who take the notion of morality as central, there are others who take that of evaluation, and whose doctrine may therefore be more suitably entitled the Autonomy of Values rather than the Autonomy of Morals. (There are also, unfortunately, a number on either side of the fence who sometimes fail to maintain a clear distinction between these two versions of their doctrines.)

Third, and as already indicated, Naturalist or Descriptivist thinkers may vary greatly between themselves in their accounts of how "morality" (or "evaluation") really is to be delimited or even defined. Some would refer to some kind of general consensus, either of society or of some class or segment of society or of mankind as a whole; others to the concept of human nature itself, interpreted in some preferred teleological way; others to concepts of basic human needs; others again to considerations of a religious or metaphysical order; and yet others to such standard Utilitarian concepts as Welfare or Pleasure or the Greatest Happiness of the Greatest Number. In other perspectives that that from which the present discussion is directed, the differences between these competing (though perhaps not equally plausible) versions of Naturalism may effectively overshadow those between any of them and the doctrine of Autonomy; and on any account of the matter, the differences between them are, of course, of very great importance.

In spite of these differences, however, there is the one central feature common to all these and other versions of Naturalism. If Autonomism is false and the facts of human nature or needs of society or of God may always place limitations on the range of meaningfully possible moral judgements (and sometimes such severe limitations as to leave virtually no choice at all), then the individual is very much less than free to determine his own moral values for himself. And in this case, to teach him the nature of morality must involve teaching him to recognize the directions in which these limitations lie.

It is important to realize that both these sets of views can be represented as views about the *logic* of moral argument and the *meaning* of terms like "morality." That is to say that the situation is not simply one of different groups of people holding rival views as to how one ought to behave. Disagreements of *this* sort, after all, are not only possible but even to be expected among Autonomists themselves; since each Autonomist considers himself and everyone else wholly and irreducibly responsible for determining his own moral values, he will show no surprise that some people should settle on different moral principles than others do. This disagreement between Autonomists and Naturalists of whatever hue, however, is one about the very structure within which any moral thinking or argument is to take place. This is what makes their disagreement a typically philosophic one.

Implications for Educators

What is the relevance of considerations such as these to the problems confronting educators? The fundamental issue, as I have tried to indicate, concerns the *kind* of thing one should be trying to do when undertaking any form of moral education or training; and in some sense or other, this issue must always be relevant. But—although I here pretend to no expertise whatsoever—I should certainly suppose that the practical immediacy of this relevance would depend very considerably upon the age and type of "pupils" with whom one were concerned. It seems clear, for example, that the Autonomist view of morality as springing essentially from the fully self-conscious decisions of maturely responsible individuals is one that can only have potential rather than direct application to very small children. There is, after all, a sense in which we must all start off as little Naturalists by learning our moral values as if they were facts.

Indeed, the Autonomist's conception of morality is in this way a peculiarly sophisticated one. The goal that he sets himself must be to bring children up to think and to decide for themselves as fully autonomous individuals; but meanwhile he will want somehow to prevent them from going altogether off what he himself would regard as the minimally acceptable rails. He is faced, therefore, with some rather tricky practical as well as theoretical problems; and up to a point, no doubt, these problems would tend to increase and to become of more direct urgency with the increasing age of his pupils or students (though this does not mean that they must not already exist in a more or less latent form from the very beginning).

So the basic issue is both educationally relevant and typically philosophic. Nevertheless, the situation is not one in which educators can simply go to philosophers in order to receive from them some professionally agreed-upon clarification of the nature and meaning of moral thinking and hence of the true goals of moral education. Faced with such systematic disagreements between the philosophers themselves, educators can hardly look to philosophy, at any rate not in its present state, to provide them with answers ready made and easily recognizable as definitive. It is nearer the mark to say that those educators who find themselves driven to work out the basic rationale of what they are or should be attempting in the field of moral training are already having to think philosophically for themselves. The most that they can expect from philosophers is that they may be able to help them in this endeavor.

But what sort of help? Help first and foremost, perhaps, in making the conflict explicit. This is already of no little importance. Where morals are concerned, it is only too easy to take the presuppositions of one's own evaluative framework for granted, noticing neither that they may be internally inconsistent nor that they may differ radically from the assumptions of others. In this way communication may be befogged and mutual understanding ruled out from the beginning. Moreover, if one lives, as perhaps most of us do, in a society of changing and conflicting outlooks, one's own thinking may very well proceed from rival and incompatible presuppositions; in such a case it is one's own communication with oneself that is befogged, and the failure to understand includes a failure of self-understanding. Philosophers may not be all that good at appreciating philosophic standpoints different from their own. But nature and training together incline them in favor of systematization and consistency, and hence both to a more thorough-going advocacy of one position rather than another and to a corresponding awareness that other people may disagree. Thus, even if they think that the views of their opponents are in the end demonstrably mistaken, their systematic expositions of their own views, their attacks on their opponents and their replies to their opponents' attacks, all help to articulate the nature, and display the characteristic strengths and weaknesses, of their respective positions.

Any serious attempt to assess these strengths and weaknesses would, unfortunately, lie well beyond the scope of the present article (which was, it may be recalled, restricted to indicating the *kind* of implications that moral philosophy might have for moral education). In any case, I am myself at present inclined to the belief that Autonomists and Naturalists can each, from within their own frameworks of concepts and assumptions, find at any rate some viable version or versions of their theses and, to their own legitimate satisfaction, deal in one way or another with any objection that the other side may bring; but that neither side can disprove the case of its opponents in the sense of showing that the case must, in whatever version it be presented, remain internally inconsistent or incomplete. Thus, the Autonomist may very well complain that Naturalism allows no room for individual moral criticism of established values; or the Naturalist, that Autonomy fails to draw a real distinction between values on the one hand and personal preference on the other. But to these complaints it may be replied that it is always open to the enlightened individual to attempt a reinterpretation of values through the recognizably fundamental categories, outside which his criticism will be unintelligible as *moral* criticism; or that the distinction between preference and value can be perfectly well made on the basis of some purely formal principle, such as that of the universalizability of genuinely moral (or evaluative) judgments. The difficulty is to find a point of neutral stability on which to rest one's balance of assessment.

I am acutely aware of the fact that this is, both intellectually and practically, an untidy and unsatisfactory conclusion to come to—that it solves very few problems and raises a number of new ones that hardly existed before. Of course, the issues involved in testing out the internal self-consistency of both the Autonomist's and the Naturalist's positions in their various versions can become exceedingly technical and complex; and it is thus entirely possible that I should be brought to recognize that my present conclusion is mistaken. But meanwhile, my most urgent problem must be to work out where the recognition of Autonomist and non-Autonomist positions as each self-sufficient and both logically and practically viable structures for understanding morality is going to leave someone like myself. It may sound in a way all very fine and superior to be able to say of two contrasting theories (or families of theories) that both may be right from their own point of view, but that neither viewpoint has the exclusive monopoly of the truth: to say this may give one the temporary appearance and feeling of being somehow above the battle. But this said, the question remains as to what, if one can no longer accept the characteristically exclusive claims of either contestant, is to be one's own view of morality.

On this question I have as yet disappointingly little to say; what is worse, that little is still so uncertain and ill-digested as to make it impossible to state it briefly and clearly. So let me say just this: it seems to me that if there is to be a third position, it is exceedingly unlikely to be something quite distinct from the other two. On the contrary, it must, I think, be sought in some kind of synthesis, a synthesis which would provide a platform from which the two previous positions could more easily be seen as intelligible than either of them can appear to a wholehearted proponent of the other. One cannot, of course, achieve a synthesis merely by sticking two opposing views together; in the process of a genuine synthesis both are bound to be subject to new limitations and modifications. To give an example of the sort of thing that I have in mind: it seems plausible (though still highly speculative) to argue that it is only in certain sorts of social and cultural conditions that such a thorough-going individualistic view of morality, as is that of the Autonomists, could become possible or even intelligible; that is to say, that it is only in the context of a certain sort of social structure—against the background of a certain level and type of social, economic and political development—that provision could be made for the kind of status necessary for the individual before he could be regarded, or could even regard himself, as constituting in his own right a creative center of values. And if this is so, it would follow that the new-style Autonomist could not coherently think of every individual as creating his own moral values for himself, but only those individuals who belonged to such a culture or society; for it is only to such individuals that the concepts would be available to think their morality for themselves. A determined Autonomist might be tempted to say that it was only in such types of society that true morality was possible. From which it would further follow that the Autonomist who wanted to preserve the possibility of morality would have to look beyond a care for individuals considered as radically discrete and independent entities to a concern for the social structure within which such a form of individualism might be preserved.

Meanwhile, to speak autobiographically, I remain more than somewhat uncomfortably poised between this possible but as yet quite unworked-out third position and that particular version of Autonomism which I myself held up to not so very long ago. My position between these two positions is one of a highly unsteady equilibrium: oscillation is probably a better word. This has both theoretical and practical inconveniences. In my theorizing there certainly seem to be moments when I reappear as an Autonomist at heart—witness perhaps my suggestion that the only reasonable help that educators can demand from philosophers is help to enable them to see and to think their problems for themselves; and while I see nothing whatsoever to be ashamed of in this point of view, I am uncertain of its proper theoretical connection with the new synthesis which I have hopefully in mind. In practice, I am still without any overall coherent view of the sort of framework within which to define and direct the purposes of moral education; and both as teacher and as parent, this is the sort of problem that one can easily ignore but cannot hope really to escape.

I have put this dilemma autobiographically because that seemed to be the clearest way to put it; but the autobiographical element is, of course, in no way interesting or important. The dilemma, however, seems to me to be both. It seems to me characteristic of much deliberate and not so deliberate moral education at the present time that it also oscillates between Autonomist and non-Autonomist presuppositions. Part of the time, children and young people (and older people, too) are encouraged to learn that they must not only think but also decide for themselves; the other part of the time, they find themselves faced with an insistence that morality is only to be understood and observed within certain very general or not so general limits, and that these they must learn—if they wish to become morally responsible—to observe and accept. It is not surprising if many find the situation confusing.

I emphatically do not claim that philosophy has at the moment any clearly acceptable solution to this dilemma. I have tried only to illustrate the very real connection at this point (as indeed at others[1]) between the interests of educators and moral philosophers. But it is not only the educator who is driven to think philosophically as he tries to get clearer on these issues: the moral philosopher, too, may be helped to see more clearly if he remembers at all times that the concepts and presuppositions of morals have to be taught and learned as they are passed on from one generation to another.

Alan Montefiore (December 29, 1926—) is one of several British philosophers who have turned their attention to the educational enterprise. He went to Clifton College and spent eighteen months on an army course at the School of Oriental and African Studies in London during his period of military service. After leaving the military he read P.P.E. at Balliol College, Oxford, where he attained First Class Honors in 1950. After teaching at Keele University for ten years he returned to Balliol in 1961. He has written A Modern Introduction to Moral Philosophy *and has contributed to such journals as* Philosophy, Mind, The Philosophical Quarterly, Ratio, La Revue Internationale de Philosophie, Geographical Studies, *and* The Harvard Educational Review.

---

[1] One such, indeed ultimately related, point is that at which problems arise concerning notions of "responsibility," and whether full moral responsibility is a necessary condition for the passing of any sort of moral judgement. I have tried to say something about the nature of these problems in "Deliberate Wrongdoing," an article which appeared in *La Revue Internationale de Philosophie*, Volume 70, 1964.

26

The Concept of Equality in Education*

B. PAUL KOMISAR
AND JERROLD R. COOMBS

THIS ESSAY addresses itself to the perennial and prodigal question: What is equality in education? Concern with this question is ubiquitious and, according to some authors, particularly germane at the present moment in human affairs. Herbert Thelen's plea is as symptomatic of this concern as any other we might quote:

> The imagination of the civilized world has been captured by the concept, pioneered but not perfected in America, of "equal educational opportunity for all." What does this mean? Does it mean, for example, equal opportunity to learn a particular body of knowledge set by the school—regardless of its meaningfulness to students having different capabilities and need? Or does it mean opportunity to learn whatever each child needs to learn in order to profit from his particular capabilities? Does it mean that every child in every state should have the same amount of money spent on him? Assuming that some teachers are better than others, who should get the best ones—the child who learns most readily or the one who learns least readily? What about the "culturally deprived" child, whose "background" has built-in resistance to learning; or the emotionally disturbed child, whose preoccupations keep him from listening; or the physiologically precocious or immature child, whose biological needs are out of step with the social possibilities for those of his age—What does equal opportunity mean here?[1]

* Komisar, B. Paul, and Jerrold R. Coombs, "The Concept of Equality in Education," *Studies in Philosophy and Education,* Vol. III, Number 3 (Fall, 1964), pp. 223–244. Used by permission.
[1] Herbert A. Thelen, *Education and the Human Quest* (New York: Harper and Brothers, 1960), pp. 11–12.

It is to this question we address ourselves, though perhaps not in quite the way Thelen poses it. Thelen's concern is with what the equality principle requires of us in different areas of education. We approach the question obliquely, by way of a linguistic analysis of the *term* 'equality.'

In the course of this paper we advance and try to justify the following claims: There are two concepts of equality—'equal as same' and 'equal as fitting' tied usually to two different uses of language—descriptive and ascriptive.[2] The sameness concept has a determinate definition and a singular meaning in all contexts of application. Equality in the fittingness sense has an indeterminate definition; its meaning shifts across contexts and language users.[3] Since the principle of equal opportunity employs the fittingness concept, it is not possible to give it a unique and definite interpretation without prior ethical commitments. Therefore, the equality principle is a second-order principle, derivative with respect to the necessary first-order ethical premises. Nor can the equality principle itself confer distinctiveness on one philosophy of education *vis a vis* any other philosophy. Philosophies with different commitments can, all the same, champion their own version of equal opportunity.[4]

Though these are the only fish we care to fry here, there is much more to the story. 'Equality' and the equality principle seem always to have been with us in American education, from the classical liberals through the recent humane welfare theories of education. And even our contemporary austere educational Calvinists do not simply pump for a crash program in excellence. They pause to ask almost plaintively, can we be excellent and equal too? Indeed these contemporary educational philosophers, engaging in what has been called, euphemistically, "The Great Debate" have shown concern for only the narrow question of whether equal educational opportunity requires a common curriculum for all students, or variegated curricula in which students with unique clusters "interests, abilities, and needs" will find a clutch of studies peculiarly congenial to them.

---

[2] This apt expression, the Fittingness Concept, was suggested to us by Harry S. Broudy. It is more suitable than our original label, the Fairness Concept. We take this opportunity to express our thanks to Broudy and James E. McClellan for their generously offered criticisms and, as custom would have it, absolve them of further responsibility.

[3] I.e., the sameness concept can be defined in the accepted way—more or less in terms of the necessary and sufficient conditions for applying or assessing applications of the term. The fittingness concept is not susceptible to definition in this way. The difference is roughly analogous to the divergence in definitional strategy one would follow with "brown" and "good" as applied to shoes.

[4] If one educational philosophy proclaims support of equal opportunity and another disavows it, to this extent they differ. But this is a trivial difference of sheer avowal or disavowal. Nothing of significance follows from it.

But in addition to the areas enumerated by Thelen, we find other areas in which equality plays a disputed role. In the legal context, even before the Supreme Court unanimously supported the words "Separate educational facilities are inherently unequal," there were attempts to broaden 'equality' to cover "intangible" factors of schooling.

In the area of school finance, the equality principle has been invoked by supporters and opponents of federal aid. But surer indications of its importance here are the dispute over the variables to be included in equalization formulae and the surprising distinction made between equal expenditures and equal educational effort.

The concept of equality, then, stands astride the path of educational thought as does no other term. Indeed, it is one of the few terms employed in nearly all the departments of educational language. Add to this the presence of disputed meanings, and conceptual analysis needs no further temptation or justification. It may be that our analysis is wrong-headed, but it is honor enough to be part of the search for clarity. When arson is the desideratum, they also serve who only blow.

I. Two Concepts of Equality

A. THE SAMENESS CONCEPT

Let us begin putting meat on these abstract bones by contrasting two speech acts—one descriptive, the other ascriptive. Consider first a common sort of case wherein we say of students that they are of equal height or ability or have read an equal number of books. This we dub the descriptive use of 'equal' and put it on a par with reports of hair color and the like.

What is the sense of the term 'equal' when it is so employed? In these cases 'equal' means 'same' as in 'same height' or 'same IQ.' One forewarning is in order, however. As Chappell[5] has recently noted, the term 'same' has itself a dual use. We can refer to an object as 'the same one we saw yesterday.' Here the force of 'same' is to identify as *one* thing what might appear on hasty, *prima facie* grounds to be distinct things. This is the *identifying* function of 'same.' But the term also serves a comparative purpose, in which it is presupposed that there are multiple objects and a comparison is made of them for this or that purpose (though

[5] V. C. Chappell, "Sameness and Change," *Philosophical Review*, LXIX (July, 1960), 351–362.

not all purposes), with respect to certain characteristics (though not all characteristics). It is in this latter role that we take 'same' as synonymous with 'equal.' Now our definition:

To say that X and Y are equal with respect to some characteristic C, is to

1. *presuppose* that an appropriate (valid) scale for measuring units of C has been correctly applied to X and Y under standard conditions; and to
2. *presuppose* that the scale applied to X is equivalent or identical to the scale applied to Y; and further to
3. *presuppose* that the units of measurement employed have a degree of fineness suitable to the context; and, then, to
4. *assert* that the resultant scores or measurements in both applications are the same.

We need not tarry here very long. Equality as sameness gives us little trouble. Our main reason for specifying this concept is to contrast it with another sense of equality yet to come. There are those, however, who would make all uses of 'equal' cleave to this sameness sense, and the temptation for such a move lies in the sameness concept itself.

Given two speakers sharing the above definition, there need not be *automatic* agreement in recognizing instances of sameness. That is, descriptive claims of equality are not *completely* rulebound. One is given one's head to a limited extent; there is room for individual judgment in even such a hardheaded task as determining whether two characteristics are the same.

The source of this freedom is criterion 3 of the definition. Thus we may say of two students that they fared equally well (or fared the same) in a course of instruction when they received the same letter grade (A or B, etc.), despite discrepancies in their test scores or their dissimilar performance at varying stages in the instruction. But in such a circumstance we could not say that their test scores were necessarily the same. A college admissions officer might want measurements on a finer scale before allowing the two candidates to be "equal in school achievement." A shift to an unexpected level of precision is the stuff of contrived melodrama.

"Yes, but they are not precisely equal," says Villain to Goodheart, who never imagined we were going to use calipers on cauliflower. So Goodheart loses the bet and coughs up his soul, his deed or daughter (for even tastes of Villains run in different directions). Goodheart's intentions were of the best but the moral is not to let your logic slide."

Consequently, there is a place for context, individual perspective to make a difference. Claims of equality are not *just* reports, not "a mere reading off of the facts." They reflect, to some degree, judgments of the speaker that can vary from case to case and speaker to speaker, depending on purpose, seriousness of concern and kinds of scales available.[6] There is a chink here in the wall of complete determinateness, but next we are considering another concept of equality wherein whole sections of this wall are absent. Our concern is that the critic not confuse a chink with a breach.

B. THE FITTINGNESS CONCEPT

Consider a second range of speech acts in which we invoke 'equality' as the operative term.

(a) "The teacher gave equal treatment to both sides of the dispute."
(b) "This school offers equal opportunity to all students."
(c) "Both candidates were given an equal chance of admission to college."

1. These assertions differ from those made with the sameness concept in several respects.

First, note that these assertions have the fore of judgments rather than reports. They avow that some practice was proper to the subjects at hand: they are expressions of approval (or disapproval in claims of inequality). Since we usually do not make a judgment of propriety or impropriety without cause, it is not surprising to find that these assertions have another function. This second function is most clearly seen in the negative case. A claim of unequal treatment constitutes a rebuke, censure of the perpetrator of it. It carries with it the presumption that the agent was responsible. Of course the responsibility can frequently be disclaimed ('I was made to change his grade'), passed on ('The school-board mandated this') or its existence denied altogether ('Really, this is the only thing we can do'). But even when such disclaimers are justified, when responsibility cannot be assigned or assigned definitely, there remains what one writer has called the 'evaluative residue.'[7] "All right, the un-

---

[6] In connection with this point and the discussion in the preceding paragraph, see Robert Crawshay-Williams, *Methods and Criteria of Reasoning* (London: Routledge and Regan Paul, 1957), Chapter 2, especially pp. 22–24, in which he discusses the role of context, i.e., purpose, in the interpretation of statements, including assertions of sameness.

[7] V. C. Walsh, "Ascriptions and Appraisals," *Journal of Philosophy*, LV (November 20, 1958), 1,062ff.; and in *Scarcity and Evil* (Englewood Cliffs, N.J.: Prentice-Hall, Inc., 1961), p. 108.

equal treatment may not have been your fault, but it's a shoddy way to treat the student all the same."

The situation is less simple with respect to a positive claim. For if a claim of inequality (impropriety) is censure, what is the force of a claim of equality (propriety)? Given a suitable contextual plot, the positive claim may exonerate an agent of presumed wrong doing ("No, he did treat the students equally") or it may give official certification to an alleged propriety ("We find there is equal opportunity here" announced by some suitable committee or office).

We found above that this use of 'equal' has affinities with evaluation. Nonetheless, a claim of equal treatment is not usually praise.[8] "You presented all viewpoints brilliantly" is commendation. "You gave ten minutes to each position" is descriptive. A claim of equal treatment hangs uneasily between. It is not praise because it is a requirement of the *concept* of teaching that the teacher be fair, impartial, just.[9] It is not description for we are passing on the legitimacy of the teacher's behavior.

2. There are two quick forays to make before the undergrowth thickens. Let us preface the first by stipulating that the approving, legitimizing, censuring, etc., acts be called the ascriptive functions of 'equal.' The sameness concept usually does not have these functions. The report that students have equal grades or read an equal number of books is not of itself approval or disapproval, censure or exoneration. Of course we may take it as such, if we care to, by suitable additions to the context.

This brings us to another point: we do not need additional information to detect that "This teacher treats students unequally" is obloquy. We want to emphasize that it is the word *'equal'* which has the ascriptive functions we are discussing. That is, we are considering the ascriptive uses of the term itself, not the presence of the term in an otherwise ascriptive speech act. *'Equal'* is the operative term making the statement 'This student was not given equal treatment' a rebuke. If the operative term were to be replaced, the whole force of the assertion would be altered. It is easy enough to note that 'You should have players of equal (same) height' is a prescription. But 'equal' does not make it so. It's more discerning to see with Benn and Peters, that:

---

[8] There is always the exception. When a teacher maintains equal treatment at a time and in a place calling for unusual skill, forebearance, etc., then it is praise. It is also unexpected.

[9] We would include it in the "restrictions of manner" made part of the concept of teaching in Israel Scheffler, *The Language of Education* (Springfield, Ill.: Charles C. Thomas, 1960), 57f, 68.

In social and political theory, however, 'equality' is more often prescriptive than descriptive. In this sense, 'all men are equal' would imply not that they possess some attribute or attributes in the same degree but that they ought to be treated alike.[10]

That is, the ascriptive functions (and Benn and Peters' prescriptive function as well) are built by convention into the very meaning of the term 'equal.' The functions don't simply arise from the syntactical form of the assertion. This is the point that is not grasped by those who analyze the concept of equality: the ascriptive functions *are part of the meaning* and must be accounted for in any definition we give.

So there is no doubt that the sameness concept can enter into ascriptive and prescriptive speech acts. It is likewise clear that the fittingness concept can be used purely descriptively, when its approving, censure, etc. functions have been revoked or neutralized.[11] But in both 'You should group students of equal ability' and 'He said there is equal opportunity here' the term 'equal' is not the operative one regulating the kind of speech act involved.

Our point, put in its most forceful manner, is that the fittingness concept of equality has ascriptive and prescriptive functions built into it. These are not part of the sameness concept. So the differences we have been discussing are truly differences between the concepts themselves. They are not differences between various speech acts in which 'equal' is merely present.

3. It is this last point that is the sticky one, and it is surely time to stop dawdling over the ascriptive *functions* of 'equal' and get to the main question. Granted that when the term is applied in contexts of the sort being discussed, it will have the force of approval or rebuke, etc. However, what is the *sense* of the term in these contexts? This sense of 'equal' is *fittingness*. To say that certain treatment is equal treatment is to be saying that it is fitting to the subjects exposed to it. It is difficult, however, to pin this sense down with a definition; for the criteria of fittingness, unlike those for sameness, shift with the ever-moving sands of context. We will offer a general defining formula to fix the concept in place. But it should be borne in mind that it is the ascriptive functions, not the criteria for application, that are common to all contexts in which the fittingness concept is applied.

Skipping further preliminaries, we offer this definition of the fittingness of equality:

[10] S. I. Benn and R. S. Peters, *Social Principles and the Democratic State* (London: Allen & Unwin, 1959), p. 108.

[11] E.g., A. H. Halsey, Jean Floud, and C. Arnold Anderson, *Education, Economy, and Society* (New York: The Free Press of Glencoe, Inc., 1961), pp. 209–214.

(a) The provisions or practices being adjudged equal be in accordance with rightful rules, properly applied.

(b) The rules employed be selected with reference to the appropriate characteristics of the subjects, correctly described.

4. The definition stands in need of further explication. But criticism being more delightful than explanation, we will postpone discussion of our own definition in order to give protracted attention to an alternative view of the meaning of the fittingness concept. The view we refer to goes something like this:

"When I say 'This teacher gave equal treatment' I may very well be approving the teacher's demeanor and what not, but nonetheless I am approving the treatment (of X and Y) because it is the same treatment (X and Y). So we can say that 'equal' has the *sense* of sameness despite differences in *functions* or *use*. On this view there is one concept of equality not two, albeit in some speech acts the single concept has ascriptive and prescriptive appendages. But even with a full complement of barnacles and weeds, a boat is a boat for all that."

We want to oppose this single-meaning view, which we call the sameness thesis. 'Equal,' we will say, has not only taken on new functions but shifted its sense as well; and it is false to claim that sameness is identical with or essential to equality in the fittingness sense.

(Two points of procedure. Since our main interest in the next section is with the fittingness concept, it seems useless to reiterate the designation. Hence we simply write 'equal' when we mean the 'fittingness concept of equal.' However, those who are already disenchanted with the single meaning view of 'equal' are advised to skip the next section and proceed to part III where we return to the problem of definition.)

II. Critique of the Sameness Thesis

There have been varied attempts in education to make sameness a defining characteristic of equality. Philip Phenix supplies us with one recent and notable example:

Equal opportunity means the distribution of schooling in such a way that the interests of each are served to the maximum, consistent with the equal claims of others. This general principle is not easy to apply in practice because different interests are not truly comparable and thus no definite meaning can be attached to their equality.

Perhaps equality of educational opportunity in the last analysis means simply that the distribution of education shall be determined through discussion and agreement within the democratic community, where each person has the same right of voice and the same standing before the law.[12]

Why should Phenix be concerned whether the students' interests (or even the curricula catering to them) are comparable? Presumably because he assumes that equal opportunity requires sameness. But since the interests cannot even be compared, we are in no position to assert their sameness. So Phenix, in the grip of the sameness thesis looks elsewhere—to the procedures followed in establishing school programs—for the necessary aspect of sameness. And here in the midst of democratic decision processes, he finds the desired identical element, viz., that each person's voice and vote count the same, i.e., as one! This is surely a desperate price to pay for retaining sameness in equality.

Myron Lieberman also champions the thesis, but by more labyrinthian paths:

At this point, it becomes important to recognize that complete equality of educational opportunity is impossible. Not everyone can have the same teacher or live in the same home environment or travel the same distance to school, to mention just a few things that could be the basis of inequality of educational opportunity. The impossibility of complete equality tells us something about what people do not ordinarily mean when they say that there is equality of educational opportunity. They do not mean that there are no inequalities whatsoever. Rather, they mean that some inequalities can be disregarded in judging whether there is or is not equality of educational opportunity.

Minor inequalities are thus disregarded in common usage. But at what point does an inequality cease to be minor? How much equalization is necessary before we are willing to say that there is equality of educational opportunity?

And farther along:

. . . equality does not mean that every student receive the same grade, but that every student be graded according to standards which apply to all. When we think of equality before the law, we do not suppose that there can be no equality unless all persons on trial are acquitted or all convicted. . . . The "equality" involved is not one of outcome but of procedure to determine the outcome.[13]

Lieberman is so insistent in his asseverations concerning the practical limits on the amount of sameness that is possible, that we are apt to over-

[12] Philip H. Phenix, *Philosophy of Education* (New York: Henry Holt and Company, 1958), p. 144.

[13] Myron Lieberman, "Equality of Educational Opportunity," *Harvard Educational Review*, XXIX (Summer, 1959). Also reprinted in B. O. Smith and R. H. Ennis (editors), *Language and Concepts in Education* (Chicago: Rand McNally and Company, 1961), pp. 133, 137.

look the fact that he makes sameness—*some* sameness to be sure—the defining element in equality. Thus the problem (to Lieberman) in equal opportunity is determining *which* conditions must be the same. His prejudice in favor of sameness forces him to overlook the obvious: *viz.*, that it is the presence of dissimilarity which *constitutes* equal opportunity in certain circumstances.

Others are less clearly supporters of the sameness thesis, but their ambiguous definitions are as susceptible of this interpretation as of any other:

In practice it [equal opportunity] means an equal chance to compete within the framework of goals and the structure of rules established by our particular society. . . .[14]
Education, we now say, equalizes when it matches equally well the variant needs, wants, and abilities of individuals.[15]

Although the quotations above do not reveal the fact clearly, the sameness thesis may take any one of several forms. We will consider each of these seriatim even though some forms are without supporters at present. However, it is likely that even the most neglected bastion, once under attack, will be found bristling with defenders.

We begin by distinguishing two general ways of construing the sameness thesis. Consider the claim 'A and B were given equal treatment.' The first approach holds that however sameness enters the picture, it obtains between A and B, the explicit subjects of the utterance. This approach we will dub the *explicit comparison*. The alternative approach is, as you would expect, more covert. It assumes that the intended comparison is 'A and B treated equally' is not between A and B as explicitly stated, but between A and other presumed A's; B and other presumed B's. The equal treatment, then exists between the asserted subjects and their respective, but unmentioned, kinsman. This naturally, we label the *implicit comparison*. What the implicit comparison does is to interpret the single claim about A and B into two separate utterances, one about A's and the other about B's.

A. SAMENESS THESIS: EXPLICIT COMPARISON

This approach itself comes in a variety of forms. These are best exemplified through consideration of the elements found in a context in

[14] John Gardner, *Excellence* (New York: Harper and Row, 1961), p. 12.
[15] M. H. Willing, *et al.*, *Schools for Our Democratic Society* (New York: Harper and Brothers, 1951), p. 139.

which we make some claim of equal treatment: There are five such elements.

(a) *Subjects:* implicitly or explicitly involved; not only students but competing hypotheses, theories, recipients of funds or other specifiable characteristics; who are exposed or subjected to some treatment.
(b) *Rule(s)* mandating how the subjects are to be treated, called often the treatment-generating rules.
(c) *Justification:* principles invoked to defend the use of rule(s) on certain subjects in particular circumstances.
(d) *Treatment:* the practices or provisions the subjects are exposed to, or the course of action taken in connection with the subjects.
(e) Finally, the *results,* in some relevant sense, of the treatment given.

1. *The Identity Form*

In this form the thesis holds that there is equal treatment of subjects if and only if the treatment (d) is literally similar or identical for each subject. This is the form we sketched earlier as the single-meaning view of equality. It posits only one concept of equality fitting all applications of the term, *viz.,* the sameness concept defined earlier. (Recall that this does not deny that some uses may have ascriptive functions. However, it is the *sense* of the term that remains the same.)

Clearly, in some cases we do require that the treatment of A and B be the same before we say that it is *equal* treatment. But this covers only those cases in which the relevant characteristics of the subjects are the same. Our use of 'equal' seems to follow the rule: when there is identity in element (a) the subjects, a judgment of equality requires sameness with regard to element (d) the treatment.

But the sameness thesis can't settle for this limited victory; it aspires to hold for all cases, including those in which subjects differ in relevant traits. Simply as a matter of fact we see that it does not hold. If two students are given the same penalties for the same misdemeanor we say that they have received equal treatment. But we judge it to be inequality of treatment to give the same penalties for dissimilar infractions. Here our use of 'equal' follows a second rule to the effect that differences in subjects require differences in treatment in order for the treatments to be judged equal.

At this juncture the sameness thesis might take one of two paths: one is to keep the identity between equal treatment and same treatment, but withdraw from the explicit to the implicit comparison. The other is to drop the identity of 'equal' and 'same' but retain sameness in some other defining capacity. We will follow up on this latter possibility first.

2. *Essential Aspect Form*

In the face of the criticism directed at the identity form, the supporter of the sameness thesis might seek some other omnipresent feature of the context as the ubiquitous element of sameness in all claims of equality. The likely candidates are the elements listed above.

(a) It might appear plausible to choose the rule(s) (element b) as the necessary element of sameness. Now we can recast our definition of 'equality' in this manner.

For treatment of A and B to be equal requires that the treatment of each be mandated by rules which are the same for each.

Now the defining element is not found in the disparity of treatment accorded but in the identity of the rules invoked to determine it.

But this definition will not hold for all uses of 'equal.' The following counter example, wherein the treatment is admittedly equal, yet not generated by the same rules, is illustrative. Imagine a teacher presenting controversial views of a topic. One side is a long, necessarily detailed inductive argument and the other a deductive, nearly stark defense (Hutchins vs. Dewey on curriculum; Catholic vs. humanist on birth control). Equality of treatment here requires not only that the actual treatment be dissimilar (in time, type of presentation); but, more relevantly, it also demands that the treatment of each alternative position be derived from rules which are *different* for the respective sides. That is, the treatment of each side will be mandated by explanatory regulations fitting to arguments of the type at hand, not by any common set of rules for all sides.

(b) In the quotation from Philip Phenix, he seems to select the justification (element c) as the necessary element of sameness in the definition of equality. However it is not clear which of the two definitions he would favor.

Treatment of subjects is 'equal' when the treatment-generating rules are justified *either*

(1) on the basis of a principle containing an element of sameness in it (e.g., same number of votes for each man principle); or
(2) by reference to one principle which covers the disparate treatment-generating rules in the situation.

Position 1 fails whenever we offer a justifying principle with no mention of sameness within it. Phenix's illustration *happens* to be a justification of type (1), justifying a rule of curriculum on the basis of the one man—one vote principle. But certainly it is not this principle, nor any other mentioning sameness within it, which justifies, say, the use of deductive rules in presenting deductive arguments or the rule that applicants for college admission exceeding a certain standard will be admitted.

So it is not the one man—one vote principle which makes an arrangement *ipso facto* an arrangement of equality. The decision, for example, made by the one man—one vote procedure, to treat *all* arguments by deductive rules, would be a violation of equality! There is a limit to the number of actions for which democracy can be conscripted as warrant.

It is the second (2) position which is the more plausible, but not so much so that another clear instance of usage does not refute it. Consider two boys applying for admission to college (or two school districts for subsidies). One applicant with below average qualifying scores is rejected (cut-off rule); another with the same scores but a religion under-represented on the campus is admitted (proportionate representation of social groups rule).

Here we find different treatment; different rules and a *different justification for each rule.* For the cut-off rule, there is the usual one about the low probability of success in such cases; in support of the other rule we are regaled with stories of the educational advantages of encountering a "balanced" college environment. Yet here is equality of treatment all the same.

It might be objected that there is more to the justification process in these cases. If the justification is pushed to its limits, the critic avers, then all justifications of presumed equal treatment consist finally in one general principle: *all treatment generating rules be appropriate to the subjects being treated.*

But this simply will not do. To defend the sameness thesis on these grounds is suicide for the thesis. For it is precisely this claim, *viz.,* that equality means fitting, we are defending *against* the sameness thesis. It trivializes the thesis to claim that the equality requires sameness because equal treatment must always be fitting treatment!

So much for the use of the element of justification as the essential aspect of sameness in ordinary claims of equality.

(c) There are probably other elements, increasingly inscrutable, more esoteric, which might be invoked as the desired element of sameness. We will consider but one more. It might be contended that equality requires that the *results* of the treatment be the same in any case of equal treatment.[16] We need not linger here long. The plausibility of the position arises in a case, for example, wherein a teacher may give different coverage to each side of a controversial topic. When charged with giving

---

[16] See Gregory Vlastos, "Justice and Equality" in Richard B. Brandt (ed.), *Social Justice* (Englewood Cliffs, N.J.: Prentice-Hall, Inc., 1962), 41ff. for a discussion of equality in terms of results of treatment.

unequal treatment, the teacher might report that students were very familiar with one alternative, thus requiring less exposure to it to reach a level of understanding commensurate with their understanding of the other side. But what if this "identity in level of understanding" did not come to pass in a case where two sides to a controversy are given divergent, yet proper, presentations? Would this render the presentation unfair? Or what if the "level of understanding (or development or achievement, etc.)" is not detectable, are we then unable to judge the fairness of the teaching? Surely not. We would judge such cases by the rules for correctness that apply to the presentation itself, regardless of outcome, known or unknown. This fact is even clearer in a case of college admissions. Equal opportunity here does not require that all candidates be admitted (same result) but that all be handled appropriately (fitting procedure).

In summary, then, we conclude that for every element that is posited as providing the sameness in a claim of equality, we can find legitimate cases where that element is not the same yet the case is a genuine and legitimate application of the expression 'equal treatment.'

B. SAMENESS THESIS: IMPLICIT COMPARISON

In the face of objections raised thus far, the defender of the sameness thesis might claim that the thesis has failed because we are seeking the comparison in the wrong place. In utterances of the form 'A and B, were given equal treatment,' the intended contrast is not between A and B, but between A and other A's; B and other B's. When so interpreted 'equal treatment' will mean 'same treatment' (the identity form), albeit not sameness between A and B.

But if this position is correct, then it must follow that every demand *for* equal treatment must be a demand for identical treatment. Consider, however, such a demand in these different contexts.

Here we can retain the sameness thesis in its pure identity form. For, as shown, 'equal' has the sense of 'same.' But this later virtue marks the fall of the sameness thesis. We need only show that *not* all demands for equal treatment are intended as demands for same treatment. This is easily done, for to interpret all such demands as claims for identity is to miss the point of the assertion in many cases and to trivialize the concept of equality.

Consider the following contexts in which demands for equal treatment can arise from different intentions.

(a) A person is correctly grouped, i.e., admitted to be an instance of X, but from oversight or intention is not actually treated as an X. For example, a community is admittedly one of a certain tax classification, but fails to receive the state funds earmarked for communities with that classification.

(b) A subject is treated as others with whom he is grouped but claims to have been wrongly grouped. E.g., a candidate for college admissions is classified as *low* in entrance examination results and rejected along with others in the group but argues that his relation to an alumnus has been overlooked. He should be *low-alumnus*.

(c) A subject is admittedly grouped properly but claims that this treatment is unfair to the entire group. The examples here are profuse. All students who would have once been rejected for further education now demanding it are illustrative.[17]

Case (a) marks the apex in the career of the sameness thesis. The request here, clearly, is to be treated the same as other members of a given group. Identity seems to hold for case (b) as well. But proponents will have to admit the fit is looser. For there are two ways of construing the claim made in (b): (1) as a demand to be treated the *same as* others of like characteristics or (2) as a demand to be treated with respect to one's *proper* characteristics. It seems to be a matter of choice as to which is the relevant description of the situation.

But the (c) type situation is a pickle from a different barrel. The issue here is *not* one of identical treatment, for that condition has already been fulfilled. The issue here is whether the treatment is the rightful, i.e., fitting way to treat the group. This shift from (b) to (c) marks the last extremity of the sameness thesis. For what has just been demonstrated is that even when the subjects and treatment are the same, it still makes sense to ask whether the treatment is equal, i.e., fitting. If "equal" literally *meant* "same," such a claim would be redundant, absurd.

Now certainly sameness is involved even in the (c) case, but only in the secondary sense that once rightful treatment is established, it should apply to all members of the group. But the sameness thesis celebrates this secondary characteristic into an intellectual way of life. To the supporter of sameness, for example, the Negro demand is to be treated the same as the white, not a demand to smash down improper differentiating characteristics. But the misconception is revealed when we realize that evidence of superior intellectual characteristics in the colored race would justify, in the name of *equality*, a demand for education superior to that given to whites.

And this reveals a deep truth about ordinary use of "equal." When we judge A and B to have fared equally, part of what we are saying is that

---

[17] These types of challenges are freely adapted from Isaiah Berlin, "Equality," *Aristotelian Society Proceedings*, LVI, 1955–56, 307ff.

each was managed according to his kind. But more importantly we are claiming that this is the proper kind, and that it is *right* to treat subjects of this kind in this way. This is the moral element involved in type (c) cases (which will be discussed in the next section).

Both Lieberman, explicitly, and Phenix, by implication, want to include type (c) cases into the class of claims of equality. The reason is apparent. To restrict the concept of equality to (a) and (b) cases is to trivialize the concept. The term would only operate, then, in cases of simple error and apparent corruption. As such the concept would be a fraud, considering the weight it is asked to carry in social and political philosophy, as well as philosophy of education. The trick is to retain the significant scope for the concept while holding fast to the sameness thesis. But when the former is done, the latter is already a dead thesis. The way to keep the horse from escaping the barn is never to bring him in.

SUMMARY

So much for the attempt to wed equality to egalitarianism by reportive, not persuasive, definition. Generally we have tried to show that to interpret 'equal' as 'same' (*in any way*) is to distort the meaning of the term in some ordinary contexts. On the other hand, to interpret 'equal' as 'fitting' retains the ordinary sense of the term in all contexts. We do not deny, of course, that same treatment may constitute equal treatment *in some contexts*, as a special case of fitting treatment. Or to put the matter differently: we are contending that 'equal' is *defined* as 'fitting' and that same treatment may on occasion be equal treatment *as a matter of fact, not definition*.

Why be concerned with this issue—so concerned that we follow the sameness thesis through its tedious convolutions? The reason is that a definition in terms of sameness offers the last best hope for a determinate, single interpretation for such a ubiquitous educational ideal as equal educational opportunity for all. To this topic we now turn.

III. The Fittingness Concept and the Equality Principle

Having assayed and rejected varied attempts to define equality in terms of sameness, we turn now to an explication of our own definition. Earlier we cited the following rules as constituting a definition of 'equality' in its fittingness sense:

a. The provisions or practices being adjudged equal be in accordance with rightful rules, properly applied.
b. The rules be employed with reference to appropriate characteristics of the subjects, correctly described.

A. INDETERMINACY

Ponder now the state of our system. If equality were defined in terms of sameness, then there would be at least one constant criterion for the application of the term in each and every context. But the upshot of our discussion in the previous section was negative with respect to this hope. The definition offered here in place of sameness is indeterminate. It is indeterminate with respect to the content of the rules to be followed and the characteristics of the subjects that are relevant.

Furthermore, the definition stands in constant danger of redundancy on the score that relevancy of subject characteristics and propriety of rules are functions of one another. That is, whether a candidate's religion is relevant in college admissions is dependent on the presence or absence of a rule about treatment of candidates with respect to this characteristic. And whether we have such rules is dependent on the importance we attribute to the characteristic.

B. PRIMACY OF ETHICAL JUDGMENT

This indeterminacy in the definition of the fittingness concept is apparently analogous to that encountered in connection with the sameness concept. With regard to the sameness concept, the selection of a suitable scale for gainsaying measures of things to be compared is a matter of practical judgment. In applying the fittingness concept, however, one is choosing the morally right rules to adhere to in a given case. This is a *moral* judgment.

It is commonly recognized that assent to equality is a moral act. What we here assert is that the decision as to what *constitutes* equality in concrete cases is likewise a moral decision and a logically necessary one. Allegiance to the equality principle as such is an empty gesture. The principle is a secondary one, depending on logically prior moral commitments to make it meaningful. For example, it is meaningless to support the idea that school subsidies should be distributed to communities on an equal basis. It is not until a commitment is made as to what constitutes rightful allocation that assent to the equality principle becomes significant. Therefore no philosophy of education is identified or made controversial by its belief in educational equality. What is distinctive about an educational philosophy is the particular way it interprets this belief, the judgments and commitments it makes along the way. For to round out this topic on a note of redundancy, the definition of equality does not dictate our educational preferences. Rather it is the case that our educational preferences constitute *our* meaning for equality.

C. ESSENTIALLY CONTESTED

Thus it is that the specific criteria or rules by which we determine a treatment to be equal are not part of the definition of the concept. As illustration, consider the distribution of state funds to local districts on an "equal" basis. A rule (read 'formula') which allocates funds on the basis of local tax *effort* is no more or less "true equality" than rules which dispense moneys to compensate for deficiencies in local tax resources or which give the same amount to each local district or which reward districts manifesting greatest educational improvements; or any combination of these. Any of these can be defended as the right, and hence fitting, way to distribute subsidies. The same holds true for, say, the allocation of teaching talent to students of differential ability. The best teachers might be allocated to the most able students; to the least able, or assigned on some compromise basis. There is nothing in the linguistic conventions which render any one rule as the "real" or "true" meaning of 'equal treatment.'

We would borrow from Gallie at this point and speak of 'equality' in its fittingness sense as an essentially contested concept, i.e., as one of the "concepts the proper use of which inevitably involves endless disputes about their proper uses on the part of their users."[18]

This does not apply, however, to the ascriptive functions of the concept depicted earlier. These functions (approving, assigning responsibility, etc.) are invariant from one context to another, and from one language user to another. However, what particular criteria a person will use will depend on that to which his moral commitments will allow him, justifiably, to apply these functions.

D. CONSEQUENCES OF THE SAMENESS THESIS

Thus it should be clear why a definition of the fittingness concept in terms of sameness is to be so vehemently rejected. For if the concept is so

---

[18] W. B. Gallie, "Essentially Contested Concepts," *Aristotelian Society Proceedings*, LVI (1955–56), 169. Our borrowing of this designation does not adhere to the strict requirements for the employment of this term as set down therein.

defined *and made to retain its ascriptive force,* the result is the thorough-going egalitarianism, so well depicted by Berlin:

In its simplest form the ideal of complete social equality embodies the wish that everything and everybody should be as similar as possible to everything and everybody else . . . I doubt whether anyone has ever seriously desired to bring such a society into being, or even supposed such a society to be capable of being created. Nevertheless, it seems to me that demands for human equality which have been expressed both by philosophers and by men of action who have advocated or attempted to reform society, can best be represented as modifications of this absolute and absurd ideal. In this ideal egalitarian society, inequality—and this must ultimately mean dissimilarity—would be reduced to a minimum.[19]

Even to hold to a less strict form of the sameness thesis is still to give priority to uniformity over variety.

So as a *reportive* definition of the fittingness concept, the sameness thesis is not only factually incorrect; it is also morally wrong. The results are no less severe if the sameness thesis is offered as a stipulated defini-tion. For if the ascriptive force of the term is retained, then the "stipu-lated definition" becomes an ethical recommendation. If the ascriptive functions are dropped, then the stipulation is pointless. We would still need a term to perform the ascriptive services of the fittingness concept.

E. OTHER MISCONCEPTIONS

1. Even those who realize that 'equality' cannot be defined in terms of sameness fall into the error of supposing that it still has a determinate definition. This is probably the source of the crude circularity in the definitions by Willing, *et al.* and Gardner, cited earlier, and in the follow-ing definition:

. . . equality does not mean identity. . . . Let me suggest again that equality in our sense involves an *equal right* of every child, . . . to achieve excellence, to excel. This is what equality means . . .[20]

[19] Berlin, *op. cit.,* 311f.
[20] Peter H. Odegard, "Education and American Values," in *Foundations for Ex-cellence,* Fifteenth Yearbook of the American Association of Colleges for Teacher Education, *Proceedings of the 1962 Annual Meeting* (Washington, D.C., 1962), p. 39. Italics added.

Dewey appears to have gone down this path also: "Belief in equality is an element of the democratic credo. It is not, however, belief in equality of natural endowments. Those who proclaimed the idea of equality did not suppose they were enunciating a psychological doctrine, but a legal and political one. All individuals are entitled to

It is quite conceivable for someone to adopt "right to achieve excellence" or "right to compete" or "right to express judgment" as criteria for determining equality of treatment in appropriate contexts. Of course, it is understood that these are not *definitions* of the term, since different and even contrary criteria might also be justified. What is fostered here is the illusion that 'equality' has a determinate sense which modifies in some way the criterion of application. But 'equal right to achieve' means no more than 'right to achieve.' One's equality with others, then, consists in the right one shares with others to achieve. It consists in no more than this, because there is nothing beyond having the right. Adding 'equal' to the right is a redundancy.

To sum up. Being given equal opportunity does not consist in being given a *special* right, *viz.*, an *equal* right; it consists in being *given* the right. The point in saying that this right is a criteron of equality (what equality means) is that it is morally justified to employ this as a criterion to apply in appropriate contexts.

2. Still another definition of the fittingness concept misconstrues the moral element in the concept and suppresses its essential contestability.

. . . the expression "equality of educational opportunity," as it is used, refers. . . . to the environmental circumstances that influence the growth and development of the individual. No reference to equal intellectual capacity or to any other native endowments is intended. The intended reference is the *chance* to get an education, *of whatever amount and kind one's* endowments make possible. It is the chance that is to be equalized.[21]

The illusion is created here that the criteria specifying what is equal treatment in some context are simply "read off" from the facts of the environment and student's characteristics. (As, for example, equal right can be "read off," merely from the facts.) But a student's endowments make different kinds of education possible. Which should we give the student a chance to get? And which of his endowments do we judge to be appropriate to encourage? The authors state that fair play is the sense of equal opportunity,' but they ignore the fact that this is a moral notion.

---

equality of treatment by law and in its administration. Each one is affected equally in quality if not in quantity by the institutions under which he lives and has an *equal right to express* his judgment, although the weight of his judgment may not be equal in amount when it enters into the pooled result to that of others. In short, each one is *equally an individual* and entitled to *equal opportunity of development of his own capacities* . . ." John Dewey, *Problems of Men* (New York: Philosophical Library, 1946), p. 60. Italics added.

21 William O. Stanley, B. Othanel Smith, Kenneth D. Benne, and Archibald W. Anderson, *Social Foundations of Education* (New York: The Dryden Press, Inc., 1956), p. 228. Some italics added.

What is equal treatment is a matter of moral choice, not factual reporting, and this yields contesting, not uniform views.

B. *Paul Komisar (January 24, 1926—) attended public school in Chicopee, Massachusetts, graduated from Massachusetts State Teachers College at Adams, Massachusetts, and was awarded the Ed.D. in philosophy of education from the University of Illinois in 1958. Professor Komisar teaches in the Foundations of Education Department in the College of Education at Temple University in Philadelphia, Pennsylvania, and holds the rank of Professor of Education. He has been active in the Middle Atlantic States Philosophy of Education Society and in the Philosophy of Education Society. He is a member of the editorial board of* Studies in Philosophy and Education *and has written quite widely for professional journals. He is co-editor of the book,* Psychological Concepts in Education.

Jerrold Coombs (November 7, 1936—) took his undergraduate schooling at Kent State University in Ohio, and in 1964 received a Ph.D. degree in Philosophy of Education from the University of Illinois. While at the University of Illinois he worked in the Bureau of Educational Research, first as a Research Assistant and later as Assistant Professor. In 1965 he moved to the University of British Columbia as Assistant Professor of Education.

Much of Professor Coombs' work has been devoted to studying the logical operations used in teaching. Results of this study, which was carried out in collaboration with several colleagues, have been described in two research reports:

Smith, B. Othanel; Meux, Milton; in collaboration with Coombs, Jerrold; Eierdam, Daniel; and Szoke, Ronald. A Study of The Logic of Teaching. *Bureau of Educational Research. University of Illinois, 1962.*

Smith, B. Othanel; Meux, Milton; Coombs, Jerrold; and Nuthall, Graham. A Tentative Report on the Strategies of Teaching. *Bureau of Educational Research, University of Illinois, 1964.*

In addition Professor Coombs has been active in the Philosophy of Education Society *and has contributed to the professional journals in the field of philosophy of education.*

Recommended Readings for Part Seven

Students are urged to consult the annotated bibliography at the end of the book for more information on the books cited here.

The following books in philosophy and philosophy of education should be especially useful.

A. PHILOSOPHY

ALFRED JULES AYER, *Language, Truth and Logic*
S. R. GOROVITZ and R. WILLIAMS *et al.*, *Philosophical Analysis: Introduction to Its Language and Techniques*
R. M. HARE, *The Language of Morals*
JOHN HOSPERS, *An Introduction to Philosophical Analysis*
SUSANNE K. LANGER, *Philosophy in a New Key*
GILBERT RYLE, *The Concept of Mind*
CHARLES L. STEVENSON, *Ethics and Language*
LUDWIG WITTGENSTEIN, *Philosophical Investigations*

B. PHILOSOPHY OF EDUCATION

REGINALD ARCHAMBAULT, *Philosophical Analysis and Education*
WILLIAM K. FRANKENA, *Philosophy of Education*
D. J. O'CONNOR, *An Introduction to the Philosophy of Education*
R. S. PETERS, *Authority, Responsibility, and Education*
ISRAEL SCHEFFLER, *Conditions of Knowledge*
———, *The Language of Education*
B. OTHANEL SMITH and ROBERT H. ENNIS, *Language and Concepts in Education*

Annotated Bibliography

THIS ANNOTATED BIBLIOGRAPHY is not intended to be exhaustive. It is comprehensive enough, or so it is hoped, that it will introduce the serious student of philosophy and the philosophy of education to some of the most important publications in the field. Through the reading of these works, and noting the bibliographies contained in some of them, the student can move on to certain other related and more technical works. For the most part textbooks have been excluded, except in certain instances where it was thought they contained material of sufficient importance to warrant inclusion. With a few exceptions, all the books were published in this century and deal with the more contemporary aspects of Western philosophy. Finally many of these books are in paperback. By a judicious selection of titles from this bibliography the student can begin to build for himself a personal library of some consequence at a modest cost.

Philosophy

AUSTIN, J. L., *How To Do Things With Words*. Cambridge: Harvard University Press, 1962. Pp. x+ 167.

A collection of lecture notes used by the author in his William James Lectures at Harvard in 1955. This book will be of special interest to linguistic analysts. It provides a program for what might be done with words.

AYER, ALFRED JULES, *Language, Truth and Logic*. New York: Dover Publications, Inc., 1946. P. 159.

An avowed logical positivist writes on the elimination of metaphysics, the function of philosophy, the nature of philosophical analysis, the *A Priori*, truth and probability, ethics and theology, the self and the common world, and solutions of outstanding philosophical disputes. Ayer holds that our sentences express (1) genuine empirical hypotheses, (2) tautologies, or (3) metaphysical expressions that are neither true nor false but "literally senseless."

———, *The Problem of Knowledge*. London: Macmillan & Co., Ltd., 1956. Pp. x+ 258.

The author begins by raising the question, "What is meant by knowledge?" He then deals with the questions of skepticism and certainty. From this, he passes on to a detailed analysis of the philosophical problems of perception, memory, and "Myself and Others." Very well written.

———, *et al.*, *The Revolution in Philosophy*. London: Macmillan & Co., Ltd., 1957. Pp. vi+ 126.

A collection of lectures on outstanding figures in British philosophy from F. H. Bradley to Wittgenstein. Traces the origins of mathematical logic, logical atomism, the Vienna Circle, and linguistic analysis.

BARKER, STEPHEN F., *The Elements of Logic*. New York: McGraw-Hill Book Company, 1965. Pp. xiv+ 336.

Covers the traditional topics in logic in concise and clear language.

BARRETT, WILLIAM, *What Is Existentialism?* New York: Grove Press, Inc., 1964. P. 218.

This volume is intended primarily to provide a comprehensive exposition of Heidegger's thinking.

————, *Irrational Man.* New York: Doubleday Anchor Books, 1962. P. 314.

This is one of the more popular volumes on existentialism. It opens with an account of the advent of existentialism, traces the sources of existentialism in Western tradition, provides lengthy chapters on Kierkegaard, Nietzsche, Heidegger, and Sartre, and closes with a discussion of integral vs. rational man. Very readable.

BLACK, MAX (ed.), *Philosophical Analysis—A Collection of Essays.* Ithaca, N.Y.: Cornell University Press, 1950. P. 429.

In his introduction to this book, Black cautions the reader against naively believing that there is but one school of philosophical analysis. The essays, which range from the mechanics of philosophical analysis to introspection, aesthetics, and ethics, substantiate Black's thesis.

BLANSHARD, BRAND, *Reason and Goodness.* New York: The Macmillan Co., 1961. P. 451.

Blanshard sets out to defend the position of reason in ethics which has come under recent philosophical attacks. He discusses tensions between reason and feeling, stoicism, subjectivism, deontology, instrumentalism, emotivism, the linguistic retreat from emotivism, goodness, thought and desire, reason and politics, and the rational temper.

BRANDT, RICHARD B., *Ethical Theory, The Problem of Normative and Critical Ethics.* Englewood Cliffs, N.J.: Prentice-Hall, Inc., 1959. Pp. xvi+ 538.

Ranges over the main problems in ethics such as tests of ethical principles, science and ethics, noncognitivism, things worthwhile in themselves, justice, human rights, retributive justice, and determinism.

BUBER, MARTIN, *Between Man and Man.* London: Kegan Paul, 1947. Pp. viii+ 210.

A collection of five works by Buber brought together in one volume for English readers. The first work, *Dialogue,* is intended to clarify the "dialogical" principle presented in Buber's I-Thou philosophy. The second work relates to politics and the third and fourth relate the dialogical principle to education. The book closes with a discussion of the essence of man.

————, *I and Thou.* New York: Charles Scribner's Sons, 1958. Pp. xviii+ 137.

A presentation of the famous I-Thou and I-It categories. Buber sees man's relation with God as the basis for true humanity. God he sees entering relations with men in "creative, revealing and redeeming acts."

CASSIRER, ERNST. *An Essay on Man: An Introduction to a Philosophy of Human Culture.* New Haven: Yale University Press, 1944. Pp. xii+ 237.

An examination of man's efforts to understand himself and to deal with the problems of his universe through the creation and use of symbols. The book is broken down into two parts: "What Is Man?" and "Man and Culture." Excellent chapters on religion, language, art, history, and science.

COPI, IRVING M., *Introduction to Logic.* New York: The Macmillan Company, 1958. Pp. xvi+ 472.

One of the standard textbooks in logic. It is divided into three sections: language, deduction, and induction.

DEWEY, JOHN, *Art as Experience.* New York: Minton, Balch & Company, 1934. Pp. xii+ 348.

A series of lectures delivered at Harvard in 1931. Dewey relates art to his concept of experience, and discusses the act of expression, the substance of art, the human contribution, and art and civilization.

———, *Experience and Nature.* New York: Dover Publications, Inc., 1958. Pp. xvi+ 443.

The method of empirical naturalism is seen as the "only way" by which one can freely accept the standpoint and conclusions of modern science and yet maintain cherished values, provided they are critically clarified and reinforced.

———, *How We Think.* Boston: D. C. Heath and Company, 1933. Pp. x+ 301.

In this well-known book Dewey discusses the problem of "training thought" in the schools, and provides an analysis of what he calls the complete act of thought.

———, *Logic, the Theory of Inquiry.* New York: Henry Holt and Company, 1938. Pp. x+ 546.

Dewey discusses the problem of logical subject-matter, the structure of inquiry and the construction of judgments, propositions and terms, and the logic of scientific method. His basic work in logic.

———, *Reconstruction in Philosophy.* New York: Mentor Books, 1950. P. 168.

A series of lectures delivered in Japan in 1919 in which Dewey tried to "exhibit the general contrast between older and newer types of philosophical problems . . . " He covered a broad range of subjects including science, logic, ethics, and social philosophy.

DRAKE, DURANT, et al. (eds.), *Essays in Critical Realism: A Cooperative Study of the Problems of Knowledge.* New York: Peter Smith, 1941. Pp. x+ 244.

A collection of essays by Drake, Arthur O. Lovejoy, James B. Pratt. Arthur Rogers, George Santayana, R. W. Sellars, and C. A. Strong on such topics as pragmatism, knowledge, the problem of error, proofs of realism, and the nature of datum.

DUCASSE, CURT J., *Art, The Critics, and You.* Indianapolis: The Bobbs-Merrill Company, Inc., 1944. P. 170.

Describes the enterprise of esthetics and outlines the essentials of the author's philosophy of esthetics. Chapter 6 calls attention to the importance of education of human feelings and suggests that "the work of the various free and decorative arts have a role to play analogous to that of scientific treatises in education of the mind for activity in the fields of science."

EDIE, JAMES E. (ed.), *What is Phenomenology?* Chicago: Quadrangle Books, Inc., 1962. P. 191.

A translation of four essays written by Pierre Thevanez with an introduction by the editor and a preface by John Wild. Wild states that he knows of no brief introduction to phenomenology that is as accurate as this series of essays.

EDWARDS, PAUL and ARTHUR PAP (eds.), *A Modern Introduction to Philosophy.* New York: The Free Press, 1965. Pp. xviii+ 797.

A collection of readings on seven problems: determinism, induction, mind, morals, existence of God, perception, *a priori* knowledge, and meaning. This book is noted for its excellent bibliographies to be found at the end of each section.

EWING, ALFRED CYRIL, *The Idealist Tradition: from Berkeley to Blanshard.* Glencoe, Ill.: Free Press, 1957. Pp. xxii+ 369.

Chapters on Berkeley, Kant, Hegel, Schopenhauer, Green, Bradley, Bosanquet, Royce, Croce, Blanshard, and others. A section on the critics of idealism.

FEIGL, HERBERT and MAY BROADBECK (eds.), *Readings in the Philosophy of Science.* New York: Appleton-Century-Crofts, Inc., 1953. Pp. x+ 811.

The editors define philosophy of science as a way of talking about science and classify it as a specialized part of analytical philosophy. The readings cover the natural, biological, and social sciences.

———, and WILFRED SELLERS (eds.), *Readings in Philosophical Analysis*. New York: Appleton-Century-Crofts, Inc., 1949. Pp. x+ 626.

Readings arranged under the headings of Language, Meaning and Truth, Meaningfulness and Confirmation, The Nature of Logic and Mathematics, *A Priori* Knowledge, Data, Reality and the Mind-Body Problem, Problems of Description and Explanation, and Problems of Theoretical Ethics. All selections are from the writings of well-known philosophers.

FRANKENA, WILLIAM K., *Ethics*. Englewood Cliffs, N.J.: Prentice-Hall, Inc., 1963. Pp. xvi+ 109.

The author seeks to do moral philosophy and not just talk about it. He clearly marks out the differences between judgments of moral obligations, judgments of moral value, and judgments of non-moral value. An excellent introduction to the subject of ethics by an analyst much interested in education.

GOROVITZ, S., R. WILLIAMS, *et al.*, *Philosophical Analysis: Introduction to Its Language and Techniques*. New York: Random House, 1965. Pp. xii+ 137.

A very helpful reference prepared by Stanford University graduate students. Chapters on elementary logic, predicate calculus and sets, assertions, sentences and propositions, extensional and intensional sentences, the Analytic-Synthetic and *a priori* and *a posteriori* distinctions, definitions, reading and writing philosophy, and divisions of philosophy.

HAMPSHIRE, STUART, *Thought and Action*. London: Chatto and Windus, 1959. P. 276.

Written for the layman, this book has been called a philosopher's essay in unphilosophical thinking. The book invites its readers to consider what it means to be one's self. Discusses such topics as freedom of the will, moral philosophy, philosophy of the mind, and the relation between knowledge and action.

HARE, R. M., *The Language of Morals*. London: Oxford University Press, 1952. Pp. viii+ 202.

Recognized as one of the most important studies in analysis and morals. The author conceives of ethics as "the logical study of the language of morals." The book is divided into three sections dealing with "the imperative mood," "good," and "ought." Must reading.

HOCKING, WILLIAM ERNEST, *The Lasting Elements of Individualism*. New Haven: Yale University Press, 1937. Pp. xiv+ 187.

Dedicated to John Dewey, this little book is called by its author . . . "a study in the philosophy of history—looking forward." Hocking is hostile to "mere pragmatism" but not to "pragmatism" for he believes it is . . . "destined to transform itself into a version of the 'dialectic method' whereby mere groping takes on a rational direction and destination." He discusses the individual as a unit of social order, liberalism, two necessities for future societies, and the Co-agent state.

HOLT, EDWIN, et al., The New Realism: Cooperative Studies in Philosophy. New York: The Macmillan Company, 1912. Pp. xii+ 491.
A collection of essays on the historical significance of realism, the emancipation of metaphysics from epistemology, a realistic theory of independence, a defense of analysis, truth and error, illusory experience, and some implications of biology for realism. Note especially R. B. Perry's essay on "A Realistic Theory of Independence."

HOSPERS, JOHN, An Introduction to Philosophical Analysis. Englewood Cliffs, N.J.: Prentice-Hall, Inc., 1953. Pp. xii+ 532.
An extremely interesting and readable book. The first four chapters are exceptionally helpful to beginning students in philosophy and education. These deal with words and the world, necessary knowledge, empirical knowledge, law, cause, and freedom.

JAMES, WILLIAM, Pragmatism and Four Essays from The Meaning of Truth. New York: Meridian Books, Inc., 1955. P. 269.
A series of lectures delivered at the Lowell Institute in Boston and at Columbia University in which James admits that he does not like the name pragmatism but goes on to explain what he means by the term. He discusses truth, religion, humanism, and several other philosophical problems. An American philosophical classic.

JASPERS, KARL, Reason and Existenz. New York: The Noonday Press, 1955. P. 157.
Translated with an introduction prepared by William Earle, this collection of lectures in existential philosophy covers the origin of the contemporary philosophical situation, basic ideas for the clarification of reason and existenz, and possibilities for contemporary philosophizing.

JONES, WILLIAM THOMAS, History of Western Philosophy. New York: Harcourt, Brace, 1952. Pp. xviii+ 1036.
Jones concentrates upon the main figures in Western philosophy, presents extensive quotations from each, and sketches in a cultural background for each. The key passages quoted are connected in the text by comment, criticism, and interpretation.

KAUFMANN, WALTER, Existentialism from Dostoevsky to Sartre. New York: Meridian Books, Inc., 1956. Pp. 319.
A collection of writings from Dostoevsky, Kierkegaard, Nietzsche,

Rilke, Kafka, Jaspers, Heidegger, and Sartre. An excellent introduction and short biographical sketches tie the selections together.

LANGER, SUSANNE K., *Feeling and Form*. New York: Charles Scribner's Sons, 1953. Pp. xvi$^+$ 431.

Langer developed her theory of art from her theory of symbolism set forth in *Philosophy in a New Key*. She discusses her philosophy of art under three headings: The Art Symbol, The Making of the Symbol, and The Power of the Symbol.

————, *Philosophy in a New Key*. New York: Mentor Book, 1948. P. 248.

A study in symbolism, the key "to all humanistic problems. In it lies a new conception of 'mentality', that may illuminate questions of life and consciousness, instead of obscuring them as traditional 'scientific methods' have done." Chapters on logic of signs and symbols, language, sacrament, myth, music, art, and meaning.

LEWIS, CLARENCE IRVING, *An Analysis of Knowledge and Valuation*. LaSalle, Ill.: The Open Court Publishing Company, 1946. Pp. xxii$^+$ 568.

A naturalistic conception of valuation is based upon a careful study of meaning and analytic truth and empirical knowledge. A sophisticated study of empiricism and naturalistic ethics and esthetics by one of our most noted philosophers.

————, *The Ground and Nature of the Right*. New York: Columbia University Press, 1955. Pp. x$^+$ 97.

Delivered as Woodbridge Lectures at Columbia in 1954. The lectures cover the subjects of "Modes of Right and Wrong," "Right Believing and Concluding," "Right Doing," "The Right and the Good," and "The Rational Imperatives."

————, *Our Social Inheritance*. Bloomington: Indiana University Press, 1957. P. 110.

Points up the complex requirements that must be met if man is to be prepared to live a civilized life. Quickly traces the social inheritance of twentieth-century Americana, discusses some of the principal ingredients in the human mentality, and concludes with a treatment of critical judgments.

MARCEL, GABRIEL, *The Philosophy of Existentialism*. New York: The Citadel Press, 1961. P. 128.

A collection of three papers written by a famous Catholic Existentialist. The first explains the main points in Marcel's position, the second is a critical survey of Sartre's philosophy, and the third seeks to define the doctrine which Marcel holds. "An Essay in Autobiography" concludes the book.

MEHTA, VED, *Fly and the Fly-Bottle*. Baltimore: Penguin Books, 1965. P. 223.

A collection of essays based upon interviews with British philosophers and historians. Exciting account of contemporary British philosophy destroying several erroneous American notions about British philosophy and history.

MOORE, GEORGE EDWARD, *Principia Ethica*. Cambridge: Cambridge University Press, 1959. Pp. xxviii+ 232.

One of the most influential books of this century covering such topics as the subject matter of ethics, naturalistic ethics, hedonism, metaphysical ethics, conduct, and the ideal. The discussion revolves about two principal questions: What kinds of things are intrinsically good? and What kinds of acts ought we to perform?

NAGEL, ERNEST, *Sovereign Reason and Other Studies in the Philosophy of Science*. Glencoe, Ill.: Free Press, 1954. P. 315.

Sixteen essays built around four themes: the relation of abstract theory to ordinary experience, the nature of reliable knowledge, the expendable nature of metaphysical systems, and the impact of new ways of thinking developed by scientific research.

——, *The Structure of Science: Problems in the Logic of Scientific Explanation*. New York: Harcourt, Brace & World, 1961. P. 618.

An examination of logical patterns in scientific knowledge and the logical methods of modern science. Sections on social sciences and history especially interesting.

NOWELL-SMITH, PATRICK H., *Ethics*. Great Britain: Billing & Sons, Ltd. Guildford-London, Penguin Books, 1954 and 1957. Pp. 283.

In the first part of his book, Prof. Nowell-Smith develops the principles of linguistic analysis implicit in moral language. These tools are applied to the general moral behaviors of choosing, advising, duty and obligation. The book concludes with a brief epilogue cautioning against unwarranted generalizations and stressing the necessary individuality of morality.

OGDEN, C. K. and I. A. RICHARDS, *The Meaning of Meaning*. New York: Harcourt, Brace & World, Inc., 1938. Pp. xxxii+ 544.

A study of the scope and task of the Science of Symbolism. Chapters on thought, words and things, the power of words, sign-situations, signs in perception, canons of symbolism, definitions, meaning of beauty, meaning of philosophers, the meaning of meaning, and symbol situations.

OTTO, MAX, *Science and the Moral Life*. New York: Mentor Books, 1949. P. 192.

Otto maintains that the impulse of our time is "life more abundant." He reminds us, however, that the crucial question is "What meaning shall we give to life more abundant?" The author is convinced that the scientific method must be put to work in man's search for the good life—"the good life richly and profoundly conceived."

PARKER, DEWITT H., *Human Values. An Interpretation of Ethics Based on a Study of Values.* New York: Harper & Brothers, 1931. Pp. x+ 415.

Parker maintains there is no separate moral interest or value but that . . . "morality is indissolubly connected with every branch of human activity." Beginning with this presupposition the author then discusses the fundamental principles of value—the values of "real life" and the values of "imagination."

PASSMORE, JOHN, *A Hundred Years of Philosophy.* London: Gerald Duckworth & Co., Ltd., 1957. P. 523.

Traces the history of philosophy from John Stuart Mill down to the present. Excellent chapters on pragmatism, logic, the new realism, logical positivism, Wittgenstein, and existentialism.

PEPPER, STEPHEN C., *The Sources of Value.* Berkeley: University of California Press, 1958. Pp. xiv+ 732.

Pepper recognizes a common problem running throughout the study of value, "how to make well-grounded decisions in human affairs?" Drawing heavily upon psychology he sets forth the contextualists' view of the source of our values. His discussion of the legislation among values is insightful.

PERRY, RALPH BARTON, *Realms of Value. A Critique of Human Civilization.* Cambridge, Mass.: Harvard University Press, 1954. Pp. xiv+ 497.

A book written to bring "unity and order" into the fields of the natural and social sciences, aesthetics, philosophy of education, and philosophy of religion by "adhering constantly to a fundamental definition of value . . . a thing—anything—has value, or is valuable . . . when it is the object of an interest—any interest. Or, whatever is object of interest is ipso facto valuable."

PITCHER, GEORGE, *The Philosophy of Wittgenstein.* Englewood Cliffs, N.J.: Prentice-Hall, Inc., 1964. P. 334.

Pitcher bases the need for this simplified and rather lengthy introduction to *The Tractatus* and *Philosophical Analysis* on two premises: that Wittgenstein is a great philosopher and that his writings are deceptively simple. One must agree with these premises to appreciate this book. His analysis is an effort to provide a general and uncritical framework within which to understand Wittgenstein's process of thought. The more obtuse sections of Wittgenstein's philosophy are untouched.

POPPER, KARL R., *Conjectures and Refutations*. New York: Basic Books, Publishers, 1962. Pp. xiii+ 405.

A collection of essays and lectures designed to develop a theory of knowledge and its growth. Discussions of three views of human knowledge and the demarcation between science and metaphysics are particularly valuable.

RATNER, JOSEPH, *Intelligence in the Modern World: John Dewey's Philosophy*. New York: The Modern Library, 1939. Pp. xvi+ 1077.

An excellent introduction of more than two hundred pages precedes more than eight hundred pages excerpted from Dewey's writings on such diverse subjects as science, social philosophy, law, education, psychology, logic, religion, esthetics, and meaning. An excellent collection from Dewey's major works.

REICHENBACH, HANS, *The Rise of Scientific Philosophy*. Berkeley: University of California Press, 1957. Pp. xii+ 333.

The author states that his purpose in writing this book is to show that philosophy has proceeded from speculation to science. The book is divided into two parts: The Roots of Speculative Philosophy and The Results of Scientific Philosophy. The final chapter compares the speculative with the scientific philosophy.

RICE, PHILIP BLAIR, *On the Knowledge of Good and Evil*. New York: Random House, 1955. P. 299.

The author holds that the language of ethics has two main functions, first to guide conduct and second ". . . to do this with the aid of knowledge, or reflective awareness of the natural and human world."

ROYCE, JOSIAH, *Lectures on Modern Idealism*. New Haven: Yale University Press, 1919. Pp. xii+ 266.

Lectures delivered at Johns Hopkins University on Kant's conception of the nature and conditions of knowledge, Kant's conception of the self, the dialectical method, later problems of idealism, and so forth.

RUSSELL, BERTRAND, *A History of Western Philosophy*. New York: Simon and Schuster, 1945. Pp. xxiv+ 895.

Russell's purpose is to exhibit philosophy as an integral part of social and political life. As a result it contains more general history than is usually found in such treatments. The book covers the period from ancient philosophy to the time of its publication. Very entertaining reading.

——, *Human Knowledge: Its Scope and Limits*. New York: Simon and Schuster, 1948. Pp. xvi+ 524.

Russell recognizes that skepticism is "logically impeccable" but "psychologically impossible." He sets out to examine the relation between individual experience and the body of scientific knowledge we possess. The book is divided into sections on the world of science, language, science and perception, scientific concepts, probability, and postulates of scientific inference.

————, *The Problems of Philosophy*. New York: Oxford University Press, A Galaxy Book, 1959. P. 161.

Russell confines himself ". . . in the main to those problems of philosophy in regard to which I thought it possible to say something positive and constructive . . ." The major emphasis in this book is upon epistemological issues rather than upon metaphysical matters.

RYLE, GILBERT, *The Concept of Mind*. New York: Barnes & Noble, Inc., 1949. P. 334.

This is one of the more important recent books in philosophy. It is intended ". . . not to increase what we know about minds, but to rectify the logical geography of the knowledge we already possess." This is the book in which Ryle identifies what he calls "the ghost in the machine."

SARTRE, JEAN-PAUL, *Existentialism and Human Emotions*. New York: Philosophical Library, 1957. P. 96.

The author sets out to defend existentialism against charges that have been brought against it. He moves on to the chief focus of his work which is that man is personally responsible for what he is and what he does; that there are no values external to man, and no given human nature he is destined to fulfill.

SCHILPP, PAUL ARTHUR (ed.),*The Philosophy of John Dewey*. New York: Tudor Publishing Company, 1951. Pp. xvi+ 718.

Brief biography of Dewey, articles on aspects of Dewey's philosophy by noted philosophers and a reply by Dewey. An extensive bibliography of Dewey's works.

————, *The Philosophy of Bertrand Russell*. Evanston, Ill.: The Library of Living Philosophers, 1944. Pp. xvi+ 815.

Russell's autobiography, descriptive and critical essays on his philosophy, Russell's reply to his critics and bibliography of his principal writings.

————, *The Philosophy of Alfred North Whitehead*. Evanston, Ill.: The Library of Living Philosophers, 1941. Pp. xx+ 745.

This is another in the series, "The Library of Living Philosophers," edited by Professor Schilpp. This volume on Whitehead contains Whitehead's autobiography, descriptive and critical essays on the philosophy of Whitehead by a number of authorities, and an extended bibliography of Whitehead's writings. Chapter 17 deals with White-head's views on education.

SCHNEIDER, HERBERT W., *A History of American Philosophy*. New York: Columbia University Press, 1963. Pp. xviii+ 590.

Traces the history of American philosophy from puritan times to the "emergence of naturalistic realisms in the twentieth century." Many references to education throughout.

————, *Three Dimensions of Public Morality*. Bloomington: Indiana University Press, 1956. P. 166.

A very general and elementary moral treatise exploring the interrelations and correlation of our traditional ideals of "Liberty, Equality and Fraternity."

SELLARS, ROY WOOD, *The Philosophy of Physical Realism*. New York: The Macmillan Company, 1932. Pp. xvi+ 487.

Sellars rejects "probable realism" and Kantian Noumena and defends physical realism.

SPIEGELBERG, HERBERT, *Phenomenological Movement: A Historical Introduction*. The Hague: Martinus Nijhoff, 1960. Pp. xxxii+ 391 and x+ 735.

Volume 1 defines the phenomenological movement and traces its development from Brentano to Nicolai Hartmann. Volume 2 traces the French phase of the movement, discusses phenomenology at mid-century and concludes with the essentials of the phenomenological method.

STEVENSON, CHARLES L., *Ethics and Language*. New Haven: Yale University Press, 1944. Pp. xii+ 338.

The author's object is to clarify the meaning of ethical terms and "to characterize the general methods by which ethical judgments can be proved or supported." A very influential book in American philosophy.

TOULMIN, STEPHEN EDELSTON, *An Examination of the Place of Reason in Ethics*. Cambridge: Cambridge University Press, 1958. Pp. xiv+ 228.

The author examines the traditional approaches to ethics, the relation of logic and life, the nature of ethics, and the boundaries of reason. He contends that the common weakness of all traditional ethical theories is that they give no adequate account of ethical reasoning.

ULICH, ROBERT, *The Human Career: A Philosophy of Self-Transcendence*. New York: Harper & Brothers, 1955. Pp. xvi+ 255.

The author examines modern civilization, views man as a self-transcending being, and declares that if our opinions are to be of worth they must be based upon criteria gained from a new understanding of the human being. This understanding lies in the direction of a restless search for new meanings.

URMSON, J. O., *Philosophical Analysis: Its Development Between the Two Wars*. Oxford at the Clarendon Press, 1956. Pp. x+ 203.

A discussion of philosophical analysis and logical atomism, logical positivism and the downfall of logical atomism, and the beginnings of contemporary philosophy.

WARNOCK, G. J., *English Philosophy Since 1900*. London: Oxford University Press, 1958. Pp. x+ 180.

A study of the evolution of English philosophy in this century. Separate chapters on Moore, Russell, Wittgenstein, logical positivism, logic, metaphysics and philosophy, and belief.

WARNOCK, MARY, *Ethics Since 1900*. London: Oxford University Press, 1960. Pp. viii+ 207.

A study of the different kinds of moral philosophy current during the past sixty years. The book begins with Bradley's metaphysical ethics, proceeds through Moore, intuitionism, the emotive theory, and moral psychology and closes with a lengthy chapter on "Existentialism: J. P. Sartre."

WHITE, MORTON, *The Age of Analysis*. New York: Mentor Books, 1955. P. 253.

Commentaries on the writings of leading twentieth-century philosophers: G. E. Moore, Croce, Santayana, Bergson, Whitehead, Husserl, Sartre, Peirce, James, Dewey, Russell, Carnap, and Wittgenstein. Selections from the writings of each are included.

————, *Foundations of Historical Knowledge*. New York: Harper & Row, Publishers, 1965. Pp. xii+ 299.

A discussion of fact, law, and value in history; explanatory arguments and explanatory statements; causal interpretations; reasons; historical narration; ethics and free will. An excellent analysis of what history is and what the historian does.

WHITEHEAD, A. N., *Adventure of Ideas*. New York: Mentor Books, 1955. P. 302.

Whitehead states that this book "is a study of the concept of civilization, and an endeavor to understand how it is that civilized beings arise." One point, emphasized throughout is the importance of adventure for the promotion and preservation of civilization. The book contains four parts: "Sociological," "Cosmological," "Philosophical," and "Civilization."

————, *Science and the Modern World*. New York: Mentor Books, 1948. P. 212.

Perhaps Whitehead's most widely read publication. A series of eight lectures delivered at Harvard in 1925 covering such topics as the origins of modern science, relativity, quantum theory, science and philosophy, abstraction, God, religion and science, and the requisites for social progress.

WIENER, PHILIP P. (ed.), *Values in a Universe of Change: Selected Writings of Charles S. Peirce*. New York: Doubleday Anchor Books, 1958. Pp. xxvi+ 446.

The editor of this book has been guided by two considerations: the introduction of the reader "to the many sides of the most versatile, profound, and original philosopher that the United States has ever produced" and to include "unpublished and inaccessible material in which Peirce presented the cultural or humanistic aspects of science and philosophy . . ." Sections on the philosophy of science, materialism, religion, and education.

WILD, JOHN, *The Challenge of Existentialism*. Bloomington: Indiana University Press, 1959. Pp. viii+ 297.

The author's aim is "to present the reader with a critical exposition of this phenomenological philosophy of existence." He gives the background of this way of thought, develops some of its basic doctrines, and discusses some of the advantages and defects of these doctrines.

WITTGENSTEIN, LUDWIG (trs. by G. E. M. Anscombe), *Philosophical Investigations*. Oxford: Basil Blackwell, 1953. Pp. xii+ 232.

A very influential publication in Western analytic philosophy. These "remarks," as Wittgenstein called them, were published to contrast his newer philosophical thought with that contained in *Tractatus Logico-Philosophicus,* a work he came to believe contained "grave mistakes."

Philosophy of Education

ARCHAMBAULT, REGINALD D. (ed.), *John Dewey on Education: Selected Writings.* New York: Modern Library, 1964. Pp. xxx+ 439.

This book is intended to promote a new look at Dewey's educational theory. Selections from his major writings in education and some basic statements of his philosophical position are included. The material is grouped under the rubrics: philosophy and education, ethics and education, aesthetics and education, science and education, psychology and education, society and education, and principles of pedagogy.

———, *Philosophical Analysis and Education.* New York: The Humanities Press, 1965. Pp. xii+ 212.

A collection of essays by British authors designed to define the philosophical study of education. The essays are arranged under four headings: the nature and function of educational theory, context of educational discussion, conceptions of teaching, and the essence of education. Many will find the editor's introduction quite helpful in explaining the present status of educational theory and the place of philosophy in it.

BANDMAN, BERTRAM, *The Place of Reason in Education.* Columbus: Ohio State University Press, 1967. P. 200.

The purpose of this study "is to determine what, if anything, qualifies as a rational argument to help us decide what should be taught." The author discusses the two senses of argument, the use of metaphysical and moral arguments in education, and the place of metaphysical and moral reasons in education.

BAYLES, ERNEST E., *Democratic Educational Theory.* New York: Harper & Brothers, 1960. Pp. xii+ 266.

The author works out what he sees as the logical consequences of the national democratic commitment and states what ought to be the major tenets of a genuinely democratic educational program. He reports on experiments with reflective thinking, discusses value theory, religion and character education, educational purposes, evaluation of pupil progress, and concludes with chapters on Dewey, progressivism, and the present status of educational theory in the United States.

——, *Pragmatism in Education.* New York: Harper & Row, Publishers, 1966. Pp. xii+ 146.

Written to promote an understanding of pragmatism and its meaning for educational practice. Chapters on relativity; the nature of man; truth, value, existence; the nature of culture; educational purpose and program; and illustrative units.

BELTH, MARC, *Education as a Discipline: A Study of the Role of Models in Thinking.* Boston: Allyn and Bacon, Inc., 1965. Pp. xviii+ 317.

A logical analysis of the structure of education with attention given to the concept of education, scope of the study of education, elements of education, educational thinking, organization of elements in the discipline, models of education, self-corrective procedure, and the curriculum.

BEREDAY, GEORGE Z. and JOSEPH A. LAUWERYS, *Education and Philosophy.* New York: World Book Company, 1957. Pp. xiv+ 578.

One of the few books in the field that provides insights into the nature of philosophy of education in countries outside of western Europe and North America. Sections devoted to "The Great Traditions," "Determinants of Policy," "National Systems," "Historical Examples," "Experimental Institutions," and "The Teaching of Philosophy of Education."

BRAMELD, THEODORE, *Education as Power.* Holt, Rinehart and Winston, Inc. New York: 1965. Pp. xiv+ 146.

A series of lectures delivered in Korea. Readers will find chapter four a clear outline of the author's position. The charter for educational leadership, given in the appendix, sets forth eight guiding concepts to which Brameld is committed, and to which he would have us commit ourselves.

——, *Education for the Emerging Age.* New York: Harper & Row, Publishers, 1965. Pp. xii+ 244.

Brameld sees the task of education as embracing "the whole complex of human dynamics through which every culture seeks both to maintain and to innovate its structures, operations, purposes." In no sense should education and schooling be considered synonymous. The author discusses the philosophical foundations of education with particular emphasis upon his reconstructionism, indicates the need for an interdisciplinary approach to educational problems, treats three current controversial issues in education, and points up the kind of education needed to bring about a "cultural renaissance."

Butler, J. Donald, *Idealism and Education*. New York: Harper & Row, Publishers, 1966. Pp. xiv+ 144.

This little book explains what idealism is, and attempts to view it critically within the context of present events. Chapter three focuses upon "Idealism as a Philosophy of Education."

Chambliss, J. J., *Boyd H. Bode's Philosophy of Education*. Columbus, Ohio: Ohio State University Press, 1963. Pp. xii+ 98.

This essay places emphasis upon Bode's criticism of various points of view in educational theory and practice, his concern for the common man, and his efforts to draw meaning from pragmatism for the purpose of humanizing education. Extensive quotations from Bode and well documented.

Dewey, John, *The Child and the Curriculum and The School and Society*. Chicago: The University of Chicago Press, Phoenix Books, (n.d.). Pp. xii+ 159.

Two of Dewey's more important works are published in one volume. The discussion of psychologizing materials of instruction is quite valuable. There are illustrations of children's work in the Dewey School at the University of Chicago. These essays are reproduced elsewhere; see: Dworkin, *Dewey on Education*.

———, *Democracy and Education*. New York: The Macmillan Company, 1916. Pp. xiv+ 434.

Intended as an introduction to the philosophy of education, this is Dewey's magnum opus on education. Must reading for all serious students in the field.

———, *Experience and Education*. New York: The Macmillan Company, 1938. Pp. xvi+ 116.

Nearly eighty, Dewey looks back upon progressive education to point out what he considers to be the diffference between progressive education and traditional education. He issues warnings to those disposed to think in either-or terms and clearly states wherein he believes progressive education, or at least some of its exponents, have failed. The book closes on an optimistic note.

———, *Moral Principals in Education*. New York: The Wisdom Library, 1959. Pp. xii+ 61.

Selections from Dewey's essay on "Ethical Principles Underlying Education," which was originally published in the *Third Year-Book of the National Herbart Society for the Study of Education*.

Subjects covered include the moral purpose of the school, moral training supplied by the school community, social nature of the course of study, and psychological aspects of moral education.

DUNKEL, HAROLD B., *Whitehead on Education*. Columbus, Ohio: Ohio University Press, 1965. Pp. xvi+ 182.

A comprehensive study of Whitehead's philosophy and his writings on education. The book is intended to establish relationships between the two as well as to offer criticisms of Whitehead's work in education.

DWORKIN, MARTIN S., *Dewey on Education*. New York: Bureau of Publications, Teachers College, Columbia University, 1959. P. 134.

A handy reference for those who wish to read John Dewey's "My Pedagogic Creed," "The School and Society," "The Child and the Curriculum," and "Progressive Education and the Science of Education." The last named is particularly pertinent today. This collection closes with the last published work on education by Dewey, an introduction to a book by Elsie Ripley Clapp, *The Use of Resources in Education*.

Educational Theory.

William O. Stanley, editor

Editorial Office

276 Education Building

University of Illinois

Urbana, Illinois

Published quarterly by the John Dewey Society and the Philosophy of Education Society. The purpose of this journal is to foster the continuing development of educational theory and to encourage wide and effective discussion of theoretical problems in education.

Encyclical Letter, *Divini Illius Magistri of His Holiness Pope Pius XI*. New York: The American Press, 1936. P. 35.

Pius XI clarifies the position of the Roman Catholic Church on Christain Education. Discusses aims of education, responsibility of family, state and Church for education, co-education and sex education. Now somewhat out of date.

FORD, G. W. and LAWRENCE PUGNO (eds.), *The Structure of Knowledge and the Curriculum*. Chicago: Rand McNally & Company, 1964. P. 105.

An examination of the nature and structure of knowledge with special reference to the natural sciences, mathematics, English, and the social studies.

FRANKENA, WILLIAM K., *Philosophy of Education*. New York: The Macmillan Company, 1965. P. 116.

Selections from the writings of Dewey, Whitehead, Maritain and R. S. Peters are arranged under two major headings: Education, its nature, aims, and principles; and education, its kinds, methods, programs, and problems. More important, however, is the introduction which provides a model for analyzing a philosophy of education.

HARDIE, CHARLES D., *Truth and Fallacy in Educational Theory*. New York: Bureau of Publications, Teachers College, Columbia University, 1962. Pp. xx+ 156.

This is a landmark volume in the philosophy of education for it is the first book in which linguistic analysis was applied to education. This edition contains a most enlightening preface prepared by James E. McClellan and B. Paul Komisar.

HENRY, NELSON B. (ed.), *Modern Philosophies and Education*. Chicago: The University of Chicago Press, 1955. Pp. x+ 374.

The fifty-fourth yearbook of the National Society for the Study of Education. One of the better-known books in the field with chapters prepared by some of America's noted philosophers: Wild, Maritain, Greene, Geiger, Feigl, and Feibleman.

HOLLINS, T. H. B., *Aims in Education: The Philosophic Approach*. Great Britain: Manchester University Press, 1964. P. 135.

In the Spring of 1961, the School of Education of Manchester University invited a number of philosophers and educators to rationally analyze the general topic of "aims of Education." This volume contains six of those lectures. The subject-matter ranges from Neo-Thomism to education and indoctrination, but the approach throughout is that of logical and linguistic analysis.

HOOK, SIDNEY, *Education for Modern Man, A New Perspective*. New York: Alfred A. Knopf, Pp. 236+iii.

A former student of Dewey surveys the contemporary scene in education, examines the ends of education, discusses the content of education, and investigates problems of method, program, and the relation of education to society.

HULLFISH, H. GORDON and PHILIP G. SMITH, *Reflective Thinking: The Method of Education*. New York: Dodd, Mead & Company, 1961. Pp. xiii+ 273.

Designed to help teachers understand how the methods of thinking can be applied. Written in a lucid style. It should be especially helpful to teachers who wish to see how Dewey's ideas may be implemented.

JAHSMANN, ALLAN HART, *What's Lutheran in Education?* St. Louis: Concordia Publishing Company, 1960. Pp. x+ 185.

This is the most recent and most complete attempt yet made by a member of the Missouri Synod—Lutheran Church to state a philosophy for the schools of this synod. Reflects the strong influence of theology on philosophical and educational thinking.

JOHNSTON, A. H., *A Philosophy of Education.* New York: McGraw-Hill Book Company, 1964. P. 463.

A Catholic educator writes on the development of human virtues and the agencies that foster their development.

JUDGES, A. V. (ed.), *Education and the Philosophic Mind.* London: George G. Harrap & Co., 1957. P. 205.

A collection of essays by British authors on Plato, Neo-Thomism, existentialism, pragmatism, behaviorism, logical positivism, scientific humanism, and dialectical materialism.

KANT, IMMANUEL, *Education.* Ann Arbor: Ann Arbor Paperbacks, The University of Michigan Press, 1960. P. 121.

A collection of Kant's lecture notes edited by one of his students. Unfortunately this volume does not have an introduction and, for that reason, should be supplemented by such a work as William K. Frankena's *Three Historical Philosophies of Education* or Kingsley Price's *Education and Philosophical Thought.*

KILPATRICK, WILLIAM HEARD, *Philosophy of Education.* New York: The Macmillan Company, 1951. Pp. x+ 465.

This is a summing up, as it were, of the author's thinking in connection with his life work of teaching philosophy of education. He sets forth in detail his philosophy of life and his philosophy of education. This is "Mr. Progressive Education's" major work in the philosophy of education.

KNELLER, GEORGE F., *Existentialism and Education.* New York: Philosophical Library, 1958. Pp. xvi+ 170.

The first full length book published on the subject. Written for the layman and educator, it is not highly technical. The author suggests educational theory and practice.

————, *Introduction to the Philosophy of Education.* New York: John Wiley & Sons, Inc., 1964. Pp. x+ 137.

A brief outline of "those elements of philosophy that are relevant to a proper understanding of education and the task of teaching." Sections on philosophy and education, traditional philosophies of education, newer modes of thinking, and contemporary educational theories. Designed for the general reader and for those who wish a quick summary of the field.

————, *Logic and Language of Education.* New York: John Wiley & Sons, Inc., 1966. Pp. x+ 242.

An attempt to relate logic to education. Chapters on the nature of logic, modes of logic, formal analysis, informal analysis, and the relation of logic to psychology, teaching, and learning.

LAWRENCE, NATHANIEL M. and ROBERT S. BRUMBAUGH, *Philosophers on*

Education: Six Essays on the Foundations of Western Thought. Boston: Houghton Mifflin Company, 1963. Pp. x+ 211.

These essays deal with Plato, Aristotle, Rousseau, Kant, Dewey, and Whitehead. The final chapter cites some contemporary problems, and develops a prologue to future philosophies of education.

MORRIS, VAN CLEVE, *Existentialism in Education: What It Means.* New York: Harper & Row, Publishers, 1966. Pp. xii+ 163.

Morris states that existentialism is a theory of individual meaning that asks each person to ponder the reasons for his existence. From this, he moves on to discuss existentialism as a philosophy and to indicate its meaning for education.

NAKOSTEEN, MEHDI, *The History and Philosophy of Education.* New York: The Ronald Press, 1965. Pp. xii+ 746.

This book begins with ancient educational theory and moves on through to contemporary problems, issues, and trends. Students of the philosophy of American education will find it particularly valuable to consult the last two sections of this book.

NASH, PAUL, *Authority and Freedom in Education: An Introduction to the Philosophy of Education.* New York: John Wiley & Sons, Inc., 1966. Pp. x+ 342.

Rejecting the school's approach, which he feels is "vestigial and anachronistic," Nash uses the analytical approach, coupled with a wide use of methods and materials from several disciplines, to develop a particular theme. His avowed goal is clarity as to ideas and commitment as to courses of action and choices among belief.

O'CONNOR, D. J., *An Introduction to the Philosophy of Education.* New York: Philosophical Library, 1957. Pp. viii+ 148.

Writing from the viewpoint of philosophical analysis, the author presents a remarkably fine discussion of the relation of philosophy and education, the justification of value judgments, explanation, and theory, and closes by commenting upon questions of morals and religion.

PARK, JOE, *Bertrand Russell on Education.* Columbus, Ohio: Ohio State University Press, 1963. Pp. xiv+ 193.

A study of the sources of Russell's theory of education and how he applied it in his Beacon Hill School.

PETERS, RICHARD, *Authority, Responsibility, and Education.* London: George Allen & Unwin Ltd., 1959. P. 137.

The last part of this book will be of particular interest to educators. Peters raises the question, "Must an educator have an aim?" This has become a rather widely discussed subject in American circles. The chapter on aims has been reproduced in William Frankena's *Philosophy of Education.*

PETERS, R. S., *Ethics and Education*. Chicago: Scott, Foresman and Company, 1967. P. 235.

A somewhat abridged edition of a book that appeared in England in 1966. It deals with the application of ethics and social philosophy to problems in education: equality, worthwhile activities, interest, freedom, respect for persons and fraternity, authority, discipline, punishment, and democracy.

PHENIX, PHILIP H., *Education and the Common Good*. New York: Harper & Brothers, 1961. P. 271.

The author maintains that "the focal point around which the entire argument of this book revolves is that the cardinal goal of instruction in whatever field . . . should be the development of loyalty to what is excellent, instead of success in satisfying desires." Sections of this book deal with intelligence, creativity, conscience, and reverence.

————, *Realms of Meaning: A Philosophy of the Curriculum for General Education*. New York: McGraw-Hill Book Company, 1964. Pp. xvi+ 391.

This book states that there are six basic realms of meaning that are characteristically human. The fundamental patterns of meaning in these six realms are set forth, and an attempt is made to draw some conclusions regarding curriculum.

Proceedings of the Philosophy of Education Society.

Francis Villemain, editor

School of Education

Southern Illinois University at Edwardsville,

Edwardsville, Illinois

Contains the minutes of the society, reports of its major committees, and the papers delivered before the membership at the annual conventions.

REID, LOUIS ARNAUD, *Philosophy and Education*. London: Heineman, 1962. Pp. xvi+ 203.

A brief survey of philosophy of education with emphasis upon the nature of philosophy, values, application of theory to practice, the self, freedom, discipline, teaching, and professional education of teachers.

RUSK, ROBERT R., *The Philosophical Bases of Education*. Boston: Houghton Mifflin Company, 1956. Pp. viii+ 176.

A statement of the philosophy of education from the idealistic standpoint. Chapters on the need for a philosophy of education, materialism, realism, naturalism, pragmatism, instrumentalism and experimentalism, and, of course, idealism which is treated in much greater depth.

RUSSELL, BERTRAND, *Education and the Good Life*. New York: Boni & Liveright, 1926. P. 319.

Russell presents his aims for education and relates them to his idea of the good life. Early childhood education and what he calls "intellectual education" are treated in depth.

——, *Education and the Modern World*. New York: W. W. Norton & Co., 1932. P. 245.

This is Russell's second and last book devoted exclusively to education. He reflects upon the social implications of education under such headings as a negative theory of education, heredity, emotion, discipline, and the individual versus the citizen.

SCHEFFLER, ISRAEL, *Conditions of Knowledge*. Chicago: Scott, Foresman and Company, 1965. P. 117.

An extended discussion of a definition of propositional knowledge with implications drawn for education.

——, *The Language of Education*. Springfield, Ill.: Charles C. Thomas, Publishers, 1960. Pp. x+ 113.

The purpose of this book is to apply certain philosophical methods to education in order "to clarify certain pervasive features of educational thought and argument." Chapters on definitions, slogans, and metaphors in education as well as two chapters on teaching and teaching and telling.

SMITH, B. OTHANEL and ROBERT H. ENNIS, *Language and Concepts in Education*. Chicago: Rand McNally & Company, 1961. Pp. x+ 215.

A collection of essays that are focused upon neglected meanings, conceptual blunders, the removal of pseudo-questions, and the logical inconsistencies in educational writing. The essays cover such topics as learning and experience, needs and the need-curriculum, explanations, and the logic of slogans.

SMITH, HUSTON, *Condemned to Meaning*. New York: Harper & Row, 1965. Pp. 94.

As the ancestral order decays and the ancient religious certainties are dissolved by science, how can modern man find meaning which binds his experience and engages his faculties and passions? The author discusses this poignant question under such pertinent headings as meaning, meaning in the academic discipline, the meaning of life, and "Import for Education."

Studies in Philosophy and Education.

Francis Villemain, editor

School of Education

Southern Illinois University

Edwardsville Campus

Edwardsville, Illinois

One of the two journals in the field of philosophy of education published in America. Excellent source of information on current thinking in the field.

ULICH, ROBERT, *Crisis and Hope in American Education.* Boston: Beacon Press, Inc., 1951. Pp. xiv+ 235.

This book deals chiefly with secondary education but includes chapters on the education of teachers, higher education, and adult education. In Chapter II Ulich describes the kind of school he desires for the future.

———, *Philosophy of Education.* New York: American Book Company, 1961. Pp. xiv+ 286.

The author's intent has been to "present substantial material concerning the basic philosophic issues and aspects of education which every prospective teacher should, sooner or later, think about." He has arranged his material under two main rubrics, "The Theoretical Groundwork" and "Education in Action." The former section deals with aims, conception of man, ethical views, while the second is concerned with religion, art, method, and curriculum.

VAN DUSEN, HENRY P., *God in Education.* New York: Charles Scribner's Sons, 1951. P. 118.

Professor Van Dusen argues against the negativism, doubt, and vain elevation of human reason ushered in by Descartes. A reaffirmation of our religious faith and the restoration of religion to a position of necessary and unchallenged centrality must be the foundation of both life and education. The last chapter is a summarization of the dissenting opinions on the Supreme Court's decision of the McCollum Case.

WHITEHEAD, ALFRED NORTH, *Aims of Education and Other Essays.* New York: The Macmillan Company, 1929. Pp. viii+ 247.

The general idea behind this great book is, in Whitehead's words, "The students are alive, and the purpose of education is to stimulate and guide their self-development." This protest against inert ideas, deals with the aims of education, the rhythm of education, technical education, classics, mathematics, the function of universities as well as with certain scientific ideas.

WIRTH, ARTHUR G., *John Dewey as Educator: His Design for Work in Education* (1894–1904). New York: John Wiley & Sons, Inc., 1966. Pp. xviii+ 322.

The purpose of this book is to answer the fascinating question, "What did Dewey stand for when he directed his Laboratory School at the University of Chicago?" The book is divided into two parts: theory, psychological and philosophical, and curriculum and method.

Index

A

Absolute, 66–69
  idealism, 222
  mind, 66, 146
Academic community, ideal, 173–75
Accommodations, 77–78
Adjustment, 77
Adler, Mortimer J., 187
Adolescence, 207–208
Adult education, 333
Aesthetics, 19–20
  appreciation, 19
  education, 18–20
  life, 220
Aim, nature of, 84
Ambiguity, 345
American Historical Association, 283–84
Analogy, 347
Analysis, 92, 337–39
  linguistic, 341
  logical, 341
  methodology, 350
Analysts, 139
Analytic philosophy, 5–6, 352
  features of, 341–44
Anti-intellectualism, 119
Anti-intellectualist, 59
Apology, 30
A priori, 58, 343–44
Aquinas, St. Thomas, 262, 265, 266
Archaeology, 285
Archambault, Reginald, 133, 388, 409
Arguments, 347
Aristotle, 226, 238, 265, 266, 270, 343
Art, 29
  united, 287
Ascriptive function, 374

Attitudes, 115
Augustine, St., 266
Austin, J. L., 395
Authoritarianism, 313
Authority, 83
  moral, 358
Autonomist argument, 356–60
Axiology, 4, 180–81
Ayer, Alfred J., 47, 389, 395

B

Baker, Bruce F.
  biographical sketch, 333–34
  "Existential Philosophers on Education," quoted, 323–33
Bandman, Bertram, 409
Barker, Stephen F., 395
Barrett, William, 334, 396
Bayles, Ernest E., 133, 409
Becoming, 310
Beliefs, 56, 61, 68
Belth, Marc, 47, 410
Ben-Gurion, 284
Ben Horin, Meir
  biographical sketch, 293–94
  "Jewish Education in an Age of Science," quoted, 282–90
  "Loyalties in Jewish Education," quoted, 290–93
Benn, S. I., 373–74
Bereday, George Z., 47, 410
Berkeley, George, 58
Berle, Adolf A., 287–88
Berlin, I., 386
Bernstein, Leonard, 287
Bible, 285